PLAYER PIANO

by the same author

COLLECTING MUSICAL BOXES

Player Piano

THE HISTORY OF
THE MECHANICAL PIANO
AND HOW TO REPAIR IT

ARTHUR W. J. G. ORD-HUME

Illustrated by the author

SOUTH BRUNSWICK AND NEW YORK
A. S. BARNES AND COMPANY

FIRST PUBLISHED 1970

© *George Allen & Unwin Ltd, 1970*

Library of Congress Catalogue Card Number: 79–81150

First American Edition published 1970
by
A. S. Barnes & Co., Inc.
Cranbery, N.J. 08512

SBN 498 07484 6

PRINTED IN GREAT BRITAIN

CONTENTS

ILLUSTRATIONS

PLATES

LINE ILLUSTRATIONS

INTRODUCTION

THIS book is about self-acting pianos. I think that one's first reaction to the reading of that statement, unless aware of the proper meaning, is to visualise magical properties bestowed upon that 'household God' as Charles Dickens referred to it, or to picture some electronic marvel coupled to a computer in a broadcasting studio. Or, most probably, to stare at the words, bemused, unimpressed and none the wiser.

If I qualify the first sentence and say 'pianola pianos', you may be a little wiser. The fact is that 'pianola' is a trade name registered by one maker of these instruments. However, in the same way that 'meccano' has come to be accepted as a word in the dictionary, having started life in a like fashion, so has 'pianola' come to mean the genus 'player-piano'.

Having established that this is something to do with player-pianos, I wonder just how many have today even seen one, let alone enjoyed pedalling their way through a roll of music. Even fewer have ever sat back and marvelled at the faithful performance of a reproducing piano, playing music recorded in perforated paper by a famous artist long since dead and buried.

There is another sort of self-acting piano which probably is known better by the term, incorrect though it is, 'barrel organ'. This is an instrument of another kind, played by a pinned barrel instead of a paper roll.

Why a book on these oddities? There are many, many player-pianos to be found and they are becoming collector's items. All, I venture to say, need some attention, unless they have just been restored. Because restoration work on these instruments is time-consuming and fiddling, to have the job done professionally is extremely expensive. And because they are basically very simple devices, this is work which the average handyman can tackle with relative ease.

There are also a number of the so-called 'barrel organs' or street pianos about. Mainly used today as charity fund raisers, there are, even so, some in private collections and these need care, attention and maintenance. All is within the capabilities of the careful worker.

I met my first player-piano when I was only just high enough to look along the keys. I failed to understand why they were going up and down and the piano was playing with nobody near it (it was an electric one) and, in fear, I fled. Various passing brushes with the things went largely without impression on me until one day I was confronted with one that did not work and, looking forlorn, it pleaded for help and a new lease of life. Being somewhat soft-hearted, I fell in with the suggestion. The lack of suitable reference material at that time meant that I learnt the hard way. Now, many pianos later, I still don't know all the answers, for there are so very many different styles and models of player. However, once the principles are mastered, the rest is comparatively easy.

My first barrel piano leered at me grotesquely from the antique shop of my good friend Graham Webb. It didn't work either and this time it didn't plead—it just challenged. Again, I learned the hard way, and again, many barrel pianos later, I think I know most of the problems and their solutions.

The idea of this book is to pass on the gentle art of preserving these things. Because player organs are akin to player-pianos, I also deal briefly with these.

The lowest point in the popularity of the player-piano was probably reached but a few years ago. However, in the last year or so, interest in the instrument has increased and they are becoming sought after not only by collectors and enthusiasts, but also by a growing number of people who, tired of piped entertainment and modern environment with all its undesirable trappings, seek respite in music and the ownership of a piano.

The current generation, with its general hatred of preservation, has deprived us of countless pianos and many a splendid instrument has ended its days prematurely on a bonfire, or been wantonly broken up in one of those demented and pointless piano-smashing competitions. Such public demonstrations of destructiveness, accompanied by dancing and chanting, are most reminiscent of the sacrificial ceremonies of the primitive tribes and seem an anachronism to twentieth century England. However, it is these people who grow up to extend their destructive tendencies to fine buildings and the countryside and thus they are the very creators of the tasteless, characterless city environments which engender in sane people a greater than ever need to seek salvation in the arts of better years.

Because today everything which savours of quiet pleasure tends to be termed 'escapism', he who seeks to enjoy music in his own home is probably thought unusual, but these conditions have insidiously spread a love of music to an ever-widening circle of ordinary people who suddenly think that they would like to own a piano. Possibly the long-term effects of the pianola of the twenties still remain with them in that they were products of the generation which was never taught to play, or probably they are able to but, as in my own case, 'just hate the sound of themselves practising'. It is this band of devotees who are calling for 'musick that Goethe with a Whele'.

When it comes to the interpretation of music using means other than musical skill, it is only in the mechanical musical instrument that one may determine to one's own satisfaction the speed or *tempo* of the performance. With the accepted means of producing personally-scheduled music in the home—the gramophone or tape-recorder—any variation in speed destroys pitch and an attempt to vary the *tempo* continuously makes it quite impossible to enjoy the music. How often have we criticicised a work by saying to ourselves 'That section should be played slower'. The mechanical musical instrument, on the other hand, possesses true and, to all intents and purposes, inviolate pitch. The speed at which the music is played upon such a machine and the number of variations in *tempo* during the performance have no effect whatsoever on the pitch of the sound. It is this characteristic which makes possible a different and personalised rendition of a music roll with every performance and enables the player-performer to achieve the utmost involvement with his music rolls and the greatest satisfaction from his playing.

The purchaser of a player-piano is forever endowed with optimism. His instrument, maybe thirty, forty or even sixty years old, has probably spent many years out of favour, perhaps relegated to a damp barn. Yet when he gets it and drags its bulk and massive dead weight into his house, he somehow expects it to perform perfectly, effortlessly and with the panache of a hidden keyboard virtuoso.

Alas! This is seldom the case. His instrument will most probably sit mute and desolate, reflecting the disappointment of its new owner. It may play badly, not at all, or sporadically. Only rarely will a newly unearthed relic surprise even the experts and work as it was built to, without drastic attention.

Player-pianos are delicately adjusted devices of wood, felt, rubber cloth, tubing, springs, slides, screws and wire. As with every machine, they deteriorate with time and lack of use, dampness and changes of temperature. Confronted with such a galimaufry of bits, the new owner may understandably despair of ever getting the thing to play. However, this need not be the case. A player-piano responds to loving care and attention and, with patience, all but the most blatantly deteriorated instrument may be brought gratefully back to another lease of life in the hands of the enthusiast. As with all forms of restoration, two qualities are paramount for the worker— patience and thoroughness. There are two ways to do every job—the quick way and the right way—and only one pays off. The mechanical piano, whether it is a barrel piano or a player-piano, demands the same personal integrity from its restorer and can give so much in return for your labours.

History is a dull subject usually, but the history of the mechanical piano (of which the player piano and the barrel piano are sisters) is rather interesting and thus I have set this out briefly. I have dealt at length with the development of the barrel piano and the pneumatic piano and described their actions in detail because these points need to be known and understood if the owner or restorer of these instruments is to become anything of an expert.

The challenge presented by a dilapidated instrument in need of a rebuild is far less demanding than that of trying to set down in an intelligent manner the processes of tackling the job. I only hope I have succeeded.

ACKNOWLEDGEMENTS

In presenting this work, I wish to express my sincere thanks to all those who have aided me so ably and encouraged me to pursue my enquiries. First, I offer thanks to Mr J. C. Allen of Steinway Pianos, Mr L. K. Busby of Blüthner Pianos, Mr D. F. Andrews of Boyd Pianos and to the staff of Broadwood Pianos for their co-operation in allowing me to use material from their archives. Mr Phelps Snr. and Mr Phelps Jnr. of Phelps Pianos Limited and Mr D. R. Heckscher and Mr M. R. Heckscher of Heckscher & Company have also aided me as have Mr W. J. Bassil of J. & J. Goddard Ltd, Mr S. J. Murdoch of Harrods Piano Department and Mr H. R. Goodall of The Aeolian Corporation, New York.

A number of fine photographs which I am pleased to include have been taken specially by the Department of Science and Industry, City Museum and Art Gallery, Birmingham, and for these I gratefully acknowledge the assistance rendered by Mr N. W. Bertenshaw and his staff. My good friend Graham Webb has been of enormous help in allowing me to examine and photograph many of the fine instruments which find their way into his fascinating shop in the Portobello Road. Mr Frank W. Holland of the British Piano Museum, Brentford, and founder of the Player Piano Group, has proved a tower of strength and has allowed me access to his truly fantastic collection, providing material of great value. Mr Lyndesay G. Langwill, as well as providing information, has helped me with translations from the German.

Dr C. de Vere Green, F.D.S., R.C.S. (Eng.), D.D.S. (Tor), Mr Ron Benton, Mr Keith Harding, Mr Rex Montgomery and Members of the Player Piano Group; Dr J. H. van der Meer of the Germanisches Nationalmuseum, Mr Bruce Angrave, Mr Gerry Planus and Mr Gordon Iles (one-time engineer with the Aeolian Company and now owner of the Artona music-roll company) have all played various parts towards the fulfilment of this book.

Special thanks are due to Mr Norman Evans of Tottenham, London, whose expertise in the restoration of instruments is matched only by his kindness in assisting with suggestions on the technical side. Next I thank the various Members of the Musical Box Society of Great Britain who have allowed me to benefit from their experience. Thanks are also due to the Society for allowing me to make use of material which has appeared under my own name and various pseudonyms in the Society journal, *The Music Box*.

Great assistance has been provided by the staff of the Patent Office Library in London who tolerated my presence in the Reading Room over an extended period of time and who so cheerfully humped heavy volumes up and down stairs for my perusal. To the various other museums and galleries who have provided illustrations, acknowledged in their proper places, my thanks also go. In conclusion, a word of thanks to Jack MacLean and Brian Bradbury, photographers extraordinary, who have produced some superb pictures for me in the most difficult of working situations.

August 1969   *Arthur W. J. G. Ord-Hume*

CHAPTER 1

Musick That Goethe With a Whele
—a History of the Mechanical Piano

T HERE was a time, not so very far distant, when you used to be able to walk through the streets
of London late at night and enjoy the Metropolis in a way no longer possible. The same could
be said of every other major town. Things were more leisurely. Traffic was still getting itself
snarled up although at a slower pace. In spite of a lack of social services and lack of drains, people
somehow seemed happier to be alive. These times are generally referred to today as 'the bad old
days', when gas lamps eschewed softer lighting, allowing sombre shadows to add a little welcome
anonymity to much of the goings-on; when the end of the autumn brought with it choking fog
and when pie-stalls, hot chestnut barrows and places for a cup of tea stayed open late, and when
stomach ulcers were almost unheard of. The internal combustion engine and its obnoxious by-
products were as yet unknown and just the rattle of the hansoms on the cobbles and the horse-
fumes filled the air. There were also the barrel organs....

The word 'barrel organ' is perhaps the largest mis-nomer in the whole field of mechanical
music, for a barrel organ is a pipe instrument—a real organ—played with a wooden barrel studded
with pins instead of with a keyboard. But, to all and sundry, a barrel organ was a large box on a
handcart. A swarthy character would stand beside it, turning furiously at a handle emerging from
its front. From the box would come popular honky-tonk piano music in a seemingly endless flow.
A colourfully-dressed monkey would often be seen sitting on top of the box holding a hat out to
passers-by who would be expected to drop in their small change in appreciation of the music.
The man who turned the handle was called the organ-grinder, sometimes grinder for short, and
the whole story would be further confused by the introduction of another name for the instrument
—a hurdy-gurdy. Now the hurdy-gurdy was a stringed instrument, played by the rotation of
a rosin-coated wheel, in the form of a violin. The strings droned continuously and the performer
would make his music by playing on a little keyboard on the side of the belly of the instrument.
The keys operated tangents which stopped off the strings, so altering their pitch.

What, then, was that instrument which once played such a part in town life and which may
still be seen today as a charity fund earner? Barrel organ? Hurdy-gurdy? It was, in fact, a street
piano. A large wooden barrel, resplendent with thick pins like headless nails and similar to that
found in the real pipe barrel organ, was turned by a worm-gear on a handle and, as it went round,
the pins engaged in sprung hammers which, when drawn back by the pin, would be let loose to
fly forward and strike tuned strings mounted in a piano frame.

The street piano on its hand-cart, and sometimes with shafts for a donkey to provide forward

21

power, was a development of a much smaller, portable street piano which first appeared during the early years of the nineteenth century. This instrument was carried by a strap, which passed around the operator's shoulder, and steadied on a single pole protruding from its base as he played it.

Not that there was anything new in the idea of the playing of a stringed percussion instrument, such as a piano, by mechanical methods for as early as the beginning of the seventeenth century, Samuel Bidermann was making spinets in Augsburg which could be played either by a pinned wooden barrel or from a keyboard. Mersenne wrote in the year 1636: 'One can still recall in our time the invention of drums or barrels employed to play several pieces of music on spinets without the use of the hand, for the Germans are so ingenious that they make them play more than fifty different pieces by means of several springs which, when set in motion, ballets with several figures leap and move to the rhythm of the songs without any need to touch the instrument after having wound the springs'.

Weigel, too, asserts some sixty years later that such instruments of automatic music: 'especially at Nahe-Kussen near Augsburg, desks, chests and all kinds of decorative cabinet-work are made and sent far and wide throughout the whole world'.

It is related that amongst the fine collection of musical instruments left by Henry VIII was such a device. The item is described in detail in the catalogue of his musical instruments prepared at the time of his death in 1547. Some doubt as to its classification must have existed, for it is included amongst the 'virgynalles' and is listed as being:

'Item. An Instrumente that goethe with a whele without playinge uppon, of woode vernisshed yellowe and painted blewe with vi round plates of siluer (silver) pounced with anticke garnisshed with an edge of copper and guilte'.

Whether it was at this time a unique specimen, or merely the representative of a class, can never be discovered, but it was clearly a barrel instrument.

Incredible though it may seem, there are at least three such instruments which are still in playing order after more than three and a half centuries. One is in the Germanisches Nationalmuseum in Nürnberg, and another is in the private collection of Mr Tagger of Paris. Both are the work of Samuel Bidermann who was born in 1540 and died in 1622 and who was thus a contemporary of William Shakespeare.

There is a possibility that a mechanical instrument of this type was in fact used by Shakespeare in an early performance of *Cymbeline*. In the cave scene (Act IV, Scene 2) one may well have been used to accompany the famous dirge 'Fear no more the heat of the sun'. This must originally have been sung, but in the text as we have it, Imogen's brother Arviragus says of himself and his brother Guiderius: 'And let us, Polydore, though now our voices have got the mannish crack, sing him to the ground', implying that their voices have broken and so they are unable to sing. Perhaps the mechanical instrument was thus introduced because the boy actors' voices broke and the dirge had to be spoken whilst the instrument provided the solemn music called for in the stage direction. Belarius says: 'My ingenious instrument! Hark, Polydore, it sounds! But what occasion hath Cadwal now to give it motion? Hark!'

A very early instrument of the mechanical spinet type is now in the collection of Lord Howard de Walden at Dean Castle, Kilmarnock. This was restored to playing condition in 1957 by Fritz Spiegl (to whom I am grateful for these notes) in collaboration with Roger Fisk and John Sebastian Morley. There is a distinct possibility that this is the instrument which belonged to King Henry VIII, or was at least made by the same craftsman. It corresponds in almost every detail with the description given in the catalogue of the musical instrument owned by Henry VIII, even down to the fact that there are six silver medallions decorated with painted figures. The costumes worn by these figures suggest Flemish origin and, indeed, the Keeper of Henry VIII's musical instruments was in fact Flemish.

Mechanical spinets or virginals which are known to survive include the following:

(1) An instrument bearing a printed label reading 'Samuel Bidermann, Instrumentmacher, Augsburg' was formerly in the Silesian Museum, Breslau. The barrel is pinned with six tunes, the titles of which are written on a label beginning with 'a joyful procession announced by the blowing of the trumpeter (by Jr. Kay, May; the procession held in Nürnburg)'. This no doubt refers to the reception of the Emperor Matthias by the city of Nürnburg in the year 1612, and this suggests that the instrument was made shortly after 1612 and was made by Samuel Bidermann the elder.

(2) Bearing the same label as (1), this instrument survives in the collection of Old Musical Instruments in the Art-History Museum, Vienna. It is reputed to date from c. 1625–30 and is thus probably the work of Bidermann Junior.

(3) In the Rück Collection at the Germanisches Nationalmuseum, Nürnburg, is an unnamed specimen which bears all the characteristics of Bidermann instruments. Its provenance is considered, by Dr van der Meer, to be Bidermann Junior and dating from 1640.

Although unhappily a victim of the Second World War, mention should be made of:

(4) An instrument in the Carolino Augusteum Museum, Salzburg which, according to descriptions, must have strongly resembled Bidermann workmanship.

The following unsigned and undated instruments also exist:

(5) In the collection of Gustav Adolf in Uppsala is an instrument which the City Council of Augsburg acquired in 1632 from Philip Hainhofer and presented to the King of Sweden.

(6) In Leningrad at the Institute of Theatre Music & Cinematography.

Items (1) and (2) are square virginals of normal size with folding front keyboard fall and compartments to the left and right. Item (3) is an octave virginal. Item (1) has a richly inlaid ebony case, the inside of the lid being decorated with a painting of Apollo and the nine Muses. Written on the wood above the printed label is the date 1651 which probably denotes the date of a repair. Item (2) also has an ebony case inlaid with different woods. A full description of this is printed in Schlosser. This instrument has a veneered and inlaid stand with two small drawers left and right. The case of Item (3) is also of veneered ebony and stands on four feet fixed to the underside. The case slopes upwards towards the back. The sides are panelled with incised mouldings and the front panel hinges downwards, serving as the key fall lid. The top of the case is hinged and bears a green velvet panel with a gold border. On the right is a nest of drawers lined with red silk. Dr van der Meer attributes this to having been made in Nahe-Kussen and on the front of the key fall lid are the emblems of Augsburg. In the inside of the lid is a mirror (not original) with the arms and motto enclosed in a moulded frame. Oil paintings on wood panels are set to the right and left of the mirror; that on the left being of a woman and that to the right the portrait of a man. They are painted in the style of Anton van Dijcks. In all three instruments, the whole casing can be lifted up and off the mechanism.

In all three, the soundboard is of pine glued to a frame which stands on four short legs on the case bottom. The soundboard displays flowers and fruit painted in water-colour (in the case of Item (2) there is also a scroll). Delicate ornament in fine line engraving surrounds the central rosette and runs parallel to the edge bridges and the row of action jacks in Item (3) and to the row of pins in Item (2). The geometrical rosettes have a herringbone pattern. The base stands on supporting mouldings, partly of hornbeam wood, the right-hand table (the left-hand table on

Fig. 1. The four compositions found pinned on the barrel of Samuel Bidermann's clockwork spinet made in Augsburg in 1640 and now in the Germanisches Nationalmuseum, Nürnberg

Item (1)) as well as the soundboard being decorated with mouldings. The action jacks pass through the soundboard in a special guide.

By removing the soundboard with bridges and jacks as one unit, the instrument can be operated from its barrel, the keyboard remaining separately in the case.

The naturals of the keyboard are overlaid with ivory (in the case of Item (2) not original), the sharps being of black-stained pear-wood with ebony veneer. The compass of Item (1) and Item (2) is C/E–c³; that of Item (3), the octave instrument, c/e–c³ without d³.

All three instruments have a wooden barrel for the automatic mechanism. These bear the characteristic ruling and dividing practised by the Bidermanns, the surface of the barrel being scored laterally and circumferentially to produce a grid of small squares. Each of these squares is divided between the six tunes of Items (1) and (2) and the four on Item (3). Vertical markings show the lengths of four crochets and the divisions numbered around the circumference in Indian ink. The pins of the quavers and the repeated crochets are of steel whilst those of the shorter notes are of brass, the longer values having brass pins bent over into a hooked shape.

In all three instruments, a spring in a brass spring barrel drives the movement. Winding is by catgut fusee and the actual gear train differs between the instruments.

The six compositions on the barrel of Item (1) are given in Protz; the six on Item (2) in Nettl and Schlosser. The four pieces of Item (3) have been transcribed by Dr van der Meer and are shown in Fig. 1.

A variation on the clockwork spinet was the so-called harp-playing clock. The name is misleading because it certainly did not pluck its strings in a harp-like way, but used small wooden hammers to strike the strings of a small wood-framed dulcimer fixed vertically behind the clock mechanism. Its music was pinned to a barrel in the self-same way that the programme was pinned to the clockwork spinet. The instrument was made in Germany and also in the Low Countries more or less contemporaneously with its more popular cousin, the flute-playing clock. Its period appears to have been from the first half of the eighteenth century through to the middle of the nineteenth century. Even so, very few examples survive, no doubt because of the fact that they needed fairly constant retuning and thus were probably considered by their owners to be more trouble than they were worth.

The technique of the mechanical keyboard instrument stemmed from the pipe barrel organ and the earliest surviving mechanical organ seems to date from the late fifteenth or early sixteenth century. The mechanical organ at Salzburg was made in 1502 and the barrel organ really came into its own in the first half of the eighteenth century, when it was developed into an instrument suitable for the mechanical production of music to accompany hymns and chants in church.

The knack of transcribing music from ordinary notation into a forest of short, thick pins on a wooden barrel was described by The Rev. Father Engramelle of Paris during the latter half of the eighteenth century and, before him, by A. Kircher. The first written words on the subject can be said to have been those of an Oxford doctor of medicine at the beginning of the seventeenth century—Robert Fludd, alias de Fluctibus, who described four different types of cylinder in his book *De Naturae Simia*. Contemporary with Fludd, a French Engineer, Salomon de Caus, illustrated part of his book *Les Raisons des Forces Mouvantes* with a drawing of a cylinder pinned with the first six bars of a madrigal by Alessandro Striggio (1535–90).

In 1752, J. F. Unger and a Berlin mechanic named Hohlfeld perfected a machine to improve the technique of pinning. This recorded the fingering of the musician on a keyboard and could also be used as a pattern for pinning. The instrument so made was called a melograph and a similar machine was constructed by an Englishman named Creed at the same time. Melography came to

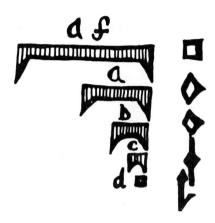

Pins of different lengths
with their corresponding note values according to Kircher's system
of mechanical musical notation

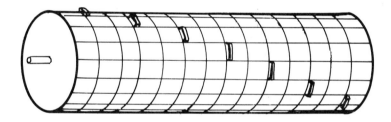

A cylinder pinned to sound different organ pipes in succession

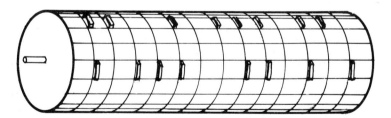

A cylinder pinned to sound different pipes at once

Fig. 2. Early mechanical music devised by Kircher in 1650

be used not just for the barrel type of music, but later on for punched cardboard and paper music, the work of Abdank and, separately, Carpentier, at the end of the last century being well documented.

Music set on a barrel is transcribed in a notation virtually at right-angles to that of printed music. The length of the music, as measured by the number of bars, becomes the length of the piece of paper. The bars thus run horizontally across the paper, and the various notes and their lengths are represented vertically. To set a piece of music of, say, forty bars length on to a barrel, the circumference of the barrel is taken as the length of the paper pattern. This length is then subdivided into forty horizontal spaces. The paper is then subdivided again, this time vertically and at a spacing equal to that of the fingers or keys of the playing mechanism. This grid is now marked in accordance with the musical notation, after which it is stuck to the barrel and the pins or bridges (in the case of an organ) inserted. In practice, more than one tune is pinned to each barrel, and therefore the paper is then marked over with different tunes, each one being displaced laterally a given distance equal to the lateral shift of the barrel needed to bring another set of tune pins under the key-frame.

Again, once the ruled paper pattern has been created, it can be used as a master for marking similar pieces of paper, either by 'pricking' the location of each pin or by lithography, only the musical notes being transferred, not the ground ruling.

The technical difficulties in reproducing, in any way faithfully, the tones and colours of stringed keyboard instruments by mechanical means were far greater than those needed to achieve the same ends for the mechanical organ. When, in 1817, Flight & Robson of London completed their remarkable Apollonicon organ, they were confident in proclaiming that it could perform with a degree of perfection at least equal to that of an accomplished performer. This organ was equipped with sets of barrels which played whole overtures and lengthy operatic selections. Many great organists also performed on this manual and self-acting instrument which was provided with no less than five separate co-lateral consoles. But for a long period the blind organist, Purkis, entertained the public with popular musical recitals, prefaced by an overture performed mechanically. This great organ was finally taken down in about 1840 when it ceased to draw sufficient public interest. Some five years later, Bevingtons built their larger Apollonicon manual and self-acting organ to illustrate the cyclorama of the Destruction of Lisbon in the 1755 earthquake, staged at Horner's Colosseum in Albany Street, Regents Park.

In the year of the demise of the Flight & Robson Apollonicon (it was dismantled and its component parts allegedly employed in the construction of other organs), Imhof & Mukle perfected their Euterpeon orchestrion organ.

An acceptably high degree of perfection from the barrel pipe organ had thus become reality with the middle of the nineteenth century, in the hands of these makers and other geniuses such as Blessing, Welte and Kaufmann in Germany.

Yet still, at this time, the mechanical piano was labouring away, trying hard to do something to offset its uncompromising tone and its unworthiness to any claim towards perfection of interpretation or purity of tone. It could not be a pianoforte—only a mechanical string-hammerer. At its best, it was unequal to the efforts of an inebriated pianist on a much-misused upright in the public bar.

Devices were invented to try to improve these qualities. Some of them worked to a greater or lesser extent, others were theoretically possible but, to all practical intents, most impractical.

The main drawback hinged on nothing more difficult to appreciate than the basic dynamics of the barrel organ versus the barrel-playing piano. With the barrel organ, all the barrel pins had to do was to raise a free-pivoting key, depress a light, wooden sticker and open a small, wooden pallet in the wind-chest. The sound was made by the passage of wind through an organ pipe connected by a windway to the opened pallet.

The barrel-operated piano, however, asked considerably more from its variant of the barrel organ mechanism. It was necessary for the musical strings to be struck with comparatively considerable power to produce the music and this had to be accomplished by the barrel pins and a key linkage. Appreciably more force was thus needed to work a piano when compared with the organ.

Since the earliest times, attempts had been made to play the piano by using some sort of frame or set of mechanical fingers which could be used to strike the piano's keys. The pinned barrel seemed to be the only practical solution. The direct association of the barrel and the keyboard, though, was not the answer to improving quality of tone.

An early mechanical piano was that produced in about 1820–25 by Clementi, Collard & Co, the musical instrument makers, in London. Muzio Clementi was born in Rome in 1752 and was a many-sided man. Infant prodigy, keyboard virtuoso, he is still known today for his sonatas for piano and harpsichord. He came to England at the age of fourteen and was a concert performer until he was almost sixty, at which point he abandoned public performances, joined the London firm of Longman & Broderip and took to the manufacture of musical instruments, among them some fine church and domestic barrel pipe organs. Upon the dissolution of that firm, he manufactured under his own name until he teamed up with Collard. As well as making barrel pipe organs and ordinary pianofortes, he made the 'Self-Acting Pianoforte'. This was a combined manual and mechanical instrument so that, if desired, the two functions could be performed together, one played by hand and the other by a 'horizontal cylinder similar to that of a barrel organ and set in motion by a steel spring' which latter was capable of performing 'the most intricate and difficult compositions' and of playing for half an hour without re-winding. The self-acting mechanism acted upon only eighteen of the piano notes.

Describing this machine, Dr Busby in his *Concert Room Anecdotes*, relates:
'The time in which it executes any movement may be accelerated or retarded at pleasure; and while by the delicacy and perfection of the mechinism the *piano* and *forte* passages are given with correctness and effect, the *forzandi* and *diminuendi* are produced by the slightest motion of the hand applied to a sliding ball at the side of the instrument.'

Another barrel organ manufacturer of the same period, Courcell, devised the Cylindrichord. In this device the piano keys were depressed by a mechanical escapement set in motion by the pinned barrel and key-frame principle.

Quoting again from Dr Busby who classified the Cylindrichord as an 'admirable and efficient substitute for a first-rate performer on the pianoforte', he says:
'In small or family parties, where dancing to the music of the pianoforte is practised, a person totally unacquainted with music, a child or a servant, may perform, in the very best and most correct style, quadrilles, waltzes, minuets, country dances, marches, songs, overtures, sonatas, choruses, or indeed any piece of music, however difficult. This instrument is extremely simple and differs altogether from the barrel or self-playing pianoforte; it can be accommodated to the height or dimensions of any pianoforte, and when not in use for that purpose, forms a piece of elegant furniture.'

How effective were these instruments we have only the eulogies of Dr Busby from which to judge. The fact remained that it was not possible to make a faithful mechanical piano. Certainly the direct linkage of a barrel to the mechanism of the piano was not good enough. The barrel pin was at its best not up to providing the motivating force on the hammer action of the period.

It may well have been instruments made by Clementi which formed the collection of mechanical pianos owned by Benjamin Flight Jnr (born 1767, died 1847) at his 101 St Martins Lane home. When Flight & Robson, famed barrel organ builders, found their business bankrupt in 1832, the whole premises and stock were auctioned, including these unnamed but interesting pianos. An examination of the auction catalogue lists four consecutive lots and the numbers given must refer to serial numbers. That all the items must be by one maker seems obvious by the disposition of these numbers. Flight & Robson are not known to have produced barrel pianos. I quote from the catalogue of the sale of Wednesday, November 14, 1832:

Lot 20   A ROSE-WOOD SIX-OCTAVE SELF-PERFORMING and FINGER-KEYED CABINET PIANO-FORTE, made on the latest and most improved principle, with Cylinder Front, Columns in the top and bottom part, Ionic Carved Caps and Bases, Carved Legs and Cornice, Radiated Silk Curtain, French Polished, &c.—No. 2795. The Self-performing part has 49 Keys, Shifts from Forte to Piano, and takes off the Damper as set by the Composer. One Spiral Barrel. No. 2815. Set to the Water Witch Quadrilles.

Lot 21   No. 2796. A MAHOGANY SIX & HALF-OCTAVE DITTO. The Self-performing part has 61 Keys, Cromatic (sic) Scale and Shift, &c. as the foregoing. One Spiral Barrel. No. 2721. Set to CLEMENTI'S Celebrated Duet.

Lot 22   No. 2781. A SEVEN-OCTAVE DITTO. The Self-performing part as the foregoing. One Barrel plays Eight Popular Airs, (No. 2791.) viz. Green Hills of Tyrol, Mazourka, Stop Waltz, WEBER'S Last Waltz, La mi Aspada, Gallopade, Der Freschutz Waltz, and March in Oberon. Cromatic Scale.

Lot 23   No. 2728. A MAHOGANY DITTO, without the Finger Keys, has 61 Keys, &c. as the foregoing, with 1 Spiral Barrel, No. 2810. Plays PAGANINI'S Set of Quadrilles.

NOTE. The Cromatic Scale has this advantage, that it performs exactly as the Composer has wrote it; whereas in the smaller Barrels they have not room to get it in as it is written, and are obliged to transpose, which loses the effect intended by the Composer.

In 1832, a mechanical piano (and a 'grand' at that!) was in use at the Grecian Hall (later the Royal Grecian Saloon), Eagle Tavern, City Road, London. The instrument was used to open the evening's performances and, in the programme for February 17, 1832, we read that 'The Self-Acting Grand Piano Forte will commence every evening at 7.0 precisely'. An undated newspaper cutting in the Enthoven Collection (Victoria & Albert Museum) refers to the fact that the self-acting piano forte 'has now been repaired and sounds very much better'. Was this one of Clementi's instruments? Can it be one about which Dr Burney wrote so glowingly? Alas! history does not relate and, sometime before 1836, the instrument had been replaced by a more conventional and probably more acceptable band of instrumentalists.

A Frenchman named Forneaux had the germ of the solution in 1863 when he decided to couple another of the features of the barrel organ to the barrel in an attempt to play the piano. He used the bellows, key-frame and sticker assembly from the barrel organ in his Pianista. Each note of the music on the barrel raised the organ-type finger key-frame and depressed a wooden sticker into a wind-chest. This opened a pallet which sent air rushing not, as in the organ, to a pipe, but into a small expanding bellows. It was this bellows assembly which actually caused the piano key to be struck. To play the Pianista, it had to be pushed up in front of the piano and over the piano keys. All the performer had to do was to turn the handle which rotated the barrel and pumped the bellows.

A device which could not really be considered a serious contender for the advancement of the mechanical piano was that patented by a Frenchman, Alexandre Debain, in 1846. His mechanism was made to fit across the keyboard of a harpsichord or spinet and comprised a peculiarly-shaped frame containing levers and stickers which rested on the keys. The music was represented by strips of wood or planchettes which were studded with pins. These wooden strips were fed along a channel in the top of the frame by rocking a decorative handle up and down. An arrangement of double ratchet levers imparted a continuous rotation to a drive cog. Called the Antiphonel, Debain's device was a hark-back to more primitive days and was certainly far less practical than even Courcell's push-up player of more than twenty years earlier.

Debain went on to make pianos which incorporated the Antiphonel. His earliest was a 'keyless' model which could only be played using the planchettes but by the time of the Great Exhibition, he was producing combined antiphonel and manual instruments. One such piano is illustrated in Plate 11. Quite long pieces of music could be played, the planchettes being numbered as sections of the music to show in which order they should be played. Sixty-one notes could be played mechanically.

The catalogue of the Great Exhibition of 1851 (Vol. III, Page 1,233) described this device as follows:

Piano mécanique or antiphonel pianoforte, an instrument which has been applied with success as a substitute for organs and harmoniums, it is said to be superior to the barrell used in church organs, and less costly.

The flat surface of the upper portion of the antiphonel is covered with a metal plate, pierced across its width with a series of openings, which admit through them a corresponding number of metal points, projecting about $\frac{1}{8}$th of an inch above the plate. These points are the extremities of small levers, which communicate with the action, then the upper level surface of the machine forms a complete keyboard, the projections are pressed down to perform the music by a piece of hard wood, studded with pins, which is forced over the level surface already mentioned. The piece is held down by a bar placed over it, and the pressure regulated by springs. Having placed the piece on the antiphonel, it is passed over the key frame by turning a handle, and as the pins on the plank come into contact with the antiphonel keys, the notes are struck, which are loud or soft as required.

The pieces studded with pins may be from 4″ to 24″ long; 8″ will contain as much as is written on a page of music paper, any number of pieces may be used for compositions of greater length. While one piece is playing; another should be had in readiness immediately to succeed it; until the piece of music is concluded.

The mode of studding the wood with pins, to produce the various effects required, is very simple and easily executed.

The antiphonel can be placed on the pianoforte as a cover, and by a simple contrivance, on opening the pianoforte, the antiphonel action is removed, and on touching the keys the tone of the instrument is not affected by the attachment. In closing the pianoforte the antiphonal resumes its place, and is ready for use.

When applied to the organ etc, as pressure on the keys is only required, the antiphonel is placed over the key frame and appears like fingers pressing down the required notes.

Perforated cardboard music originated in 1842 and was variously applied over the years without much success until it came into its own at the end of the 1880's at which time it appeared likely to oust the wooden barrel for both organs and pianos which worked automatically. In 1884, Thibouville–Lamy of Paris advertized their Pianista (a name which many subsequent makers adopted) which could be pushed up in front of a piano keyboard. Perforated cardboard music,

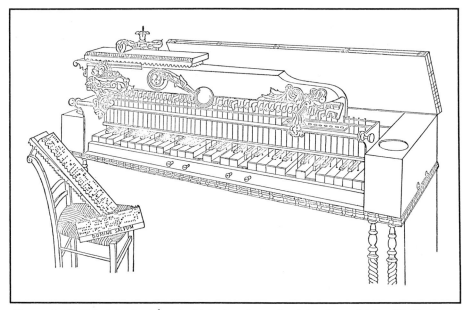

Fig. 3. A. F. Debain's *Antiphonel* which played wooden 'planchettes' (after Dr Buchner)

folded into a zig-zag 'book', was fed through the Pianista by turning a handle. This caused little fingers to push down on to the piano keys. A similar contrivance was made for organs and this was called the Organina. It is related that if the operating handle was turned quickly, the music came out loud and fast; if it were turned slowly the music came out soft and slow. There was no method of regulating volume and speed independently.

The period 1878–80 saw the introduction in America of a small table musical instrument called the Organette. Precursor of a very large number of different makes, designs and styles, this was a pneumatic instrument which played free reeds using a perforated paper roll. The performer turned a small handle to feed the music through the machine and also to reciprocate a pair of small bellows which continuously drew the air out of the case. When a perforation in the paper engaged with a passage leading to a particular reed, the suction of the bellows or exhausters would draw air through the reed, so making it speak.

Although a Londoner, Anthony Baynes, had taken out a patent as early as 1846 for the playing of a pipe organ using a perforated paper roll, the concept was not developed and thus it was not until the advent of the organette that the clue to the pneumatic playing of a piano was understood. The table organette was built both in Germany and in America in a large variety of shapes and sizes, some playing perforated metal discs similar to those used on the disc musical boxes. In these, the projections on the disc engaged in levers which opened pallets over the reeds. The true pneumatic organette, playing a paper roll which was fed over a perforated tracker-bar, was the first step towards the pneumatic action, already being exploited in organ construction, and its application to the piano.

When, in 1887, the Welte Company of Freiburg-im-Breisgau perfected and patented a piano playing system using a pneumatic action controlled by a perforated paper roll, the stage was set for the ultimate in piano mechanisation.

Up to this time, the barrel piano and most of the cardboard-playing pianos had employed, to a greater or lesset extent, a mechanical action. The new discovery was the power of air. Used in conjunction with a method of modifying the pressure of air in a vessel relative to that surrounding the vessel, air could be made to perform a variety of operations quickly and positively. The pressure modification was achieved by bellows or exhausters, and the performance of duties by small bellows (termed motors), and valves. The music sheet was no longer expected to make physical contact with a lever or to do any work other than to control the access of air to a small wind passage. It could thus be made of a thinner substance—paper.

The paper-roll pneumatic action was used mainly in the production of orchestrion organs in Germany by Welte who later expanded their interests to America where they set up a factory. The next major advance came in 1888 when William D. Parker of Meriden, Connecticut, devised a player reed organ called the Symphony which was produced by the Wilcox & White Company. He followed this in 1891 with a combination manual and paper-roll operated piano. In England, the paper-playing Maxfield reed organ was perfected. Alfred Dolge, one time head of a great piano manufacturing empire and American piano historian, suggests that R. W. Pain produced the first self-acting pneumatic piano in 1880 as a complete unit for Needham & Sons. This had 39-notes and was followed in 1888 by an electrically operated 65-note instrument.

In 1897, an American, E. S. Votey, perfected the Pianola piano-player. This was the first provenly successful example of a number of the odd devices which, although short-lived and soon discarded in favour of later inventions, played a vital part in piano history. The Pianola was intended to make any piano into an automatically-played instrument. It was, in fact, a completely separate appliance which was used in conjunction with an ordinary piano.

Known as a cabinet-style player or 'push-up', it consisted of a set of bellows (more properly termed 'exhausters'), worked by the feet of the performer, a paper-roll transporting device which fed the perforated music over a tracker board containing small windways leading to a set of pneumatic valves, and a row of small fingers at the back of the player which rested on the piano keyboard. Votey's first model, which played on only a few of the piano keys, is preserved in the Smithsonian Institute in Washington.

The first production Pianola was a cumbersome contrivance and, although it only played 58 or 65 notes of the piano, it was so large that it obscured even the largest and most grandiose of uprights. In due course, the fruits of development resulted in a smaller and quite compact instrument.

Backed by the enormous drive and business acumen of William Barnes Tremaine and his son, Henry B. Tremaine, plus the facilities which were later to add up to the largest player-piano consortium in the world, Votey's piano-player was soon being sold all over the world. So were the similar products of many other firms who wheedled their various ways around the Votey patents to build virtually the same machine.

Even so, the piano-player enjoyed but six or seven years of unequivocal favour. It was at best a cumbersome contraption, tricky to position at the piano and with the ever-present risk of damage to the slender, felt-covered piano-key fingers at the back. By 1908, its sales had dropped almost to nil in favour of subsequent improvements. And this in face of the belief firmly held by experts such as William Braid White who maintained that the cabinet player would not lose its popularity in favour of 'the inner player'!

Nevertheless, the advantages of the 'push-up', advanced more and more plaintively by r makers, paled into insignificance in the face of one instrument which could be both player and played upon manually.

Notwithstanding the claim by Dolge of the existence of a single unit player-piano in 1880, by 1901, Melville Clark—another American—had discovered a method of packing all the player action components inside the piano. He produced the first documented player-piano and, within a year, the Aeolian Company in New York was advertising 'The Pianola Piano—The First Complete Piano'. He was also the first person to produce a pneumatic player action in a grand piano in 1904.

So was born the pneumatic roll-playing piano, and with it all the trappings of a new industry. In America, specially modified Ford trucks were made which had piano loading attachments so that the piano salesman could take an instrument to a prospective client, demonstrate it and, he hoped, make an on-the-spot sale. Some $2\frac{1}{2}$ million player-pianos were sold between 1900 and 1930.

In England, where such sales methods were considered distasteful to say the least, refined advertisement in the best newspapers and such magazines as *Punch* and *The Illustrated London News* together with displays in piano showrooms produced a comfortable growth of sales.

In 1912, a concert was held at the Queen's Hall in London at which the London Symphony Orchestra conducted by Arthur Nikisch played Grieg's Pianoforte Concerto in A Minor, the solo part being played by Easthope Martin on a player-piano. Elena Gerhardt sang several songs to 'pianola' accompaniment at the same concert. The programme was repeated a year later with Camille Chevillard conducting the Lamoureux Orchestra.

Among the many devices employed to popularize the instrument in England besides many concerts such as these were the early endeavours of Britain's largest manufacturers of piano rolls, the Perforated Music Company. In 1913 they started their 'Riddle-Roll' competition in which an unlabelled roll (usually an abstruse piece of music) would be supplied to subscribers for identification. Together with their 'Popular-Puzzle-Roll' contest, the first prize was a year's free subscription to the roll library.

Demonstrating that the modern do-it-yourself enthusiast is no new specimen of humanity, only his tools, materials and ideas being with the present-day, the magazine 'Work' spent many issues during 1914 instructing its readers on how to build the player-piano. This must have been no mean feat for an amateur although in very recent years Mr Reg Best, an officer of the Greater London Council, has achieved just that in constructing a charming and practical 'push-up'.

There was still the ultimate in player-pianos to be invented—the reproducing piano. The ordinary player-piano would produce all the notes, but left the actual expression (soft and loud pedalling, theme expression and phrasing) to the performer who achieved these effects by small levers on the piano which operated pneumatic bellows controlling the actual action of the piano and quite independently of the musical playing action.

The problem of making the whole system automatic was not insurmountable by any means. It just demanded that the roll of music be provided with some extra perforations to control special action pneumatics directly. As early as 1904, the German firm of Welte built a reproducing piano known as the Keyless Welte since it had no keyboard but was purely mechanical. Hupfeld followed with an electric reproducing piano of more conventional layout in 1906. However, it was not until just before the first war that the Duo-Art reproducing action was perfected in America, followed soon afterwards by the Ampico.

So absolutely perfect were these instruments and the interpretations which they could give, that each roll was specially recorded by an artist who would add his name to the roll. Many famous pianists did just this and, thanks to their co-operation and to the reproducing piano, we can actually hear today the performances of such masters as Edvard Grieg, Claude Debussy, Theodor Leschetizky, Josef Lhevinne and Rachmaninov to name a glittering handful.

Fig. 4. The difficulties associated with obtaining a faithful recording of a piano – the scene in an early phonograph recording studio. ......

The implications of this statement need time to sink in and thus, to paraphrase it, we may hear from a music-roll the identical performance and interpretation of a pianist long since dead. Admittedly, some of these artists made phonograph recordings, but these are inferior on many counts. Not only was the microphone and sound apparatus of the time distressingly primitive by today's standards, but the range of sounds picked up on the phonograph cylinders was limited. To all intents and purposes, this meant that the performer could not play *pianissimo*, but had to pound out the music, largely with disregard for the soft pedal. Also, each cylinder played for a set time, and so the performance had to be tailored to that duration. The reproducing piano roll had no such shortcomings, for it was a timeless mute transcription, faithful in every respect and demanding for its rehearing just to be placed on a reproducing piano.

The importance of the player-piano during its life cannot be over-emphasized. It was certainly regarded as of greater interpretational significance than the gramophone by such famous pianists as Leschetizky—who firmly averred his disappointment that it had not arrived on the musical scene a century earlier—and Busoni, who is reputed to have thought it as important an invention as the cinematograph.

There is no doubt that during its lifetime the player-piano was in no small measure responsible for the growth and development of musical knowledge amongst people who might otherwise have never had their latent musical interest aroused. A spokesman for the Perforated Music Company said, in 1913, 'A man buys a player, and the first month he plays rag-time. Then he goes rapidly through the comic opera stage, till he reaches Chaminade and MacDowell. Often he gets no further than that, but an increasing percentage go on to the classics'. Certainly more people were inclined to take 'the classics' into their homes when they could 'play' themselves and it has been averred that the reputation of MacDowell in this country was largely due to the influence of the player-piano.

The potentials of the music roll are best demonstrated in a story told some years before the first war by a well-known American roll-manufacturer. A famous singer was about to take part in a piano-player promotional recital and, the preceding afternoon, was taken on a conducted tour of the factory. She showed such a great interest in the roll-making department that after a while she was invited to sit at a piano and sing one of her own songs. At the conclusion she was asked if she would sing that particular song in the recital due to begin a few hours later. 'But it isn't even in manuscript', replied the artiste. 'I haven't had time to write it down and no one could accompany me and I cannot do both satisfactorily'.

She was then told that, although the new song was not written down, she had in fact just cut the master roll by playing upon the recording piano. The song was performed that evening.

A foretaste of later trends in public libraries occurred in 1914 when that institution in Kansas City, Missouri, added 500 player-piano rolls to its music library. Non-musical ratepayers, however, had little cause for grievance; the rolls were the outcome of a gift from a private individual.

An understanding of just why player-piano rolls and, later, reproducing rolls, give us a far better idea of musical interpretation of the time than the few gramophone and phonograph recordings can best be appreciated from the following extract from a letter which Busoni wrote to his wife in November, 1919.

'...My suffering over the toil of making gramophone records came to an end yesterday, after playing for $3\frac{1}{2}$ hours! I feel rather better today, but it is over. Since the first day, I have been as depressed as if I were expecting to have an operation. To do it is stupid and a strain. Here is an example of what happens. They want the Faust Waltz (which lasts a good ten minutes) *but it was only to take four minutes!* That meant quickly cutting, patching and improvising, so that there should still be some sense in it; watching the pedal (because it sounds bad); thinking of certain notes which had to be stronger or weaker in order to please this devilish machine; not letting oneself go for fear of innacuracies and being conscious the whole time that every note was going to be there for eternity; how can there be any question of inspiration, freedom, swing or poetry? Enough that yesterday for nine pieces of 4 minutes each (half an hour in all) I worked for three and a half hours! Two of the pieces I played four or five times. Having to think so quickly at the same time was a severe effort. In the end, I felt the effects in my arms; after that, I had to sit for a photograph, and sign the discs.—At last it was finished!'

In a later letter, just before he gave his last public concert in 1922 at the age of fifty-six, he wrote from his London hotel to his English manager:

'...The conditions are most unfavourable. The room, the piano, the chair not inviting. I have to start like a racehorse and to end before four minutes have elapsed. I have to manage the touch and the pedal differently from how I do it usually.

What, in heavens name! can be the result of it? Not my own playing, take it for granted!...'

Busoni was, admittedly, best described as an interesting if unconventional performer whose personality and creative imagination often coloured his renditions to such an extent that, as Claudio Arrau once said, 'very often the composer was almost totally lost'. Be that as it may, his comments on the techniques and demands of the recording studio remain extremely valid and demonstrate forcibly the enormous value of the reproducing piano and its music and, albeit to a slightly lesser extent, the ordinary player-piano.

These highly sophisticated reproducing pianos and their actions were expensive and there materialized a number of attempts at achieving partial expression from music rolls by simpler methods. The Themodist, for example, was one of many which provided automatic soft/loud pedalling and theme accentuation by the expedient of extra holes in the paper roll when used on a player-piano equipped to interpret this system. This was what might be called un-graduated pedalling as compared with the Duo-Art which provided no less than sixteen different 'shades' of dynamic intensity to cover all extremes of *fortissimo* and *pianissimo* and to produce the most finely-graded *crescendos* and *diminuendos*.

The American Aeolian Company used the Duo-Art action in their pianos and the mechanism was also fitted in Steck and Steinway models, both grand and upright.

In the course of its advertizing campaign, the Aeolian Company promoted a series of concerts at Aeolian Hall, New York, at which the New York Symphony Orchestra performed piano concertos with the piano solo part being supplied by an un-manned Duo-Art playing a roll. Remembering that these rolls were always signed by the artist who had originally recorded them, it was widely publicized that the soloist at one such concert—Harold Bauer—would be in Chicago at the time of his New York 'performance'.

At a London concert, a performance of a Liszt Rhapsody was shared between the pianist Cortot playing 'live', and a previously-recorded music roll by Cortot. The effect, we are told, was so dovetailed that music critic Ernest Newman said: 'With one's eyes closed, it was impossible to tell which was which'.

The system by which Duo-Art recordings were made was ingenious to say the least. The celebrated pianist performed upon a grand piano which, in outward appearance, was no different to an ordinary instrument. However, from the piano ran a multi-core electric cable carrying two different sets of wires, one from contacts beneath each piano key and one from positions near where the hammers struck the strings. The cable led out of the recording studio into a sound-proof room in which was situated the Duo-Art Recording Apparatus. Here the wires were attached to electro-magnets which operated punches in a perforating machine, each punch corresponding with its proper note on the piano. As the pianist played, so the punches perforated the paper master roll, thus making a permanent recording.

This method of recording thus achieved accuracy of reproduction, the length of perforation being determined by the length of time during which the key was held down. The punches in the machine repeated at the rate of 4,000 cycles per minute, so making possible the accurate recording of the most rapid of staccato notes struck by the pianist. The resultant punched hole for the briefest note would be just 1/32 inch in diameter.

Rhythm of the music was determined by the spacing of the perforations in the master roll as it passed through the recording machine, at a constant speed which was normally eight feet a minute. So long as the rolls made from the master so cut were played back at the same speed, faithful *tempi* would naturally result.

Dr John B. McEwen, then Principal of the Royal Academy of Music, prepared a graphic illustration (Fig. 5) to demonstrate the different *tempo* phrasing used by two great pianists of the time when playing the first four bars of Chopin's Prelude No. 15 in D flat (the so-called 'Raindrop' prelude).

The melodic outline is shown by its position in the horizontal sections whilst the vertical columns represent the regular divisions of rhythm, each one being of the value of one quaver. The bar lines are indicated by thicker vertical lines. The middle section represents the rigid metronome *tempo* with the notes occurring exactly upon the rhythmic positions indicated in the printed music.

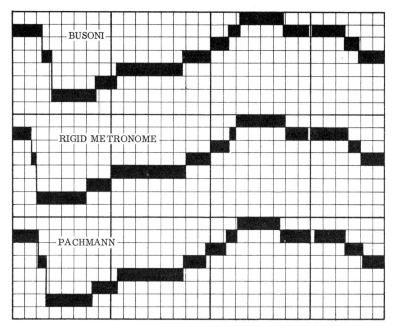

Fig. 5. McEwen's chart demonstrating *tempo* phrasing

The upper section is taken from the Duo-Art recording by Busoni whilst the lower section shows the amount of *tempo rubato* used by Pachmann in his Duo-Art recording.

In both recordings, the first note can be seen to be in excess of its actual value. Busoni held it an extra quaver while Pachmann increased its normal length by a dotted semiquaver. The short notes are all extended beyond their value by both artists and the excess of time is balanced by a reduction of some of the longer notes, particularly the dotted minim in the second bar. Where the note F is repeated at the beginning of the fourth bar, theoretically the previous note should extend exactly to the commencement of the bar, but if the note has to be played twice as called for in the score, there must be a point at which the finger is raised. This can be seen as a slight division in the marking of the two notes just before the bar line in the middle section. It is interesting to observe that, whilst Busoni raised the finger for a very short time and played the two notes with the different values indicated by Chopin, Pachmann made a wider space between the notes and played them as though they were of equal value. Both pianists shortened the highest note of the phrase, but it is almost certain that if a vocalist had had to sing that melody, the top G would have been considerably extended.

The touch of the pianist was similarly recorded and reproduced, using the same technique of perforations in the music-roll following electrical impulses from contacts within the recording piano. With four dynamic controls, sixteen different degrees of touch could be produced (see Chapter 9), extending over the whole range of finger power from the lightest *pianissimo* to the strongest accent. In combination with the Themodist device already mentioned, the melody could be differentiated from the accompaniment, each having its own set of dynamic controls and full range of touch.

When the original recording was made, it more than likely contained stray wrong notes which no pianist may entirely avoid when playing passages requiring speed and force. One of the finest pianists of the time noted to his chagrin no fewer than 360 false notes in a single performance! Fortunately, these wrong notes could be detected and corrected under the supervision of the artist himself. Every blemish to the performance could be removed and omitted notes cut into their proper places. Even the touch and rhythm could be improved upon if the artist was dissatisfied with his recording.

It is obvious that, with such revision carefully carried out with the artist, the result was a most polished interpretation. This explains the statement of Percy Grainger (who studied with Busoni) that his records on Duo-Art represented him not merely as he did play, but as he 'would *like* to play'. Possibly the greatest tribute to the Duo-Art came from Paderewski who, speaking of the music roll of one of his compositions, said that listening to it gave him the same feeling in his heart as when he played it himself.

The Aeolian Company of New York produced a series of player reed organs between 1898 and 1914. Called Aeolian Orchestrelles, they played mostly 58-note paper rolls but some larger models played 116-note music. They were all arranged to speak with a tone resembling flute, trumpet, French horn or whatever the particular stop might be. Instruments ranged in size from a large upright piano to 9 foot high monsters in richly ornamented cases with as many as twenty-eight different speaking stops. The Wilcox & White Company of Meriden, Connecticut, built a similar range of player reed organs called the Symphony. As with the Orchestrelles, the Symphony played paper rolls and the performer was left to use his own discretion as to the stops to use, guidance only as to speed and expression being provided.

The reproducing piano technique was applied to these reed organs and also to special pipe organs made by a number of American companies including Aeolian. These were very beautiful instruments, both in tone and appearance, and they played 176-notes on two manuals. All functions of the organ, including the swell shutters, could be operated automatically from the paper roll as well as the stops, the result being a perfect performance from a fine instrument.

Wilcox & White reflected the trends with their early reed player instruments and one of their Angelus models could be pushed up to a piano keyboard in the same manner as the contemporary piano-player. Playing from the music-roll, the organ would perform on a small number of stops —usually about seven—and, when a stop-knob marked 'Piano' was drawn, it would let down upon the piano keyboard a set of fingers which would then function in the same way as those on a conventional player. The device could thus play a piano/organ duet, a 'dual-solo' or whatever the performer demanded just by the arrangement of the stop knobs.

In America, the electrically-driven nickelodeon—basically a player-piano to which was added percussion effects and sometimes a few ranks of organ pipes—became the rage. Both in Germany and in the States, many varieties of these instruments were made for the bars and cafés, dance-halls and amusement arcades. The centres of production were, respectively, Leipzig and Chicago. With the spread of Prohibition in the 1920's, the market for these diminished considerably and many makers went out of business or changed to making cinema 'Photoplayer' orchestras (see Chapter 5).

The complexity and intricacy of some of these devices brings home to one that it is not just the present-day technician who knows how to pack a large number of pieces into a small space. The only difference lies in the fact that components packed into a player mechanism tended to be larger than those packed into, say, a modern computer today.

The player-piano inventors of the period were not short of ideas and a great number of patents were taken out for various improvements to the instrument, its action and construction. Some were of lasting value, such as the invention by the Aeolian Company in 1901 of the printed *tempo* line on the ordinary music-roll, and the primary pneumatic action. Others, such as the electro-magnetic player using sheet metal music-rolls, were destined not to make the grade.

A vast industry had been created and the number of player-piano manufacturers is impossible to estimate. Almost every maker fitted either his own player action or, more commonly, a recognized action available as a kit or unit from a player action maker. The psychological impact of the instrument on the public was profound and sales boomed. Pianos with player capabilities went to ocean liners, troopships, dancehalls, hospitals and private homes. Interest and demand for the player-piano spread throughout the world and by 1920, Japan had a thriving industry manufacturing *ji-do pianos* (player-pianos, literally 'self-moving piano') which cost from 1,400 yen to 3,800 yen for a player grand. Also in full manufacture at this time in Japan were electric coin-freed barrel pianos for cafés.

The popularity of the player-piano can in some measure be judged by the fact that the 1922 London Trades Directory listed agents and manufacturers for no fewer than fifty-two different types of instruments including reproducing pianos. Some of these were inferior instruments but these figures prove the existence of a very considerable demand in Britain. Since the demand here was but a fraction of the American sales, the number of makers in the United States was extremely large and, in the way of things, the precise figure may never be known.

Considerable artistry could be employed in the playing of a music-roll and, indeed, a performer who had both a flair for musical interpretation and an understanding of the mechanism of his instrument could produce a performance of extremely high quality using the manual expression controls fitted to an ordinary player-piano. The logical argument was that, with all the musical notes ready to play and requiring no mental effort, the performer could concentrate all his skills and faculties into the method and style of interpretation. The serious player-piano operator could produce a perfect interpretation from an ordinary roll, given a good piano and the desire to master it and to learn the roll.

Notwithstanding the two more obvious elements of the player-piano which were responsible for its popularity—entertainment and personal gratification—the instrument could be used by the serious music lover for the analysis of a piece of music. Even the accomplished pianist could learn much from the music-roll that the musical score and his interpretation might otherwise pass over. The Aeolian Company's introduction of 'annotated rolls' was engendered by just this demand. Considerable explanatory text and a wealth of detailed information—including the musical score—was actually printed on the rolls to 'educate whilst playing'.

Indeed, in one interesting experiment to demonstrate the art of the contrapuntal as employed and developed by J. S. Bach, a piano roll of one of his compositions was reversed so that the high notes became the bass and the low notes the tenor and treble. The result, so it is related, sounded just as melodious as before!

This more serious side to the player-piano is further demonstrated by the activities of the German Honorary Committee for the Promotion of Musical Studies, by means of the Duo-Art and Pianola. Although savouring strongly of a publicity 'gimmick', this group held their inaugural meeting in Berlin on Wednesday, May 18, 1927, and included such musical personalities as Max Bauer, Siegfried Wagner, Bruno Walter and Percy A. Scholes. The objectives of the Committee were (a) to further the educational use of Duo-Art and Pianola instruments and music-rolls; (b) to comment technically on the music available from the Aeolian catalogue, and (c) to recommend to the company a choice of new compositions to record.

Also at this meeting, Percy A. Scholes introduced 'The World's Music' series of music-rolls in their various forms. There was the Biographical Roll, the Analytical Roll, the Running Commentary Roll and Rolls with Explanatory Introduction. Aeolians were certainly the most enter-prising of the roll makers.

Late in the 1920's, more in an attempt to stimulate the dying market than to foster perfection, American dealers organized player-piano proficiency contests for students. Two authoritative books were written by contemporary musicologists on the techniques of playing the player-piano and the British Broadcasting Company employed a reproducing piano to play not only interval music, but also scheduled piano music programmes. The instrument had not only become accepted, but was most definitely respectable.

True as this was, the player-piano had a profound sociological effect on the community. As Roehl reflects, a whole generation grew up without the need to learn to play the piano. Hitherto, piano playing was part of home life, part of growing up. Almost everyone could perform to some degree. With a self-acting instrument, there was no longer any call for tiresome five-finger exer-cises. All that was wanted was a roll of music, for technical competence had been superseded by rubber tubing, valves and air motors. The *Saturday Evening Post* cartoonist summed up the situation in one sentence. His cartoon showed a young girl rather stolidly pumping her way through a roll of music. The mother, in conversation with another woman relates: 'Yes, my daughter has a great foot for music'.

The President of the Aeolian Company, H. B. Tremaine, was honoured for his work with the company and, indeed, for his pioneering work in the field of the player and reproducing piano, by the staging of an International Duo-Art Week on November 20–25, 1922. Commemorating Tremaine's twenty-five years' service, Duo-Art recitals took place in many parts of the world and they included Paderewski's Duo-Art performance of his 'Minuet' to mark also his return to the concert platform.

One hundred distinguished musicians under the chairmanship of Walter Damrosch and including all the famous Duo-Art pianists, formed the Tremaine Tribute Committee to arrange the events. Tremaine received many awards including one from the Pope (as 'purveyor to the Papal Palace'), the Belgian Order of Leopold and the French Legion of Honour.

The London Duo-Art concert was held at the Queen's Hall with Sir Henry Wood conducting and the Duo-Art as soloist in Saint-Saëns' G Minor Concerto. Photographs of Aeolian Halls and showrooms in Australia, New Zealand, Capetown, Johannesburg, Gibraltar, Java, Gothen-burg and Trondhjem (Norway), Denmark, Holland, France, Germany, Spain, Italy, China, Japan, Argentine, Brazil, Chile, Venezuela, Columbia, Ecuador, the West Indies, England and both North and South America were on show.

An interesting display was mounted tracing the history of the player-piano and organ from 1885 through the organette, Aeolian Organ (46 notes), Aeolian Grand (58 notes), Aeolian Orchestrelle, Pianola Cabinet (65 notes) to Pianola-piano (65 and 88 notes) and thence to the electric Duo-Art Grand.

It is interesting at this late juncture, to reflect upon all these events in the light of the years which were to follow. By 1931 a financial crisis affected most of Europe and America was similarly embarrassed. The few short years that followed saw the end of Tremaine's empire.

The player-piano remained in favour until the mid-1930's, but the peak of its popularity was between 1920 and 1925. Almost every manufacturer of pianos both in England and in America fitted player actions to their instruments. There was no question of its being beneath the dignity of the great names amongst makers to build player-pianos; indeed some of the finest instruments bore such famous names as Steinway, Blüthner, Broadwood and many others. Naturally, the better the piano, the better the player action fitted and, understandably, it was the practice of these top-brass makers to fit the reproducing actions such as Hupfeld, Welte, Ampico and Duo-Art.

With the progress of wireless and the introduction of television during the years immediately prior to the 1939–45 war, not to mention the improvements in the gramophone industry, the player-piano suffered a progressive decline. This did not apply solely to player-pianos, but also to ordinary instruments. Production tailed off and many makers went out of business or were absorbed by larger firms. The onset of war marked finis to the era. In the short space of about forty years, the pneumatic player-piano had developed from a rather primitive and largely impractical machine to a set of components which fitted inside the piano and by which perfect reproduction might be obtained. As with so many great inventions, having gone through the processes of evolution, it emerged as the quintessence of its designed specification, only to find that standards had been altered so much that it was no longer required. Thus in its very prime it became obsolete.

Happily, though, after a period of quiescence, there has been a resurgence of interest in the player-piano and in 1950 the Aeolian Corporation produced a new instrument. Oddly enough, this was a hark-back some half century for, whilst small, compact and electrically-operated, it was a piano-player as distinct from a player-piano. Called the Key-Top Pianola, it was simply lifted on to the keyboard of an ordinary piano and performed by pushing down on the keys as would a human performer—or Forneaux's Pianista of 1863! This was not a trading success and was sold only in America on limited scale.

A few years after the Aeolian revival, the Gribble Music Company, of Kansas City, produced a device called Magic Fingers which had to be permanently attached under the keyboard of an ordinary piano. Engineered by the Midwest Research Institute, it was, so it seems, unsuccessful and was both expensive to make and to fit.

These two modern failures could justifiably have been taken as evidence against the likelihood of any successful attempt at resuscitating the mechanical piano. However, in 1957, the P-37 Hardman Peck Duo was introduced to the American market by the Aeolian Corporation. Possibly because the public had more money to spend by this time and probably because they were becoming more musically aware, the measure of success enjoyed by this instrument was surprising. Selling at about £465 each, these well-engineered, full-scale player-pianos sold well. Encouraged by this, a new Pianola, styled the P-67, was marketed late in 1960. Stylishly modern in appearance, garnished by present-day trends and advertised in the now-accepted soap-powder and cigarette style, this was not a true piano, but a 64-note spinet costing £300.

In 1964, Dynavoice Incorporated of Plymouth, Michigan, produced another key-top player, and then the Ivers & Pond, Cable and Winter Musette player-pianos followed. These were all produced by subsidiaries of the Aeolian Corporation. The name 'pianola' is thus once more before the public in the shape of a new, modern instrument, but perhaps more interesting still is that the makers have seen fit to name some of their range Duo/Art. The new Duo/Art is not in any way a reproducing instrument, though, the words being used to emphasize nothing other than the ability of the instrument as both a manual and a self-acting piano. To distinguish between the new and the old, Duo/Art is written with a stroke instead of being hyphenated.

The price of the new Duo/Art runs from $1540 to $1580 depending on the design of case selected. For an extra $240, the instrument can be supplied with an electric motor in which variant automatic re-roll, re-play and expression pedal control is included. Whether electric or otherwise, the new Pianola is also supplied with the 'Ukelano' which, states the advertising literature, 'allows a wide range of Mandolin-like effects. When a knob located under the keyboard is pulled forward, a rink-a-tink sound reminiscent of a mandolin or "treated" piano is produced'. All this does is to lower a strip of leather with a metal tag on its end between each piano string and its hammer—a system used in almost all the coinola-type pianos and nickclodcons made in the twenties.

This rebirth of the player-piano is of great interest and obviously has as its basis deep socio-logical undertones. It can be seen as an example of yet another demonstration of the latent rebelling by the ordinary person against the electronic age. More overt manifestations of this are seen in the rapid and largely sincere increase in popularity of antiques and Victoriana in general.

In certain quarters, though, the player-piano's following has never really waned. In Australia, for example, the instrument is almost as popular now as it ever was, there never having been any marked recession in interest. There is still a rich trade in restored player-pianos and also in new rolls which are still being produced in quantity. In both England and America exist small firms, often one-man outfits, who will produce new ordinary rolls, or make a copy of an old roll. The use of modern electro-mechanical methods in roll copying is a problem to which I have given much thought in recent years as a result of which I now have my own automatic roll copier. Interest in player-pianos is mounting daily now. They are becoming more and more sought after; their ownership, once considered a liability, is now being cherished and owners are taking a second look at their pianos and even taking the trouble to learn the proper way to make them perform a roll. Even so, as an industry, it is still a little precarious and one may confidently predict that it may never again be so lucrative a line as it was half a century ago.

The basis of the player-piano has very recently been the breeding ground for an interesting and promising development known as the Pamplin Electronic Keyboard Control System. Invented and patented by Mr Terence Pamplin of Worcester Park, Surrey, in 1965, the principle purpose of the system is to use modern technology to proceed beyond the pneumatic piano playing action and to produce something capable of recording music so that it may be played back with a degree of perfection and touch hitherto impossible.

With the reproducing piano (see Chapter 9), a high degree of control could be imparted to the keyboard but, even with the Duo-Art system's fifteen degrees of touch and Hupfeld's 'floating expression lever', individual notes could not be expressed adequately, such as the three notes of a triad for example. An early exception and one which came very near to this ideal was the Tel-ektra made in 1905 (see page 272). This used an all-electro-magnetic lever system, controlled by perforations in a brass music roll, some one hundred small fingers being employed to effect the necessary switching.

Mr Pamplin's first experiments consisted of mastering the electrical control of one note of a piano action. The control system chosen was that of an audio-frequency signal of known frequency which was released on depressing a key of the piano, passed to a band pass filter and from there to switch a power solenoid and thus set in motion the action for that piano note. The second stage of experimentation comprised the construction of a three-note model. In this, storage of information was introduced by means of a tape recording. For the three notes, three different frequencies were chosen—3000, 3600 and 4200 Hertz—and signal generators of these frequencies were incorporated in the system to be controlled by the key switches. On depressing one or more of the keys, the corresponding signal or signals would be passed via an amplifier to the tape storage unit. On replay, the signals passed to a bank of three band pass filters, each tuned to one of the control frequencies. After selection, the signals would actuate the appropriate solenoids and thus complete the cycle. It is worth noting that the solenoids for this experimental model came from a derelict Violano-Virtuoso (see Chapter 5).

The third stage was the development of touch control, the sensing of key depression velocity and using this to modulate the control frequency to give infinite reproduction of the degrees of touch. The fourth and final stage is the control of a complete piano keyboard, expanding on the three-note experimental system and incorporating stage three.

The advantages of the new system are claimed by Mr Pamplin to be many but are best revealed in the two fundamental assets—firstly, the remote control of a piano with infinite touch and, secondly, a recording and reproducing piano with infinite touch.

For the piano teacher, the first of these points suggests an entirely new conception of teaching, making possible class instruction in the form of a piano-teaching laboratory. It would allow one teacher to take a class of up to ten pupils, each at different standards, and in a similar way to that practised in language tuition.

The complete recording/reproducing piano has many obvious advantages. In the home it would serve as a normal fully-expressioned player-piano, taking magnetic tapes instead of paper rolls. In this form, teaching tapes from a piano-teaching laboratory could be put into the piano's 'memory' to teach the pupil at home. Thus the old problem of finding a performer of suitable standard with whom to play duets would be overcome. It would only be necessary to play one part into the memory of the piano, then replay that particular magnetic tape whilst performing the second part. For the composer, the advantages are at once apparent. Instead of having to write at the keyboard, he would be able to compose directly on to the piano, where his music would be ready to replay from the piano's memory at any time, allowing transcription into regular notation at leisure.

Mr Pamplin's system, at present being developed by the old-established London piano manufacturers, Monnington & Weston, who hold the patent rights, is capable of further applications such as the provision of couplers for octaves and harmonics, pedal boards with touch, and detached keyboards. The results here would undoubtedly be more satisfying than those envisaged in 1852 by Dr John Henry Gauntlet and in 1863 by Goundry who, patenting an idea for the playing of organs electro-magnetically, projected that from one keyboard situated in St Paul's Cathedral, every organ in London could be operated by one organist! Of all the possibilities, the educational aspect appears to be the greatest and this is a development which, although possibly outside the scope of the normal player-piano, promises to be an important one in future years.

CHAPTER 2

The Barrel Piano

THE barrel piano is a direct application of the principles of the mechanical pipe organ, properly termed 'barrel-organ', in which a wooden drum, studded with metal pins, is rotated by a worm-gearing and a handle. The pins on the drum represent the music and operate metal levers in a key-frame which in turn move stickers into a wind-chest, open pallets and let air through to certain musical pipes.

In the piano application of the system, however, the barrel with its pins and gearing is all that remains. The idea of a rotating drum or cylinder having pins to operate a musical device is of some great antiquity and the mechanical horn organ at Salzburg used just this system in 1502. Later on, smaller versions were used in musical clocks to play simple tunes on bells, dulcimers and glockenspiels.

The introduction of the practical barrel piano in the form in which it has come down to us is widely claimed to have been the work of a piano maker named Hicks of Bristol, in the first few years of the nineteenth century. The Hicks family were prolific workers and, from 1805 up to at least 1850, they produced many such instruments, both in Bristol and, later, in London.

Joseph Hicks of Bristol seems to have been the inventor of the device later to be called variously cylinder piano, barrel organ (incorrect), street piano, piano organ (travesty), hurdy-gurdy (incorrect), grinder organ (incorrect), mechanical dulcimer (perhaps the most apt). Even the word 'piano' must be adopted with reserve for, certainly at the beginning, it was incapable of varying its sound output and was far more 'forte' than 'piano'. Although 'mechanical dulcimer' is thus nearer the truth when terminologically speaking, cylinder piano or barrel piano may more readily be understood.

The date of the invention is claimed by Scholes as 1805; Clark says 1810. Certainly the techniques and skills necessary to construct such an instrument were known well before that time and I feel rather inclined to suggest that the earlier date is more probably correct.

Joseph Hicks was the son of a famed cabinet-maker named Peter Hicks who was admitted a freeman of Bristol on October 12, 1812. The last entry in the Rates Books which Langwill has traced for Joseph is 1847.

A specimen of this type of small street piano exists in the George Brown collection, New Jersey, and bears the mark: 'George Hicks, Hand-Organs and Cylinder Pianos, Brooklyn, L.I.'. This instrument is identical to those made by Hicks in England and, in the absence of concrete evidence, it may be suggested that George was either the brother or the son of Joseph Hicks, emigrating to America probably about 1820.

One John Hicks of Clerkenwell, London, was building the same type of instrument c. 1850 and it is more than likely that he, too, was related to Joseph. The name Joseph Hicks crops up again on a much larger instrument in which the barrel paper watermark is 1846. The address given is Pentonville, London. Whether this implies that Joseph (of Bristol) died in 1847 and Joseph (of London) was a son, or whether Joseph left Bristol in 1847 and came to London, remains unknown. There is a close similarity between all the instruments bearing the name Hicks and the trade of cabinet-maker is certainly evidenced in the good workmanship and appearance of their cases.

With the apparent exception of the large one by Joseph Hicks in London, referred to above, these early pianos were intended for use by street musicians. Street music is as much part of life as any other form of music and was particularly so at this time. Indeed, a study of this subject, its sociological influence and its general effect on the public at large would itself require a large monograph. The wandering musicians either played ordinary musical instruments (where they had the ability) or relied on mechanical ones.

The small barrel pianos, barrel pipe organs and the barrel harmoniums of later years were extremely popular—at least with their players. This enthusiasm was not shared by the town residents, however, and the mass medication of citizens in their homes by noisy musicians in the road outside, invariably playing the same tune over and over again, jarred nerves, encouraged high blood pressure, fostered questions in Parliament, engendered ineffectual bye-laws—which still did not stem the remorseless tide of mechanical music in the streets. The Victorian writer, John Leech, was sent to an early grave because, he apparently claimed shortly before his demise, he was being driven mad by the noise of 'organ-grinders'.

Professor Charles Babbage, mathematical visionary, inventor extraordinary and a cantankerous genius to boot, justly earned the title of the organ-grinder's Public Enemy Number One. Like Carlyle, his concentration was extremely sensitive to distracting sounds and he considered that a quarter of his life's working power was destroyed by the audible nuisance of 'organ-grinders' and other street musicians performing outside his house in Dorset Street, London. Babbage took up petitions against them, complained to his Member of Parliament, badgered the police to arrest them and, so it is related, once persued a fleet-footed member of this maligned fraternity for a mile across London before finding a policeman who was willing to run him in.

Nevertheless, the closing years of the reign of George III saw the resurgence of street music using mechanical barrel pianos. Pall Mall in London was the first street to be illuminated by gas light in 1807, breaking for the first time the Stygian gloom of London's night-life. The itinerant musicians could now play after dark and gain revenue from the theatre-goers and promenaders.

When Joseph Hicks died, his teachings survived in the hands of his one-time apprentice, Henry Distin. He produced instruments very similar to those of Hicks, playing eight or ten tunes on 23 notes. All these pianos had wooden frames; indeed with the exception of the hammer shafts and the sundry brass springs and steel linkages, they were made entirely of timber. The iron frame for normal pianofortes, an American invention, did not come until 1825, so there was nothing unusual in this style of construction. With the pianoforte, the total pull of all the strings on the wooden frame was often as much as 30 tons and thus it was common practice during the interval of a concert or piano recital for the tuner to come to the rostrum and retune the instrument. The smaller street piano suffered, to a lesser extent, from the same inherent problem and thus there was plenty of work to be had for the Distins and the Hicks, maintaining their products in service. The fact that these street pianos went out of tune so quickly and also that usually their operators either couldn't care less or, quite probably, were not musical enough to notice, only fanned the rising distaste of the public for this sort of music.

Henry Distin later moved to Philadelphia where he was still alive in 1898—his eightieth year. An interesting story concerns Distin's father who was a solo bugler in the Grenadiers. In that capacity he was supposed to test all the musical instruments for the British bands. One day he chanced to try a bugle which had been sent down from the Tower. It had been badly packed and a nail from the packing case had been driven through it. Distin tried the instrument and found that it played a new note (bugles at this time, in keeping with most horns, had no pistons). Thus inspired, he bought an old bugle and filled it full of holes until he found the new notes which would be usable. Henceforth, the keyed bugle was perfected.

There was a trend for the musicians to favour the street barrel-organ playing pipes rather than the barrel piano. Although its initial cost was probably greater, it did not require frequent attention and, with normal use, remained in tune. Jos. W. Walker, a parlour apprentice to organ-builder George Pike England, was prompted to manufacture a barrel organ almost identical in appearance to the Hicks/Distin type of barrel piano. Only one of these has ever been seen and the average street barrel organ tended to be a smaller, more compact instrument taking the best advantage of the ability of organ pipes of excessive length to be mitred into compact shapes.

The strong similarity between the concept of the barrel piano and the barrel organ led to the manufacture of mechanical pianos by several barrel organ makers. William Rolfe of Cheapside, London, built both barrel organs and normal square pianos. His son, Thomas Hall Rolfe, concentrated more on the mechanical piano and, in 1825, took out patents for improvements on the self-acting pianoforte which comprised a method of pinning the barrels to produce loud or soft notes by regulating the length of the pins—a device later perfected by Schmidt in Germany as we shall see further on.

William Youens built a mechanism patented in December 1859 which could be placed on to the keyboard of a piano or harpsichord for mechanical playing. Unlike Alexandre Debain's Antiphonel playing mechanism of 1846, which used flat, studded wooden boards or 'plan-chettes' to produce movement via stickers to the keys, Youens fell back on the time-tested barrel as the musical provider. This was fixed in a frame with a set of weighted levers, one for each piano key. The music was represented not by pins on the barrel, but by holes or depressions. When the ends of the levers dropped into these openings in the barrel surface, their opposite ends contacted the keys. The force of contact, and thus the volume of sound produced, could be varied by the form of the barrel note holes. This keyboard-player could be operated either by hand or by clockwork.

During the 1850's, thoughts were turning towards larger barrel pianos and two other famous barrel organ manufacturers—Imhof & Mukle and T. C. Bates, directed their attentions to the making of fine instruments which would blend with the fashionable styles and décor of the period.

Imhofs made some particularly attractive hand-wound pianos in ornamental cases richly endowed with ormolu decoration. These had 54 notes and were provided with storage space for a second barrel beneath the first. Extra cylinders could be bought for £10 and many were pinned for dance music and pop music of the period. One example I have seen plays selections from *The Bohemian Girl* by Balfe (1843). The tone of these Imhof instruments was comparable to that of the pianoforte.

T. C. Bates & Son of Ludgate Hill, London, produced a clockwork cylinder piano which stood 7 feet high, was 4 feet 7 inches wide and 2 feet 3 inches deep. It played 85 notes and had a manual keyboard. The 3 foot 9 inches long cylinder for mechanical playing was placed in the bottom of the case along with the action. Bates also built weight-driven pianos standing 4 feet 6 inches high and playing 3 foot long cylinders.

William Gillett and Charles Bland improved the Hicks system in 1869 when they devised a barrel piano having continuously-beating hammers, allowed to contact the musical strings only when the correct key was lifted by a barrel pin. Their invention was not a success, though, and in 1874 Daniel Imhof devised a combined damping and sustained device for barrel pianos played with ordinary Hicks-type hammers.

Daniel Imhof had amassed a tremendous amount of experience using pinned barrels for the orchestrion organs which his firm, Imhof & Mukle, manufactured at Vohrenbach in Baden Baden, and he produced a number of improvements to the basic mechanism, particularly with regard to the tonality.

Instead of a crank handle, the manual/mechanical piano made by J. Lecape & Co. in 1882 was operated by a foot treadle which turned the barrel for mechanical playing.

For the major developments in the barrel piano, we have the Italians to thank. During the second half of the nineteenth century, a large number of Italian musicians and artisans came to England to find work. A number of these settled down to producing large barrel pianos for the street musician.

In the ensuing years, the history becomes a little confused because these Italian workers formed companies, moved from one address to another, re-formed with other workers from other firms and reorganized time and time again. Practically every one of the London Italian makers, for example, worked at some time or another with his contemporaries. We must therefore steer a path through this period by examining some of the improvements and commenting on their influence on the barrel piano.

One of the Italian migrants was Giuseppe Chiappa who founded a street-organ and piano works in the Clerkenwell district of London in 1864 with a fellow Italian, G. Fersani. This particular quarter of London, the Farringdon Road area of the watch and clock-making district of Clerkenwell, a few miles to the east of the City centre, was to become the home of the street barrel piano industry and practically all of the subsequent firms made their homes either here or in near-by Warner Street and its environs. In the immediate vicinity were the lodging houses of Saffron Hill where the street musicians, mainly Italians, made their homes.

Chiappa and Fersani produced large barrel pianos which were transported on hand carts or donkey carts. Whether or not they were the first to make these large street instruments is unknown, but they were certainly the first of the recognized builders. In 1878, they took out a patent for a combined street piano and organ played by one barrel. Half the instrument was a piano played by pins on the wooden drum, and the other half played a 'cornet accompaniment' from pins and bridges over that half of the barrel. In true barrel-organ fashion, the worm-gear which drove the barrel also manipulated bellows through reciprocators to provide wind for the pipes. No such instrument has been seen and it is to be assumed that either few were manufactured, or their degree of durability rendered them short-lived.

In the following year, J. Y. Smith patented a method of controlling the action of barrel organs and pianos but it fell to Alexander Capra, J. B. Rissone and S. Detoma jointly to make the first worthwhile improvements to barrel piano action in 1880.

The instrument of this period comprised a vertical wooden frame, substantially built to resist the enormous strain of the combined string tension, a pivoted key-frame or, more properly, hammer-frame which supported one sprung hammer for each note, and a pinned wooden drum. Each drum would play eight or ten tunes and was advanced manually by a snail cam controlled from the outside end of the case. This cam was linked to the hammer frame so that, when the barrel was shifted, the delicate hammer-tails were lifted clear of the barrel pins to prevent damage. Unlike the cylinder musical box, to which there was a mechanical family likeness, the tune could be changed at will, even in the middle of a performance by indexing the cam with the handle provided.

Each musical note was represented by wire strings as in the ordinary pianoforte. The base strings were copper-covered and usually the extreme two or three bass notes would be represented by single strings. The remainder of the wrapped strings would be bichords, that is to say that there would be two strings tuned in unison. The central portion would be represented by trichords—three strings in unison. Some makers later used four or even five strings in unison for the extreme treble register. This was due to the fact that thin strings, of short length to produce a high note, are weak in volume for a given hammer force. This volume can be increased by increasing the number of strings which sound that note.

Alexander Capra devised a barrel piano with 'mandoline harp' effect in 1890. Each string was plucked by a rotating cylinder holding three spring-wire plectra. The plectra throughout the piano compass were kept in rotation by a linkage from the crank handle and were brought into contact with the strings by the normal aegis of the barrel key and connecting levers.

Capra was an inventor who also gave thought to the problems of mechanizing the ordinary pianoforte and, in 1882, he had devised a piano-player using a pinned barrel and stickers but, for the same reason no doubt that the later pneumatic push-ups fell out of favour, this was not a money-spinning idea.

Capra and Rissone now turned their attention towards the other possible markets for the barrel piano. The public house was an obvious thought and for such use they devised the first clockwork-driven barrel piano. This was powered by a fusee-wound spring motor and would play a tune to order without the need for cranking a handle all the time. The first of many such clockwork pianos, termed 'automatics', this appeared in 1884 and proved an immediate success.

Just as Bidermann had mechanized his keyboard spinets by the addition of a barrel mechanism, so did similar solutions receive consideration from inventors. Ludwig Potthoff and Hilmar Golf of Berlin devised a most complicated barrel attachment to a keyboard piano which they patented in 1884. The barrel mechanism was mounted under the keyboard and, when played mechanically, the barrel pins operated a linkage of primary and secondary levers and cams, terminating in a secondary piano key which set in motion the piano action in the same manner as the pianist's fingers.

Johann Gerhard Gottfried Schmidt of Köpenick near Berlin was soon to realize that his compatriot's endeavours to set in motion the piano action via the barrel was rather like burning down the farmyard to achieve bacon. All that had to be moved was the actual hammer, not the action, and so, in 1887, he perfected a simple barrel mechanism, again under the piano keys, to do just that. He also patented the principle, first registered by Rolfe in 1825, that the volume of the note depended on the force exerted on the hammer-tail by the return spring

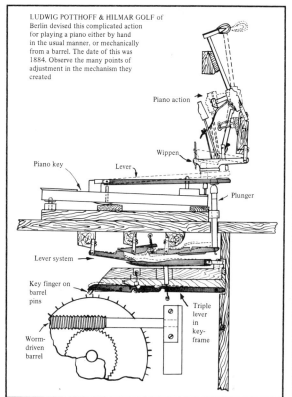

LUDWIG POTTHOFF & HILMAR GOLF of Berlin devised this complicated action for playing a piano either by hand in the usual manner, or mechanically from a barrel. The date of this was 1884. Observe the many points of adjustment in the mechanism they created

Piano action

Wippen

Piano key

Lever

Plunger

Lever system

Key finger on barrel pins

Triple lever in key-frame

Worm-driven barrel

JOHANN GERHARD GOTTFRIED SCHMIDT's patent for a combined keyboard and barrel-operated piano - 1887. Because the travel of the mechanical hammer action could be so short in this system, much shorter barrel pins could be used, allowing longer tunes to be pinned than normal practice for a barrel of a given size. The barrel could therefore be turned slower. When not played mechanically, the mechanical hammer rest-rail held the action clear. The mechanical key-frame bears a resemblance to the early Hicks style

Hammer

Normal rest rail

Tie

Piano string

Hopper or Wippen

Normal piano key

Mechanical hammer action

Hand-cranked worm drive to barrel

Rest rail for mechanical action

Short barrel pins

Barrel

Pivot

Hammer tail

Mechanical action key-frame

Fig. 6. Potthoff & Golf's barrel-and-finger piano action

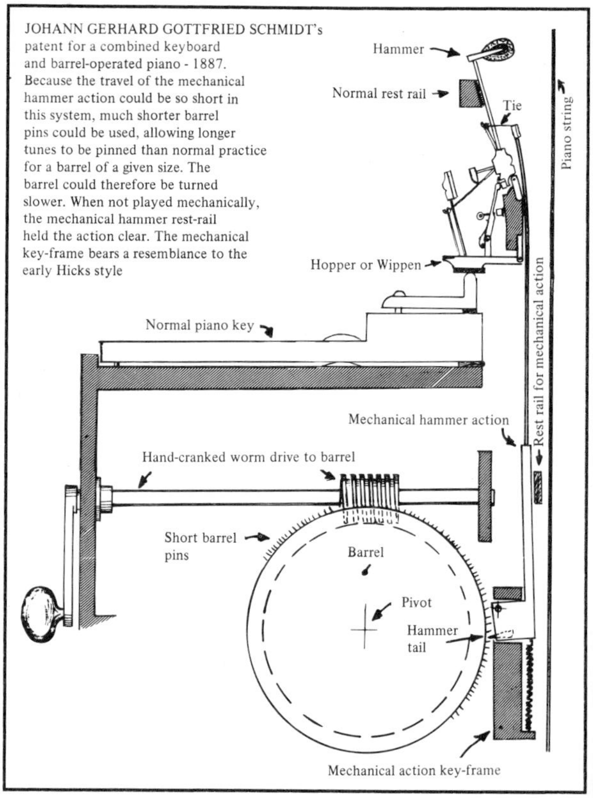

Fig. 7. Schmidt's simplified barrel-and-finger mechanism

and thus the intensity of a note could be varied by the distance which the pins protruded from the surface of the barrel.

In Bologna, Italy, Giovanni Racca and W. Seward were making barrel pianos for use in indoor public places, and Francesco Getto of Ivrea, Italy, produced small portable street pianos similar to those of Hicks. Getto, however, improved on the detail of Hicks' concept in many ways, not the least of which was the use of thinner music strings to produce a brighter and more singing tone.

When Gillett and Bland contrived their design for continuously-beating string hammers in 1869, they were on the threshold of perfecting what was later to be known as the 'mandolin' effect in which, when a note is sounded, the hammer strikes the strings several times in quick succession. With sustained notes, the effect is supposed to resemble the sound of a mandolin.

J. M. Grob & Co., of Eutritzsch near Leipzig, was the first to devise a practical mandolin effect from a street piano. A fluted steel shaft was arranged between specially-shaped sprung hammers and the piano strings. The hammer-tails, which were not rigidly attached to the hammers themselves, were moved by bridges on the barrel, in the same way that a barrel organ works. The bridges raised the hammer-tails and held them for the appropriate length of musical time, drawing the actual hammer against the rotating shaft by means of a spring. The result was the staccato striking of the string. Some two years later, in 1890, Capra improved on Grob's

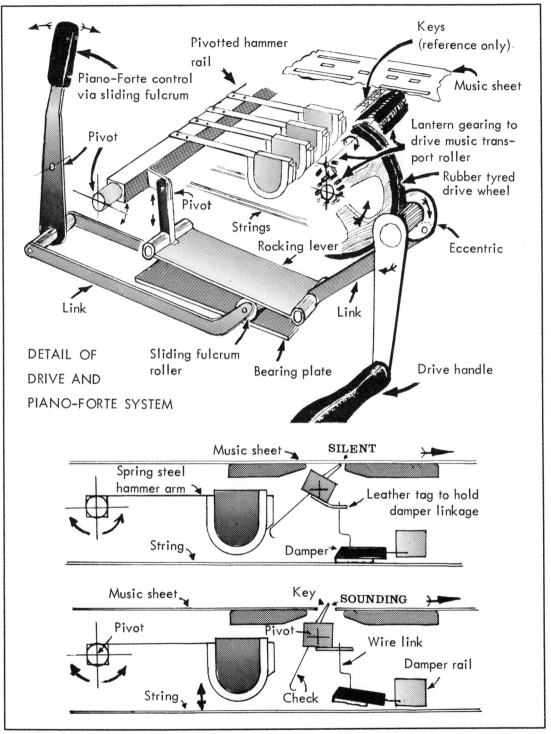

Keys (reference only)

Pivotted hammer rail

Piano-Forte control via sliding fulcrum

Pivot

Pivot

Strings

Rocking lever

Link

Link

Music sheet

Lantern gearing to drive music transport roller

Rubber tyred drive wheel

Eccentric

DETAIL OF DRIVE AND PIANO-FORTE SYSTEM

Sliding fulcrum roller

Bearing plate

Drive handle

Music sheet

SILENT

Spring steel hammer arm

String

Damper

Leather tag to hold damper linkage

Music sheet

Key

SOUNDING

Pivot

Pivot

String

Check

Wire link

Damper rail

Fig. 8. The 'Piano Melodico', made by Giovanni Racca in 1886, featured an ingenious system of continuously-beating hammers. Several makers of hot-air engine-driven pianos used this same method of striking. (See page 73)

invention and, so successful was this modification of the barrel piano, that during the next twenty years, almost every manufacturer of consequence perfected his own system of achieving this effect.

The clockwork barrel piano had caught on very well and was now being built by several makers. In an endeavour to break fresh ground, Gregori Pasquale & Co., which firm comprised Charles Romano and Pasquale Amato at this time, placed the clockwork motor actually in the end of the wooden barrel and wound it through a hole in the barrel access door. This was in 1898. It was obviously necessary to let the spring run right down before attempting to remove the barrel for changing and it meant that each replacement barrel had to have a spring motor built into it.

The following year, P. Rossi, C. Rossi and Loreto Spinelli made a barrel piano which could be either hand-turned or clockwork driven and this included tuned bells and a drum. The spring motor was again in the barrel.

The bane of all street pianos was the warping of the wooden frames. Manufacturers tried numerous forms of construction to avoid this trouble including cross-boarding the backs. Not only were the frames prone to warping, but they also showed a tendency to split along the wrest-plank due to the string tension and this usually meant the end of the instrument to all practical intents and purposes. So great was the tension that the wrest-pins often worked loose. Even at its best, the piano could not be expected to stay in tune for very long.

It was in an endeavour to cure these shortcomings that Rossi and Spinelli produced some clockwork pianos having iron frames. These were intended for indoor use but they were not a success since the tone suffered badly.

The iron frame was never adopted for the street instrument. This was primarily due to the greater weight which it would have entailed. However, if any application of the barrel piano called for an iron frame, then it was certainly the poor street model with its erroneously supposed stoic disregard for climatic changes and the exigencies of the London weather.

In America, Eugene deKleist of the North Tonawanda Barrel Organ Factory near New York was devising a barrel piano, later to be known as the 'Tonophone', for the Wurlitzer company. DeKleist, who heralded from Düsseldorf in Germany, went back to Forneaux's system in that he used a barrel and key-frame system combined with pneumatic bellows. The pins on the barrel lifted a key which connected with a tracker to a wind-chest, admitted air into a small pneumatic motor or bellows and thus allowed the string to be struck by a hammer connected to one of the bellows boards. Driven by an electric motor, deKleist's Tonophone was patented in July of 1901.

The coin-freed piano had been in existence for some time and was probably the invention of Gregori Pasquale who set up his firm in London in 1895 and remained in business until 1940. This attachment to a clockwork barrel piano allowed a tune to be played by the insertion of a penny. It was usual for the tune to be played twice for one coin and it speaks well of the design and execution of these instruments that, although there was only the smallest gap in the pinning between the beginnings and ends of the tunes, the mechanism always stopped in the right place after its two revolutions. Chiappa made improvements to this mechanism in 1901 and became one of London's largest manufacturers of this type of instrument, probably ranking very close to Pasquale who was a prolific maker.

Because the power of the wrist remained in excess of that afforded even by the best clockwork motor, the clockwork automatic barrel piano was unable to strike more than five strings at once without 'jumping'. The hand-wound piano, however, could strike eight or more notes

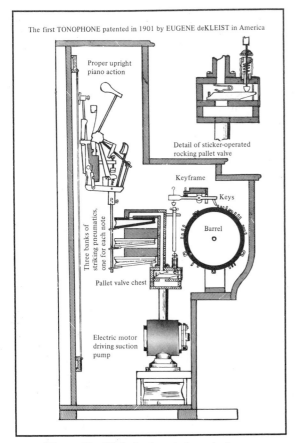

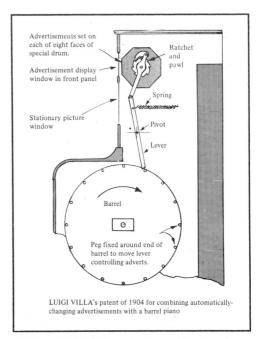

The first TONOPHONE patented in 1901 by EUGENE deKLEIST in America

Proper upright
piano action

Detail of sticker-operated
rocking pallet valve

Keyframe

Keys

Barrel

Three banks of
striking pneumatics,
one for each note

Pallet valve chest

Electric motor
driving suction
pump

Advertisements set on
each of eight faces of
special drum.

Advertisement display
window in front panel

Stationary picture
window

Ratchet
and
pawl

Spring

Pivot

Lever

Barrel

Peg fixed around end of
barrel to move lever
controlling adverts.

LUIGI VILLA's patent of 1904 for combining automatically-
changing advertisements with a barrel piano

Fig. 10. Villa's barrel piano with changing
advertisements

Fig. 9. De Kleist's electric barrel piano –
the Tonophone

at once and thus manufacturers were able to make the street piano into a more florid interpreter of music by employing many more barrel pins and exercising their transcription skills to the full.

Several of the London makers had branches elsewhere in the country and the two cities most favoured were Manchester and Glasgow. At some time or another, a number of the larger manufacturers opened works in these places, as did some of the barrel organ makers. Gavioli, for example, was making organs in the Great Ancoats Street part of Manchester.

One piano-maker who, it seems, remained indigenous to the Manchester area was D. Antonelli who specialized in clockwork barrel instruments. He patented in November 1901 a method of removing the barrel for changing without disturbing the rest of the mechanism. This was a very great step forward and the Antonelli improvements were to be felt throughout the entire industry in a short space of time. Hitherto, to change a barrel was a fairly lengthy business, demanding, for example, great care in realigning the new barrel. Antonelli retained his barrels in a fixed location in the piano case, pushing them into the right position with a leaf spring on the access door.

Joseph Piana Canova of Clerkenwell was one of the many makers who thought up improvements to the beating hammer tremolo or mandolin effect in 1902. In the following year, Luigi Pesaresi coupled a fortune-telling device to a street piano, which consisted of a wheel set spinning inside a window in the front fall of the piano case.

Another maker in Clerkenwell, Luigi Villa of Granville Square, Farringdon Road, also directed his inventive thoughts to utilizing the piano case for secondary purposes—this time with strong commercial leanings. In April 1903 he took out a patent for a method of displaying advertisements through a large window in the front fall. A system of levers and links, inter-mittently moved by pins in the end of the music barrel, converted the continuous rotary motion of the barrel into an intermittent rotation of vertical rollers at each end of the case. These rollers carried a travelling blind upon which were mounted advertisements.

Across the Atlantic, deKleist's Tonophone pneumatic barrel piano was selling well, spon-sored by Wurlitzer. He improved his original mechanism and took out subsequent patents covering his new thoughts in both 1902 and 1903.

Rose, Coop & Rissone of Regent Street, London, applied the coin-freed mechanism to a pneumatic piano-player which they made in 1903 and, after that, they seem to have discontinued barrel instruments. Pesaresi & Son concentrated mostly on 40 and 44 note automatic street instruments, usually fitted with tremolo or mandolin effect, but they were only made in small numbers, not receiving much encouragement from the users with whom, for some reason, they were unpopular.

The clockwork barrel piano was in wide use in cafés, public houses and such-like. In the same way that the modern juke-box may be controlled remotely from customers seated at their tables in a café, so did Thomas Linforth Jones contrive to set clockwork pianos playing in 1905. He used 'electro-magnetic energization' by the insertion of a coin in a remotely-mounted coin-slot box to free the detent on the piano's clockwork mechanism. Any number of such coin-slot boxes could be connected to the one instrument.

The so-called mandolin or tremolo effect on a street barrel piano seems to have been very popular and every maker of consequence devoted efforts to perfecting the system. The general concept was substantially the same as that first conceived by Grob in Leipzig in 1888. The hammer was made in two parts, usually connected by a spring. Between the two parts rotated a splined shaft. A sustained note on the string was represented by a bridge or staple on the barrel, instead of the usual pin. This bridge held the lower part of the hammer in such a way that the hammer arm and head was placed in engagement, under the load of the spring, with the rotating shaft, thus imparting a staccato beating to the string.

A drawback to the rotating-shaft system for creating a mandolin effect was the appreciably greater wrist-power needed to play the instrument. Even when in good order, more than twice the force was required and one can imagine that after a few hours' playing, the operator would be somewhat fatigued.

In 1905 Julius Carl Hofmann of Vienna again modified the beating-hammer system and, in the same year, Spinelli built the first split-bridge mandolin barrel piano. This piano had a sound-board with two bridges which effectively divided it, providing two sets for each of the treble notes to permit two hammers to be used for one note. By pinning the barrel to work each hammer alternately, a mandolin effect could be achieved without the complication of bevel gears and beating hammers.

Simon Robino, described as a musical instrument maker of Manchester, patented his own version of the beating-hammer tremolo in 1906 but his system involved a complex movement of the hammer as compared with the eclectic trends. His hammers were drawn down by bell-

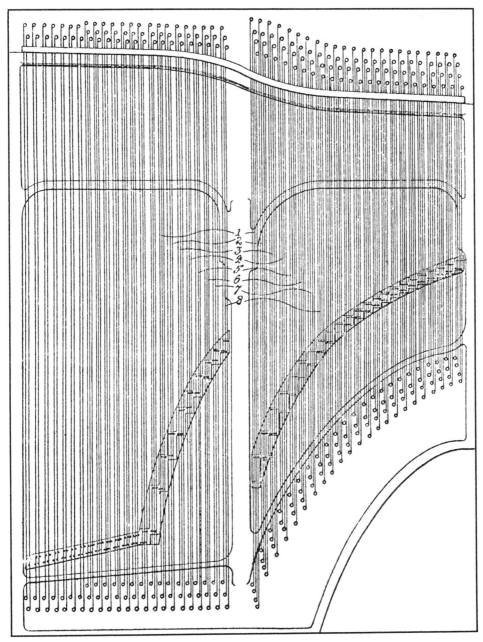

Fig. 11. Loretto Spinelli devised this 'split bridge' for street pianos in 1905, to produce a mandolin effect by doubling up on the treble strings

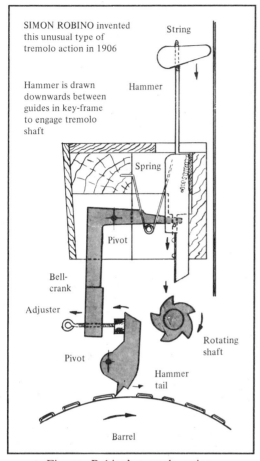

SIMON ROBINO invented this unusual type of tremolo action in 1906

String

Hammer

Hammer is drawn downwards between guides in key-frame to engage tremolo shaft

Spring

Pivot

Bell-crank

Adjuster

Pivot

Rotating shaft

Hammer tail

Barrel

Fig. 12. Robino's tremolo action

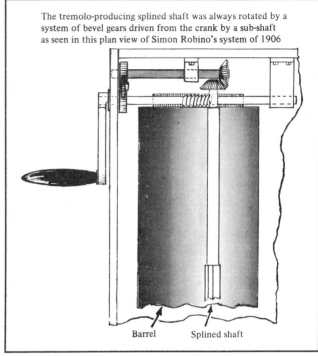

The tremolo-producing splined shaft was always rotated by a system of bevel gears driven from the crank by a sub-shaft as seen in this plan view of Simon Robino's system of 1906

Barrel Splined shaft

Fig. 13. Typical tremolo gearing

crank-shaped hammer-tails until they engaged in a star wheel which kicked them against a return spring.

Clerkenwell's Warner Street was, as we have seen, a haven for the barrel piano makers and another maker there was Vincenzo Pozzouli. He shunned the complex trappings of the tremolo devices of his contemporaries and made, in 1906, a mandolin piano having four bridges—the first being a mandolin, the second a piano, the third a second mandolin, and the fourth a base piano. He also used hardwood hammers.

Even so, this cannot have proved very successful, for still the rotating-shaft tremolo method was being improved upon by the larger makers and, in April 1907, Luigi Pesaresi sired another patent for yet another different system.

One would think that there would have been a limit to the variations on the same theme but the ultimate had, so it seems, still not been reached, for in the following year Ernesto and Benedetto Tomasso, who made barrel pianos in Leeds, devised another such system. This one was different insomuch as that the rotating shaft was in front of the hammers as distinct from being between hammers and strings.

A type of barrel piano introduced about 1910 was the 'zither-banjo' which produced a

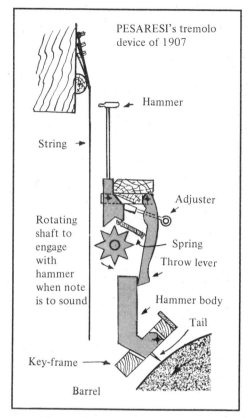

Fig. 14. Pesaresi's tremolo system

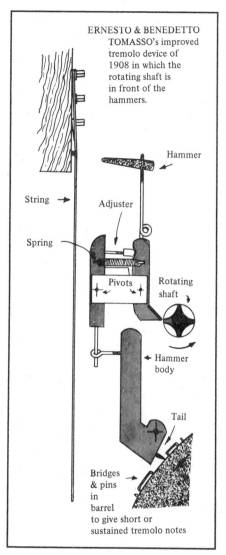

Fig. 15. Tomasso's tremolo action

distinctive, clear sound not at all unlike that of a banjo. It was, however, very loud and Canon Wintle asserted 'that it could be heard a mile away'. The secret lay in the mandolin-like duplication of strings and a very thin soundboard.

At this particular time the book-music piano was in vogue. Chiappa was probably the first to change to this type of instrument in the mid-1890's. Whilst the barrel continued to have its staunch devotees, cardboard music was favoured on several counts. To begin with, the piano was not so bulky and certainly lighter in weight. Furthermore the music was readily available and could be carried or stored with ease, as compared with the heavy barrel together with its limited repertoire represented in pins which were liable to damage.

The cardboard-music street piano was not, however, a success, for it carried with it its own individual shortcomings. The Italian musicians soon tired of the books of music which rapidly wore out, tore or got lost. Whilst book music was fine for an indoor piano or even a fair organ, the street piano was an instrument exposed to rough use, the exigencies of the weather and the wear of continual movement along cobbled streets. Moreover the barrel makers offered a very quick and cheap re-pinning service and could set new music on to existing barrels with great finesse. It is thus perhaps not surprising that few, if any, of these cardboard-music instruments for street use have survived.

The clockwork barrel pianos did not reach as high a state of perfection in England as in other parts of the world. Probably related to the popular trends in entertainment in public places, they were to reach their zenith in America where they proceeded onwards through the whole gamut of mechanical musical instrumentation. The Wurlitzer company, which first commissioned deKleist's Tonophone pneumatic barrel piano, went on to make mechanical banjos, harps, zithers, guitars and even jazz bands. The call for musical entertainment has always been greatest in America and the later machines made to accompany silent films in picture theatres achieved a remarkable degree of perfection and flexibility. The Photo-players of the twenties combined a wide range of effects in a basic roll-operated, pneumatic piano mechanism and Wurlitzers constructed an incredible number of full-orchestra theatre organs, some of which were installed in this country.

The clockwork barrel piano, other than for the entertainment of the British working classes as they drank, never ascended very far above its street hand-cranked brothers.

In Italy, Austria, Belgium, Holland and France, however, mechanical pianos with percussion accompaniment were popular in cafés and restaurants. Rossi made a number of these in Italy as did Crubois in France during the second decade of the twentieth century. Crubois continued making these pianos at least until the late 1920's and they featured a partial iron frame, drum and triangle and castanets. These were coin-freed and driven by clockwork motors.

In the same way that the barrel piano industry was established in England by Italian immigrants, so were similar industries established in other parts of Europe at more or less the same time. Spain, in particular, possessed a large and flourishing manufacturing industry.

One of these Italians named Apruzzese came to Salamanca, Spain, in 1883 and began making barrel pianos. The firm he formed moved to Madrid in 1906 and, in the same year, the present owner, Mr Antonio Apruzzese, was born. He is today the last remaining member of the family to be engaged in piano work and he is also the last remaining barrel piano restorer in Madrid.

Perhaps the best of the Spanish makes were the instruments built by Luis Casali, another Italian. He came to Barcelona and set up business early in the 1880's. The firm comprised three partners—Casali, Pombia (who was responsible for the actual construction), and Subirands whose job it was to transcribe music for the wooden barrels. So successful were their instruments that they were awarded gold medals at the Brussels Exhibition of 1895, having earlier received a similar award in Spain in the year 1886.

Spanish instruments usually included percussion instruments such as the drum, bells and, most common of all, the castanet. Triangles were sometimes to be found as well. It is interesting to note that the instruments built in various countries by these Italian immigrants rapidly became musically acclimatized to their area and developed distinctive regional identities. The Spanish piano invariably included at least one *pasodoble* in its programme and these dances and other music of similar *tempi* came over particularly well.

The Spanish piano was built with 60, 56, 45, 40, 35 and 30 hammers and the larger ones were made to be fitted to a donkey cart. Felt-covered hammers, common elsewhere at the

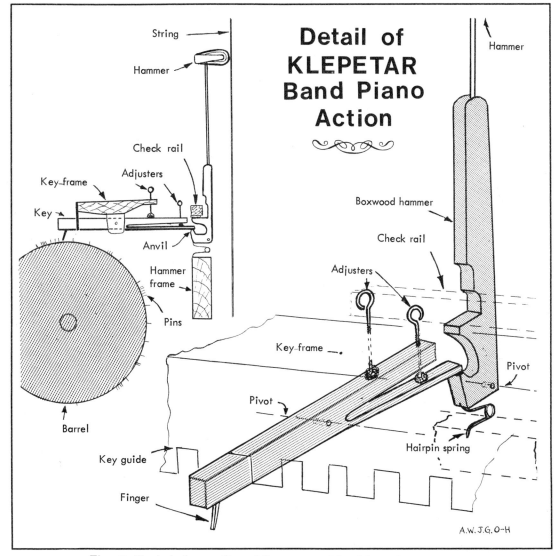

String

Hammer

Check rail

Key-frame

Adjusters

Key

Anvil

Hammer frame

Pins

Barrel

Key guide

Finger

Detail of KLEPETAR Band Piano Action

Hammer

Boxwood hammer

Check rail

Adjusters

Key-frame

Pivot

Pivot

Hairpin spring

A.W. J.G. O-H

Fig. 16. Typical of many Central European weight-driven piano-orchestrions and band pianos is this action by Klepetar

time, were soon scrapped in favour of plain walnut hammers when it was discovered that they produced a brighter and louder sound. Wooden unfelted hammers had, of course, been used by Hicks and others in England for tenor and treble notes and, indeed, Tomasso and others were to use uncovered hammers on their tremolo hammers by the beginning of the twentieth century.

The Prague firm of J. Klepetar built an imposing piano-orchestrion comprising a 34-note iron-framed piano, two drums, a triangle and a cymbal. This was powered by a clockwork mechanism using a slowly descending iron weight which transmitted its power to the driving train through pulleys and gearings. All but the four lower strings were trichords, the lower ones being bichords. This was coin-operated and would play two or three times for the insertion of a coin. Dating from the early part of this century, the Klepetar piano played eight tunes from a barrel $9\frac{1}{2}$ inches in diameter by $25\frac{1}{2}$ inches long.

J. Stychs, also of Prague, was another maker of piano-orchestrions worked by pinned barrels. They flourished during the 1890's along with a number of other manufacturers in Eastern Europe.

Eduard Jacques Bourquin of Paris was to contribute the last significant improvement to the barrel piano in the summer of 1922 when he made use of the revolver-barrel mechanism first used by barrel-organ makers Flight & Robson, and later by Forster & Andrews on some of their church barrel organs. Bourquin mounted a large number of tune barrels between the flanks of a pair of large wheels. Each barrel was indexed in turn against the piano-string hammer-tails and was played. The barrels turned on a spiral as they played, thus enabling quite lengthy tunes to be performed from one barrel. On the completion of a barrel, the mechanism would disengage, rotate sufficiently to bring the next barrel into place, and then play again.

No account of the barrel piano and its history would be complete without reference to the contribution of the late Canon A. O. Wintle. During the agricultural depression following the 1914–18 war, he provided employment for men home from the war in the repairing and restoration of barrel pianos at the Old Rectory, Lawshall, near Bury St Edmunds in Suffolk.

He founded the East Anglian Automatic Piano Company and specialized in the restoration, tuning and re-pinning of old and new barrels. No new pianos were made and the instruments which were rebuilt were either sold or hired out to charitable organizations.

Canon Wintle unquestionably gave a new lease of life to many instruments which would otherwise have fallen into decay and been destroyed. However, in so doing, he almost always saw that the name of the original maker was obliterated and replaced by that of the E.A.A.P.C.— usually in the form of an oval, blue rubber stamp on the barrel paper prior to re-pinning. When Wintle died in 1959, the firm closed and the remaining stock of sundries was destroyed.

Many people believe that the existence of a barrel piano today reveals the survival of an instrument dating from the turn of the century. In truth, this is probably far from the case since the life of these instruments was comparatively short in service. They were still being built in the 1930's and the late Canon Wintle extensively rebuilt many, many instruments up to the end of the 1950's.

The majority of surviving pianos date from the years between the wars and, with a few exceptions, these earlier models have not survived. One must remember that the life of these machines was arduous to say the least. They were out in all weathers, usually stored in the open, and generally misused. As the discerning reader will already have gathered, the close relationship of makers and the inevitable swopping of workers all engendered instruments of similar appearance and performance. Where no original name survives, or where it has been removed, it is almost impossible to discover the true maker and to date it. The tunes which it plays are also unacceptable as a clue to its date because barrels were frequently re-pinned or replaced.

And what of the repertoire of these instruments? The late Canon Algernon Wintle (who, as a boy, used to spend much time with the 'organ-grinders' as well as Simon Robino, the Manchester manufacturer of street pianos) analysed their music. Of the ten tunes pinned to each barrel, the first two were invariably waltzes, the third a quick-step in two-four time, then a jig, hornpipe or Scottish reel followed by a fox-trot in four-four time. The sixth would be a two-step in six-eight time whilst the seventh was usually reserved for a special tune to suit the customer. This might be a 'pop' song or something more exotic—Wintle once set Mozart's

Eine Kleine Nachtmusik on one! The eighth tune on the barrel would be another waltz or perhaps a march whilst the ninth could again be a march or perhaps an aria from the opera. The tenth and last tune might be from the opera, a hymn or a sentimental song. Musically speaking, the street piano catered for a wide variety of tastes and it was nothing uncommon to find so-called 'classical' music on the clockwork pianos used in public houses.

The art of barrel-pinning was jealously guarded amongst the various makers, 'the secret of the clock-face', as it was termed, being passed on only to their own children.

New barrel pianos are being produced today in Spain and these are usually small instruments having 32 notes, two clappers and one triangle. Featuring nylon and plastics in their construction, they are pleasing little devices and are referred to as *'pianos a manubrio'*.

To all intents and purposes, though, the barrel piano has departed from the street scene forever and remains only as a curio—a nostalgic memory of the hansoms, trams, fog and the 'tuppence-a-pint' pubs of the early part of this century.

The mechanism of the barrel piano is extremely simple and the illustrations readily show the primary parts.

The case of the instrument comprises a solidly-built back, usually of heavy-section framing, with a spruce or clear pine sound-board upon which is set the bridge (in the case of some pianos, the bridges). The top member of the piano frame carries the wrest-pins for the strings, the other ends of which are hooked on to sprags (hitch pins) driven in at the lower end.

The side-boards to the frame, as well as forming part of the enclosure, also locate the action parts, simple that they are. A wooden block positioned on each inside face of the side-boards holds the key-frame on a pivot, so that the entire frame can be rotated towards and away from the strings. This key-frame carries the hammer-tails which are usually formed in two parts lapped and glued together from close-grained ash or beech. A flat-sectioned iron pin is provided in the lower part of this tail to engage with the barrel pins. From the top of the hammer-tail projects a stiff wire which carries the actual hammer-head, usually of wood wrapped with felt, often with a sheepskin overwrap. Some makers used plain wood hammers, leather faced or not, particularly in the treble register where a much more percussive sound was required to enable the note to sing out above the more resonant bass strings.

Each hammer was pivoted on a continuous wire hinge and fitted with a safety-pin-type spring beneath to keep it firmly engaged with a felt strip when the hammer was not in use striking the string.

The tune barrel, sometimes mounted on a wooden carrier to facilitate loading and in the same manner that barrel organ barrels were usually made, was slid into the case through a circular, removable door in the right-hand side panel. With hand-cranked pianos, the left end of the barrel was equipped with a broad wooden gear-wheel which engaged in a brass worm-shaft fixed in the case at the left side of the front. Later pianos employed a cast gear ring screwed to the end of the barrel. Pianos which were driven by a clockwork motor—automatics, as Pasquale and others preferred to call them—had, in place of the wooden or cast iron gear, a thin iron gear-wheel to mesh with a broad pinion on the motor which was usually fixed below the barrel at the left side of the case.

To allow for the changing of the tunes, remembering that most barrels were pinned for eight or ten tunes, a snail cam was fixed to the left end of the case and against this rested the steel axis of the barrel. In the same way that a musical box changes its tune using a snail cam, so did this cam serve to shift the barrel laterally sufficient to bring another set of barrel pins to bear on the iron pins in the hammer-tails.

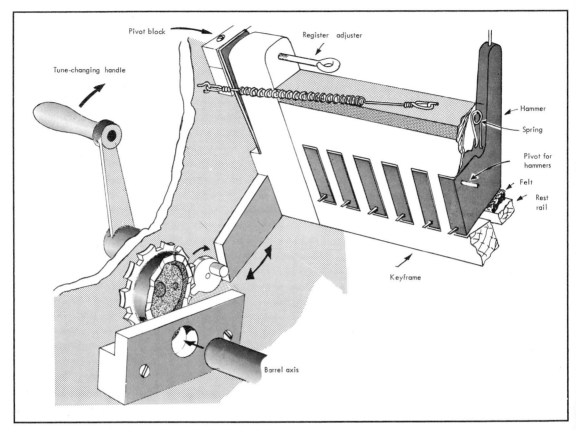

Fig. 17. The tune change mechanism of a street piano

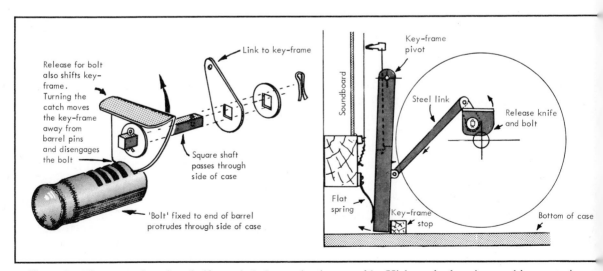

Fig. 18. The tune-changing knife and bolt mechanism, used by Hicks and others in portable street pianos

This snail was controlled by a handle on the outside of the case. To avoid damaging the hammer-tail pins and the barrel pins, operation of the snail cam control-handle served also to rotate a cam which automatically lifted the key-frame well out of the way. In this way, it was possible to change the tune at any time—even in the middle of a melody—without risk of damage to the instrument.

Those familiar with the musical box will know that, after playing the repertoire of tunes pinned on the musical box cylinder, the final change of the snail is to let the cylinder move back from the furthest tune position to the first again—usually a distance of little more than an eighth of an inch. The musical box cylinder, moving laterally against a spring to effect such a change, makes this jump with a slight bang. On some larger musical boxes, the probable dele-terious effect of this hammering of the cylinder against the snail on this large change was minimized by the provision of a short intermediate step so that, as the snail turned, the cylinder made two jumps in rapid succession.

With the barrel piano, however, the barrel was much heavier and the distance from the first tune position to the last was more in the order of an inch. To have the barrel jumping back that distance could only lead to a loud bang and ultimate damage through wear and so the change snail was designed so that it moved up for half the number of tunes, and back again for the other half. To express this another way, on an eight-tune barrel, the changes would be 1, 3, 5, 7, 8, 6, 4, 2, and then back to one again. This made for smoother action as well, for the barrel was shifted by a large and powerful leaf-spring contained in the barrel access-door on the right of the case.

The small barrel pianos, it should be added, together with the earlier instruments employed the barrel-organ change system—a completely manual movement of the barrel using the notch-plate and knife.

Coin-freed automatic pianos used a counter-balanced coin tray which freed a sprag from the governor on the motor. At the end of the tune (they frequently played twice for one coin), the coin would have tipped out and the balanced tray would rise up and re-engage the motor governor.

The clockwork motors were most commonly wound directly from a handle on the outside of the case. Sometimes, though, chain-driven winding handles would be used in cases where the motor was mounted too low in the case for practical direct hand winding.

Since the inventions and improvements of Antonelli and others, most street and clockwork barrel pianos enjoy the same basic mechanisms. An appreciation of the governing factors as outlined in the chapter on repair and overhaul, will enable other instruments of irregular design to be tackled with success.

CHAPTER 3

From Cardboard Music to Pneumatic Action and the Paper Roll

W E have seen how the mechanization of both piano and organ depended from the earliest times on the wheel. The first carillons were sounded by a wheel with projecting peripheral teeth which engaged in the hammer linkages. By extending the wheel in thickness, more pins and hence more musical notes could be provided. Extending the wheel still further in width produced the barrel.

The brass cylinder—a refinement of the barrel and used in musical clocks from their earliest times—was destined to remain as the *modus operandi* of the ordinary musical box right up to the present day. Even the modern, mass-produced Swiss and Japanese musical movements still use this archaic, but never bettered, principle. Of course, the musical box produced its off-shoots in the way of those variants which played metal discs, perforated card strips and even one worked by a perforated paper roll. The disc musical box was an undoubted success, offering changeability of music easily, quickly and for little cost. However, this important feature of the later musical box was effectively killed, as was the need for the musical box industry itself, when the phonograph was introduced. Musical boxes then degenerated into devices to produce soothing tinkling rather than the more serious business of interpreting a melody, and thus the brass cylinder was reverted to.

Pianos and organs, though, called for barrels of such large dimensions that they presented a serious disadvantage. Indeed, on the large barrel-playing orchestrion organs and military bands, the barrels reached such prodigious proportions that it required two men to change the music and needed a large amount of space in which to store the barrels when not in use.

A form of music programme for such instruments which would be less cumbersome and less liable to damage through careless handling and bad storage was thus needed. A solution was to come from a completely different direction and one far removed from music.

Lyons, France, was the home of a straw-hat maker named Joseph Marie Jacquard. His business involved, or was associated with weaving cloth and he sought to improve the existing looms upon which patterned cloth was woven. The looms were made to weave different designs in different colours and the selection of the proper colour controls on the loom had to be executed deftly by highly trained personnel. Jacquard worked on the idea that if he could bring all his loom controls together as small keys on a control board, they could be selected in any prearranged order by passing across them a strip of cardboard, suitably punched with

1. The oldest surviving barrel-operated percussive stringed instrument is probably this mechanical spinet in the collection of Lord Howard de Walden at Dean Castle, Kilmarnock, Scotland, by whose courtesy this picture and also Plate 2 are reproduced

2. Driven by a clockwork motor, this instrument bears a remarkable resemblance to an instrument which was described in the catalogue of the collection of musical instruments owned by King Henry VIII, at the time of his death in 1547, as follows: 'An Instrumente that goethe with a whele without playinge uppon, of woode vernisshed yellowe and painted blewe with vi round plates of siluer pounced with anticke garnisshed with an edge of copper and guilte'. Whether or not this is the King's instrument, there is evidence to point to its having come from the hands of the same craftsman

3. Formerly in the collection of Doktor Rück of Nürnberg, this mechanical spinet
was made *c.* 1575 by Samuel Bidermann and is preserved today in the Germanisches
Nationalmuseum, Nürnberg

Picture by courtesy of Dr J. H. van der Meer

4. The fusee-wound clockwork motor driving the pinned barrel can be seen in this exploded view, together with the 36-note keyboard. Only 20 of the notes could be sounded from the mechanical components
Picture by courtesy of Dr J. H. van der Meer

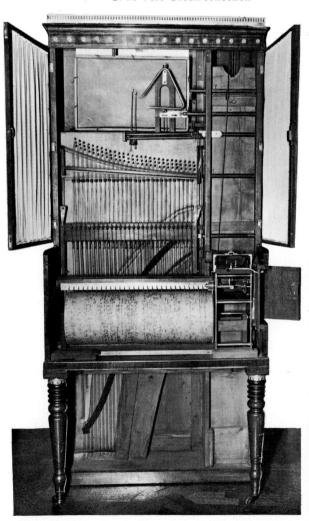

6. The interior of this 30-key instrument shows the large wooden-framed harp and, at the right, the enclosed box which runs from top to bottom of the case and provides a guide for the heavy weight which drives the clockwork. The wire can be seen stretching upwards to the pulley in the case top. The small door in the right side gives access to the stop/start and speed control

C. de Vere Green collection

5. A clockwork piano of French origin and probably dating from late eighteenth or early nineteenth century. The cabinet is richly decorated with ormulu. The two front legs are later additions. Protruding from the right side can be seen the five *stops* controlling *piano/forte*, mute, drum, triangle and dampers

From the collection of C. de Vere Green

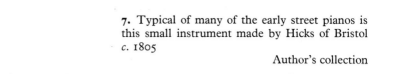

7. Typical of many of the early street pianos is this small instrument made by Hicks of Bristol *c.* 1805

Author's collection

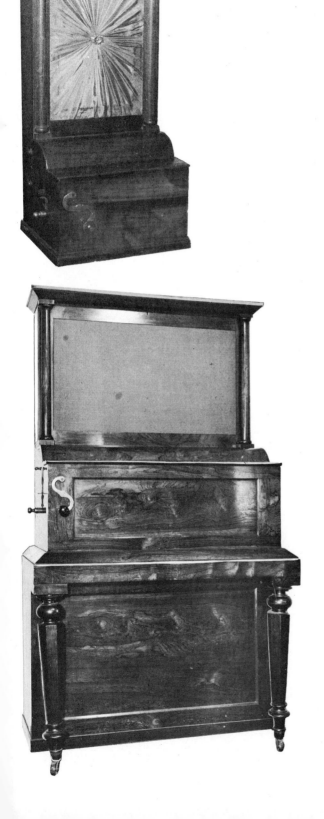

8. The early Hicks style continued for some years and this example, seen with its front removed, was probably made between 1860 and 1870 for sale by Alfred Hayes of London. This piano is very well made and has a more 'piano-like' tone than the mechanical dulcimer of Hicks. Although of the same proportions as the one shown in Plate 7, the fruitwood case suggests that it was not made for street use. It bears no sign of ever having had the usual straps attached to it

Restored by the Author for Mr Keith Harding

9. A much larger barrel piano is this handsome 41-key instrument, in a rosewood case, made by Joseph Hicks in London *c.* 1846. The cabinet base houses two spare barrels

Keith Harding collection

10. The style of the early 'Bristol Hicks' is clearly evident in this inside view of Joseph Hicks' instrument. The block to the left of the line of hammers is a sprung bearing for the winding shaft; a wooden bar keeps the worm engaged with the barrel cog, regardless of any irregularities which might be present

Keith Harding collection

11. *Antiphonel* mechanical piano made by Debain *c*. 1850. This instrument was once the property of the Empress Eugénie, wife of Napoleon III of France, and was auctioned when her Farnborough, Hampshire, residence was sold in 1927. It is now in the Norman Evans collection. The piano contains two distinctly separate actions. As shown, the instrument is ready for mechanical playing. The top lid of the piano lifts up to expose at the left front the planchette key-frame. The 61-note mechanical player is worked by turning the large central handle. For manual playing, the lever seen below the keyboard to the right of centre is moved over to the left. This raises the whole upper part of the piano by about three inches, lifting the player-action hammer frame up and away from the strings. whilst at the same time bringing forward the normal key action full-compass hammer frame

Debain's *Antiphonel* keyboard instrument playing attachment. The stickers which depress the keys can be seen. A toothed rack on the lower edge of the planchette engages with the winding handle

Picture from Mr Ron Pearsall

12. A particularly fine piece of furniture is this ornate barrel piano made by Imhof & Mukle during the first half of the last century. This 54-note instrument has a damper or 'loud' pedal to allow the operator to introduce his own expression

Rex Montgomery collection

Inside shot reveals the storage ~~ce~~ for the second barrel beneath ~~~~ one in playing position. A long ~~r~~ on the right side of the case ~~~~s access to both. The dampers ~~~~ be seen over the bass half of ~~~~ strings above the hammers. The ~~~~k-like projection on the left side ~~~~e tune indicator

14. London in 1888. The hansoms negotiate Oxford Circus whilst two street musicians haul their piano on its two-wheeled cart, no doubt headed towards Clerkenwell where the makers of street pianos and their hirers could be found. Itinerant musicians could hire a piano for a shilling or two per day, returning it each night to its owner. Some hirers were not so honourable and quite often the owner would have to roam the streets looking and listening

Radio Times Hulton Picture Library, photograph

15. Street piano made by Pasquale at 5 Phoenix Place. The barrel has been repinned and bears the stamp 'R. Hall, Piano-Organ Specialist, 19b, Wilbury Grove, Hove, 3'

Lancaster House, collection

16. A street piano by Tomasso of London, which featured a tremolo attachment to the treble

Graham Webb collection

17. This detail shot clearly shows the operation of the Tomasso tremolo attachment. The pins used by the ordinary hammers can be seen together with the bridges for the tremolo hammers (right). An extra shaft is driven in line with the normal worm shaft by gearing from the crank handle. This shaft carries at the other end a bevel gear, meshing with a similar gear on a shaft which traverses the width of the piano between the strings and the hammers. The exact mechanism is shown in line drawings elsewhere

Graham Webb, collection

CHIAPPA & SONS,

Manufacturers of all kinds of Musical Instruments,

PLAYING BY BARREL OR PERFORATED CARDBOARD.

6, LITTLE BATH STREET, HOLBORN, LONDON, E.C.

~ TRADE PRICE LIST. ~

PIANO FOR STREET PLAYING.

Class	**A**—40	Hammers,	10	Tunes...	...	...	...	...	£16	10	0
,,	**B**—44	,,	10	,,	...	..	...	..	...	17	10	0
,,	**C**—48	,,	10	,,	...	...	...	...	...	18	10	0
,,	**D**—55	,,	10	,,	...	...	...	...	21	0	0

EXTRA BARRELS FOR ABOVE PIANOS, £5 10 0 EACH.

ALL THE ABOVE PRICES ARE STRICTLY NET.   *TERMS CASH.*

18. This early advertisement shows a hand-turned street piano which could be had with either barrel mechanism or perforated card action. Chiappa was one of the first to make pianos for street use which played cardboard books

19. No four-ale bar worth its spit-and-sawdust
was considered complete without its 'automatic'
—a coin-freed barrel piano. This one, beautifully
preserved, is typical of many

Graham Webb collection

20. With the fall-boards removed, the driving
motor, coin chute and money box can be seen

21. An interesting feature of this clockwork piano is its automatic 'soft pedal' action. A damper runs the full width of the piano and carries a strip of felt. By raising the damper, the felt is interspaced between the hammer-heads and the strings. Control of the damper is from special bridge pins set in the end of the barrel via a linkage

Graham Webb collection

CHIAPPA & SONS,

6, LITTLE BATH STREET, HOLBORN (near Hatton Garden),
LONDON.

Automatic Penny-in-the-Slot Piano.

Telegrams- "CHIAREZZA, LONDON."   Telephone - 12930 Central.

MODEL E.

22. Coin-freed barrel pianos of this type were a feature of most public houses in past years. Chiappa was one of several makers of 'automatics' as they were called

23. Detail shot showing the winding gear on a Rossi & Spinelli street piano. This once featured a travelling picture front, long since discarded, which was driven from the short vertical shaft and pinion, just to the right of the unusual worm pressure block

Author's collection

24. This café piano was made by Crubois of Granville, France, early this century. It plays 51 notes with drum, triangle and castanets

Graham Webb collection

25. Instruments of this type were not popular in this country. France and the Low Countries, on the other hand, favoured pianos of this type and many are still in use today. The Crubois features a part-iron frame and the largest spring motor the author has ever seen in a piano

Graham Webb collection

26. A barrel-operated piano orchestrion probably made about 1890. This instrument has a 33-note piano, 12 notes of which are repeating or mandolin hammers, 8-note set of chimes, snare drum, bass drum and cymbal. It is driven by a descending weight at the back of the case. Details of the clock-work are evident in this picture and the open lantern wheel, which drives the tremolo effect, can be seen above the left end of the barrel. Eight tunes are played and the Geneva style tune-change mechanism can be seen on the extreme left of the inside case. The music played on these pianos was always well set up and usually comprised bright folk dances, national songs and marches

National Museum, Prague

27. A modern street piano complete with other attractions, photographed in 1964 in Madrid

Jackson Fritz, picture

28. This cardboard-music playing mechanical piano was made in 1886 by Giovanni Racca of Bologna, Italy, who also made barrel pianos. It has 73 notes and features a system of continuously-beating hammers which was patented by Racca and W. Seward. A diagram of this action appears elsewhere

G. Webb collection

29. The *Piano Melodici* as Racca called it, has a friction drive set in motion by a crank handle as shown. The lever protruding from the lid of this grand-shaped-piano controls the *piano* and *forte* expression. There is also a small lever which raises the dampers from the strings

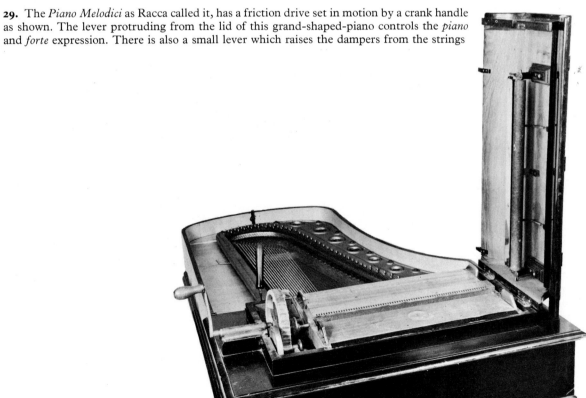

30. The iron frame can be seen in this view, also the small levers which are pressed down when the music is in place. When a lever is allowed to rise through a slot in the cardboard, that note sounds

31. In this detail shot of the action and drive mechanism can be seen the adjustable hammer-rocking mechanism which gives *piano* and *forte* effects and also the damper lifting lever

G. Webb collection

32. The action is displayed in this view with the mechanism removed from the case. Note the graduated felt-covered hammers, each mounted on a spring steel strip and connected to the rocking bar. Racca produced a smaller variant of this instrument which, unlike this 73-key model, had a rectangular case

G. Webb collection

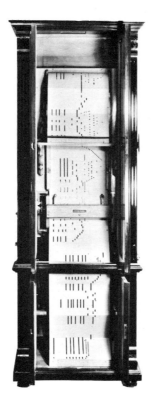
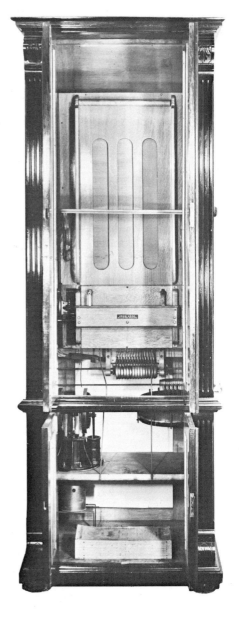

33. The handsome cabinet of a German cardboard-playing piano powered by a hot air engine
City Museum & Art Gallery, Birmingham, collection

34. With the two pairs of front doors opened, this view shows the music in place. It passes from top to bottom, refolding on the floor of the case. The key-frame is the wide bar at approximately the middle position

35. The hot air engine of this piano is seen at the lower left. The mechanism features continuously-beating hammers, rather like those employed in the Racca piano (Plates 28 & 29), and plays piano strings (behind the silk-panelled deck in the upper half of the case), chromatic bells, drum and triangle. The book of music can be seen lying in the bottom of the case

36. Another hot air engine-driven instrument is this Piano-Orchestrion which again plays folded cardboard music. The music book is placed on an extending shelf on the left-hand side, passes across the instrument and re-folds on a similar shelf at the other side. The hot air engine, with its methylated spirits burner, is housed in the cupboard beneath. If required, the mechanism can be played by hand by turning the wheel

Henry A. J. Lawrence, Leamington Spa, collection

37. Probably of German origin and dating from the late 1880's, this instrument again featured continuously-beating hammers, the sound produced being not unlike a mandolin or balalaika and extremely pleasant

Henry A. J. Lawrence, Leamington Spa, collection

38. J. Carpentier's Melotrope of 1889, which played on a piano keyboard using perforated cardboard music

Conservatoire des Arts et Métiers, Paris

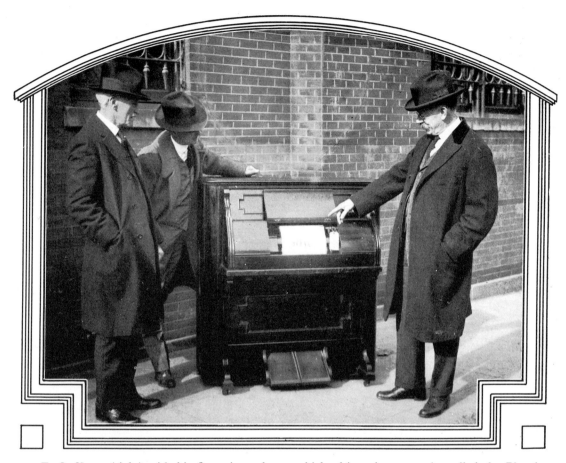

39. E. S. Votey (right) with his first piano-player, which ultimately was to be called the Pianola. This model is now preserved in the Smithsonian Institute, Washington

40. An early push-up piano-player was the Simplex, made in America by the Simplex Piano Player Co. at the turn of the century. Playing 65-note music-rolls, it was fitted with a clockwork motor to drive the music-roll, which was 28·7 cm. wide. The instrument stands 39¾ inches wide, is 17 inches deep and has an adjustable height of about 40 inches

British Piano Museum (Frank W. Holland collection)

41. A very rare instrument is this Melville Clark Apollo push-up piano player, which was made in America at the turn of the century. It was presented to the City Museum and Art Gallery, Birmingham, in an extremely dilapidated state as can be gathered from these illustrations. The case, broken and rotted, and the pneumatics well and truly perished, the instrument is to be preserved and restored

City Museum & Art Gallery Birmingham, collection

42. This rear view of the Apollo shows the horizontal exhausters and the small, central equaliser mounted beneath it. The key-frame plungers can be seen beneath the remains of their operating pneumatics

City Museum & Art Gallery, Birmingham, collection

43. Melville Clark fitted his Apollo with a clockwork roll re-wind system. All the time the music-roll was being played, a linkage from the treadles wound up this motor through a friction clutch. At the end of the music, the large knob on the front was pulled and the motor re-spooled the roll. The knob seen in the music-roll compartment, above the left side of the take-up spool, is the screwed adjuster for the 'transposing mouthpiece' which moved the tracker-bar

City Museum & Art Gallery, Birmingham, collection

E. S. VOTEY

AN IMPORTANT AEOLIAN INVENTION

Two views of the earliest model of the Pianola—later reduced in size and greatly improved—invented by E. S. Votey, now Vice-President of The Aeolian Company

44. The early production model of the Pianola was indeed a large and cumbersome device, in most cases dwarfing the instrument which it was designed to play. E. S. Votey (top right) was made Vice-President of The Aeolian Company

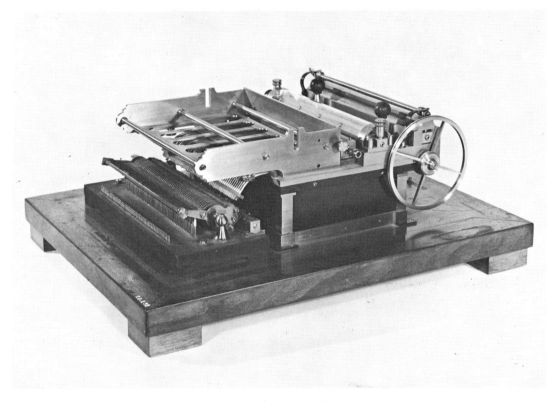

45. An early machine for perforating paper rolls for pneumatic player-piano actions

Conservatoire des Arts et Métiers, Paris

46. Roll drive on later piano players was provided by the air motor. In this picture can be seen a motor of the 1905 period, as fitted to the Angelus player

Author's collection

"I Love the Moon"

A SING SONG
WITH THE
'PIANOLA' PIANO

THE words of the operas, of the old ballads, of the latest song hits, are all printed in large type on the 'Pianola' Song Rolls, so that they can be read easily, as the music plays, by a large group of people standing around the 'Pianola.' Everybody joins in with that special pleasure found in doing things together.

AEOLIAN MADE AND AEOLIAN GUARANTEED

The latest models of the genuine 'Pianola' Piano are equipped with a transposing device for playing songs in the key to suit the voice. The 'Pianola' single lever tempo control makes song accompaniment a delight.

Special Demonstrations of 'PIANOLA' SONG ROLLS

are being given at Aeolian Hall during this week.

All those who are interested in music in the home are cordially invited to call and hear them. The Song Roll repertory is practically unlimited. Anyone can sing with the 'Pianola' Song Rolls, and the instrument is so easy to operate that everyone is a good accompanist. This is one of the many pleasures that a 'Pianola' will bring into your home.

SOME OF THE MOST POPULAR SONG ROLLS

"She's a Great, Great Girl"
"All by Yourself in the Moonlight"
"Old Man Sunshine"
"Love's Old Sweet Song"

"I Love the Moon"
"Sonny Boy"
"My Ain Folk"
"Danny Boy"

If you are unable to call, 'Pianola' Piano Catalogue J.F. and particulars of the wonderful range of 'Pianola' music, will be sent on application.

THE AEOLIAN COMPANY LIMITED
Aeolian Hall · 131-137 NEW BOND STREET, LONDON W.1

---

47. Typical of the player-piano advertising this side of the Atlantic was this full-page piece from *The Sketch* of March 6th, 1929

48. Pianola – the most famous name in player-pianos – was the name given to Aeolian's cabinet-style piano-player, a 65-note instrument seen here in position with a piano. These were produced from the beginning of the century until about 1909, by which time manufacture had tailed off in favour of the so-called 'inner player' which appeared about 1904

Ron Benton, Shanklin, collection

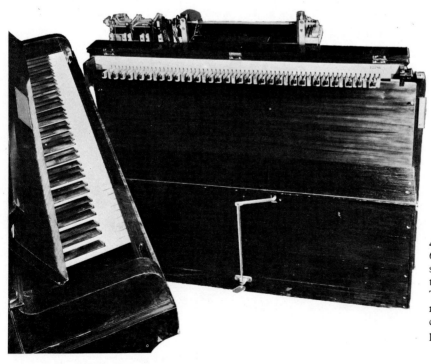

49. The Pianola was originally 65-note cabinet-style player and i seen here drawn back from the pia to show the piano playing finge The linkage on the back of the inst ment is the lever which pres down on the sustaining pedal of piano

Ron Benton, Shanklin, collect

THE

CHASE & BAKER PIANO PLAYER.

Easiest to Pedal.
Simplest to Manipulate.
Most Human in its Reproduction.

Guaranteed for five years.

PRICE :

£52 : 0 : 0

NET CASH.

If unable to call, please write for Catalogue B.

THE
Chase & Baker Co.
(LIMITED),
CHASE AND BAKER BUILDING,
45 & 47, WIGMORE ST.,
LONDON, W,

50. This ornate player by Chase & Baker, together with matching grand piano, was advertised in 1905
Picture by courtesy of the Robbins Music Portrait Collection

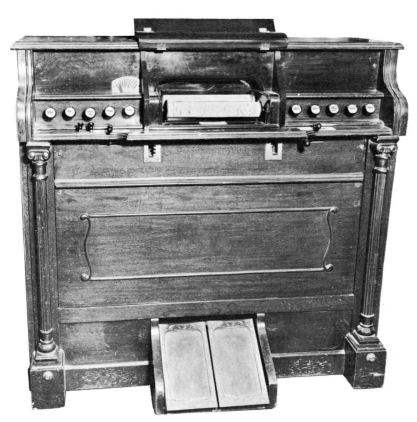

51. The Angelus cabinet-style player was made in two styles, one as a straight 65- or 88-note player and the other, illustrated here, as a player organ as well as a piano-player. A number of sets of reeds could be played within the instrument from 58-note 'Symphony' rolls made by Wilcox & White mainly for their player organs. When the stop knob, at the far right of the console, was drawn, the piano-player fingers were lowered to the keyboard of an ordinary piano. It was thus possible to use the instrument without a piano, or to play a 'duet' for reed organ and piano

Graham Webb collection

52. The first of the reproducing pianos was the Welte-Mignon, known as the 'Keyless Red Welte' because it had no keyboard and also because it played 13½-inch wide red paper rolls. Its classic-styled cabinet contained a beautifully-made and remarkably advanced mechanical-pneumatic action. Very few were made, mainly because it could only be used as a mechanical piano, not enjoying the occasional manual use to which an ordinary player might be put. It was made between the years of about 1904 and 1909. Only two examples are known in this country, one in the Norman Evans collection, London, and the one illustrated from the collection of the City Museum & Art Gallery, Birmingham

holes or slots. By feeding long strips of cardboard across these keys, intricate and varied patterns could be woven accurately by scmi-skilled operators.

Jacquard's control system for looms called for the design of the cloth for weaving to be set out on graph paper in such a manner as to represent a greatly magnified plan of the finished cloth, showing the weave interlacings in detail. The design was then transferred to cards into which holes and slots were punched on a machine known to this day as a 'piano machine' worked by a foot treadle.

The complete bundle of cards was then laced together into an endless chain and fixed to a square drum on the Jacquard machine normally situated above the loom. As each card was presented to a matching set of needles or tiny levers, the interlacing of one pick of weft was completed according to the instructions passed on by the perforations in the card.

Jacquard, who was born in 1752, is credited with this invention in the year 1801. He was awarded a medal at the Paris Exhibition of 1801, and, after interviews with Napoleon and Carnot, he was seconded to work at the Conservatoire des Arts et Métiers in Paris. Here he worked on his loom, incorporating ideas from a loom conceived in 1745 by Vaucanson (who is perhaps better known as a maker of spectacular automata). Messrs Bouchon and Falcon had done similar work in 1725 and 1728 respectively.

Jacquard perfected his special loom and its method of control, returning to his native Lyons in 1825 only to be given a hostile reception by the local silk-weavers who feared redundancy should his machine be adopted. Just as James Hargreaves had seen his 'Spinning Jenny' smashed up by those who gave vent to similar sentiments in England in 1764, Jacquard witnessed the burning of his loom by the angry mob. As with most revolutionary inventions, there is always an initial predominance of hot-headed pessimists whose misplaced loyalties and passions can generate such conduct. Today, though, labour forces go on strike as a more civilized method of taking up the cudgel against things which might upset the fine balance of industrial relations.

Once the initial furor regarding Jacquard's loom had died down, the importance of its capabilities and the increased trade potential created by its adoption were gradually recognized and Jacquard lived to see happier times with his looms in almost universal use and bringing prosperity to his native city. The new loom could weave delicate patterns in carpets and could make fine cloth quicker and cheaper than by the old hand methods. Napoleon, ever appreciative of any technical genius that would further the industrial reputation of his country, rewarded him with a pension of £60 and a royalty of £2 on each loom erected, along with the Cross of the Legion of Honour. Jacquard died in 1834 and, six years later, a statue of him was erected in Lyons on the spot where his first loom had been publicly burned.

The casual reader may ponder on the connection between the weaving industry and the mechanical piano. The answer lies in the ability to correlate a pattern of behaviour to a set of keys. Axminster carpets, rugs, complicated stitches—all were being automated by cardboard strips which passed over the control keyboard of looms. The keys were held firmly down as the strip moved steadily along. When a hole or a slot came up to a key, the key would rise through the cardboard and some mechanical linkage at its opposite end would conduct a function of the loom. The fact that a spring-loaded key could be made to rise and fall by the passage of a perforated card strip was the making of mechanical music to come. Whether the end of the key was connected to a loom shuttle control, or to an organ wind-chest, or to a pneumatic lever to strike a musical string was of no consequence. The cardboard could still be made to move the key.

A Londoner, Alexander Bain, patented in 1847 a mode of playing wind instruments by using a perforated paper surface and this was probably the earliest application of paper or card to control wind.

Duncan Mackenzie patented improvements to the Jacquard card system specifically for playing musical instruments in August 1848 and, three months later, Charles Dawson used perforated card to replace the barrel in his barrel organ. Dawson's device was not a success, for he used the openings in the card to control directly the access of the wind to the pipes and this meant that the wind supply was opened up slowly and closed down slowly to play each note, producing a most undesirable wavering in the note from the pipe and destroying the most attractive feature of the barrel organ—its very promptness of speech.

The 'self-acting piano or seraphone' patented in 1849 by William Martin, was also played by a system of Jacquard cards.

Joseph Antoine Teste applied the Jacquard system to the playing of mechanical organs in 1863 and improved upon it during the next year, taking out several patents. J. Amman, two years later, produced an electro-magnetic piano playing system using a Jacquard card moved between the two contacts of a primitive solenoid. In England, Alfred Barlow played a reed instrument using an endless band of paper which had holes punched in it. This was one of the forerunners of the reed instruments later to be called organettes and the date was 1870.

An electro-magnetic system was used in the following year by E. Molyneux to open the pallets of his reed organ which played a perforated paper strip.

Determined not to permit one chink in his patent specification, Charles Abdank de Laskarewski and Thomas Herbert Noyes specified either the pinned barrel or the perforated card or paper strip on their mechanical musical instrument of 1873 which played on tuning forks.

Paul Ehrlich of Leipzig was a prolific inventor of improvements in both the musical box and organette field. He patented a system of perforated tune sheets for organettes in the summer of 1876. These were intended for the mechanical playing of 'automatic organs, harmoniums &c' and had wedge-shaped holes so that the keys passed slowly through the slots and the opening of the pallet could be controlled to produce louder or softer notes. The system, Ehrlich claimed, could also be used for musical boxes and pianos.

The philosophy of the perforated tune sheet had now been established. A cardboard strip could be made to push small levers up and down. Perforated paper was easier to

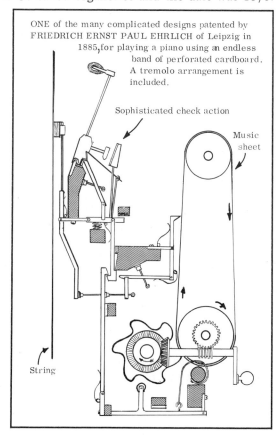

ONE of the many complicated designs patented by FRIEDRICH ERNST PAUL EHRLICH of Leipzig in 1885, for playing a piano using an endless band of perforated cardboard. A tremolo arrangement is included.

Sophisticated check action

Music sheet

String

Fig. 19. Ehrlich's endless-band tremolo action

make and to store, but it was impossible to use it to do mechanical work. It could, however, be used to open and close a small air passage leading to a reed or musical pipe.

At this time there were thus two distinctive methods of producing music using a perforated substance as compared with the traditional barrel. As we have shown, there was on the one hand perforated paper used to operate a pneumatic valve. On the other hand, perforated card could be used to move a mechanical lever.

The earliest use of pneumatic principles in playing music was the work of a mechanic from Lyons in France, C. F. Seytre. His Autophon, patented in 1842, played 'all kinds of melodies by means of perforated cards with square or oblong holes according to the length of the notes to be played'. The holes were connected by tubing which led air pressure from pedal-operated bellows to small cylinders attached by each key in the keyboard. In each cylinder was a small piston which, when subjected to air pressure, could move a jack to engage with the tail of a hammer striking the string from below.

Probably the first satisfactory method of utilizing air was devised by another Frenchman, J. Carpentier, who, as related by Buchner, constructed his first pneumatic instruments for the International Electricity Exhibition in 1880. His repeating melograph, first used for the harmonium, punched holes directly in paper strips which were then used to play the music in a specially constructed electrically operated harmonium. Carpentier developed two more instruments in 1887—the Melograph and the Melotrope—which he put before the French Academy. The Melograph recorded music performed on any keyboard instrument whilst it was being played. It worked by means of electrical conductors leading from contacts beneath the keys of the instrument. As the key was pressed down, current passed to the Melograph which operated along similar lines to a teleprinter. A wooden plaque with a row of flexible metal strips was attached to the instrument in such a way that the strip of metal came beneath each of the keys, forming the contact when the keys were moved. The strip of paper upon which the music was recorded was moved along by an electric motor with a speed regulating device. Underneath the paper was a perforated cylinder inking-roller which was kept wet with black ink. Above the paper was a row of vertically mounted impression rods which could be actuated by electro-magnets which caused the rods to press down on the paper whenever particular magnets received the current. There were thirty-seven magnets to play thirty-seven keys on the instrument. The recording thus produced consisted of inked lines and the distance between these marks and the edge of the paper indicated the notes to be played and also their duration. In order to obtain from this Melograph perforated strips for use in suitably-equipped mechanical instruments, Carpentier invented a hand-driven perforating mechanism equipped with punches. The punched strip thus obtained was used to make large numbers of copies in a mechanical perforating machine. To play these strips, Carpentier invented a crank-driven mechanism—the Melotrope—which was placed on the keyboard of the instrument to be played. It was in the form of an oblong box and contained thirty-seven mechanisms for the playing of that number of the piano keys. At the right-hand end, the perforated tune sheet held down lightly-sprung metal fingers. A slot in the music allowed one of these fingers to lift up into a grooved brass pressure roller above it in the manner which Anselme Gavioli was to use on his book-music-playing show organs in later years. The Melotrope's levers were each connected to rocking levers spaced along the length of the box. The wooden plungers which sounded the piano keys were themselves spring-loaded and loosely attached to the rocking levers by a cord which also passed twice around a rotating wooden shaft running the length of the instrument. When a key was raised by the music slot, the rocking lever would cause this cord to be drawn tightly against the rotating shaft. The friction would at once cause the plunger to be pushed downwards on to the piano key. Musical expression was obtained by using the pedals (in the case of a piano), and the volume of sound was controlled by a lever which raised or lowered the key plungers. Both the Melograph and the Melotrope were very popular at the end of the nineteenth century and a large number of pieces of music were 'recorded' in this way.

Elias Parkman Needham, in America, exploited the paper roll system and, from 1877 onwards, presented many improvements in the development of the pneumatic system. He invented the upright player action used in reed organs, which was the step that paved the way for the entire later development of paper-controlled music.

The first person to make significant improvements to the simple pneumatic system was John McTammany of Worcester, Massachusetts. He was a far-sighted inventor who patented a remarkable series of improvements to the paper-roll system from 1868 onwards. He applied his techniques to the manufacture of organettes but the venture was not a success. Unable to pay the renewal fees on his patents he had to see each one taken up and successfully exploited by other companies. McTammany, whose name is almost forgotten today, did much to give us the player organ and organette as well as the player-piano, yet he was to die penniless in 1915.

Merritt Gally of New York patented in 1881 a pneumatic device for use in playing pianos. In concept, this was some years in advance of its time. For various reasons, Gally concentrated on perfecting the principles of the small organette rather than those of the pneumatic piano. Gally and, separately, McTammany laid these foundations. Between the years of 1896 and 1902, the progress and perfection of the external player can largely be attributed to men such as Tremaine, White, McTammany, Gally, Goolman, Doman, Parker, Votey, Kelly, Paine, Brown, Davis, Clark, Hattemer, Winter, Healy, Weser, Salyer, Klugh, Ball, Wuest, Gulbransen and Welin. In England, Bishop & Down patented a pneumatic system for keyboard playing in 1882, whilst C. A. Custer of New York contrived what must surely have been the first 'expression' device in 1887. His system graduated the power of touch and operated the piano pedals from 'either barrel or perforated roll'.

The so-called American Organ, soon to become known almost universally, was developed in the United States and worked on the principle that air was sucked down through the reed, so producing a sound. This differed from the first harmoniums in which air was blown through the reed. The precursor of the American organ was the organette and in 1881 M. Harris controlled the mechanical performance of one such device by passing a strip of perforated paper across the air passage to the reeds. He mounted his bellows above these passages. Harris later used the same system on a keyboard reed instrument and also a pipe organ and was thus one of the first to follow E. P. Needham's system. In subsequent years, Wilcox & White and The Aeolian Company were to exploit the pressure or blown reed in their paper-playing organs, as this system produced a louder note with a greater purity of tone which could be voiced almost like a pipe organ sound.

The barrel was now relegated to a third-rate position, superseded by perforated paper and punched card. Barrel organs, however, were still to be made for a number of years to come and, indeed, a wide range of these instruments was included in the 1905 catalogue of Thibouville-Lamy of London and Paris. The barrel piano for street use, as we have seen in an earlier chapter, was soon to regain its former position in spite of the infiltration by perforated music, such makers as Pasquale continuing in this line of business until the 1930's. However,

Beethoven on the Æolian

Kreutzer Sonata, Op. 47 ; Adagio Sostenuto, Andante con Variazioni, Presto
Moonlight Sonata, Op. 27
Adelaide
Coriolan Overture
Egmont Overture
Leonore Overture, No. 3
Namensfeier Overture
Prometheus Overture
Die Weihe des Hauses Overture
König Stephan Overture
König Stephan Triumphal March
Fidelio, Abscheulicher
Fidelio Potpourri
Trauermarsch
Turkish March from Ruins of Athens
Andante Favori, Op. 35
Hallelujah Chorus from Mount of Olives
Klavier-Concert No. 3, Op. 37 ; Allegro con brio, largo, Allegro Molto
Klavier-Concert No. 3, Op. 37 ; Allegro con brio, rondo Allegro
Klavier-Concert No. 4, Op. 58 : Allegro Moderato, Rondo Vivace
Nocturne, Op. 42 ; Allegro, Minuet, Andante quasi Allegro
Septet, Op. 20 ; Adagio, Allegro con brio
Serenade, Op. 25 ; Andante
Serenade, Op. 41 ; Scherzando, Adagio, Allegro Vivace
Sextuor, Op. 81 ; Allegro con brio Adagio, Allegro
Sonata No. 1 ; Allegro, Adagio
Sonata, Op. 2, No. 2 ; Largo
Sonata, Op. 2, No. 3 ; Allegro Assai, Scherzo and Trio
Sonata, Op. 10, No. 1 ; Allegro Molto, Adagio Molto
Sonata, Op. 10, No. 3 : Minuetto and Trio, Largo
Sonata, Op. 13 (Pathetique) ; Grave, Allegro Molto, Allegro, Adagio
Sonata, Op. 14, No. 2, Allegro
Sonata, Op. 22 ; Adagio
Sonata, Op. 26 ; Marcia Funebre, Andante and Var, 1 and 5, Scherzo and Trio
Sonata, Op. 31, No. 3 ; Allegro
Sonata, Op. 49, No. 2 ; Tempo di Menuetto
Sonata, Op. 81 ; Les Adieux, l'Absence, Le Retour
Symphony No. 1 ; Adagio Molto, Allegro, Andante Cantabile, Menuetto Adagio, Allegro Vivace
Symphony No. 2 ; Adagio Molto, Allegro con brio, Larghetto, Scherzo, Allegro Molto

T HE STATEMENT that the Aeolian will play any piece of music ever composed is so broad and sweeping that it many times fails to impress the reader with its wonderful significance. As a means of affording a better idea of the enormous repertoire of the Æolian we present herewith partial list of the works of a single composer, BEETHOVEN, that are included in the Æolian music catalogue.

These are all arranged from the full orchestral scores, complete and unabridged. Many of them are never attempted upon the piano, and are played only by large orchestras ; yet it is possible for any one to play them on the Æolian correctly, and with all the changes of tempo and expression.

Aeolians, £24 to £175.

Aeolian Orchestrelles, £350 to £600.

May be purchased on the Hire System if desired. Visitors always welcome. If unable to call, send for catalogue 33 giving full description.

The Renaissance. Price £400

The Orchestrelle Co., 225, Regent St., London, W.

The Aeolian is sold at no other address in London.

Liverpool—J. Smith & Son, Ltd.
Manchester—Hime & Addison
Glasgow—Marr, Wood & Co.
Edinburgh—
    Methven, Simpson & Co.
Bradford—Joshua Marshall, Ltd.

Birmingham—Stockley & Sabin
Bristol—Milsom & Son
Dublin—Cramer, Wood & Co.
Sheffield—
    Arthur Wilson, Peck & Co.
Leeds—Mitchell & Briggs, Ltd.

Fig. 20. An advertisement of about 1900

69

the 1880's evoked a spate of playing systems which, with but a few exceptions, left the barrel out cold.

Bishop and Down produced a paper-operated piano player in 1882, followed closely by A. Wilkinson who used a calico tune sheet.

The perforated tune sheet became more sophisticated. The Automatic Music Paper Co. in America made many improvements to the paper roll, starting with such a basic thing as a method of attaching the paper to the wooden spool.

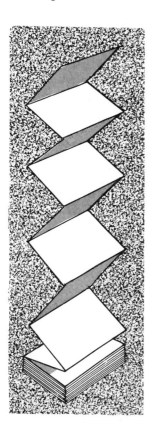

Fig. 21. A book of music for a fair organ, piano or other book-playing instrument looks like this before perforating. The laminations of pre-folded card are glued up, allowed to set for several days and then trimmed to this appearance prior to putting on the punching table, when the master stencil is laid on top, stencil paint applied and then the marked card book punched

As the paper roll was perfected, so came a demand for a means of making the rolls cheaply and speedily. The Auto Music Co. in the U.S.A. devised a machine for punching out music in 1881. This made stencils from which could be punched the music rolls themselves.

The means employed to perforate the paper were indeed diverse. In 1883 J. Maxfield devised a system of perforating organette rolls using an instrument which was equipped with a number of gas jets. The music-roll was burned against a template or pattern to produce the holes. The most common system was to punch the paper with closely-spaced holes or slots with a metal punch but in the late 1880's several makers were sandblasting their paper tune sheets against a pattern.

In shotblasting or punching the paper, loose paper fibres would be created and the suction through the tracker-bar would draw this dust, together with any other dust in the atmosphere, into the intrument, ultimately clogging the tiny valves and exhaust ports. F. Engelhardt and A. P. Roth solved this problem in 1901 by splitting the tracker-bar, over which the paper trayelled, horizontally and interspersing a removable filter which was supposed to trap the dust.

Claude Gavioli in Paris was at this time producing street organs and he perfected a pneumatic-lever action in which the air valve in a high-pressure wind-chest was opened by a servo valve in a low-pressure wind-chest using a key lever moved by the perforated card tune-sheet. This was in 1881.

Gavioli was among the earliest to make serious use of perforated cardboard music and he applied this technique to mechanical organs and pianos, perfecting the zig-zag folding of the music into a book which could be fed through the instrument. He patented a piano-player which worked on this principle in 1884–85. By 1895, Gavioli was using cardboard music to work the keys of all his show organs and, four years later, was using the servo-pneumatic system which came to be known as the 'keyless' system, in use on fair organs to this day. This was really just a form of suction tracker-bar.

A number of people devised methods of joining the card into a continuous length and the methods used included metal hinges, cloth strips and wire hinges. Gavioli used a simpler and more practical method. He glued his music strip from machine-creased, overlapped card. This produced a hard, durable board which could

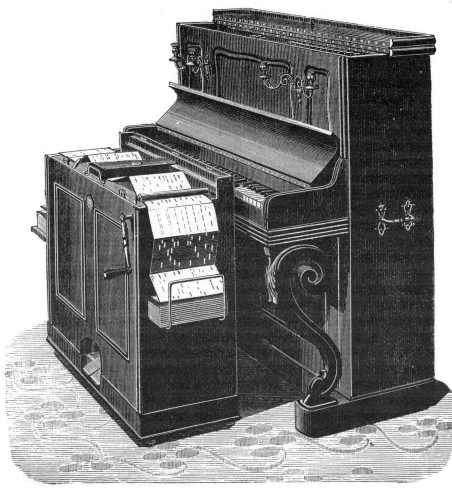

PIANISTA THIBOUVILLE.

View of the Pianista placed before the Piano.

This apparatus can be adapted to any piano either of English or foreign make.

View of the Pianista ready to be played.

LATEST IMPROVEMENTS.

Pianista Patented S. G. D. G.

Fig. 22. Thibouville-Lamy's 'Pianista' piano-player which played book music

be punched cleanly with the music apertures, yet at the same time was capable of easy unfolding and refolding in the organ.

Chiappa applied this music principle to the street pianos he was building in place of the barrel in the early 1890's, using it also in his military band organs. On the continent, Bruder in Germany and all other fair-organ makers gradually changed from the pinned barrel to the perforated cardboard music form.

Paris was at this time the traditional home of the fair organ and thus when, in 1884, Thibouville-Lamy produced their Pianista piano-player, it was not surprising to find that it scorned paper music, but played Gavioli-type book music. The Pianista was matched by the production of the Organina which applied the same principles to organ playing.

Nevertheless, perforated paper had seized the imagination of many inventors, particularly in America. Organettes were cheap to make and sold well at a price far less than the cheapest average-quality musical box. Hundreds of different styles were made and many inventors found improvements to patent. Ithaca, New York, was the home of the Autophone Company and they produced small organettes from about 1880 onwards. These mostly played paper rolls or endless paper bands, although they also made the Gem roller organette which, in true barrel organ tradition, played small, wooden rollers bristling with pins. These barrels were pinned spirally and made three revolutions to complete the tune—a system well known in barrel-orchestrion making.

F. E. P. Ehrlich of Leipzig made a machine in 1885 for the mechanical playing of an ordinary piano, which used a perforated tune sheet and an escapement cocking mechanism worked by small levers to strike the piano strings with sufficient force. He was to produce a number of such interesting variations but all were basically punched-card players. Ehrlich applied these techniques in his many types of organette which culminated in the successful and widely-sold Ariston of 1885 (which played a circular punched card disc), and his little Orpheus disc-playing piano of 1887 which played Ariston cards. Both Ehrlich and Lochmann later made large 'long-case' pianos which were played by metal discs rather like Polyphon's Concerto (q.v.).

Activity was not centred just in Northern Europe and America, for Italy was a centre of mechanical music and, of course, mechanical pianos. Giovanni Racca of Bologna was a maker of barrel pianos who devised, in 1886, a system of playing a piano using perforated book music. He used a variation of the tremolo system invented by one Signor Caldera in about 1875, applied in England to the ordinary piano-forte by Kirkman and known as the Melopiano. This was a *sostinente* attachment wherein each hammer was attached by a flat spring to an oscillating rail set in motion by a foot pedal and flywheel. The hammers were restrained by checks which were freed when their respective piano keys were touched, so causing the strings to be struck repeatedly. Racca, with his co-patentee Seward, achieved this with the mechanism shown in Fig. 8. Four sizes of these attractive machines were produced under the name 'Piani Melodici' and they were of horizontal layout, the largest one closely resembling a small baby-grand. These were operated by small spring-tensioned levers normally pressed down by the card in the same way as Ehrlich's card-operated organettes were being made in Germany. . . . Whilst many barrel instruments of all types were being converted to book music, for the piano at least, this was but a passing phase.

J. M. Grob, A. O. Schultze and A. V. Niemczik in Berlin jointly perfected in 1886 a playing machine for pianos which could also be used with organs. Unlike Thibouville-Lamy's instrument of the same period, this was worked by a perforated tune sheet. Levers were moved

Pianos Mélodieux

de la fabrique   [289

G. Racca à Bologne (Italie).

Ces instruments mécaniques n'ont rien de commun avec les autres instruments congénères comme les Aristons, Simphonions etc.

Les Pianos Mélodieux ont une voix aussi forte qu'un bon Piano, et la note tenue comme les harmoniums.

Avec ces instruments on peut obtenir les plus délicates nuances d'expression.

Exiger la marque de fabrique sur les Pianos et cartons musicaux pour n'être pas victime d'ımperfectes contre-façons.

10 000 instruments vendus.

Exportation. — 4 differents modèles à 4 et 6 octaves.

Fig. 23. Popular at the turn of the century was the Piani Melodici (see Plate 29)

Fig. 24. Another cardboard-operated piano-player was made by J. M. Grob of Leipzig. Sold in London in 1881 by F. Payton & Co, it was described in this catalogue as follows: 'The Piano Player, a wonderful invention, by means of which any kind of music can be played on any piano, by merely turning a handle; it is played in a proper way by automatic keys which supply the place of the fingers. Price, with 6 tunes £7.15.0 Extra tunes, each 0.1.8'

By courtesy of Mr John Payton, Islington

mechanically by the cardboard disc, allowing segmented arms to wedge cam-fashion on a rotating drum, thereby cocking the piano hammer and striking the string. It was Grob and, separately, Ehrlich who first applied a variation of the Christofori hammer action to the mechanical piano. This action was a considerable improvement on the direct striking hammer principle inasmuch as the hammer mechanism for one note was progressively cocked by the action (with the ordinary piano, the action is cocked by the depressing of the piano key), finally bringing the hammer against the string and allowing it to fall back immediately, regardless of whether or not the operating lever is returned to normal position. This made for a prompt action, allowed notes to be sustained by a separate damper connected to the cocking mechanism and also permitted free and easy repetition of the note. Grob's player acted upon thirty-six of the piano's keys.

Whereas Ehrlich and some of his contemporaries used the progressive movement of a lever, pulled by the tune sheet, to cock the hammer and release it, Grob, and those who favoured this other method, relied on the mechanical fact that a cam can be wedged on a rotating lever, thereby applying a relatively considerable amount of force for the initial expenditure of a very light force at the opposite end of the cam lever.

A number of very ingenious cardboard-playing pianos were made, particularly those driven by hot air engines. Of German manufacture and more than likely the products of the Leipzig area, rich as it was with mechanical music expertise, these were intended for domestic use. The Organista, made about 1890, played in addition to piano strings, a glockenspiel, drum and a triangle. Another such instrument, the Piano-Orchestrion, was a horizontal instrument and played on strings only. Both these instruments derived their power from a methylated spirits burner and a hot-air engine located in their lower portions, or could be played by turning a handle.

C. A. Custer in the United States made a keyboard player for a piano which graduated the power of touch and actually operated the pedals of the piano from the music-roll in 1887. This was quite probably the first attempt at built-in expression.

Favouring the principle of a device clamped to a piano keyboard, G. P. le Dan patented his player for keyboards in 1887. This worked using a series of metal plates having projections which engaged in levers connected to the keys. It was thus similar to the Antiphonel of Debain.

The invention of the first proper pneumatic system to be controlled by a perforated paper roll specifically designed to play an organ can be attributed to Emil Welte of M. Welte & Söhne of Freiburg in Germany. Between 1887 and 1889, Welte took out patents for such an action to replace the barrels in their large orchestrions and barrel-playing military bands. Welte produced at this same time an air-motor for driving the music-roll (a trefoil cam-controlled motor which was, in modified and improved form, to remain a feature of all subsequent Welte mechanical organs and pianos) and made an elementary device to reduce the characteristic tendency of paper-roll music to speed up as it played, due to the driven take-up spool gradually increasing in diameter as more paper was wound on. Welte minimized this by making the take-up spool of large diameter.

A handful of inventors gave thought to the use of electro-magnetic player actions using the perforated tune sheet. The 1880's saw the production of many of these instruments which must have been, to say the least, illuminating to watch with their showers of blue sparks as they played. Tune rolls for these were often of thin brass or special paper, sometimes coated with a non-conducting substance such as shellac. In place of perforations, some of these had the musical 'notes' printed on the roll, as electrically-conducting portions of the roll where there was no shellac or other insulating material.

To avoid oxidization of the electrical contacts, silver terminals were used, even platinum tips. Perhaps it was the unreliability of the Victorian electricity supply which killed these electro-pianos—but it was more likely to have been due to an understandable fear of the machine, for, with its lack of earthing, it was no doubt capable of dispensing electric shocks *gratis* to those who chose to lean upon it whilst presenting their party pieces to the family gathering on a Sunday afternoon.

One of the more unusual of these electrically-played pianos was that thought up by R. K. Boyle in 1884. His piano had no hammers, the strings being set into vibration by energizing them in conjunction with an electro-magnet.

Another of these monstrosities was the invention of A. P. S. Macquisten whose piano played an 'electro-magnetic pattern or Jacquard device' using copper wire feelers to make electrical contact through the tune sheet.

Mr Henry Klein, of 84 Oxford Street, London, was already established as a musical box importer when, in the summer of 1898, he secured the agency for the electric pianos manufactured by Hupfeld and distributed throughout Europe by H. Peters & Son of Leipzig. The instrument sold for the sum of £128—a very costly instrument by contemporary standards. The action was pneumatic, every one of the keys in the seven octaves capable of being played from the music-roll. Driving power was provided by an electric motor and, at the end of the roll of music, rewinding was automatic. The piano was coin-operated and represented a considerable advance on the types of instrument available anywhere else in the world at the time. A combined manual and mechanical model sold for £110. For both types the electric power came from storage batteries which held sufficient current 'to play a thousand tunes before the need of re-charging'. In Berlin, no fewer than four firms were engaged in producing electric batteries for driving mechanical instruments such as orchestrion organs and pianos.

The United States Krell Piano Co. spent some years developing an electric piano attachment in the late 1890's which was claimed would be one of the most perfect on the market and also would be available at a reasonable price. Power could come either from the mains or from storage batteries. The inventor was a Mr Simpkins who believed that he had devised something to revolutionize the piano attachment industry. The pious belief of its creator proved unjustified.

William Gerecke, of 8 and 9 Goring Street, Houndsditch, London, advertised themselves as manufacturers and importers of musical instruments. In 1901, they introduced the Pneuma which was a 'self-playing patent apparatus on the *Pneumatic Principle*—fitted to any New or Old Piano—requires no alteration of the Instrument, which can still be played as a Piano after the apparatus is attached—worked by Storage Battery, or direct from the Lighting Current, or by crank.' The Pneuma, an electrically-driven attachment, could be supplied with a piano for £50 or, alternatively, the mechanism could be installed into any existing piano. Gerecke was also a musical box agent and stocked the largest disc-playing musical box ever made—the Komet.

An early attempt at making a reproducing piano was made in 1910 by the Harper Electric Piano (1910) Co. in England. They produced an electrically-operated piano in that year but, after expending much time, effort and money for limited success and market, directed their manufacturing capacity towards the making of more conventional, pneumatic players. The Harper played 65 notes from 13½-inch wide perforated paper rolls, most of which were punched out by the Up-To-Date Music Roll Company at Hammersmith.

Electro-magnetic action was, however, successfully developed in later years, specifically in America, where the Wurlitzer and Mills Novelty Company made a variety of instruments played electrically from a perforated paper roll.

With the acceptance of the paper tune sheet, certain physical properties of the early papers used had to be taken into consideration, not the least of which was its expansion and contraction in varying moisture conditions. Quite often a roll of paper would swell so much as to wedge

75

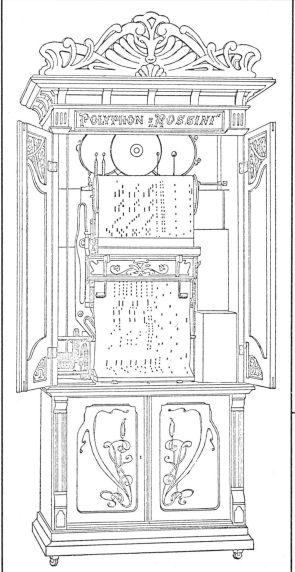

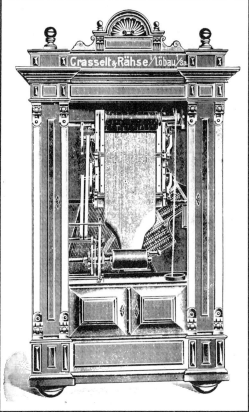

Fig. 25. Piano Orchestrions (a) This stringed instrument with persussion was made in Leipzig by the Polyphon musical box company in 1904. It played perforated card music Piano Orchestrions (b) Similar mechanically is this instrument made for restaurants and public places in 1901. The piano had an iron frame

itself firmly between the wooden spool ends. Again, the paper would not track properly or wind on to the take-up spool in damp weather. Adjustable spools had to be invented until the introduction, early this century, of music paper which had a low expansion rate. Another problem was fluff, dust and paper fibre from both the surface of the paper roll and also the sometimes ragged edges of the perforations. After a while, the suction at the tracker-bar would dutifully draw any such undesirable debris into the mechanism, upsetting the seatings of the valves and so causing malfunctionings. Filters and dust traps were incorporated until better paper was adopted. The Aeolian Company were the first to fit their piano-players with a

TABLE SHOWING TYPES AND WIDTHS OF COMMON MUSIC ROLLS		
Instrument	Paper Width	Type of Spool Drive
Aeolian Orchestrelle	$10\frac{1}{8}$ inches	Projecting pivot on left end of spool, projecting pivot with drive lugs on right end of spool
Aeolian Pipe Organ	$10\frac{1}{8}$ inches	As above (Reproducing organ rolls are $15\frac{1}{4}''$ wide)
Wilcox & White Symphony	$10\frac{1}{4}$ inches	As above but roll is wound in reverse on spool
Piano, 65-note	$11\frac{1}{4}$ inches	Projecting pivot on left end of spool, projecting pivot with drive lugs on right end of spool
Piano, 88-note, Full-Scale	$11\frac{1}{4}$ inches	Recessed hole in left end of spool, recessed hole with drive slot in right end of spool
Piano, Hupfeld Phonola range	$11\frac{5}{8}$ inches	Projecting pivot on left end of spool, projecting pivot with drive lugs on right end of spool
Piano, Welte-Mignon (original red paper rolls)	$13\frac{1}{2}$ inches	As above

NOTE: The *Orchestrelle* and *Symphony* rolls are for player reed organs. *Symphony* rolls also fit the *Angelus* reed organ/cabinet-style piano-player combination. Both of these instruments play 58-note rolls. The *Aeolian Pipe Organ* plays 116-note music rolls of the same width as the 58-note *Orchestrelle* rolls. The method of driving the music spool on rewinding, perfected by Aeolian, was adopted almost universally. The only variation is the 65-note rolls as described above.

transparent sliding lid to the spool box to keep out the dust whilst the instrument was not in use.

By the 1890's, the sheer simplicity of the basic principles of the paper-controlled pneumatic piano ensured that the quest for a piano-playing system had been completed. Indeed, the perforated-paper player-piano was to be one of the last contributions in the field of musical instruments of the classic generation. The second generation instruments are, of course, no longer recognizable as musical instruments. Being nothing more than musical noise-generators, they rely on the principles of electronics controlled by perforated-paper computer tape developed from the telegraph transmitting tape perfected as another offshoot from the Jacquard system.

There remained the trickle of odd systems for a few years but, seeing that paper music was easy to make, cheap to sell and quite compact, the piano industry latched on to making pneumatic actions almost overnight. Indeed, far from having his first player-piano burned by a gathering of irate music teachers, Needham's principles were warmly welcomed universally. Everyone wanted a self-acting piano and he who made the best and simplest action would be a hero. 'Make a better mouse-trap and the world will beat a path to your door!'

With the polished rosewood player pushed up to the piano and a good selection of popular rolls including, perhaps, some virtuoso pieces to impress visitors, every home of 'with it' Victorians was suddenly complete. All that had gone before was relegated to being old-fashioned and valueless. In the same way that today few, if any, would consider forming a collection for the preservation of obsolete television receivers, the precursors of the piano-player were cast out. In but a few short years, the piano-player was to suffer the same ignominious end.

Before this century was more than a few years old, perforated-paper-controlled pneumatic actions were being made to install inside pianos, upright instruments to begin with and then, as skills developed, into grand pianos. The sheer convenience and simplicity of the paper roll closed the book on the subject of inventing devices to play the piano. The job was done.

CHAPTER 4

The Development of the Player Piano

As one may well imagine, progress in the development of the pneumatic piano followed the same pattern as that which applied to the street piano and, contemporarily or earlier, to the musical box and the barrel organ. Whilst an invention, discovery or improvement would be adopted by one maker, others did not necessarily follow suit for some while. Again, whilst many, many inventions were patented as improvements to almost every conceivable part of the mechanical piano from the disposition of the valves to the shape of manual control levers, other and more important developments are difficult to place as to date of inception and name of inventor.

This is not hard to understand when one realizes the huge number of manufacturers on both sides of the Atlantic. Initially, the practical piano-player and player-piano emanated from the United States where resources and promotion were already geared to production of instruments. The European players of the time, although probably of better specification, workmanship and performance, were not launched at the market with anything approaching the gusto and financial backing of, say, the Aeolian Company which published expensive colour brochures, mounted a nation-wide advertising and marketing campaign—and had the production facilities to cater for the resultant demand.

This must not be taken as in any way denigrating the European achievements for, as we shall see, instruments of both ability and quality were produced on this side of the Atlantic. The products of Ludwig Hupfeld and Emile Welte, for example, were outstanding in their own way. Significantly, England produced no worthwhile contributions until fairly late on in the story although the British market for American and European products was extremely keen. Such pneumatic actions as were later produced had little to offer over imported products (with the possible exception, as we shall see, of the Boyd Pistonola) and, as with the British-designed and built Carola reproducing action made for Blüthner by Sir Herbert Marshall Piano Company at Acton, manufacture was soon abandoned. Invariably, imported actions, already produced elsewhere in large quantities, were cheaper and of equal performance.

Whereas in England the barrel piano found its birthplace in the poorer parts of East London, the player-piano came from the much more sophisticated Mayfair showrooms of plush manufacturers whose names and reputations were already firmly established. The Camden Town area of North London was as much the home of the piano-making industry as Hatton Garden that of the jeweller and watchmaker or Shoreditch the domain of the cabinet-maker. But to begin with we must go back and follow the development of the instrument.

The player-piano is the result of experiments which took place in three places—in France, Germany and the United States. In the beginning France was the scene of much pioneering work and a lot of early development study. However, France seemed to lose its early interest and world lead in the mechanical piano several years before America forged ahead. Both Hupfeld and Welte in Germany successfully devised and produced instruments, but it was America where the commercial know-how and the necessary brains were available to push an idea rapidly through development stages and into production.

Germany's position as the first in the field is not hard to accept when it is realized that the largest mechanical music industry in the world was in Eastern Germany, Leipzig being the centre with Berlin a close second. The art of the musical box, first evolved in the Swiss Jura, was systematically developed in Leipzig where the disc-playing musical box was invented and the great orchestrion organs made. Thus Leipzig was in the best possible position to devise a pneumatic action for piano playing. Welte in Freiburg had shown that an organ could be made to play in this manner and the Leipzig industry immediately applied itself to the exploitation and improvement of the system. There was only one dissonant note of any consequence to retard these formative years of Leipzig's self-acting piano and organ industry and this was the antiquated copyright law in Germany which prohibited the making of perforated rolls of musical compositions for which copyright existed. The simple expedient of taxing rolls had yet to be adopted.

It was partly due to these omnipresent wrangles which occasioned the formation of a society of German mechanical musical instrument manufacturers at the turn of the century. President of this society was Wilhelm Spaethe whose organ and piano manufactury was situated at Gera and it was due to repeated pressure brought on the authorities by the society that the Reichstadt finally passed Paragraph XXII of their new copyright law which decreed that copyright need not apply to the playing of music from a tune sheet, but that the tune sheet or music-roll must have a copyright or performing-rights tax levied on it at the time of sale. Spaethe naturally had a personal interest in the matter since his firm was one of the largest manufacturers of pneumatic instruments. It is interesting to note that the Polyphonmusikwerke in Leipzig, makers of the Polyphon disc musical box, was deprived early on of the rights to make discs of the music of Gilbert and Sullivan because of a dispute over the copyright act prevailing at that period, as applied to their first—and only—disc of their music which was the *Mikado* waltz.

The ideas conceived wholly in America were the ones which made the largest contribution, if not necessarily the first, in the field of the player-piano and thus it is to America that we must go to start our story. The pneumatic piano-player, as distinct from the European cabinet-style mechanical machines, appeared in the States in the late 1890's.

Driving the music-roll presented its own problems. With the organette, it was quite sufficient for the roll to be wound on to the take-up spool by hand. With the piano-player, however, it was not feasible to expect the performer to pedal with his feet, juggle with levers and at the same time maintain a regular rotation of a handle. Early instruments transported the roll by a mechanical linkage from the foot treadle—a belt, a chain or even bevel gears and shafting. These all suffered from the same intrinsic defects—the speed of pedalling directly affected the speed of the music. Whilst these worked up to a point, they did not make provision for rewinding, unless one was prepared to pedal the roll back again, and nor did it respond adequately to anything other than regular pedalling.

The use of the clockwork motor was favoured by a number of early makers and an early

THE APOLLO
PIANO PLAYER.

Have you a Piano ? Almost everyone has. But can you play it ? Ah! only a little. By buying an APOLLO to attach to your Piano, you can have the most perfect music of all kinds played on your own instrument in a faultless manner.

YOU SUPPLY THE EXPRESSION & SOUL. WE SUPPLY THE TECHNIQUE

A child can play all music—either operas, oratorios, chamber music, or accompaniments, in ANY KEY at will; and no knowledge of music is necessary.

VLADIMIR DE PACHMANN says :

"I was surprised at the advance you have made in your 'Apollo Piano Player.' Its artistic purpose is achieved by rapidity and correctness of execution, the delicately adjusted tempo stop, and the transposing attachment. I wish you well-deserved success."

L. EMIL BACH says :

"I have just made a careful examination of your 'Apollo Piano Player,' and confess I am surprised at its possibilities.

"I am astonished at its faultless execution of the most difficult passages in works, and at its artistic expression by use of the tempo stop. This instrument opens up the whole field of piano literature to anyone who wishes to draw from that unfailing source of pleasure. I consider it a most wonderful success."

Price £52 10s. Nett.

Some points why the **APOLLO** is the best Piano Player ever offered to the Public :—

The Music-rolls are **SELF RE-WINDING.**

All Music can be played **IN ANY KEY**

by means of a transposing screw.

It is easily pedalled, and responds quickly to the action of the foot. There is no strain on the muscles, as in other attachments.

The Pedals are adjustable to suit the Performer.

Anyone can p'ay it.

It is constructed to suit extreme climates.

In fact, it is the most perfect attachment.

THE CLARK APOLLO CO., Ltd.,
"D" DEPARTMENT,
119, REGENT STREET, LONDON, W.

Fig. 26. Advertisement for the Clark Apollo player c.1901

piano-player was the Simplex which employed a large three-spring motor to drive the roll. The Simplex—a 65-note player—used rolls which were somewhat narrower than the normal ones used and a good proportion of the music for these comprised accompaniment rolls for songs.

Melville Clark made ingenious use of clockwork in his first Apollo 58-note player of 1899. The action of treadling turned a crankshaft on a train of gears which rotated the take-up spool and also wound up a clockwork motor through a friction clutch. At the end of the roll, a handle was pulled and the gearing was rearranged so that the roll was rewound by the motor.

In spite of the 'innovation' of clockwork, G. H. Davis saw fit to equip his piano-player of 1901 with a weight-driven rewind. As the roll was played, so was raised a large weight and the potential energy thus stored was used to rewind the music.

The clockwork motor invented by the Smith Lyrophone Company in America in 1902 could be used for driving the roll and rewinding it independently of the foot treadles, spring winding being effected by a suitable handle on the front of the player.

The first vacuum air motor in which the action of sucking in air through a system of bellows and valves produced rotary motion, was probably that invented in America in 1884 by J. Morgan for driving the tune sheets in automatic reed instruments.

Air motors on pianos, oddly enough, were sometimes worked by air pressure instead of suction, a small compression bellows being supplied in conjunction with the foot treadles for this purpose, but George Kelly in America invented the most convenient and straightforward suction drive with his slide-valve motor in 1886. Kelly's motor consisted of a series of sliding plates fitted to a board, each with a matching pneumatic bellows fixed to the other side. Inlet and exhaust ports were cut in the dividing board and each slide was linked with a connecting rod to a crankshaft. Suction applied to the exhaust side of the system would cause each bellows to open and close alternatively, the slides regulating the admission of atmospheric air into the vacuum chamber of the motor and serving to turn the crankshaft.

An advantage of this system was that the motor could develop a good deal more power than the earlier pressure motors and was also capable of much smoother action by the provision of four or even five sets of bellows and slides, having the effect of a multi-cylinder car engine as compared with the erratic low-speed behaviour of a single or twin cylinder engine. The wind motor provided more or less constant speed which could be variably controlled by a gate valve. The motor maintained its speed under almost all conditions of pedalling—fast or slow or erratic—so long as there was some pressure differential in the piano system. A flywheel was usually provided on three-valve motors to help even out the motion, but the multi-valved successors usually did not need such an addition.

A further device was the suction air motor perfected in Freiburg, Germany, by Emil Welte in 1887 and first used to drive his paper-roll-playing orchestrion organs. The Welte motor consisted of a cone-shaped body carrying along its length three pneumatic bellows arranged at 120°. These were linked at their wide ends by connecting rods to a crankshaft which ran through the centre of the body and carried at the opposite end a rotating cam which alternately uncovered and covered in turn the entry and exhaust passages to each little bellows. When suction was applied to the 'exhaust' side of the motor, air would be drawn into one of the three bellows, so causing it to turn the crankshaft via its connecting rod and, at the same time, advancing the inlet and exhaust port cam. When a further inlet port was uncovered, the adjacent bellows would begin to inflate, advancing the crankshaft and so collapsing the previous bellows, the air from which would be passed down the suction exhaust passage to the inlet side of the main bellows assembly of the whole organ. The continuous application of suction to the exhaust side of the motor kept the system working smoothly, the crankshaft turning with sufficient power to drive the take-up spool. So successful was the Welte rotary motor that, in improved form, it was to remain a feature right through the subsequent range of pianos which Welte made.

Transposing devices, thought of as later improvements to the player-piano, were in fact embodied by Melville Clark in his Apollo of 1899. His 58-note tracker-bar could be moved to permit the music to be played in any one of the five keys from B^b to D and the change was effected by the turning of a thumb screw to shift the tracker bar laterally, its lower connections being of flexible rubber tubing. This also served to cater for the irregularities in paper and spool width which, with the early players, varied quite greatly. He called it a 'transposing mouthpiece'.

In later years, with the introduction of quality-controlled paper music and 88-note actions, tracker-bars had to be made of brass and these could be shifted through several keys (the Hupfeld Phonola pianos through no less than nine!) by a small transposing lever. Whilst it was common to shift the tracker-bar to transpose, some actions were made wherein the music roll and take-up spool were moved instead.

Hand in hand with transposing came the problem of maintaining the paper roll in perfect alignment with the tracker-bar holes during playing and this was achieved by an automatic device which moved the spools fractionally. Operation was achieved by special holes in the tracker which aligned with the margin of the paper. So long as these were both covered, tracking was perfect. If the paper tended to drift to one side, it would expose one hole, allowing air to transfer to a special bellows assembly which would gently push the spools over until alignment was once more achieved. The Standard Player Action Co. in America produced such a system. Aeolian, on the other hand, used a system worked by delicately-balanced fingers which followed the edge of the paper and which were connected to bellows as before. Another system ran the paper between two small brass 'fences' set in the tracker-bar which performed similar functions. A variation of the 'uncovered hole' method was patented by J. J. Walker in 1909 and this used special music-rolls having a continuous line of central perforations, which ran between two holes in the tracker-bar. If the roll wandered, so allowing air to enter one or the other of the holes, so the bellows would gently ease the roll over the opposite way.

Players were fitted with wheels to allow them to be pushed up to the piano and all the better ones were fitted with devices for adjusting the height of the player to the keyboard. The Angelus, for example, had two large handles which engaged in a ratchet slot to each side of the front of the case, and so the height of each side of the player could be adjusted independently. Better class models were fitted with wheel brakes or wedging devices so that, in the middle of a *fortissimo* passage or when the performer was pedalling hard, the player would not roll away or shift its position on the keyboard.

The Aeolian Company's cabinet-style Pianola piano-player sold for £65—quite a considerable sum at the turn of the century. The only British-made player was the 'Boyd' which sold for £27 10s 0d cash or £32 8s 0d by monthly instalments of 13s 6d. But something appreciably cheaper and, by all accounts, easier to work, was about to be put on the market. This was called the 'Pianotist'.

The New York firm of Emile Klaber was already well known in the field of pianos. Emile's son, Augustus David Klaber, worked in London at 29 Queen Victoria Street where Klaber pianos were distributed in this country. On May 29, 1900, he filed a whole series of patents

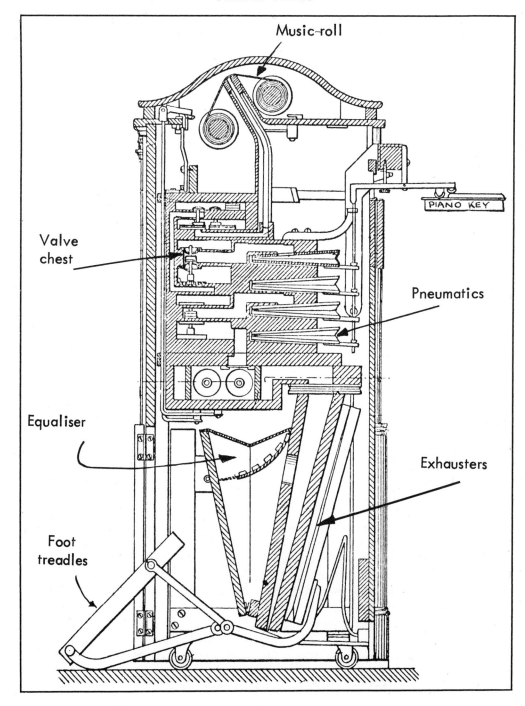

Music-roll

Valve
chest

Pneumatics

PIANO KEY

Equaliser

Exhausters

Foot
treadles

Fig. 27. The Aeolian Co. patented this piano-player in 1901

for various details of a mechanical piano, including detachable treadles for a player action which could be fitted to a normal piano, a method of driving the tune sheet from the treadles, a pianoforte system for mechanical playing and a device for playing the piano by hand 'when the feet are not available'—assumedly the *mechanical* piano. Paradoxically, he concluded this flurry of British patents with one for a tuck-in envelope for printed-paper rate mail as the normal type of tuck-in envelope was '. . . often cast to one side remaining unopened'.

Klaber's efforts towards the mechanical piano continued and a few months later he formed the Pianotist Company with offices and showrooms at 56 Regent Street, London. His father, Emile, was managing director and the American parent company was the Adek Manufacturing Company of New York. An elaborate machine was perfected for punching out music-rolls in May of 1901 and in September they perfected a device for 'varying the loudness of automatic piano-players by adjusting the force of hammers on the strings'.

In the summer of 1901, the Pianotist Company carried out an ambitious (by current British standards) advertising campaign to popularize their instrument and gave free piano recitals using their player attachment at their Regent Street showrooms. Five styles of the Pianotist were offered, the lowest of which was priced at twenty guineas.

Lamentably, no working example or even complete installation remains. A fragmentary Pianotist in the British Piano Museum shows it to have been operated by a music-roll made of thin card and to have been operated by a mechanical linkage wound by a handle. Little else survives to tell us just how the Pianotist worked and the patents relate only to small details of the whole. It was obviously eclipsed by other inventions, yet a long article entitled 'Evolution of the Piano Player' in a 1901 issue of *The Illustrated Sporting and Dramatic News* praised the device.

I can do little better than relate verbatim an extract from this article which reveals that the Pianotist was an 'inner player', did not rely on treadle-power and was considered excellent value for £35. Having sung the praises of the ordinary piano-player, the writer continued:

'Hardly are the words uttered in praise and endorsement of these instruments before a veritable genius arises and condenses the whole operative mechanism into such small space that it can be fitted into *any piano, out of sight*, thus not interfering at any time with the use of the piano in the ordinary manner. Not content with this unquestionable advantage, the inventor of this instrument has provided what he is pleased to call "melody stops", whereby "the otherwise fatal accuracy and equal dynamic force" of all the fingers of a mechanical player may be varied at the will of the performer. The bass notes of a composition may be subdued, and the melody in the treble accentuated, or if desired a melody brought out in the bass, while the treble provides merely a whispered accompaniment. This is a great achievement hitherto unknown in mechanical piano-players, and in the opinion of those best qualified to judge, it places this instrument far ahead of any other instrument of its kind. A simple frictional device (sic) has been substituted for pneumatics, with a consequent result that only 2 lbs. pressure is required as against 14 lbs. necessary to operate the cabinet form of piano-players.

'In the opinion of some of the greatest artists and musicians who have seen this invention, it is considered artistically superior to anything of its kind, and such artists and musicians as Adelina Patti (Baroness Caderstrom), Mark Hambourg (the great pianist), Henry J. Wood (conductor Queen's Hall orchestra), Wilhelm Ganz, Tito Mattei, Landon Ronald and many others, have not hesitated to put such opinions to paper over their own signatures. From the fact that the *Pianotist* (this is the name of this remarkable instrument) when fitted to a piano in no way interferes with its use, or injures it in any way, it may be reasonably prophesied that

Growth of Appreciation.

The Pianola does not injure the piano in any way. Its felt-covered fingers rest upon the piano-keys and strike the notes in their proper relation one to another as indicated on the music-sheet, With its aid any member of your household may play upon the piano even if he or she literally does not know one note from another—not only one or two selections, but every piece of music ever written for the piano-forte. Grand and light operas, Liszt's Rhapsodies, Sousa's marches and the latest popular airs are practically "at your fingers' ends." You have all the pleasure of hand-playing because you control the expressor, which is the soul of music. Estimate for yourself the profit and pleasure the Pianola would bring you in a single year.

An Instance

A CAREFUL investigation of the Pianola invariably leads to surprise and delight. The more you see and hear the instrument the better you enjoy and appreciate it. This is invariably the rule, and the more musical a person is the more appreciative he becomes.

Josef Hofmann, the famous pianist, when he first saw the Pianola, said of it :

"I anticipate much pleasure from learning to play this exceedingly ingenious device which reproduces with such astonishing accuracy the masterworks of music."

A month later, April 18, he wrote :

"I find that your instrument offers facilities for expression that will enable an intelligent player to give a very close imitation of hand playing. I have been surprised to discover to what an extent one can, with a little practice, control the dynamic effects."

Hofmann also says in the same letter :

"In all the essentials of artistic piano playing, the Pianola is the best instrument of this type."

We are demonstrating the possibilities of this remarkable instrument to all who call at our exhibition rooms. We are always glad to show the instrument to anyone sufficiently interested to visit us. You need not feel the usual hesitancy about going to see a thing you do not expect to purchase. as we have rooms especially set apart for displaying the Pianola, and employ a large staff of men whose sole duty it is to play the instrument and explain it to visitors.

The marked popularity of the Pianola in the home leads to the belief that an examination of this instrument is to the interest of everyone.

The Pianola *can be bought by monthly instalments if desired.* **Price £65.**

Send for Catalogue G.G.

THE ORCHESTRELLE COMPANY,
225 REGENT STREET, LONDON, W.

Fig. 28. Advertisement for the 1901 Pianola

The Pianotist.

AN INSTRUMENT BY MEANS OF WHICH ANYONE CAN PLAY ANY PIANO.

The above shows the **PIANOTIST** fitted to an upright piano, and illustrates its operation.

Price **35 guineas, fitted complete.**

FREE RECITALS DAILY.

THE . .

PIANOTIST

Enables anyone without any musical knowledge to play on any Piano with taste and expression even the most difficult composition. It is extremely simple in construction, has no pneumatics, and no clumsy cabinet to interfere with the use of the piano in the ordinary manner.

It is exceptionally easy to operate, there being no air pressure to be overcome.

With a few hours' practice, such results may be obtained that even a critic cannot distinguish the playing from that of a human performer.

Write for Descriptive Illustrated Catalogue F, Mailed free on application.

56 Regent Street, W.

(NEAR PICCADILLY CIRCUS.)

Fig. 29. Advertisement for the Pianotist, 1900

the piano of the future will be capable of performing the dual role of "an old century piano" and a "new century piano player". Such manufacturers as Erards, Steinways, Pleyels, &c., &c., are eulogistic in praise of the *Pianotist*, and all those contemplating the purchase of a piano-player would do well to call at the showrooms of the Pianotist Co. Ltd., 56, Regent Street (near Piccadilly Circus), and see and hear this latest invention before finally making their choice.

'A strong Company has been formed for the manufacture and sale of the *Pianotist*, and as indicative of the success of this instrument it may be stated that a number of prominent people have already availed themselves of an offer made by the Pianotist Company to change their old style instrument for the *Pianotist*, the Company making a fair allowance in exchange therefor.'

The lack of more detail and, surprisingly, the failure of exhaustive attempts to locate any surviving complete Pianotist is tantalizing, yet must serve as proof that the instrument was not generally favoured in consideration of other players on the market at that time.

The Angelus player was produced by the Wilcox & White Company of Meriden, Connecticut, who patented on April 8, 1902, a new approach to the problem of adjusting the height of the player to the keyboard—undoubtedly a problem of great concern to all makers since the fingers had to be at the precise height over the piano's keys in order to do their job adequately. Each note pneumatic of the Angelus after 1902 lifted a pitman which carried a number of notches in its back edge. The keyboard fingers were all carried in a frame which could be moved up and down on guide rails provided at each end, so bringing the adjustable fingers into suitable notches in the pitmans. Adjustment, although positive, required careful preparation but, once set, would stay that way. The Angelus also featured a transposing device, as much for the correct alignment of rolls as anything else. This was worked by a knurled screw which moved both the take-up spool and the music roll chuck laterally across the fixed tracker-bar.

The compass of an 88-note or full-scale player and roll is from Contra-A to C^7 whilst the range of the 65-note instrument is from A to C^6. The physical proportions of the tracker-bar and roll are six perforations to the inch in the 65-note roll; nine to the inch for the 88-note.

With the 65-note players and their precursors such as the 58-note early Apollo by Melville Clark, the tracker-bar was of wood. Larger scales called for closer, smaller and more accurate holes and this could not be achieved in wood. The Aeolian Company took out the first patents in 1902 for a tracker-bar made of brass tubes, their upper ends flattened into a rectangular shape and cast into a strip of Britannia metal.* Connections from the other ends of the tubes to the valve chests could then be made with rubber tubing.

Brass tracker-bars of this type were soon adopted throughout the industry and they did permit of neat and simple registration and transposing devices to be applied to them.

The Angelus cabinet player was built with a full-scale 88-note action as late as 1909 but this instrument, a specimen of which is in the author's collection, must be considered to be rare. By this time, the 'inner player' was well on the way to perfection and the market for a push-up had dwindled to almost nothing. It was about this time that Wilcox & White changed their name to the Angelus Piano Co. with offices in New York.

Music-roll manufacturers were faced very early on with problems associated with the quality of the paper which they had to use. Being hygroscopic, it was extremely susceptible to moisture and a roll would swell so much that it would not unwind from its spool. Perhaps even worse, if it could be induced to unwind, it would split across the edges on being wound on to the take-up

---

* Britannia metal: an alloy of tin with antimony and a little copper.

spool. A roll with split and torn edges rapidly got worse until it reached the point where it began to sound marginal notes unintentionally.

The adjustable spool for pianos was probably made first by the Aeolian Company and was simply a spool having one flange loose to slide along the wooden arbor. However, Welte had made adjustable spools for orchestrion rolls since the turn of the century and these were well made affairs wherein one end of the spool spindle was hollow and carried a telescoping end complete with flange.

Most of the roll makers later adopted the adjustable roll spool to allow for paper expansion and, with greater accuracy in both tracking and paper quality, take-up spools did not have to be so close-fitting to the paper width.

In the manufacture of rolls, it had been usual to cut sustained notes as one long slot in the paper. These long cuts frequently tore or, where a sustained chord resulted in the paper 'ribboning', discords would sound. These disadvantages were largely countered in 1914 by the introduction throughout the roll-making trade of the so-called 'contigious' perforation where long notes were represented as a series of closely-spaced but separate perforations. Broadwoods and the Perforated Music Company were among the first to adopt this in England. The positioning of the holes for sustained notes was critical; too wide a spacing produced staccato notes and too closely spaced holes easily tore into the long slot which was to be avoided.

Since the era of the organette, attempts had been made to strengthen the edges of the paper but all this did in effect was to make the edges thicker than the centre. Even so, the Hupfeld Company's Animatic music-rolls of the 1920's for their Duophonola reproducing piano had their edges reinforced for a width of about $\frac{3}{8}$ inch by varnish. This must have been a mixed blessing since, whilst it undoubtedly reduced the chances of edge damage, it had the effect of making the rolls spool up loosely—not the best way to prevent moisture warping the paper, for even the best paper will track badly if loosely spooled.

The ability of air at a reduced pressure to perform work by collapsing or expanding a bellows motor was soon applied to the control of the action and damper rail. By connecting the soft pedal action to a large pneumatic and linking this with tubing to suitable extra perforations on the tracker-bar, the action could be moved by placing additional holes in the music-roll. Likewise, the sustaining pedal action could be controlled. It was thus possible to play softly and loudly from the paper roll. The first person to contrive automatic operation of the dampers and rest-rail of the piano action was E. M. Skinner, who patented such a system on March 21, 1900. He used additional marginal perforations in the music-roll, a trend rapidly followed by most other makers.

Subsequently, various inventions were made to bring out the theme of the music from the accompaniment, to accentuate the first or last note of a chord and so on. Most of these worked on the simple, if not always wholly desirable, principle of doing what so many budding keyboard virtuosi do—holding down certain notes longer than others, thereby holding the damper off as long as possible. In the music-roll, this could easily be effected. Whereas, for example, the *tempo* of a piece of music would call for notes to be a regular half-inch in length of perforation, by extending the perforation to perhaps an inch or more, the note would sing out for longer.

The so-called accented or accentuated rolls had a subtle device to enable the theme of the music to be emphasized, certain notes being sounded louder. This was achieved by a very simple yet ingenious method first thought of by T. Casson in 1900.

The notes to be accented—the theme notes—were picked out by the addition of theme holes. These theme holes appeared in the edges of the music-roll as two small perforations, placed close to each other side by side. Since most theme notes occurred in the treble half of the piano scale, it was usual for these to appear only in the right-hand margin. Certain dance music, on the other hand, featured a dominant bass theme and, in such instances, notes throughout the scale would be 'themodized' by theme holes at each edge of the roll.

These holes were placed very slightly ahead of the note which was to be accented and served to inflate partially the pouches at that instant so that when the particular note was instructed to sound (by the normal roll perforation) some of the work had already been done and the available power could be used to produce a stronger blow to the strings for just that one note (see Chapter 7).

Although from a musical standpoint, the arbitrary theme emphasis offered by these 'expression pianos' tended to be insincere, these efforts at a more realistic performance were aimed at making it easier for the player-pianist to produce good music and to get away from the mechanical, toneless effects produced by the earliest piano-players. They were on that count very popular. Many music-rolls were made which incorporated such features, the most common being the Themodist and Artistyle.

Around these largely experimental early days of the player-piano and piano-player, there were many schools of thought as to how many of the piano's complement of notes should or, indeed, could be sounded by a mechanical or pneumatic action. Actions were being made which played 58, 65, 70, 82 and 88 notes and this complete lack of standardization did not engender a progressive industry. It was not until 1910 that actions and rolls were standardized at 65-note and 88-note. The decision for this was taken at a convention of player manufacturers at Buffalo, New York. This regularizing of the piano and roll industry did not affect player-organs which normally used 58-note rolls.

By 1913, there were three systems of music-roll note accenting in use. First was the 2-slot device employed by Broadwood, Pianola, Hupfeld Solophonola and other better-class players. Then there was the 88-slot (marginal) which had one accent slot for each note on the tracker-bar and, finally, the 'Dalian' system of double tracker-bar with actual note perforations which determined the playing of accents. This last-mentioned method was used in the Crowley player-piano (see below) but was never produced in quantity. The second was used only on a limited scale and the first was again used only with a few actions. Note accenting for the popular piano consisted of the Themodist pattern.

At the British Music Exhibition held at Olympia in September 1913, a number of manufacturers exhibited player-pianos, among them Messrs George Rogers' 'Rogers Player-Piano', William Sames & Co.'s instruments (which were fitted with either Hupfeld or the very successful and cheap Higel action London-made and sold by Heckschers of Camden Town), and Malcolm player-piano (Malcolm & Co. used at one time to make a player-organ), and the Direct Pneumatic Action Company with their Stems player-piano fitted with the Arrow action.

Also on show was the Dalian player-piano exhibited by John H. Crowley. This was an unusual type of expression piano which, although of excellent potential, was dependent on costly apparatus with which to manufacture the special paper rolls. Each note was provided with a damping pneumatic and a regulator. One common vacuum pressure was used, but the strength of the piano hammer blow to the string was variable by the amount of atmospheric air admitted through the tracker-bar. This was regulated by having perforations of different widths in the paper, loud notes having wider holes than soft ones. As an alternative, ordinary 88-note rolls could be played. Here, in theory at least, was the ideal expression piano, indeed *reproducing* piano, where every note was characterized by its very own interpretational value.

It was, of course, highly impractical and was never produced.

The Olympia exhibition also showed the range of mini-player-pianos made by Barratt & Robinson which were small enough to be taken on a small yacht or boat. The Pedaleon was one of the smallest players ever made. Following early organ-building techniques, the keyboards on some of these pianos were both hinged and sliding, folding up out of the way when not in use.

Brinsmead showed examples of their Mignon and Aluminium players, the former being of traditional wood construction and the latter a highly durable all-metal action. From Murdoch, Murdoch & Co. of 461 & 463 Oxford Street, London, came the Connoisseur Player Piano. There was also the Connoisseur Reed Organ and the Connoisseur Pipe Organ, both player instruments. The piano was equipped with all the usual controls. Each maker strove to give his own distinctive names to these expression levers or buttons and to employ these euphemisms in their advertising. Murdoch's instrument, for example, had the Tempola, Phrasiola, Solo-theme, Diminuent, Transposa, Automelle (theme isolator controlled by additional holes in the ends of the tracker-bar), Autoforte and Autotracker. Armed with that lot, it is a bit of a come-down to find that the performer still had to pedal and one wonders why no enterprising manufacturer, tongue in cheek, didn't call his foot treadles 'Pedairolas'. Murdoch's also made the 'Golden Tube' music rolls for 65- and 88-note music. These dispensed with having to have a spool for each music-roll; the paper was attached to a tube into which one spool could be fixed for playing.

The player-piano opened up certain opportunities for the musician. The instrument had, for example, the ability to play more than ten notes at once (assuming the normal pianist never to be able to play more than one note per finger). It could be made to play in a manner which the human player could never achieve. Such abilities as these not only encouraged arrangers to extend the tonality of the instrument by adding octave unison accompaniment or a bass line, but also fired the enthusiasm of composers such as Moszkowski, Malipiero and Stravinsky who wrote pieces of music especially for it. Another composer, Casella, composed a fox-trot for pianola in 1918 in which all the notes within a chromatic scale of two octaves were struck at once!

Fortunately, perhaps, such musical mutations were few and the mechanics of the instrument were put to better use by skilled musicians in setting up pieces for four hands on to one roll, transcribing orchestral works and suchlike. Two typical examples are the Overture *Fingals Cave* and also the Suite, opus 15, by A. S. Arensky played by Bauer and Gabrilowitsch. This duet, Duo-Art roll number 5849, contains some remarkable expression shadings between the four hands.

By the 1920's, the range of rolls available for the player-pianist was enormous. Not only were most of the great piano and orchestral pieces transcribed in roll form, but so were the best of the popular songs, dance music, hymn tunes—in fact the whole gamut of music.

Popular songs tended to demand either a knowledge of the words or an additional musical score. Rolls were printed which had the song words stencilled along one side and these were introduced some time about 1906, although Roehl states that the Vocalstyle Music Company of Cincinatti, Ohio, were the first to make this type of roll 'as early as 1908'. Be that as it may, song rolls were certainly in full production by most companies by 1909. The words were rather disconcertingly printed in lines corresponding to the correct musical note to which they were to be sung. This necessitated them being read virtually from bottom to top and the music-roll songster had to become adept at reading one line above the other—not so simple as it at first seems, particularly with hyphenated words:

ling
dar-
my
ways
al-
love you
ll
I'

Along with the 'pedal line' or expression line (which indicated whether a section was to be played *pianissimo* or *fortissimo* and also gave advance warnings of such changes as *crescendo*, *diminuendo*, pause, *tempo* variance and so on) the words were printed on a rotary stencilling machine which pressed a suitably-marked stencilband on to the paper roll as it was passed under it. A similar system was used by the advanced makers of music-rolls who printed their *tempo* lines in different colours (often red or green) and other marks in more colours.

Player-pianos and piano-players were made which would perform from both 65- and 88-note music-rolls. The tracker-bar had two lines of openings in it, one for each roll type, and a simple change-over lever in the roll box could be moved to select which set of openings was to be used.

The 88-note or full-scale rolls were much more popular than the limited scale ones but even so there was still a market for the 65-note instruments. To fit into the smaller compass a degree of alteration was required to the score and, in certain pieces, the transformation from the original full-scale to the 65-note roll was nothing short of mutilation. From the mechanical standpoint, though, 65-note actions were more reliable. Component parts were slightly larger and, most important of all, the tracker-bar was not so finely pierced and therefore was not so likely to become clogged with dust and paper fluff.

Ordinary music-rolls cost from 5s upwards. In 1920, Aeolians categorized their Themodist music-rolls as A, costing 6s, B costing 8s 6d, and C priced at 11s. 65-note rolls were 1s cheaper in all three classifications.

One of the largest manufacturers of music-rolls in England was the Perforated Music Company. With showrooms at 94 Regent Street and a library at 81 Beak Street, off Regent Street, their head office and factory was 197–199 City Road, North London. Their trade mark was 'Imperial' and in 1910 they advertised as manufacturing rolls for many instruments including Pianola, Orchestrelle, Symphony, Amphion, Broadwood, Apollo, Angelus, Hardman, Forte, Metzler, Simplex, Humana, Aristo, Neola, Humanola, Aeriola, Pianotist, Kimball, Chase & Baker, Sterling, Triumph, Rex, Imperial, Electrelle, Cecilian, Autopiano, etc. All their rolls were made at City Road and, by 1914, their premises were extended with the acquisition of the adjacent buildings, numbers 201 and 203. In March 1918 a disastrous fire gutted the entire factory, destroying all the plant and equipment as well as hundreds of thousands of rolls. The firm subsequently re-established on a much smaller scale at 6 Bride Street, London E.C., where it continued for a few years until the general slump in the music-roll trade in the late twenties and early thirties.

Shortly before the first world war, two young London engineers, H. C. Coldman and C. F. Webb, bought a player-piano and took it apart to see how it worked. They were surprised by the seemingly large components and consequently the large amount of air which had to be moved in order to play the instrument. They believed that, by rethinking the entire action, a much simpler, cheaper and more reliable action might be made. The result of their labours was the Pistonola manufactured by Boyd Limited, whose first head office was at 19 Holborn, London. Boyds had already entered the self-playing piano market with a 65-note piano-player of very angular appearance which sold for £32 8s od together with six rolls of music.

Boyds showed their Pistonola to the public at a concert held in Ilford Town Hall on November 26, 1913, the programme including both solo and accompaniment pieces for the player-piano. April 1914 saw a public demonstration of the Pistonola at the Corn Exchange in London under the auspices of the London music dealers, H. Payne & Co. With Mr Stanley Harris at the controls, the Pistonola performed in concert with a tenor, a contralto and a violin.

The Pistonola was an interesting device, its very name perhaps indicating the principle upon which it operated. Widely acclaimed as the all-metal player action, every function of the player was achieved by the use of a piston moving in a cylinder. The foot treadles drew air out of a master cylinder using pistons. The master cylinder itself had a spring-loaded piston within it through which vacuum tension could be achieved. Pressure-reducing valves provided both low and high vacuum pressures to operate the roll-drive motor (which was again a piston motor) and the valves. The valve chest and pneumatics of the ordinary action were replaced by a compact bank of eighty-eight tiny cylinders each no more than half an inch in diameter and each having a small free-moving piston made of compressed graphite within it. Being self-lubricating, the graphite pistons required no other lubrication. Each piston was connected to its respective piano-action hammer by a cord. When a hole in the music-roll opened a hole in the tracker-bar, the piston would move, setting in motion the hammer action. When the tracker-bar hole was once more covered, the suction would be removed from the piston which would immediately drop back under its own weight. Appreciably less air was required to be shifted to play the Pistonola as compared with a normal player-piano, and when it was launched it was widely acclaimed in the press. Two models were available, one selling for £75 12s od and the other, fitted with the so-called Modulist and Crescodant manual expression devices, sold at £84 os od.

After the 1914–18 war, an improved version was marketed called the Terpreter. Three versions were available, the Models One and Two, each costing 160 guineas, and the Model Three at 150 guineas.

When properly adjusted, the Pistonola and Terpreter were very good players and were capable of easy and immediate expression from their controls. The action was, nevertheless, prone to malfunctions which were not always easy to trace and rectify. Mr D. F. Andrews of Boyd Pianos remembers these instruments and relates how some were 'jinx' instruments which were always temperamental. Thus it is perhaps no surprise to find that, by the 1920's, Boyd's were producing a more conventional player with imported action. This was the Boyd Autoplayer, available in a number of different styled pianos for as little as 108 guineas. One of the controls on the Autoplayer was called the 'Deletor'. The advertising literature wrote of this:

'If a section of the music-roll is not required, this wonderful device will allow the roll to travel in silence at high speed. . . .'

The call for the accented piano roll, sometimes referred to as 'Hand-played', and the instruments upon which to play them remained in demand right up to the thirties. However, the need for a player-piano which could reproduce faithfully the performance of a concert pianist without requiring any dexterity on the part of the owner of the player-piano was recognized very early on.

The instrument so conceived was called a reproducing piano—a name actually patented by

93

the Aeolian Company but one which, as with 'pianola', came to be the generic term for all makes of piano which produced a concert rendition of a piece of music from a music-roll recorded by a concert pianist whose name would appear on the roll.

Surprisingly enough, the first such instrument came with the so-called 'Keyless Red Welte' made in the opening years of the present century. This piano did not have a keyboard (a feature which undoubtedly cost the Welte company many sales and which led to its having a very restricted market) and performed electrically. Requiring neither pedalling nor touch from its owner, it would perform at the pull of a switch.

The original Welte-Mignon or 'Red-Welte', so termed after the music-rolls which were of red paper, played $13\frac{1}{2}$ inch wide rolls and the action used remained practically the same from the keyless reproducing piano of 1901 to the end of the 1920's. The system was usually fitted only in grands, particularly the Steinway, and was different from other installations in one major respect—it was fitted above the action on top of the piano as distinct from the later Ampico which was fitted beneath.

Welte were the first makers of reproducing pianos to dispense with the most awkward component in the player action—the pump which created the vacuum. In the non-electric players, the vacuum was manufactured by large exhausters. Electric players used either a four-lobe rotary pump belt-driven by an electric motor or a self-contained electric motor and exhauster pneumatics built into a sealed metal case. With the grand installation, the pump tended to spoil the side appearance of the instrument since it protruded below the instrument. The player action itself took up little space. Welte put the pump in a completely separate cabinet, finished in matching style to the piano and connected to it with a flexible rubber hose. In addition to dispensing with the bulkiest part of the player action, it also eliminated any mechanical noise. The Aeolian 'Key-Top Pianola' of the 1950's also used a separate vacuum system.

Welte also produced cabinet-style piano-players right up until at least 1931. These push-ups were very different from the short-lived players of the turn of the century for they were expression players. Tastefully constructed, beautifully finished and driven by an electric motor, these played Red Welte $13\frac{1}{2}$ inch rolls and performed on the keys of a piano with all the sensitivity of a real pianist. Each of the four wheels of the player could be adjusted with a screw-jack so as to position the fingers correctly. The illustration (Fig. 30) shows a 1912 cabinet style push-up of this type. Known as the Welte Vorsetzer, it made any ordinary piano into a 'reproducer'.

As John Farmer relates, the immediate success of the Welte and the very fulsome and doubtless sincere tributes which they were paid by almost every important musical figure, impressed the Germanic personalities of the co-inventors, Edwin Welte and Karl Bokisch, with a Wagnerian sense of destiny. The Welte system in its original form became imbued with mystic significance and was seen as the embodiment of perfection. In consequence of this, no important modification was made either to the recording mechanism or to the playback piano action throughout the quarter of a century or so of manufacture.

The Welte reproducing piano-player cabinet first appeared about 1904. It differed from the ordinary player in that it was a full reproducing machine which played on an ordinary piano with 'pianists fingers'. When not in use, the player could be pushed against a wall where it looked like a tasteful sideboard, there being neither pedals nor doors to belie its contents. It used the Welte system of triple exhausters to the suction reservoir and, of course, used the triple radial wind motor characteristic of Welte. As with the Ampico and Welte internal actions, it performed on eighty of the piano's keys, the remaining holes in the 100-perforation tracker

THE WELTE CABINET PLAYER

THIS Instrument is attachable to, and removable from, any piano in a few seconds, and achieves the same perfect reproduction as the combined models.

Height	-	3 ft. 4 ins.
Width	-	4 ft. 1 in.
Depth	- -	1 ft. 9 ins.
Nett Weight	-	354 lbs.
Packed Weight		548 lbs.
Measurement	-	41 cub. ft.

Fig. 30. The Welte Cabinet Player – known as the Vorsetzer – was a true reproducer. The mechanism is shown in Plates 54 and 55

operating the expression and other functions of performance.

1911 saw the start of the manufacture of the Welte-Mignon in America. However, under the provisions of the Alien Property Act, the company was confiscated upon America's entry into the First World War. It was later reformed as a subsidiary of the Auto-Pneumatic Action Company and named the Welte-Mignon Corporation. The Welte patents were used under licence and a re-engineered instrument produced which was called the Welte-Mignon (Licensee) Reproducing Piano.

In 1924 the Welte-Mignon Corporation of 297–307 East 123rd Street, New York, copyrighted the name 'reperforming piano' as their personalized answer to the 're-enacting piano' of Ampico and the 'reproducing piano' of Aeolian's Duo-Art. It should be noted that all makers of reproducing pianos referred to them as such and, as already pointed out, this became the generic term for them just as pianola had come to mean a player-piano.

The Welte-Mignon Corporation produced the Welte-Mignon (Licensee) action which played standard width $11\frac{1}{4}$ inch paper rolls and was generally accepted as being not quite as good as the original German Welte-Mignon with its much wider, red-paper rolls. Red Welte music had tended to be almost exclusively of a serious nature, the popular music repertoire being limited.

Welte-Mignon Licensee reproducing actions were fitted in a hundred and twelve makes of American piano including those by Baldwin, Bush & Lane, Conover, Hardman, Kimball, Kranich & Bach, Mehlin & Sons, Packard, Sohmer and Stieff, also Acoustigrande, Hazelton, Ivers-Pond, Kurtzmann. Pianos by Schulz used both the Welte-Mignon and the Aria Divina (q.v.) mechanisms.

In 1927 the Steinway-Welte Grand in a rosewood or mahogany case cost £550 and the upright version £350. The Welte Cabinet Player reproducer cost £195. It is interesting to note that whilst the ordinary 'push-up' piano-player went out of fashion by about 1910, Welte's reproducing player was still in production until 1931 in which year they produced their last reproducing instrument. Edwin Welte, son of the great Emil, died in 1957 at the age of eighty-two having lived right through the entire history of the pneumatic piano.

As I have shown, Welte reproducing pianos, made in Freiburg-im-Briesgau, Baden Baden, Germany and, also, later in New York,* were expensive items and, initially, the special music rolls for use with them were certainly far from cheap. The Welte (Licensee) catalogue of rolls, published at Steinway Hall, London, in October 1922, listed 3,755 titles of which the most expensive was Fanny Bloomfield-Ziesler's performance of Beethoven's Sonata, op. 111, in C minor (second movement) which cost all of £3 19s 0d. Song rolls and accompaniment rolls were generally cheaper and short pieces of music could be had for as little as 10s 6d.

By 1926, however, Welte perfected new paper-perforating machinery and, in the face of competition from other manufacturers whose roll prices were less and becoming lower still, they lowered their charges appreciably. Beethoven's Sonata referred to above now became available for only 24s. Even so, it was expensive for the enthusiast to build up a repertoire of music-rolls.

These catalogues of Welte rolls reveal a glittering parade of performers ranging from top concert pianists to composers themselves. Some idea of the fascination of these paper rolls can be gathered from the following considerably shortened list of performers who 'recorded' the music: Tosta di Benici, Edward Brightwell, Ferrucio Benvenuto Busoni, Claude Achille Debussy, Erno Dohnányi, Manuel de Falla, Gabriel Urbain Fauré, Alexander Konstantinovich Glazunov, Enrique Granados, Edvard Hagerup Grieg, Hans Haase, Engelbert Humperdinck, Wanda Landowska, Theodor Leschetizky, Josef Lhevinne, Gustav Mahler, Ignace Jan Paderewski, Maurice Ravel, Max Reger, Charles Camille Saint-Saëns, Artur Schnabel, Georg Alfred Schumann, Alexander Nicholaevich Scriabine, Dr Richard Strauss, Paul Felix Weingartner.

The methods by which Welte rolls were recorded are shrouded in mystery. In an article contained in the Journal of the British Institute of Recorded Sound, John Farmer states that, unlike Aeolian and Ampico, Welte always insisted that their recording system was fully automatic and did not ask for the services of the pianist in the later stages of preparation of the master roll. It seems that the recording piano had a trough of mercury beneath the keyboard. Each key had a light carbon prong suspended from its lower side which dipped into the mercury when that note was played. This was said to have enabled the recording of the exact force and duration of the note. This does, however, seem unlikely, but Mr Richard Simonton, who befriended Edwin Welte during his later years, told John Farmer that the carbon prongs

* Givens relates that evidence shows all Welte-Mignon (Licensee) instruments in America to have been made at the Estey Piano Company factory in New York City.

were in fact suspended from the key by a fine coil spring and consequently the depth of penetration of the carbon rod in the mercury would have varied with the force with which the key was depressed. From this, it would follow that the resistance to the flow of current would vary slightly with this depth of penetration and if this could be traced against each note, a fairly good idea of the pianist's dynamics would be obtained. But, as John Farmer rightly asserts, the techniques of electrical measurement with the limited knowledge available at that time makes this a little doubtful. Undoubtedly this is not as reliable a recording system as one which directly measures hammer velocity and Farmer suggests that this may be one reason why some of the passages in Welte rolls tend to sound a little rough.

The De Luxe Reproducing Roll Company was a branch of the Auto-Pneumatic Action Company which produced the Welte-Mignon (Licensee) reproducing action for sale to independent piano manufacturers, relates Roehl.

By 1913, the first Ampico action had been produced by the American Piano Company in New York, taking its name from the first two letters of each word in the company's name.

Although first made in 1913, it did not make its début until 1916 when it was demonstrated to a distinguished gathering at the Hotel Biltmore in New York (today overshadowed by the giant Pan-Am building) on October 8th. Pianist Leopold Godowsky played four pieces of music which were then repeated by the Ampico playing rolls which he had previously recorded.

The action underwent several modifications, culminating in a major re-engineering in 1929, but all models would play the same Ampico music-rolls.

Ampico used as their trade mark the words 're-enacting'. Artists, among whose ranks were some whose music, recorded in Europe for Ludwig Hupfeld, had been 'scientifically adapted for the Ampico', included: Wilhelm Backhaus, Harold Bauer, Alexander Brailowsky, Ferruccio Busoni, George Copeland, Erno Dohnányi, Edvard Grieg, Mark Hambourg, Fritz Kreisler (whose talents are today better associated with the violin), Theodor Leschetizky, Misha Levitski, Alexander MacFadyen, Pietro Mascagni, Benno Moiseiwitsch, Sergei Rachmaninov, Artur Rubinstein, Camille Saint-Saëns, Artur Schnabel, Alexander Scriabine and Richard Strauss.

The Ampico playback action had been invented by Charles Stoddard and, although he was already a successful inventor with no prior connection with the music industry, its subsequent development and the evolution of the company from that date on absorbed almost his entire activity.

In 1923 Rachmaninov, who had scorned the overtures from other and wealthier roll-manufacturing rivals to the Ampico organization, sat down with the directors of Ampico to listen to the finished master rolls of a recording of his G minor Prelude. At its conclusion, he puffed a cloud of smoke into the air and calmly remarked: 'Gentlemen, I have just heard myself play.' According to Adam Carroll, American popular music arranger and performer who headed the light music section of Ampico, this one remark caused a sensational rise of Ampico stock on Wall Street.

A few months before his death, the great pianist Moiseiwitsch was discussing his recordings for Ampico with a BBC interviewer in London, relates John Farmer. One of the pleasures of working with the company, he said, was that the editing staff with whom the pianist was expected to co-operate closely in the final stages of correction of the master recording, were not only engineers with complete command of their craft but also consummate musicians. When asked if he considered that the Ampico recording system and the playback piano could adequately and faithfully realize his artistic intentions, he paused a while and then replied, 'Absolutely!'

One of these Ampico technicians was Edgar Fairchild, today living in California. Under the name 'Milton Suskind', Fairchild made a number of Ampico recordings of his own playing for the serious music department, making some superb arrangements of popular music of the 1920's which, as piano transcriptions, would not have done dishonour to Liszt. Fairchild finally assumed responsibility for the editing of all recordings by the great pianists, a course of action largely dictated by the fact that many of these performers, particularly Lhevinne and Rachmaninov, would only discuss matters arising out of their performances with Fairchild and no one else.

Ampico's recording apparatus comprised two separate moving sheets of paper on which were recorded all the movements of the piano keys and pedals, together with exact measurements of hammer velocity at the moment of impact with the strings. This was done by the spark chronograph technique, firing one spark through the sheet of paper as the piano hammer approached the string, and a second spark in the final instant of travel before it struck the string. The integration of the data from the two sheets was the work of skilled artist engineers. The men who formed the Ampico team were a uniquely creative and happy band. 'Every day,' according to Adam Carroll, 'was a holiday.' This was certainly reflected in the quality of the music rolls produced and in the company as a whole.

The Ampico recording pianos were no 'run of the mill' instruments. Carrying no maker's name, they were built to the special order of Ampico using the best parts of the best makes of American pianos. In this manner was produced a piano with a perfectly even tonal quality throughout the keyboard, thus ensuring that reproduction of the music-roll on other instruments would be the nearest possible to the original.

One reason why few Ampico instruments survive today is that the entire player action was attached to the underside (of the grand) by bolts which could readily be removed to return the piano back to normal. There being few tuners or repairers who have either the interest or talent to regulate these (or any other player, come to that) owners have long been advised to 'throw away the player and rolls and restore (!) the piano as just an ordinary piano'.

The actions were expensive—Marshall & Wendell, for instance, offered an Ampico baby grand piano in 1929 for $995—but perfection and subsequent modification enabled the piano firm of William Knabe & Company to produce a 'baby *Ampico* and piano combination' for $495 in 1938 and made a point of offering to 'exchange your old, silent piano at good allowance'. Some of the finest American-made pianos with Ampico action were those made by the famous house of Chickering.

A British company—Ampico Limited—was formed with offices at 233 Regent Street, London W.1, and the action was distributed in England by Marshall & Rose. The Ampico action cost £200 and a further £200 to install and the 6 foot 1 inch grand Ampico cost 659 guineas. In 1928 the installation was modified by the introduction of the Model 'B' tracking device and electric drive. They ceased production in about 1936 but continued making rolls until 1940.

Perhaps the finest of the Ampico grand installations and also the finest reproducing pianos were the Grotrian-Steinweg and Steinway. The main parts of the player action were mounted in a sliding drawer which ran the full width of the piano under the keyboard. A five-valve slide motor was fitted to the left of the spool compartment and all controls were neatly displayed on the top panels either side of the drawer. The Grotrian-Steinweg Ampico was also one of the most expensive of the reproducing instruments. In 1929 Ampico introduced the so-called Model 'B' drawer which was intended to replace the standard one where desired. This had electric roll drive through a constant speed, series-wound motor in place of the air-motor and was also capable of taking rolls which would play for a full half-hour.

The Ampico reproducing action was fitted into many pianos. In America it was installed in the Knabe, Chickering, Mason & Hamlin, J. & C. Fischer, Marshall & Wendell and Haines Brothers, whilst the Canadian maker, Willis, also fitted it. In Great Britain, it was fitted in pianos by Broadwood, Chappell, Collard & Collard, Challen, Hopkinson, Marshall & Rose, and Rogers. The German maker, Grotrian-Steinweg, and also Bosendorfer in Austria, used it.

As a result of negotiations begun in 1909, the Aeolian Company in New York established a tie-up with Steinway pianos and, in the autumn of 1913, introduced the Steinway Duo-Art reproducing piano. Aeolian purchased Steinway pianos built into special cases and then fitted their Duo-Art mechanisms into them. Their actions were also fitted into other famous makes of pianos, and, in order of price, they ran Steinway, Weber, Steck, Wheelock, Stroud and Aeolian.

It seems that Aeolian used several methods by which to record their artists. A recording piano with electrical contacts was used, movements of the keys, dampers and pedals being traced on to a sheet of paper by the action of a series of relays. Although giving an accurate recording of the length and duration of notes, this did not provide for the degree of force assigned to each note. This was, at one stage, applied to the roll after recording, editors of varying degrees of skill working in collaboration with the recording artist. The company also made gramophone records of performers so as to compare the roll with the actual performance. Later on, though, the direct measurement of the individual hammer velocity in the recording piano was introduced. This was probably similar, if a little less refined, to the spark chronograph method used by Ampico.

The Duo-Art had the advantage of being available on the market several years ahead of the Ampico and scored over the newly-introduced Welte-Mignon and Hupfeld in that the music-rolls were much cheaper. Multiple roll-punching machinery at the Aeolian factory worked twenty-four hours a day to keep down costs and also to meet the fantastic demand for this instrument which could play as all the great instrumentalists.

The Duo-Art was produced until 1935 when the New York factory was destroyed by a disastrous fire. At this point, the Aeolian Corporation merged with the American Piano Co. and moved to the Ampico factory at East Rochester. From that date forward, Duo-Art and Ampico actions were under the same roof and there was much interchanging of rolls, and Roehl states that the very late Duo-Art rolls are sometimes to be found fitted with Ampico labels.

As with all reproducing piano rolls, Duo-Art had its own selection of the masters and this leads one to wonder whether or not a keyboard virtuoso would go to the bother of recording a roll for, say, Welte, Ampico, Hupfeld and Duo-Art (and probably others), or whether, as Ampico admitted, some of their rolls were 'scientifically adapted' from a master reproducing roll cut elsewhere and for another company. Be that as it may, the Aeolian Duo-Art artists included the celebrated I. J. Paderewski, George Gershwin, Victor Herbert, Harold Bauer and Rudolph Ganz.

The interesting ethics of advertising of the period, particularly those practised in America, may come as a revelation to us today. Testimonials, blatantly solicited, were printed from famous artists. Paderewski, so one was led to believe, was perfectly content to have no less than two 65-note Pianolas (and countless other makes of player) and sit at the piano with them, pedalling his way through music which he could far better perform by hand. In later years wide publicity was given to the fact that Benito Mussolini had a Weber Duo-Art in his palace at Rome and there was also one to be found at the Elysée Palace, the official Paris residence of the President of the French Republic.

One of the most amusing advertising stunts was pulled off by the Ampico makers. Under a large headline proclaiming BECOMES SO ENGROSSED IN THE AMPICO THAT HE NEGLECTS TO PERFORM HIS LITERARY WORK, the dramatic critic of the *New York World* is credited in this story with having written to the Ampico Corporation officials that he wanted arrangements made to have the piano removed at once. 'I shall miss it acutely,' goes on the story, 'but everyone flocks here to play the instrument. . . . I never will get any work done while this beguiling attraction remains on the premises.' The scruples of advertising!

Aeolian issued a number of Duo-Art 'Author's Rolls' which were song rolls. These had printed on the leader paper details of the writer and the words of the song *in toto*. This was one further example of the enterprise of the Aeolian Co., who also produced reproducing rolls with complete musical scores and synopsis, with notational examples on the leaders of some rolls. Quite often the first eight feet of paper on the rolls were intended to be read prior to making mechanical music.

Even so, the Duo-Art and the Welte-Mignon (Licensee) actions were surpassed in excellence of performance by the Ampico action.

The firm of Hupfeld was formed in Leipzig in 1892 by Ludwig Hupfeld with the aim to produce on a large scale all types of mechanical musical instruments. In that year he took out patents on the principles of pnuematic action for pianos and organs. His work is probably better known today in the field of large orchestrions and also for the remarkable Dea-Violina pneumatic violin and piano, yet he was responsible for some very forward thinking on the subject of the pneumatic player-piano. As with all other makers, his first instrument was a cabinet-style 'push-up' player and his factory was engaged in the production of these until about 1901, by which time he had perfected an action which could be fitted to the underneath of the piano keyboard. Adaptable to both upright and grand pianos, the attachment was available as a hand-cranked unit costing £30 or could be driven by a 100-volt electric motor at a cost of £58. A third choice was a model powered by a 25-hour accumulator. This cost £66 inclusive of the battery.

By 1902, Hupfeld was producing pianos with an electrically-operated pneumatic player action. The compass was 5 octaves, C to c^3, and models were available which were coin-operated and/or remotely controlled from separate wall-mounted coin boxes.

In 1908, Hupfeld produced an electric expression piano capable of playing 73 notes and having five central expression holes in the tracker-bar. At the time of the Hupfeld 73-note expression instrument, the American makers were still producing 58- and 65-note ordinary pianos. Shortly afterwards, Hupfeld had perfected the full-compass or 88-note player and devised melody- and theme-emphasizing systems, pedal control and tracking for his ordinary player-pianos as well as the fully automatic reproducing instruments.

Europe greeted the Hupfeld player-piano with enthusiasm but it was not until 1910 that the first Hupfeld actions, fitted into Blüthner pianos, came into England. They were an immediate success, particularly as the action was far easier to fit to an existing piano than contemporary makes. The Hupfeld technical know-how at this time was extremely advanced—the firm possessed no less than 250 patents, the vast majority on the subject of pneumatic actions.

By 1920, wood and rubber tubing had been almost entirely dispensed with in construction and the action was largely fabricated in metal. At this time also they made models which could

TWO LETTERS FROM PADEREWSKI

THERE IS A STRIKING FACT ABOUT THE PIANOLA AND THE ÆOLIAN, WHICH GIVES THESE TWO INSTRUMENTS A UNIQUE POSITION IN THE MUSICAL WORLD—THEIR ENDORSEMENTS. To the casual observer, or one unfamiliar with the instruments, these endorsements seem inexplicable.

It is not alone the fact that this latest new instrument the Pianola has received the commendation of some *one* or *two* musicians of note, but there would appear to be a miraculous power about it, like that connected with the Pied Piper of Hamelin, with the difference that it charms—not the children, but *all the great musicians* of prominence in this country, the Continent, and America.

Scarcely a month or a week passes but the name of another recognized authority is added to the long list of those who have endorsed the Pianola, and each endorsement evinces an enthusiasm uncalled for, unless felt to a marked degree.

Paderewski would be the last one, perhaps, to tolerate a mechanical aid to piano-playing; yet he undoubtedly is one of the warmest admirers of the Pianola, and derives the utmost pleasure from it himself.

Aside from all other considerations, the fact that he took a Pianola home with him to Paris a year ago, and six months later ordered a second one sent to his residence in Switzerland, shows the value of this dextrous little piano-player to the greatest pianist; while the pleasure experienced by those who are otherwise unable to play the piano is beyond computation.

Broadly speaking, the Pianola is an instrument by means of which any one can play the piano. This includes those who literally do not know one note from another.

The Pianola does the finger-work, striking the notes in the right relation one to another as they are printed on the music-sheet—the performer still being the pianist, with all the pleasure of producing the music, because he has full control over the expression.

Visitors welcome. We are glad to show the Pianola to every one, knowing that the instrument will gain another friend, whether a direct purchase results or not. If you are unable to call, send for pamphlet 33 our most recent publication.

The Pianola is sold at no other address in London.

Pianola in use with upright piano

Private Car "Riva,"
En Route to San Francisco
March 24, 1900.

Gentlemen—As an admirer of the Aeolian, the wonderful merits of which I have attested to in a former letter to you, I have much pleasure in adding my tribute to your latest invention, the Pianola, which I consider still more ingenious. It is astonishing to see this little device at work executing the masterpieces of pianoforte literature with a dexterity, clearness, and velocity which no player, however great, can approach.

Everyone who wishes to hear absolutely faultless, free from any kind of nervousness piano - playing, should buy a Pianola. It is perfection.

Wishing you well deserved success, I am,

Yours very truly, I. J. PADEREWSKI.

Chalet Riond-Bosson Morges, Nov. 7, 1900

Gentlemen—I desire to order another Pianola for use in my residence. Will you kindly select an instrument in rosewood, and have packed with it rolls of music, and ship by steamer?

Yours very truly, I. J. PADEREWSKI.

The Orchestrelle Company

225 REGENT STREET, LONDON, W.

And HENRY M. BIRGE, Sydney, Australia.

Fig. 31. Typical of the advertising stunts of the time is this published in 1901

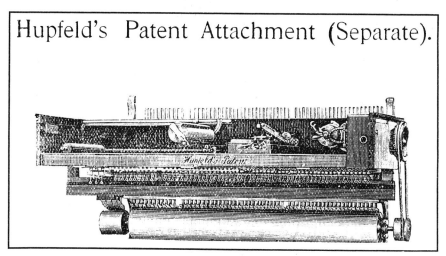

Fig. 32. Hupfeld's 1901 player attachment fitted under the keyboard of an upright piano and was a mechanical action using perforated paper on a similar principle to the Melotrope

operate by 'the electric light current'. Remember that at this time domestic electricity was used almost exclusively for lighting and the thought of using it for operating any form of machinery was practically unheard of.

Three models were put on the market—the foot-operated Solophonola, the electric reproducing piano called the Duophonola and the Triphonola which could be used as a foot-operated instrument playing ordinary rolls, as a reproducing piano with electric drive or as an electrically-driven ordinary player. Unlike most other reproducing pianos, the Duophonola played the full 88-note scale, additional holes in the tracker-bar taking care of expression facilities in the same manner as the original Welte.

The famous German firm of Blüthner, who distributed their pianos in England through their London office in Wigmore Street, fitted the Hupfeld action to their grand and upright instruments. The last Hupfeld installation was made about 1937. In the early part of the 1930's, Blüthner designed their own player action which they called the Carola, and this was built at their factory in Southfield Road, Acton. The Carola, however, was if anything more costly-for Blüthner to make than the cost of importing the Hupfeld action and, since there was very little difference between the performance of both actions, the Carola was dropped.

Hupfeld actions showed distinctive characteristics as compared with their American counterparts. The automatic tracking device, for example, used the horizontal see-saw bellows principle and the air motor was a straight-line, three-valve, slide-action unit. The Solophonola and Triphonola models had automatic expression and theme accentuation built in, and the theme emphasis was a patented system called the Soladant.

Each note of the Hupfeld action comprised a self-contained, individual unit which could, if need arose, be removed and replaced in a few moments. This system, the so-called unit block board, was used by a number of makers in later years. The one-piece unit valve-assembly was patented in 1929 by the Leipzig firm of player-piano makers, Kastner-Autopiano Akt.-Ges.

The Hupfeld music-rolls thoughtfully bore the watermark 'Phonola' and also the year of manufacture within the first yard or so. This also applied to their violin-playing rolls.

Blüthner made a great point of the system known as 'Aliquot' stringing in their pianos. The system made use of a sympathetic string on each note above the so-called break in the keyboard (bass to treble). This string was not struck by the hammer but was allowed to vibrate in sympathy with the struck strings. In the middle treble register, the aliquot was tuned an octave above (producing a distinct brightness of tone) and in the extreme treble the aliquot was tuned to unison. This feature, still used today in Blüthner concert grands, was always emphasized on the Blüthner-Hupfeld grand instruments.

The Aeolian Company operated a lending library of both Duo-Art and ordinary music-rolls at Aeolian Hall in London's New Bond Street. They issued rolls in boxes which bore a yellow label proclaiming 'The World's Music—a New Aeolian Library of Illustrated and Descriptive "Duo-Art" and "Pianola" rolls. Edited by Percy A. Scholes'. These rolls featured a lengthy printed leader which, in addition to giving concise instructions as to the use of the music-roll, gave brief details of the piece of music and often of its composer as well, usually with a line illustration pertinent to the music. Each roll was divided into bars by being ruled across at the correct place. Justly called the 'Annotated Series', these rolls were an undoubted valuable asset to the student, to the singer and also to the performer of the live instrument as they gave a true insight as to the breakdown of the music. The library was formulated in conjunction with the well-known musicologist, Percy A. Scholes, known for his classic work *The Oxford Companion to Music*.

The Aeolian Music Roll Library was probably the first lending library of its type in the world and would supply to subscribers up to twelve rolls at a time as frequently as they chose to use the facility. The cost was four guineas per year. Other libraries were soon established and Steinway's operated a library and approval service for Welte-Mignon rolls from Steinway Hall, Ampico doing the same from their Regent Street showrooms.

The firm of Broadwood, who are famed for the production of the so-called square piano (of which they made no less than 65,000 between 1770 and 1854) and of the piano used by Chopin for his London recitals, made a quantity of reproducing pianos using bought-out actions. They also equipped Steck pianos with Duo-Art actions by arrangement with Aeolians.

Other reproducing pianos were the Solo Carola, the ArtEcho, Apollo, Angelus Artrio, Aria Divina and Celco, all of which stemmed from America. The ArtEcho and the Apollo were mechanically the same and both were developed by the American Piano Company, the former for sale to independent manufacturers and the latter for Wurlitzer. The Solo Carola never sold in great quantities, although, claims Roehl, it was potentially very good. The Angelus Artrio was used in Hallet & Davis, Conway, and Merrill pianos, all built by the Conway Music Industries. The Celco action was incorporated into pianos built by Chase, Emerson and

Fig. 33. The Orchestrelle Company's lending library roll label

Lindeman. In Germany, the Stuttgart firm of Lipp & Sohn produced the Duca-Lipp which sold for £300. The Leipzig firm of Popper made the Stella reproducing piano.

How good were these non-starters in the world of reproducing pianos? Why did they fail to catch on? And why did the three big names of Aeolian, Ampico and Welte succeed? The simple answer is just that they were 'big names'. The giant Aeolian Company and the American Piano Company together comprised most of the biggest and best of the American piano trade. Welte held a high reputation in Germany. In favour of the Ampico action, Celco, ArtEcho and Apollo—all produced by subsidiaries of the American Piano Company—were not allowed the chance to make much of an impact. The Solo Carola, Artrio and Aria Divina tried to find a chink through which to break into the market. That they did not succeed does not directly imply that they were poor reproducers or in any way inferior actions. They failed due to the fundamental fact that they did not have the backing to forge and maintain a standing in the market. Indeed, it is an interesting thought that one or more of these may well have been a candidate for a better action than those produced by the great names—we can never know.

The Solo Carola apparently took two years to develop and cost $175,000. Manufactured by the Cable Company of Wabash and Jackson, it was introduced in the summer of 1916.

It should again be stressed that 'expression' pianos were a cheaper form of the reproducing piano and usually offered up to five degrees of expression applied to the entire keyboard.

It is worth mentioning again the rival method of musical reproduction of the period—the gramophone. The first electric recordings were in production and a 12-inch 78 r.p.m. record would play for almost five minutes. Tone arm pick-ups were heavy and the essence of reproduction was the steel needle which could only be used once as its passage in the record groove ground it (and, ultimately, the groove!) into a different shape. Needles came in tins marked 'Loud Tone' (fat ones), 'Soft Tone' (thin ones) and 'Medium Tone'. A novelty was the dual-purpose spear-shaped needle which could be used as either loud tone or soft tone just by rotating its odd-shaped body through 90 degrees angle in the sound-box chuck. Commonest defect of all was the ever-present 'needle hiss' caused by the rotation of the disc under the needle and accentuated by the quite ridiculous weight of some of the pick-ups which seemed more intent on wearing through to the groove on the other side than in concentrating on the one on top of the record. Gramophones worked by clockwork. Records were made to be played at about 78 r.p.m. although several makers produced ones to be played at 80 r.p.m. and one at least at 82 r.p.m. Speed naturally affected pitch and thus pitch was arbitrary. My gramophone-loving colleagues will no doubt accuse me of 'knocking' the gramophone but all I am doing is showing that as regards piano music, in which field an alternative method of reproduction was available, the reproducing piano was far, far superior since it was in truth a real piano giving forth a real performance by an accredited artist.

Marshall & Rose fitted the Angelus action made by Wilcox & White and first patented in 1895. Their Model 43 grand had the action in a drawer under the keyboard very similar to the Ampico and it also had foot treadles.

Some grand pianos were made which housed fold-away treadles in a box extension under the instrument and forming part of the ordinary pedal support. One characteristic instrument of this type was the player built by C. R. Taylor of Wood Green.

Chappells produced an upright player for 158 guineas and a grand for 240 guineas in the 1930's. They also built a special upright player for King Edward VII.

Early in 1930, the Aeolian Company in London went into liquidation. This was brought about by a number of circumstances which jointly cost the Company its resources. The depression had reduced the demand for pianos of all types below an economic level. A large and grandiose advertising programme—just an extension of the lavish promotional campaigns undertaken during the Company's lifetime—did not bring forth the anticipated fruits. The roll library must be considered as another heavy overhead, for it is doubtful if this far-sighted venture ever paid off. It was the largest of its kind in the world. The last complete roll catalogue to be issued by Aeolians was in July 1932 and, from thence to the closure, only monthly supplements were added.

When the crash came, Harrods, the large London department store, bought up the remaining assets and took over some of the staff of Aeolian Hall.

The perfection of the techniques of the gramophone, the effects of other entertainments such as wireless and, later, television, and perhaps above all else the gradual trend of the family home to become smaller, all set the scene for the close of the pneumatic piano era. War was the catalyst. What remains today is the afterglow of an age of musical achievement which, in its own scale of sphere, was quite as remarkable as the present space age.

CHAPTER 5

Other Forms of Roll-Playing Instrument

IT may seem hard to visualize in this era of computers, which can compose and play music electronically, the marvel of a musical instrument which played all by itself or with the minimum of human assistance. Just as, in the time of William Shakespeare, people no doubt gazed in wonderment at Bidermann's clockwork spinet, so did people stare in amazement three centuries later at the Wurlitzer automatic harp and the Mills self-playing violin.

It is a sobering thought that almost every one of the so-called orchestral musical instruments was automated by one process or another between the years 1500 and 1930, from the saxophone of the dance band to the harp of the symphony orchestra, from toy trumpet to banjo, from xylophone to violin.

The early ones derived some measure of perfection from their music by using the pinned barrel, but, with the advent of perforated music, the whole gamut of the orchestra in perfection became a mechanical possibility. Whether the best results were achieved electro-magnetically or pneumatically, the programming of the impulses to produce sound was undertaken by paper. From Aeolian's expression pipe-organ down to the elementary triangle, paper music encouraged and inspired inventors all over Europe and America.

Strange as it may seem, one of the earliest instruments, other than the piano and organ, to inspire the creative genius of inventors for paper musical adaptation was perhaps the most difficult to mechanise—the violin.

The Paris organ-builder, Antoine Corvi, patented in 1854 a method of playing '. . . violins, tenor violins, violoncellos and other common stringed instruments' using either a pinned barrel turned by a handle or by finger keys. Corvi's system used rubber-tyred wheels as bows to each string and mechanical fingers to stop off the strings. Best known for his fine portable street organs, Corvi went on to patent the playing of almost every orchestral instrument but it is not known whether he actually built such an automaton.

Many mechanical organs contained stops which were named 'violins', but these were hardly stringed instruments, being in truth wooden pipes carefully voiced with 'beards' to the lip to produce string tones. All the famed makers of orchestrion organs incorporated violin pipes in their instruments and many of the so-called piano-orchestrions also had a rank of violin pipes for tonal effect.

One of the earliest of the genuine mechanical violins was that which was contrived by Professor Wauters of Binghamton, New York. Wauters was development engineer for the Binghamton

Automatic Musical Company, later to be taken over by the Link Piano Co. The Automatic Musical Company, founded by two brothers named Harris, concentrated mainly on modifying pneumatic pianos made by other concerns but they did contribute some considerable research and experimentation in the realm of other mechanical musical instruments, producing in 1903 the Automatic Xylophone which, as Roehl says, was undoubtedly the forerunner of the marimbaphones and xylophones produced by American manufacturers in later years. In Europe, of course, such makers as Welte had been using similar accompaniment techniques for some years.

Professor Wauters joined the company in about 1900 and spent seven years perfecting a 65-note pneumatic violin. The resultant instrument was remarkably sophisticated and featured pneumatic devices for the automatic application of rosin to each of the four circular 'crystal' (sic) bows, variation of bowing speed and the ability to play on all four strings at once. Wauters' instrument, although contemporary writers speak well of it, was probably too temperamental, too demanding of repeated human attention to maintain its perfection, for it to be a viable manufacturing proposition. The firm continued selling their other lines which included the Encore Automatic Banjo which played paper music rolls $9\frac{5}{8}$ inches wide. By 1913, they were in debt as a result of which the firm was taken over and re-named the Link Piano Company (see Chapter 11).

There were three European contributions to the self-playing violin. At the Brussels Exposition of 1910, Hupfelds presented their Phonoliszt-Violina. This consisted of a Rönisch piano with player action above which were mounted three vertically-set violins played pneumatically and, like the piano, controlled by perforated-paper roll music. Upon the first violin, sixteen fingers worked on the E string; on the second violin ten fingers worked on the A string and on the third violin ten fingers worked on the D string—the G string was not used. The fingers were little pads of felt attached to arms fitted to collapsing pneumatic motors. The three violins were arranged vertically with their necks lowermost. Each was pivoted so that it could be moved outwards to bring its single string into contact with the bow. The group of violins was encircled by a horizontal continuous hoop-shaped bow rotated by an air-motor. The bow, patented in 1910, consisted of some 3,000 horsehairs each about twelve inches long and forming a short tangent inside the circular bow. They each overlapped slightly so as to provide, in effect, a complete, circular interior bow. The rotational speed of this bow could be varied automatically by the control of its driving air motor.

Tonally, the Hupfeld Phonoliszt, when properly adjusted, was considerably better than the Mills instrument made in America. Hupfeld scored in having full-compass piano accompaniment and the violin emphasis on each note came very close to that of a live performer.

The Phonoliszt-Violina was produced in several different styles, equipped with one, three or six violins. The most common was the three-violin model and these were popular in England in amusement arcades, funfairs and seaside shows as well as cafés and restaurants. Their success was not confined only to Europe, and these large instruments, over twice the height of a normal large upright piano, were also distributed in America.

One of the Hupfeld range of reproducing pianos was the Dea and this was sometimes combined with the violins to form the Dea-Violina.

The Hupfeld instrument was preceded by the Violina, invented in Vienna by Stránský in 1911. This was almost identical to that made by Hupfeld and again mounted three violins within a rotating circular bow on top of a piano. Pneumatic roll-playing action was used.

The abortive attempt to produce a mechanical violin playing fifteen strings, which was the brainchild of J. W. Whitlock, is described later in this Chapter, but by far the most outstanding achievement in this field was the work of Henry Konrad Sandell in conjunction with the Mills

Novelty Company of Chicago. Sandell was born in Sweden in 1888 and went to America at the age of ten. By the time he was eighteen, he was chief electrician for the Adams Westlake Company and at the age of twenty-one, he began taking out his first patents for a coin-operated, mechanically-played violin. Up until the time of his death on January 29, 1948, he had secured over 300 patents, mostly on violin-playing machines.

By 1904 Sandell was employed by the Mills Novelty Company, who remained his employers for the following twenty years. In 1907 the first of Sandell's automatic violins appeared. It was called the Mills Automatic Virtuoso and consisted of a normal violin played electro-magnetically from a perforated-paper roll. Metal fingers were used to stop off the strings and bowing was achieved by rotating celluloid discs after the fashion of Professor Wauters whose work was contemporary.

Thanks to the historical research of Q. David Bowers, much of the history of this unusual and fascinating instrument has been recorded for posterity. In the spring of 1908 an Automatic Virtuoso was brought to England and put on display at Waring & Gillow's department store in Oxford Street. The effect it had on London was astonishing and it created a sensation. The instrument was subsequently sent on tour and everywhere it went it was loudly acclaimed. During its tour, something like two thousand separate references or news items concerning it appeared in the British press.

King Edward VII commanded that the instrument be brought to Windsor Castle for him to hear but this great honour was never to come to pass, for Queen Alexandra's father, Prince Christian,* died the evening before the command performance and all arrangements were automatically cancelled.

It seems that, whilst touring England, a pianist was hired on frequent occasions to accompany the concerts which the instrument gave. Word of this got to Sandell and he immediately gave thought to combining the two instruments—a requirement which he rapidly met. The result was the Violano-Virtuoso. The first of these instruments contained a 44-note piano of regular lay-out, with the bass strings on the left and the treble on the right. However, subsequently the piano was made with a symmetrical lyre-shaped frame having the long bass strings in the centre and the strings extending shorter on each side, so that the treble was at both ends. This unusual form, proven to pose almost insuperable problems to the ordinary piano-tuner, was selected since it distributed the string tension evenly on the frame, thereby reducing the need for regular tuning.

News of the earlier Automatic Virtuoso and its successful tour of England reached officials of the U.S. Patent Office in Washington. They considered the machine worthy of exhibition at the Alaska-Yukon-Pacific Exposition to be held in Seattle and, unaware of the makers or owners, they requested the U.S. Consul in London to investigate. Patent experts then visited Mills in Chicago where the first Violano-Virtuoso was being finished and, upon invitation to exhibit at the Seattle show, the instrument was hurriedly finished and delivered to the American Government. At government expense, it was then taken to Seattle and exhibited together with seven other inventions which received similar honour. These included the steam turbine, the Telepost system, an early colour photography device and the Parallax Stereogram—a stereo projector.

Mills cannot be criticized for seizing this excellent opportunity to gain kudos for their instrument, and thus every Violano-Virtuoso to be produced from that date forward carried a legend reading 'Designated by the U.S. Government as one of the Eight Greatest Inventions of the Decade'.

* Prince Christian of Schleswig-Holstein Sonderburg-Glücksburg.

After the Seattle display, the U.S. Patent Office moved the instrument to the National Land and Irrigation Exposition in Chicago—the home town of the Mills Company. The Company records show that another feature of this particular show was the Mexican National Band. 'The swarthy little bandsmen stood and listened to the Violano-Virtuoso play their favourite and intricate Spanish dances by Sarasate and other composers', relates Mills. From Chicago, the instrument was taken to other exhibitions, all at Government expense and at no cost to the Mills concern. Indeed, no finer publicity agent could hope to have been found in the whole country— and entirely free of charge!

The list price of the Violano-Virtuoso was between $2,000 and $2,500. The *DeLuxe* model, which played two violins, cost $3,000. From its inception until the time when production ceased *circa* 1930 (a specimen in a London collection was shipped in 1930 and remained mint and un-opened in its packing case until 1963!) between 4,000 and 5,000 were built. Today it has survived in larger numbers than many of its contemporary mechanical musical instruments and some 200 or so are known to exist. In England there are known to be about a score, Norman Evans of North London owning three. The British Piano Museum at Brentford possesses a number in-cluding a fine specimen of the *DeLuxe* twin-violin instrument.

The operation of the Violano-Virtuoso was ingenious. To begin with, the Mills Company discovered very early on in their history that the ordinary violin, regardless of make, was unable to stand up to almost continual playing and expensive hand-made ones by famous craftsmen soon went out of tune and became unplayable. The only answer was to make a special violin and to this end Mills set up a production line of instruments. From their literature, it would seem that great pains were taken to produce an instrument that was both mechanically perfect and aesthetically satisfying. The greatest care was taken in selecting timber and in construction. The tuning, how-ever, was quite different from that of a normal violin. Instead of turn-keys in the neck of the instrument, the Mills violin passed its strings over a lever to which was attached a weight on a threaded arm. Tuning was achieved by moving this weight along the arm. Once the correct position was found, the instrument would stay in tune for long periods. Other than this, and a special linkage to provide a most life-like *vibrato* effect to the playing, the violin was quite standard in appearance. Indeed, it could have been taken from the playing mechanism and played quite satisfactorily by hand.

Bowing was effected by an electric motor which drove four shafts, each terminating in a pack of small celluloid discs. Each shaft was arranged in line with one of the violin strings and was also universally jointed, so that it could be moved up and down by solenoids whilst rotating. The motor itself had a variable resistance so that its speed could be varied continuously from slow to fast. This permitted the effect of light bowing for *pianissimo* playing, and strong bowing for *forte* pas-sages. Before playing each tune, a block of rosin was pressed on to each of the bows.

The tailpiece of the violin was connected by a lever to a cam so that, all the time the instrument played, the strings were in lateral movement. This produced an excellent *vibrato* effect. Beneath each string was arranged a number of cleft fingers, one for each note and semitone capable of being played on that string. These fingers were each controlled by a solenoid corresponding to the position of a slot in the music roll.

The roll itself was situated in the lower half of the instrument and was driven by a governed motor so that, regardless of the amount of paper on the driven spool, the speed of travel of the paper across the 'tracker-bar' remained constant. This was a most important feature since the rolls played five or more tunes each and were of large diameter. A brush of copper finger contacts made the complete electrical circuit between the tracker and the playing mechanism, the paper music passing between. Operating, as did most of the contemporary electro-magnetic mechanical musical instruments made in America, on 110 volts direct current, the playing was accompanied by a shower of bright blue sparks, normally hidden from public gaze by the doors in the base of the cabinet.

The piano part was again fully electrically controlled, each hammer having its own operating solenoid. The rest rail, adjustment of which gave *piano* and *forte* playing, was likewise controlled by a solenoid. The only contact between the piano and the player was a thick electrical cable and, since the piano was mounted in the form of a hinged door to the rear of the stoutly-built case, it could be removed and stood against the wall several feet from the rest of the Violano-Virtuoso where it would play quite happily. Though in no way an intentional or optional feature of the machine, this characteristic demonstrates the simplicity of the electric piano as compared with the pneumatic action.

Having made such a success of the Violano-Virtuoso, the Mills Novelty Company chose to capitalize still further on the mechanism, producing the Viol-Cello in about 1912. This variant had no piano, utilising the violin and playing mechanism of the Virtuoso combined with a vertically-mounted cello to the right of the case. Whilst contemporary sources state that, 'famous cellists who have heard this instrument have marvelled at its wonderful execution of the great violin concertos which have never before been arranged for cello playing', the machine was not the hoped-for success. Bowers recently questioned a man who was a Mills distributor about 1922–24 and was told that, 'the instrument was unsuccessful as no way was found to finger it successfully'.

Another Mills product was the Viol-Xylophone which was similar to the Virtuoso but employed xylophone in place of a piano. This also appears to have been unsuccessful and, if any were built, none has survived.

Accessory cabinets were produced for the Violano-Virtuoso and these, standing alongside the instrument, contained percussion effects which could be 'plugged in' and played from the same standard roll used for violin and piano.

The next Mills product was the 65-note all-electric Expression Piano. This used a design concept similar to the Violano-Virtuoso in that the bass strings were in the centre of the frame. The 'orchestra box' or accompaniment cabinet for the Violano-Virtuoso could also be connected to this piano. There were several variants of this peculiar piano, including one with a horse-race diorama. Said to have been one of the most complex and intricate devices ever sold by any manufacturer, the Mills Race-Horse piano operated its horses electro-magnetically in conjunction with a moving belt. A sophistication of the London street pianos with moving picture fronts! Even so, the success of the early days was never repeated and little remains now save the Violano —incredible even by today's standards and remaining a focal point and discussion topic amongst collectors both in America and England. A number are still in regular use in the way originally intended and one example in an American tourist resort still earns upwards of $500 in a four-month season. Many were shipped to England and were in use in funfairs and seaside shows right up to the outbreak of the 1939–45 war. Lamentably, with the altered set of values engendered by war, many were unnecessarily destroyed or 'cleared' and left to rot.

Mention was made earlier of one which survived in London in mint order. This machine turned up in a shop specializing in mechanical musical instruments in the Portobello Road, in 1963. Never unpacked from its shipping case, it was complete with original instruction manuals, spare parts and so on. The shipping documents with the model showed that it was sent from Chicago in 1930 and must thus have been one of the last to have been built. Unfortunately, in spite of its outward mint appearance, a large proportion of the metal castings proved to be quite useless. Having been cast in a zinc alloy called 'mazak', and then nickel-plated, electrolytic corrosion had taken place, reducing the metal to powder. In the hands of collector Norman Evans, the instrument was carefully rebuilt, new castings being made in bronze from the remains of the originals. Now beautifully restored, it performs regularly before gatherings of admirers in his basement workshop.

The Mills system for operating violins was later put to use in another application—the Mills Melody Violins. In this case, the violin was played by a keyboard and as many as one to one hundred violins could be played by one operator seated at the keyboard console. Of course, this was not strictly mechanical music.

One more mechanical violin remains to be listed. This was the Violonista perfected in 1926 by two French engineers, Gabriel Boreau and Emile d'Aubry. Their instrument resorted to pneumatic action controlled by a roll of paper music. Bowing was achieved by using an ordinary type of violin bow which was mounted on a trolley and driven by a cable actuated by small pneumatic motors. These caused the bow to be pulled backwards and forwards and the speed and direction of bow travel could be controlled realistically by perforations in the music-roll. It seems that the Violonista was purely an experimental prototype and was never put into production.

Banjos, mandolins, guitars, harps 'or other stringed instruments' were all embraced in the patents taken out in 1892 by J. Vose for his electromagnetic device worked by perforated paper. Unfortunately it is not known whether or not any of his instruments were ever made. Likewise the mechanical banjo of the American, W. S. Reed of 1893 seems to have come to nothing.

E. Tippmann and O. Keller thought up similar ideas for their automatic harp (or other stringed instrument) of 1895. This was worked by a simple, perforated-card tune sheet.

Leipzig's piano makers J. M. Grob and K. A. Gutter invented the Autoharp in 1884. This was a small zither-like instrument across the strings of which were arranged a number of wooden bars. Each bar was fitted with spring studs, so that it could be moved up and down on to the strings, and carried felt pads in certain positions. These pads muted certain notes and thus, by depressing one bar and strumming the strings, only the free strings would sound and these would be arranged into one of the standard accompaniment chords. Each bar would mute different strings and so give forth different chords.

The Autoharp would not strictly be termed an automatic instrument, but it was soon to be modified for mechanical playing. Paul Riessner who had been one of the founders of the Polyphonmusikwerke in Leipzig, invented many systems for plucking stringed instruments from mechanical linkages. In fact, he and F. E. P. Ehrlich (of the Monopol musical box fame), both individually patented a large number of such devices during the first two decades of this century.

By 1919, Riessner had perfected the Mandoline-Zither, a mechanically-played version of the Autoharp. This played twenty-five strings from a narrow paper roll. This was transported across a key-frame by turning a handle with the right hand. The left hand was used for the manual plucking of the accompaniment chords. These chords were numbered and the appropriate number stamped on to the music roll at the point at which it was intended to be played. Also known as the Triola, this instrument featured a reciprocating frame carrying short springs, which actually plucked the strings when a note was to be sounded.

A mechanical zither called the Chordephon was produced in Leipzig by Claus & Co. at the turn of the century. The strings were plucked by a linkage set in action by musical-box type projections from a disc, and models were made which could be hand wound or worked by a clockwork motor.

INSTRUCTIONS

FOR PLAYING THE

"TRIOLA"
Mandoline-Zither.

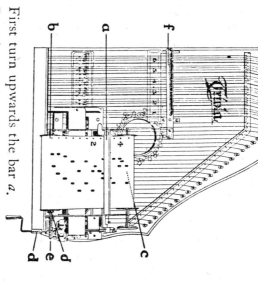

1. First turn upwards the bar *a*.

2. Put the music-roll in its place *b b*. Slip out the end of music-roll underneath bar *a*, and fix it into the slit *c* on wooden roller. Turn roller until the mark $\frac{|\ |\ |}{|\ |\ |}$ shown on music-roll comes just underneath bar *a* ; turn bar *a* down. The printed figures on music-roll should now show uppermost.

3. Fix handle on spindle *d*. The instrument is now ready for playing. Turn handle to the right only.

4. Choose first a song or other simple piece, in order to learn the accompaniment by sounding with thumb of the left hand the accord, which is indicated by figure on the music-roll Care should be taken to sound the strings just at the moment when the figure goes beneath the bar.

5. The *quick and proper reading* of the figures on the music-roll for the accompaniment, is the main point :—

A figure with a ring means : Sound only the bass string.

A figure underlined means : Sound the whole accord.

A figure only : Sound the bass string only, and the holes following mean : Sound only the three strings of the same accord as many times as the holes appear. This fits in with the proper time of the piece, such as in a Valse (3/4 time), the bass is one, and the two following holes, the three accord strings sounded twice, being two and three.

6. To re-roll, turn the handle and fix it on the re-rolling spindle *e.* To keep the paper flat and firm, place the left hand on the music-roll while turning.

7. To play soft or loud, move the bar *a* forward or backward. *p* means play soft, *m f* medium, *f* loud.

8. Care should be taken to keep the music-rolls dry and rolled up.

Fig. 34. Instructions for playing the Triola paper-operated zither

About the same time was produced the Guitarophone, also disc-playing but using a striking hammer action for its 47 playing notes.

The small organette was one of the first practical instruments to make use of the perforated paper music-roll. The instrument stemmed from the brains of several inventors, both in America as well as in Europe where J. Carpentier made several machines in the early 1880's. Maxfield and McTammany in the States probably did more to develop the machine into a worthwhile and cheap instrument, although McTammany was denied the reward of his inventive genius, seeing his expired patents exploited by others. The American Orguinette Company, basis of the subsequent Aeolian Company, was the largest manufacturer. Instruments were made which played endless paper bands, paper rolls, cardboard discs, zinc discs, metal discs and annular rings.

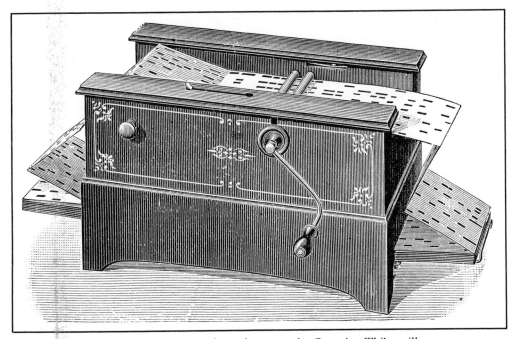

Fig. 35. A book-music reed organ – the Organina Thibouville

In operation, three systems were used. First there was the type which used mechanical levers, held down by the tune sheet, to lift pallets so as to allow air to pass through a reed. Then there was the style which featured a tracker board over which the perforated paper was drawn. In one type of this style, air from the atmosphere was drawn in through the reed to a chest from which the air had been reduced in pressure by means of exhausters. The other type compressed air in a wind-chest using bellows and then allowed it to escape to atmosphere through the reed, when a hole in the tracker board was uncovered. The German Ehrlich brothers favoured the use of mechanical levers and produced the highly successful 24-note Ariston played with cardboard discs. Other European types, such as the Mignon, were complex in operation, having a set of 'primary pneumatics', made of thin skin, to operate valves in the reed chamber. In all these, however, driving power was achieved through a cranked handle and there was no other form of motive power.

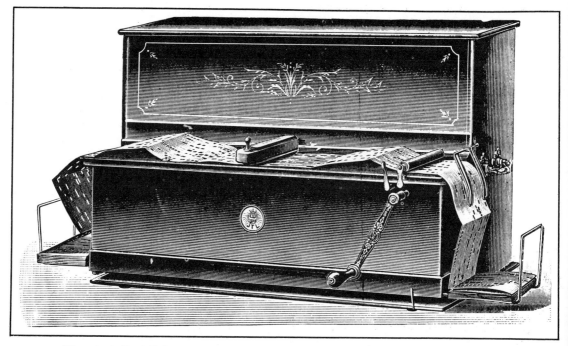

Fig. 36. A Gavioli Coelophone street organ made c. 1904 and sold by Thibouville-Lamy

The English manufacturer, J. M. Draper, was the first to make an organette with two or more stops of reeds and he took out patents for such a device in 1887. It must be added that multiple reed stops were common in reed organs at this time, but nobody had applied the technique to the little organette before.

The Mechanical Orguinette Co. also made some larger organettes, one of which stood in a cabinet some four feet high, and another of which resembled a cabinet-style piano-player in that it had foot-operated exhausters and a handle to transport a wide band of music across a tracker board. This had two stops or banks of reeds, the second one being controlled by a small knob. A swell effect was also provided. Many small organettes at this time also had this device, usually in very rudimentary form and comprising a hinged flap over the reeds.

I have chosen to devote a separate short Chapter to paper-roll playing, large organs, both reed and pipe.

Reminiscent of the mechanical trumpeter made by Kaufmann in the 1840's, J. P. Browne devised an '. . . automatic instrument for teaching bugle or trumpet calls', in 1887. 'The calls are played on an automaton reed musical-instrument actuated by a tune sheet and similar to the Ariston. The number of notes on the instrument is equal to that used for calls'.

I am indebted to Q. David Bowers for his research into the history of a machine which must vie with the Violano-Virtuoso for originality. This machine, the self-playing harp, was certainly a most curious and interesting mechanical musical instrument. In spite of this, and also the words of the Rudolph Wurlitzer Company which stated that 'as a money maker the Wurlitzer Harp has proven itself the king of them all', Bowers has found that ten years after its introduction in 1905, it had all but disappeared.

The automatic harp was first thought of in the 1890's by a Cincinatti harp player and band leader named Harry Connor. He interested his friend, inventor J. W. Whitlock, in the idea and Whitlock began experimenting. The first patent for the instrument was taken out in Whitlock's name in 1899 and covered an upright wooden-framed harp housed in a rectangular case. Pneumatic action operated by a perforated paper music-roll $8\frac{1}{2}$ inches wide operated small mechanical fingers which plucked the strings, there being one finger for each note. The sound produced by this mechanism was not unlike that of a guitar and was softer than that of a piano. Although a most pleasant and mellow sound, it did not sound very much like a harp.

The subsequent years saw the production of a small number of automatic harps by Whitlock in a small wooden building next to his home in Rising Sun, Indiana. In 1905 Whitlock put several instruments out on location in various Cincinatti, Ohio, taverns. Whitlock's choice of Cincinatti, about 35 miles from Rising Sun, as a trial ground proved fortuitous, for Cincinatti was also the home of the Rudolph Wurlitzer Company. Wurlitzer had been in business with coin-operated musical instruments since the 1890's, having begun with the Regina disc-playing musical box which was produced in a coin-freed variant. In 1899 Wurlitzers sold the first cylinder-playing, coin-operated piano (deKleist's Tonophone), followed a few years later by the 44-note Pianino. These were such a success that thousands were sold and the factory could only just cope with the demand. Having introduced coin-music to the American public, Wurlitzer was out to corner the market in all types of this music.

And so it was that one day Howard Wurlitzer, then business manager of the Wurlitzer Company, chanced to visit a certain Cincinatti café and was confronted by an ideal machine to add to the Wurlitzer range—an automatic harp! Wurlitzer travelled to Rising Sun and signed a contract with J. W. Whitlock for the purchase of 1,000 instruments. Whitlock constructed a new factory and set up his production line.

The Automatic Harp sold through Wurlitzer for $750 each and music rolls cost $7.50 apiece. Alternatively customers in the neighbourhood of Cincinatti could hire out instruments for a percentage of the profits. By early 1906, 135 different places in Cincinatti alone had the Automatic Harp installed. A year or so later the Style 'B' harp was introduced and this was built in the shape of a real harp as distinct from the rectangular case of the earlier model. This cost $100 extra. Soon afterwards, though, demand fell and the Style 'A' price was dropped to $650, thence to $500. By 1916 they were being remaindered for only $375. By 1920, the instrument was finished. In all, 1,500 had been built.

Following the success, short-lived though it was, of the Automatic Harp, Whitlock experimented with a self-playing violin which was intended to comprise fifteen strings, each with its own rosined disc bow. The instrument was never finished and is today in the Bowers collection. Whitlocks subsequently went into business building furniture, which work they still do to this day. J. W. Whitlock died in 1935 at the age of sixty-four, being succeeded by his son Stewart who died in 1966.

The forerunner of the accordion, itself played pneumatically in latter years in the Belgian Mortier and Arburo café organs of post-war years, was the concertina. This used a reed plate in which were set reeds facing alternate sides and controlled by small pallets worked by finger buttons. Wind was passed through the reeds by the inward and outward moving of the bellows and each reed would have a leather flap over the speaking side so that, on moving the bellows inwards, the inner reeds on the plate would speak, the others muted by the flaps. On moving the bellows inwards, the process would be reversed.

Mechanizing the concertina, beloved, or so tradition would have us believe, by the mariner and country dancer alike, was attempted by several inventors, among them M. A. Wier in 1883. He used a perforated tune sheet transported across the pallet linkages by springs and bridges between the two ends of the instrument. Wier also made many other mechanical instruments playing perforated music, including a trumpet-shaped reed instrument blown by means of a mouthpiece and playing music by a hand crank. Similar instruments were made in Leipzig by O. Meinhardt from 1886 onwards, whilst G. A. Cole's toy trumpet of 1888 played its tune from a fixed disc against which a handle rotated a reed plate.

L. A. Klepzig shunned perforated music in his mechanical concertina of 1884, favouring a pinned barrel rotated by a linkage between the two ends as used by Wier. G. Richter, probably of the Richter manufacturing empire which produced the Libellion, Imperator and other musical boxes using plucked combs, devised a type of inertia motor to drive his tune sheet. This was in 1885 and the inertia motor was set into motion and boosted on each compression of the concertina bellows. J. M. Farmer's concertina-like instrument of 1889 again played perforated music and was similar to that thought up by M. A. Wier.

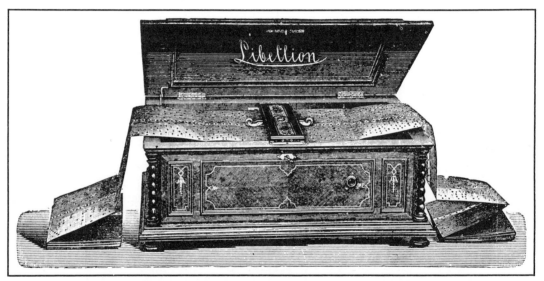

Fig. 37. The Libellion was a comb-playing musical box played by book music and was made by Richter of Schwarzburg-Rudolstadt

The name Richter, this time Friedrich Adolf Richter, the musical box maker, appears on another patent dated 1893 for a concertina. In this one he used a coil spring to drive the music roll, and wound it by a ratchet lever from the normal playing action of moving the bellows in and out. However, the successful self-playing concertina—as automatic as it could be—was the work of P. Fehling in 1895. Fehling used a motor of the inertia type which had a large fly-wheel which was driven by a ratchet lever within constant easy reach of the performer's fingers. This lever could be flicked back and forth whilst 'pumping', and the music-roll was thereby transported across a key-frame. The music paper held down a row of lightly-sprung keys. Where a hole in the paper indicated a note to be sounded, the key rose through the hole, and its other end lifted a pallet. R. Wunsch patented a similar device in Leipzig in 1896.

These mechanical concertinas were produced with 14 or 28 single notes or 28 quadruple reeds and were in production right up until the 1930's. They were known as the *Tanzbär* or 'dancing bear' for some unknown reason, although it seems likely that this was a registered trade mark. Many hundreds were built and they were particularly successful in the field of the old music hall where it was often desirable for the comic to be able to play a few bars of music to get himself off the stage. The instrument lent itself admirably to such harmless little pieces of deception. Each bore a small circular emblem showing a dancing bear and with the word Tanzbär (which is German for a bear-dance).

Toy trumpets have been mentioned already, but paper-roll playing toy saxophones (the $2.89 Play-a-Sax) were marketed in America as late as the 1920's. Other instruments were also made such as the Clarola clarinet and all worked by looping a band of perforated paper around the body of the instrument. The paper covered the 'key' holes and, acting as a sliding valve, played a tune as the holes were uncovered by the passage of the paper. A smaller application of this principle was to be seen in the Rolmonica patented in May 1928. The Play-a-Sax, the Clarola and the Rolmonica—a paper-roll playing mouth organ costing $1—emanated from America, the first two from the Q.R.S. music-roll company.

In an earlier Chapter, I mentioned the geographical boundaries to which certain types of instrument strictly adhered. The café piano with drum, castanets and triangle was common in France, Italy and Spain, yet never caught on in England. The coin-operated café piano, common enough in its basic form in the British Isles, was to be developed and perfected, improved upon and embellished almost beyond recognition in America and to find markets where no comparable market existed—or was pursued—elsewhere in the world. Teutonic piano-orchestrions were Europe's nearest counterpart. The habits of people and their conditions of living, their surroundings and temperaments can all be said to have an influence on this demarcation.

Styles of furniture and also, surprisingly enough, architecture have a considerable bearing in the study of the development and environmental acceptance of mechanical instruments. Many of my readers are no doubt familiar with the rich, Gothic-style cabinets of the larger Polyphon musical boxes, frets, curlicues, Stephensonian-order turned columns, richly-carved, almost overpoweringly heavy pediments surmounted by spikey finials. This is typical of the furniture and, in fact, of the architecture of the age.

It is obvious to see that in the eighteenth century, furniture of the cabinet type was largely controlled by the proportions of classical buildings. Work boxes, automata, nécessaires became architectural microcosms. They simulated not only town houses and country villas in mahogany and other hardwoods but also portrayed in their façades all the current fashions and conceits of Palladian mansions, Gothic churches, Indian pavilions, Chinese pagodas and French châteaux. Many cages for live birds of the period were epitomes of this trend and resembled some of the most palatial of the contemporary doll's houses.

This tendency, to take architectural criteria into consideration when styling furniture, was broadly adopted by almost all of the creative cabinet makers and designers to follow. Indeed it can be argued that even today we still practise this odd form of syllepsis in creating modern furniture which is quite as unbeautiful as our modern architecture. One has only to examine a tubular chair or a cocktail cabinet-cum-television receiver to see, in miniature, the influences of those depressing monstrosities of concrete, glass and plastics which are variously scattered about our land as offices and living machines ('homes', other than for the mentally ill and the aged, are dictated no longer to be in fashion).

The Germans brought the trends of the Gothic edifice (often, one finds, even the Hellenic) to bear on their mechanical musical instruments. I have already mentioned the Polyphon cabinet. Indeed, all the disc-playing musical boxes made in Germany displayed a similar Teutonic appearance. When such orchestrion makers as Popper, Hupfeld, Gebruder Weber, Losche, J. D. Philipps & Söhne, and Welte went to work, they built, no doubt unconsciously, miniature examples of the most solid endemic architectural constructions as cases for their devices. In Paris, the father of the fair-organ—Gavioli the Italian—styled his façades in the rococo and the *Art Nouveau*. This feature of the fair-organ undoubtedly captured a world-wide acclaim, for cases in this style became characteristic of many fair-organs the world over, so demonstrating a diversion from our arbitrary geographical limitations. The rococo or Louis XV style became known almost universally. Molinari in New York and Limonaire in Paris and Camden Town, London, built a range in austere cases (perhaps even more Teutonic than Italo-Parisian!) as did others in the trade, but Gavioli's display of the ornate had set the trend. The Dutch street organs, *draai orgels*, today display a charming façade quite in keeping with the best of the Gavioli foundation —the architecture of Louis XV, Versailles, Paris in the 'eighties.

This treatise on cabinet trends is given to explain in part the great variety of styles to be found over the years and to help in the regional identification of work. Mission oak finish, for example, coupled with casework after the best Colonial pattern, characterized many of the American products in the field of mechanical musical instruments in the early years of this century.

A particularly interesting species of roll-playing pneumatic—or electrically-operated instruments is one which, to the best of my knowledge, remained almost unknown in Europe. I refer to the American theatre orchestra, known variously as a 'photo-player' or just plain 'fotoplayer' (the trade name of a product of The American Photoplayer Company). These go back to the days of the silent picture and were produced by many manufacturers to meet a need for music and sound effects to accompany films. The only European equivalent was Hupfeld's Clavimonium designed for 'kine-theatres'. This combined a player-piano with a 5-stop harmonium.

The photo-player was made in countless styles and combinations. It was basically a piano, containing also a pipe-organ, chimes, drum and cymbals, xylophone and other effects. The instrument frequently comprised a piano console with one or sometimes two matching attached cabinets to contain the various other effects. The whole could be operated manually from the keyboard and pedal clavier, or could be operated from roll music. Some could play two music rolls at once, others were made with complex arrangements for selecting instantaneously any part of any one of up to half a dozen or more rolls fitted into a self-changing mechanism.

Typical of the advertizing media of the period and typical of the literature circulated by the makers of photo-players, is the following extract from an advertizing booklet published by the house of Seeberg, one of the leading makers of this type of instrument. Their Pipe-Organ Orchestra was available in models ranging from $3,500 for a console and one case, up to the vast Style 'A' De Luxe with its towering ranges of pipes on either side. 'Price', it adds darkly, 'by arrangement'. But to quote from their publicity:

'It is Tuesday night and you are showing a five reel feature of undoubted merit; but it is *more* than a film which has filled your theater to the last row. With an orchestra at his finger ends, your piano player sits at his keyboard and watches the film flit across the screen. He is only a single person, an individual, mind you, and yet he had at his instant command the resources of a pipe-organ with its wonderful variety of stops, the tender, true tones of a violin, the brisk notes of a xylophone, the gay click of the castanets, the silver rattle of the tambourine, and the syncopated beats of the drum.

'There is no descriptive demand which a film story can make but he is able to meet it— no episode in movie land that he cannot make more thrilling, more touching, more enjoyable to the audience. As his fingers run over the keyboard he is master of every situation. He is the living

118

interpreter of every shade of emotion registered by the silent players. He can express the sorrow of the life stories enacted there in the heart-searching melodies of that great organ's voice; or he can add zest and life to a comedy film with an instrumental accompaniment which puts a new bustle and spirit into the funmaking of the screen comedians.

'The silent audience sitting there with eyes glued on the screen as yard after yard of film un-winds may not be conscious that this one man holds their emotions in the hollow of his hand. They may not realize that it is his perfectly fitting accompaniment which make a photo play in your theater twice as enjoyable as in the movie house across the street, but when the final "close up" of the lovers clasped in each other's arms fades away with the sweet *pianissimo* tones of the organ giving the scene new meaning, then they turn to one another and say "What perfect music".

'And that is just what the SEEBURG Pipe-Organ Orchestra is—"perfect music". It enables you to have the same sort of music in your theater that only an orchestra and a $10,000 pipe organ could otherwise give you—and in addition you have all the sound effects which add so much to the showing of any film.

'If a messenger dashes up on a foam covered horse, your pianist presses a single button and hoof beats are perfectly imitated. If the wind is howling around the miner's cabin, the effect is correctly achieved by the SEEBURG—the ring of a 'phone, bird call and any number of other realistic effects are in your SEEBURG instrument at the player's finger tips.

'Who can overestimate the value of a perfect musical accompaniment to a moving picture? Who can say what a great effect such music has on the box office receipts?

'Isn't that the sort of music you want in your theater? It certainly is. But, you object, the cost is too great. No longer, however, can this objection hold true because since the advent of the SEEBURG Pipe-Organ Orchestra such perfect music is within the range of any good motion picture play-house. The SEEBURG instrument not only gives you a piano, an organ, the resources and traps of an orchestra, but it has the further advantages of both hand and self-playing operation.

'Note that we say "self-playing" and not "mechanical" because there is nothing to even sug-gest the "mechanical" when the SEEBURG is operated by a roll. It still has the human touch and the human soul found in no other instrument on the market—the quality of tone shading and personal expression which have made the SEEBURG the choice of the proprietors of America's best motion picture theaters.'

There were many other 'fotoplayer' makers, among them the Cremona made by the Mar-quette Piano Co. of Chicago, the Capital Symphony Orchestra by the Capital Piano Company, New York, the Banjorchestra by F. Englehardt of New York and the Link produced by the firm which was later to pioneer the Link Trainer for instructing aircraft pilots in blind flying. There was also the Reproduco, the Nelson-Wiggen, Coinola, North Tonawanda, Berry-Wood, Wur-litzer and so on. This was a vast industry the likes of which we were never to see in Europe. With the arrival of the 'talkies', this industry was wiped out almost overnight and the many thousands of theatre orchestras thrown out and destroyed. Thanks to the efforts of present-day enthusiasts in America, such as Q. David Bowers and Harvey Roehl, remaining machines—and their litera-ture—are being preserved.

The keyless piano became popular in the United States in the form of the coin-operated nickel-odeon. This type of instrument was available in a number of sizes and styles to suit the needs of the café, bar and silent picture-house. Casework was often embellished with *appliqué* carving and panels of leaded coloured glass through which the mechanism, illuminated by electric light-ing, could be watched. The music-rolls were standardized into several sizes and types which could be used on instruments having xylophone and other percussion accompaniments. It was not uncommon to find a row of violin-toned organ pipes to provide a sometimes uncompromisingly transparent chorus.

The smaller keyless nickelodeons, such as those made by the Nelson Wiggen and Link companies, were much smaller than a comparable player-piano and could thus be fitted easily into the smallest bar or diner. Larger instruments often played an endless 'roll' of music which, without the facility of a spool, would be allowed to uncoil and pack into a compartment provided for it, subtly approaching the zenith of entanglement, but never actually jamming and shredding, several hundred feet of paper in its meanderings preceding and succeeding its passage over the tracker-bar.

At which point the nickelodeon became an orchestrion or piano-orchestrion is not possible to determine with any degree of accuracy. The terminology of the time, both in Europe and America, tended to be imprecise. The Wurlitzer Bijou Orchestra, for example, included a piano, mandolin effect, string-toned pipes, snare drum and xylophone. The same firm produced a larger model named the PianOrchestra as well as the Mandolin Quartette, which last-mentioned was really a pneumatically-operated tremolo piano. Another coin-operated tremolo piano was the Regina Sublima which played from rolls of stiff perforated paper $19\frac{5}{8}$ inches wide. This used the same type of beating hammer action as the *Piani Melodici* invented by Racca in Italy, only the 'pianoforte' effect was achieved automatically by a ratchet wheel, eccentric inched back and forth by twin pawls. Generally speaking, the reciprocating cycle of this type of action caused rapid wear so that in some respects the instruments were unintentionally self-destructive.

Nickelodeons with keyboards could be depended upon to entertain even when the resident ivory-tickler was out having a beer and sometimes they were fitted with the famed Wurlitzer roll-changer which systematically played six rolls of music one after the other, rewinding each at its conclusion. Unfortunately, many of the parts of these ingenious and complex devices were cast in a metal alloy which has swollen over the years and thus a number of collectors have experienced various malfunctions including the miserable results of a roll-changer going haywire and attempting to change its rolls in the middle of a tune.

Roll-playing instruments once ruled the realms of mechanical musical instruments, usurping the reputation of the pinned barrel. All that remains today of this breed are but a fraction of the many thousands of instruments made and, of these, most are ordinary player-pianos.

CHAPTER 6

Overhauling the Barrel Piano

THE simplicity of the barrel piano makes the task of restoration comparatively straight-forward. However, as with all mechanisms, simple or otherwise, a thorough understanding of the principles of operation and of the functions of the various components, severally and individually, is vital before proceeding. The illustrations should therefore be studied carefully, together with the details of mechanical variants shown in Chapter 2, where such instruments have to be tackled. Once the fundamentals are understood, repair and regulation is largely a matter of common sense.

Three types of barrel piano are most likely to be encountered—the small portable piano of the Hicks style, the hand-turned street instrument and the clockwork piano. A basic knowledge of these three instruments will enable the workings of all other types to be understood.

As with every specialist job, the repairman should first equip himself with certain tools and sundries, to enable him to carry out his work efficiently. These comprise ordinary hand tools, but specifically call for the following: a large screwdriver having a $\frac{3}{8}$-inch wide blade and a good hand grip, a long, slender 'watchmaker's' screwdriver with a $\frac{3}{16}$-inch wide blade, a 6-inch general purpose screwdriver, an 8-oz. hammer, heavy pliers, long-nosed pliers, round-nosed pliers (for forming eye ends on music wire), a pair of stout cutters for music wire, a pair of side cutters and a wire brush.

Special tools comprise a piano-tuning key or lever (you will need one with a rectangular slot for early pianos and a square or 'star' key for street and clockwork instruments), and either a chromatic pitch-pipe or a set of tuning forks. These last-mentioned can probably be dispensed with if you have immediate access to an ordinary piano for comparative tuning, or if you have a good ear for musical pitch. As we shall see, however, pitch is seldom critical.

Stiff bristle brushes, emery-cloth and probably a vacuum-cleaner will all come in handy as well.

We will deal initially with the portable street barrel piano which can be worked upon on the bench or kitchen table. Study the illustration, Figure 38, thoroughly to start with. This variant of the instrument is more akin to the antique and frequently displays the best-quality work-manship.

The first task is to dismantle the instrument. The barrel access door on the right-hand side of the case is usually secured either by a wire which passes down through the case side (seen when the front fall and barrel lid are removed), or by a turn-button on the inside of the door.

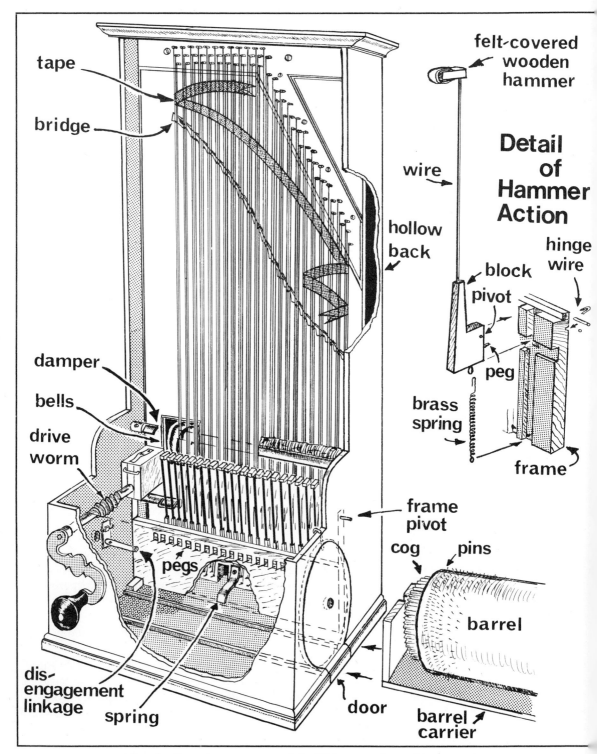

felt-covered wooden hammer

tape

bridge

wire

Detail of Hammer Action

hollow back

hinge wire

block

pivot

damper

bells

drive worm

peg

brass spring

frame

frame pivot

cog

pins

pegs

barrel

dis-engagement linkage

spring

door

barrel carrier

Fig. 38. General arrangement of the Hicks type of portable street piano

Note that this door should have two studs in its lower edge which engage in holes in the bottom of the case side.

The action of the key-frame is controlled by a cam on the outside left of the case. Turning the cam pushes the key-frame away from the barrel, so moving the hammer-tails clear of the barrel pins, to prevent damage to both when the barrel is shifted. The key-frame must be moved to this position before shifting the barrel and if it does not move, due, say, to the linkage being loose, missing or broken, then you must push the frame back against its spring with a long screwdriver and hold it there whilst the barrel is withdrawn from the other side of the case.

Take out the door and you will now be able to see the end of the barrel. Usually this is supported in a wooden cradle to facilitate sliding the barrel in and out, but sometimes this is missing. Its absence does not affect the working of the instrument, although it is a good idea to make up a simple cradle so that, when the door is removed, the barrel does not drop down on the pins at that end.

Hold the barrel end by the protruding spindle with the right hand, raise the tune-selecting knife (Fig. 18) on the other end of the case with the left hand, and draw out the barrel, watching carefully to see that the pins do not foul the case round the doorway. Because barrels are made of softwood, they are often found to be infested with woodworm. More often than not, this can be cured and all made well again. At this stage it is a good plan to treat any infestation with a proprietary worm-killer. Use this liberally and let it soak well into any infected parts, particularly the barrel ends and the drive cog. Because several applications will be needed to do this job properly and because it is advisable to allow a day or so between each treatment, the sooner you apply the first treatment the better.

With the barrel out of the instrument, you can now remove the crank handle by turning it anti-clockwise whilst holding the worm-shaft still. Originally, these handles were threaded on to the end of the worm-shaft as far as a protruding stop so that they could be removed easily without the handle having become 'thread-bound'. Sometimes this protruding dog is missing and so you may have to apply a little force to unscrew the handle. Now take off the bearing block which supports the inside end of the worm-shaft. This is fixed with two screws from the outside of the left of the case. When the block is free, a little juggling is often necessary to free both it and the worm-shaft from the case, the worm-shaft having to be moved back a little to free it from its bearing in the case front.

Disconnect the tune-selecting knife, the key-frame linkage and cam and set them aside for cleaning. All the brass parts, including the handle and worm-shaft, can be treated with good quality metal polish. Stubborn dirt stains—common enough on these parts—can be removed with a brass wire-brush or the application of a piece of fine, worn emery-cloth lubricated with metal-polish.

The key-frame is next on the list and this is taken out by springing the right-hand side strip clear of its pivot in the case. Insert the blade of a screwdriver between the strip and the case and twist gently to do this. The frame can now be turned a little to clear the bearing, disengaged from the pivot at the other end, and lifted clear of the case.

You are now left with the empty piano case complete with the stringed portion, commonly known as the harp. If the strings are all present and in fairly good condition, there is no need to remove them unless the wrest plank is badly split or the wrest pins loose. The wrest-pins should all protrude from the wrest-plank at the same angle—a little above the horizontal. If any are at variance with this norm, it is a good indication that the pins are set loose in worn, oversize holes, or that the wrest-plank itself is split.

Most of these pianos employed a harp having twenty-three notes. On better instruments the tuning scale was marked above each pin, there normally being three strings to each note over the tenor and treble parts of the scale, the bass notes being two or just one string. Only the bass notes are what is called 'wrapped'. Wrapped strings have copper wire coiled round them so that they vibrate at a low frequency without having to be too loose to be practical.

Assuming that the piano is in the worst condition, we will continue to strip the instrument but do bear in mind that, if the instrument is basically sound at this point, there is no need to proceed further and you can continue with replacing any broken or missing strings, tuning and re-assembly.

As in full-sized pianos, the strings are not all of the same thickness, there usually being at least three different gauges of wire used, the thinnest wire being provided for the highest notes. Again, the bass notes are wrapped strings, so these have to be considered separately. If possible, measure the gauge of the wires before removing them, or at any rate keep specimen strings and mark which groups of notes used the same gauge of wire. There are some more points to make on wire later on.

To remove a string, slacken off the wrest-pin first, unhook the string from its peg (hitch-pin) at the bottom of the harp, and then uncoil it from the wrest-pin. It is not advisable to remove the actual wrest-pin unless it is so loose that it can be pulled out with the fingers. This is because the wrest-pin was originally a very tight fit in the board and its unnecessary removal will make it looser on replacement. Again, if the pins are taken out to be cleaned (they are often rusty), do *not* clean the portion which fits into the wood.

If the wrest-pins are loose, then the piano will not stay in proper tune, since the tension of each string will exert a torque greater than the frictional resistance offered by its wrest-pin in the wrest-plank. This can often be improved by removing the pin and thoroughly rubbing the shank with powdered rosin. If the wrest-plank holes are slightly oversize and the pins still turn, then you must carefully re-drill them very slightly larger, making sure that the drill goes in at the proper angle. Fit new oversize pins which you can get from the piano-sundries supplier. Should the new pins be a little too long, you may legitimately drill the holes sufficiently deep so that the string hole on the new pin lines up with those in the other pins. If the wrest-plank holes are very badly oversize, ream them out to a clean circular shape and plug them with a hardwood peg well glued in. Trim this off flush with the plank when dry and drill slightly undersize to take the pin. At all times when removing wrest-pins, use plenty of rosin on them before replacing. Remember, by the way, that the shanks of these pins are, in fact, slightly threaded and so they should be screwed in with the tuning key. But to return to the dismantling of the piano.

With all the strings removed, brush out all the accumulation of dust and dirt from inside the instrument and you may choose to scrub the inside of the case with hot water and detergent but do not overwet the wood, or allow it to soak up too much moisture. Again, do not wash the actual sound-board which is of thin spruce or clear pine. Wipe this with a damp cloth and detergent and this should be sufficient to restore its brilliance. You can rub this down with fine sandpaper and revarnish it if you wish. Stains are best removed by scraping with the grain, using a single-edged razor-blade before sanding.

Examine the bridge very carefully for looseness, splits and missing sprags. This must be securely glued to the sound-board and the sprags which align each string must be all present and correct. Missing or broken ones can be replaced by panel pins but these must be inserted at the proper angle—do not try to knock them to the proper angle after driving them in straight—this will split the bridge.

Make good any loose joints or splits in the case. If the sound-board is bowed—a frequent failing—you should leave it well alone. If it is split, then force hot brown glue into the crack and let it set. Remember that the sound-board is the resonator of the harp. If it is split, the instrument cannot produce its full volume of sound and, if you attempt to patch it by gluing a strip of wood on to it, you will muffle it and again produce less sound. However, if the sound-board is badly damaged, you must remove the back of the case and support the sound-board face down on a solid block of wood covered with a sheet of polythene to prevent the glue sticking to the block. Pour hot glue over the damaged area and fit over it a small patch of $\frac{1}{16}$-inch veneer arranged so that its grain is across that of the sound-board. The patch must be no larger than necessary and it must not be nailed or screwed on but left to set under a heavy weight. Patching will affect the sound, but, as a last resort when the sound-board is damaged, this is permissible since it cannot easily be replaced in entirety.

Check the wrest-plank for splits, particularly around the pin holes. If there are any, you should replace the wrest-pins (if already removed), tap them home with the hammer, lay the harp on its back and force synthetic resin adhesive into the cracks using a cake-icing syringe with a fine nozzle. Where no splits are evident, but the wrest-pins are loose, there is a preparation available from piano-tuners and sundries stockists which will tighten them up. To use this, you must again lay the case down so that the wrest-plank is horizontal and then paint the special liquid round the loose pins, leaving it overnight to soak in and do its job.

The next job is re-stringing. Equip yourself with a one-ounce coil of each of the necessary gauges of wire for the unwrapped strings. Cut each string about six inches longer than is required and form a small eye on one end with the round-nosed pliers. See that the loose end is securely wrapped round the body of the wire as otherwise it will unwind under the tension needed to tune it.

Begin with the longest unwrapped string and hook it on to its proper peg at the bottom of the harp. Lead the wire straight up to the wrest-pin, threading it under the stringing bar just below the wrest-pins—make sure that you line up with the right one—and cut the wire exactly $1\frac{3}{4}$ inches longer so that you have that much wire protruding above the pin. Take a pair of flat pliers and bend over the last $\frac{3}{8}$ inch to a right-angle. Thread this bent end through the hole in the wrest-pin and, using the tuner's key, turn the pin in a clockwise direction to take most of the slack out of the wire. You will find that the amount of overlength on the wire gives you about two and a half turns on the pin. The exact number is immaterial—two to three is usual—but they should all be the same. See that the coils do not overlap each other. Before applying the last half turn of tension, tap the end of the wrest-pin with a hammer to make sure that it is properly home in the wrest-plank. Now thread the lower end of the wire around its proper bridge sprags. This serves to stop off the correct length of string which is capable of producing the desired note for a given tension. Bring each string just tight and no more until all the wires are in place. Proceed with all the strings in this manner, lining each one properly in place on the wrest-plank and also its bridge sprags.

A word now about the gauge of wires on these pianos. Without overstepping the limits of justifiable restoration, one can decidedly alter the tone by restringing with slightly thinner wire. The effect is to brighten the tone and often to accentuate the treble and tenor registers—these last frequently being 'woolly'. It is entirely up to the restorer what he does here, but I have been agreeably surprised at the improved tone achieved by restringing a 23-note Hicks piano with strings two gauges thinner throughout, i.e. for 36-gauge wire I used 38-gauge. Needless to say, you should not try to thin the wrapped bass strings as these are best left as intended.

There are other things you can do, legitimately, to amend tonality and these again will be discussed a little further on.

Wrapped bass strings are readily obtainable very cheaply and, since it is not possible to cut down regular piano strings because of the resultant loosening of the winding, it is far better to get a piano-repair merchant to make them up for you. He will need to know the gauge of the music wire and also the gauge of the copper-winding as well as the exact distance from hook end to wrest-pin. Ideally, of course, the original string should be given as a pattern. Large merchants will usually make you a new string whilst you wait. Confide in them that you are restoring a barrel piano—a little cultivated interest will always get you a better and quicker service!

The next stage is tuning, and this is a job which will take several days—sometimes a week— to do properly, for the strings must be allowed to stretch and the piano harp-frame allowed to move. The combined load on the wrest-plank when all the strings are tensioned is quite considerable and it is perfectly normal for the plank to warp a little. Excessive deformation now or at any time in its previous career will result in splitting.

The technique of tuning these street pianos is somewhat arbitrary. They were never intended to produce concert music, nor were they intended to be tuned to a set pitch. The fact that the notes may be lettered to the scale again means little for, as any person with the slightest knowledge of music will know, you can call any pitch of sound 'C', for example, and create a perfect scale to that note. What you actually call a note is purely of interest where the instrument is to perform music with other instruments or with a singer. For this reason, it is sometimes not only difficult but quite impossible to tune a street piano to the correct concert pitch of the notes shown on the wrest-plank.

The tuner therefore has to lay out the foundations for his scale without necessarily being influenced too much by his letter 'C' tuning fork and the note 'C' on the normal piano. When tackling a piano which has some or all of its original strings still *in situ*, then it is sometimes possible to find the scale by plucking the bass notes, for these are the least likely to have got out of tune as they are subjected to less tension. From this a note can be found—preferably C— from which to set off a tenor c or middle C. If the piano harp is badly warped or if it has been split, then it is a good idea and perfectly acceptable to lower the pitch slightly (throughout the instrument, of course) to reduce the tension of the strings.

Having found the strings on the harp lettered C and tuned them to a pitch (note that I am not necessarily saying that these should be to concert pitch C), proceed up the scale. For the non-musical, the tonic sol-fa scale is quite sufficient and this corresponds to the normal musical notation as follows, starting the scale at C:—

C	C♯	D	D♯	E	F	F♯	G	G♯	A	B♭	B	C
doh		ray		me	fah		soh		lah		se	doh

Because the scale starts and stops with the letter C, we have set out an octave. At this point, do not worry about the intermediate notes (the black notes on the pianoforte) which are C♯, D♯, F♯, G♯ and B♭. Just concentrate on the 'natural' notes of the scale.

A treatise on piano tuning here is out of place and I intend only to set out the very rudiments of the science. For those who wish to delve further into the art, there are several good handbooks on the subject. Back, however, to our amateur tuning which will suffice for the street pianos. The chances are that we shall end up with an instrument sounding far better than it did at the time of its intended use in spite of our limited experience.

If you can tune to a pitchpipe, so much the better. But if you have had to set off your own scale, then you must usually resort to what we will call *comparative tuning*. Briefly, this consists of producing notes which are in perfect harmony with each other. If you have a good ear for music and for pitch, you will easily be able to detect the notes which fall in harmony and the steps are as follows, starting with the foundation of C.

> C
> C & E
> C & G
> E & C (octave)
> E & D
> D & B
> C & F
> F & A

Having concentrated on one octave and tuned the naturals in that, you can proceed downwards from the 'middle C', and then upwards to the treble. You can do this easily by tuning notes in octave unison from the foundation notes you have already established in the centre of the piano harp. At this point, go back and check through the first octave to see that it is still in tune. Having applied tension to the wrest-plank, it may have warped slightly, so flattening the pitch of the notes. If this has happened, re-tune it to the same principles.

Now you can tune the sharps and any flats. Few of the small pianos are fully chromatic, that is to say few of them have all thirteen notes in the scale and so you will only have to bother with perhaps F♯ and G♯ and C♯.

Having tuned the sharps and flats in the foundation octave, tune those in the octaves above and below. If you have restrung the harp, it is better to set the instrument on one side for a day or two and allow the strings to stretch and the frame to warp.

Do remember one of the fundamentals of piano tuning and that is that the tuning lever has to be treated gently when 'pulling up' a string. The higher up the scale you go, the greater the tension of the strings relative to their length and gauge and also the less you must turn the lever to adjust them. Also, because the string is in two parts (the part between the wrest-pin and the bridge and that between the bridge and the hitch-pin), it is necessary to over-tighten the string a semi-tone and then bring it down to the correct pitch to help to even out the tension in the two halves. Even so, a piano needs frequent adjustment until it will hold its tune for a reasonable length of time and this is because the bridge pins effectively break the string into two lengths and by tightening on one end it takes a while for both halves to assume the same tension.

As I have said, a treatise of piano tuning here is unwise. To tune a concert grand requires a practised ear and several years of training. Because you can tune a barrel piano does not mean you are a piano tuner. You are an amateur and may remain so for good! I recommend your reading the little book *How to Tune a Piano* by H. Staunton Woodman. Before passing over tuning, I would add that the barrel piano, with its wooden frame, will not hold its tune for long. I expect to have to tune my own instrument at least once a week, particularly if it is in regular use since the act of hammering a string helps to stretch the string and loosen the wrest-pins a fraction. Not that you will have to lay your foundations all over again—it is just a question of a little polishing up the pitch here and there and need take no more than fifteen minutes.

Next you must service the key-frame. The Hicks and Distin type used very long, thin, brass springs on the hammers—shown in the illustration—and these frequently become brittle with age and disintegrate. Whilst a very good temporary repair is the ubiquitous rubber band, this is neither permanent nor practical and you should make new springs. Use the thinnest possible music wire which is called 'oo' in music wire gauge or ·oo8 inch in diameter and wrap your new spring around a piece of 16 s.w.g. piano-wire obtainable from a model maker's store. Ideally, you should hold the thick wire in the chuck of a slow-turning drill and wind on the music wire to make a tight, even-coiled spring of sufficient length (about $\frac{1}{2}$ inch less than the overall length between hammer and spring-peg). Slide the new spring off the wire mandrel. Form the loop ends and fit the new spring, noting that at the hammer end it is fixed with a thread loop. If the loop is broken, make a new one of button-thread poked through with a needle and knotted into place.

All the hammers should have the same spring tension—this is important. When the springs have become weak, either shorten them if they will take such treatment without breaking, or make new ones. See that the hammers move freely in their slots in the frame. Do not remove them unless absolutely necessary (this is achieved by withdrawing the hinge wire) as this will necessitate the probable undoing of all the springs, risking breakage. If the hammers are stiff, pump powdered graphite into the gaps each side to lubricate. *NEVER USE OIL OR GREASE* —this will clog them even worse and attract dust and dirt. The ideal graphite to use is that sold by locksmiths in a plastic puff-can and intended for freeing and lubricating door locks. It is marketed under the trade name Foliac.

Now look at the hammer heads. If they are leather-covered, see that the leather is properly attached—it often springs away at the top and bottom of the hammer. If the leather is badly hardened and grooved where it has been in contact with the music strings, then you may be able to tease it with a wire brush (on larger hammers you can 'needle' the felt). If not, then it is better to replace all the leathers.

See that the frame hinge-pivot supports are not loose and at the same time see that the strip steel spring in the bottom of the case, which pushes the frame out from the back, is in good order.

A frequent point of wear and damage are the hammer-tails. These are hardened steel and are very brittle—they may be bent slightly but respond to rough treatment by breaking off. Once broken flush with the hammer heel, it is highly unlikely that you will be able to get the broken piece out even by using watchmaker's pliers. This is because the metal rusts into the wood. The repair scheme is to make a new tail out of hard steel. You can use a 2-inch domestic wire-nail for this. First of all, heat it blood red and then, holding it with pliers, hammer it until it is evenly flattened to about $\frac{1}{16}$ inch thickness for a distance of about $\frac{3}{4}$ inch from the end. Cut this to the shape shown in the sketch and file the ends up true. Drill a $\frac{1}{16}$-inch hole in the hammer-body *immediately* above the broken piece and drive in the new tail. The square section of the tail in the round hold will ensure a tight fit. Support the back of the hammer properly otherwise it will break as you hammer in the steel. Line up all the tails so that they are (a) all straight and in line horizontally; and (b) extend from the hammer ends at right-angles to the axis of the hammers.

Refit the hammer frame and reconnect the linkage which moves the frame out of the way whilst changing the tune.

The next stage is the barrel. If it is dusty and dirty, then you must first brush it all over with a stiff brush to remove loose dirt. Then wash the barrel by brushing it with benzine applied

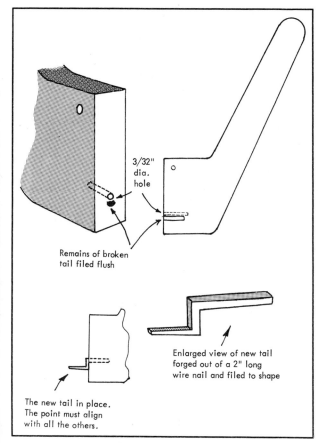

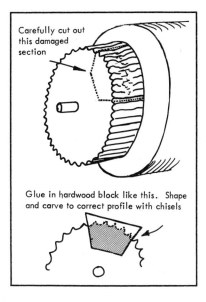

3/32"
dia.
hole

Remains of broken
tail filed flush

Enlarged view of new tail
forged out of a 2" long
wire nail and filed to shape

The new tail in place.
The point must align
with all the others.

Fig. 39. How to fit new hammer tails

Carefully cut out
this damaged
section

Glue in hardwood block like this. Shape
and carve to correct profile with chisels

Fig. 40. Repairs to barrel teeth. On larger
street pianos, the barrel cog was frequently
cast in the form of an iron ring screwed on
to the wooden barrel

liberally to the surface. Remember benzine is highly inflammable. I do not recommend petrol for this purpose since this leaves a deposit on the paper covering to the barrel. If the barrel is fitted into a carrier, check that this is not loose or broken and make good any slack joints. See that the carrier slides easily in the rails provided for it in the bottom of the case. Check that the tune changing stud is tightly fixed to the barrel.

Any badly-bent barrel pins should now be straightened with fine, flat pliers. The pins were almost always made of thick, fairly soft, brass wire, so there is little danger of their breaking off.

At this point, carry out any final treatment of the case which you think necessary. To finish the cases, French polish or wax polish should be used rather than paint or varnish.

Refit the brass-work to the case (tune-change knife and so on), refit the crank-handle and worm-drive shaft, firmly screwing its block to the case. See to it that the sprung, adjustable bearing piece for the inside bearing of the worm-shaft is working properly—this is intended to diminish wear and tear on the barrel cog.

One tricky job may yet remain to be done to the barrel. Sometimes the wooden barrel cog-teeth become worn away. Where worm has infested the barrel, the cog-teeth may have been weakened so much that they have crumbled to a useless state. Where the cog is extensively crumbled, then you will be far better off to have a new cog fitted. There is a firm of cabinet makers in London who have made some excellent new cogs for the barrels of one of Dr de Vere Green's barrel organs (pipe organs!) and they can make such cogs for all wooden barrels. However, any skilled cabinet-maker should be able to do these for you. He will want the barrel, though, and you should first of all show him the pins, tell him how fragile they are—and then wrap the barrel in thick, foam-plastic wadding before handing it over.

Where the cogs are only partly worn, you can make a new insert yourself, spiling off the profile for the new piece from part of the existing cog. Where one or two teeth only are damaged, you can cut in a new tooth by notching the cog and gluing in a strip of straight-grained ash, carving it to shape when set. The illustration shows these steps clearly.

Fit the barrel back into the piano, seeing that it is located properly in the bearing provided for the brass pivots at each side. The right-hand bearing is in the barrel access door. If these bearings are loose or sloppy, then the instrument will not work properly and you should have new ones made to fit into the woodwork. There should be about $\frac{1}{64}$ inch maximum side play in the bearings—some play is not only unavoidable but actually desirable otherwise the access door cannot be angled into its location when supporting the barrel bearing.

Check two things at this point—first that the key-frame does in fact clear the barrel pins when in the proper position, and secondly that the key-frame is parallel to the barrel and not leaning closer to one end than the other. If the former applies, you must adjust the linkage and probably make a new connecting link of slightly different size. If the latter is the case, then there are two small wooden blocks in the case-bottom against which the key-frame is encouraged to rest by its spring. One or both of these may be missing, or they may need replacing. This is easy—they are only small pieces of $\frac{1}{2}$ inch square lumber.

With the tune-selector knife engaged in the first slot in the barrel stud, see that the hammer-tails are in line with the pins. Play the instrument and see that it performs a recognizable tune and is not in fact playing part of two tunes at once. On some instruments, there is a small screw through the side of the case with which the key-frame can be moved laterally just sufficient to bring the hammer-tails into register with the barrel pins. Where this is not fitted, you must pack one or the other of the key-frame pivots with a thin washer to move the frame over a little.

It is quite likely that the instrument will sound very tinny and devoid of resonance. This is because the hammers instead of just striking the strings and springing back clear of them, are remaining in contact after striking, so muting the strings. Earlier I mentioned the importance of having all the hammer springs of the same strength so that the hammers all offered the same resistance to the barrel pins on the hammer-tails. Now you must ensure that the hammers, when at rest, are not touching the strings. As the hammer-heads are fixed to stiff wires which pierce the hammer block, all you have to do is to bend the hammers to achieve a nominal clearance of about one-sixteenth of an inch. When bending the hammers, bend the wire by holding the end of the wire close to the hammer block and do not, for example, take hold of the hammer-head and try to use it to lever the wire. This will split the head and can crack the block. Bend only the wire.

At this point the piano will begin to produce acceptable music. Bear in mind that the hammer-tails must lie in a straight line parallel to the axis of the barrel both in plan and elevation, that the pins must be straight in the barrel and that the hammer-tails must all be firm in their blocks.

The last job on the mechanism is to damp off the 'dead' portion of the music strings above the bridge. This is done by threading cotton tape through the strings as shown in the illustration (Fig. 38). Use $\frac{5}{8}$ inch or $\frac{3}{4}$ inch wide cotton bias binding and, to match the original, in red or crimson. The tape is easily threaded with a wire hook. The fish-mouth ends serve both for decoration and to prevent fraying.

Your portable barrel piano should now play perfectly. Where a damper is fitted, this is usually nothing more complicated than a round wooden rod traversing the strings just above the hammers and carrying in a slot along its length a strip of felt. The rod, protruding through the case side, has a knob by which it can be turned to press the felt strip on to the strings. You may have to replace tattered or moth-eaten felt here. Some pianos were also equipped with two small bells let into the sound-board and struck by the two left-hand hammers. There was usually a method of disconnecting these consisting of another knob on the case side which rotated a U-shaped wire bracket against the relevant hammers, so pushing them clear of the barrel pins which controlled them.

I have so far dealt with the portable piano and in some considerable detail, to boot. Having mastered the action of the little piano and having understood both the principles and practice of overhaul and repair of such instruments, it is but a small step to the much larger, street barrel pianos, café or clockwork pianos and piano orchestrions. All contrive to achieve the same end—the striking of strings by hammers controlled from pins on a barrel. And all may be treated by the intelligent application of the foregoing. There are notable differences and some important points to watch, so let us now look at the popular street piano of the type usually seen on a handcart.

In an earlier chapter, we saw how the tune-changing of the large piano was effected using a progressive snail cam to work the barrel 'odd numbers' one way and then back on the 'even numbers'. Because the instrument is so much bigger than the small piano, it is far, far easier for it to get out of adjustment, out of register and, consequently, out of order.

To strip the instrument, first of all you must open the door in the right end of the case. This door is dowelled into the case at the bottom and is locked in the proper position by one or sometimes two stout, wooden turn-buttons. The door also carries a stiff leaf-spring to hold the barrel firmly against the change cams at the other end of the case.

On the left-hand side of the case will be found a handle. The action of turning this handle is twofold. As you can see from Figure 17, it works exactly the same way as a Geneva stop-work on a clock spring motor. One rotation of the handle indexes the snail cam one position. However, as well as doing this, it also lifts the key-frame away from the barrel for the duration of the critical lateral shift of the barrel from one snail cam to the next, so avoiding the chance of damage to the barrel pins and the hammer-tails. Thanks to this contrivance, it is possible to change tunes in the middle of playing the instrument without fear of damage, since the key-frame is only lowered to the barrel pins again when the lateral shift is completed. Set this handle in such a position that the key-frame is at the limit of its travel away from the barrel and see that, in fact, the pins are clear. If not, then you can wedge the frame further away by using one or more large screwdrivers pushed between case block and key-frame at each end.

There is no knife or bolt to secure the barrel—it is now quite free to be removed. Some barrels originally had carriers or cradles but these may have been lost or discarded. The removal of the barrel is best achieved with an extra person to guide the far end of the barrel whilst you gently lift and pull from the right end. Watch that you do not lift the barrel so much that the pins catch on the access door surround. With the barrel out of the piano, lay it on the floor, preferably on sacks or cloth so that the pins will not be damaged.

To remove the key-frame, the first step is to take off the tension spring which connects the left end of the frame to the left side of the case. This spring is looped around a stout wire lug threaded into the metal capping of the key-frame. Hold this lug firmly in the pliers and rotate it anti-clockwise for 180° so that it is in line with the loop of the spring. Put a piece of cloth over the spring and hold the coiled part firmly whilst springing the loop from the lug with a screwdriver. The spring is then easily unhooked from the case side. This is shown in Fig. 17.

Remove the two large wire springs which hold the key-frame in contact with the tune-change cam. These stout wire springs usually have their top ends bent over to form a handle and they are fixed to the case as shown in the drawing. Hold the spring by the handle, push it forward, move it towards the centre of the piano to disengage the screwhead locating its upper portion, let it back and then jigger it off the large centre pivot-screw which passes through its two or three centre coils. Remember which spring came from which end—it will save time and frustration on re-assembly.

Now unscrew the two small capping pieces from the key-frame pivots. The frame is now free to be lifted out. However, it is comparatively heavy, awkward and a tight fit in the case and, whilst with practice you can take it out single-handed, you would be better advised to have someone to help. Ensure that the hammers do not jam between the strings as you get it free and, most important, avoid the hammer-tails as not only do they have a certain predilection for catching in the clothing, but they also may be murderously sharp if the piano has had a lot of use, and can slice the flesh.

Pianos fitted with tremolo arrangements are but a little more complicated to strip and the techniques are largely a matter of common sense since I assume none to be foolhardy enough to meddle with even the simplest mechanism unless they can recognize a screw, a bolt or a wire and take the necessary action to suit the task.

Clear away any broken strings and proceed to give the inside of the case a thorough clean. Where the harp is not in bad condition, you can, as before, proceed immediately with re-assembly. However, as with the smaller piano, we must consider every eventuality in the process of resurrection. Where the strings are all present, but rusted, you can largely restore the tone by giving them a stiff brushing with the wire brush. However, bad rusting does really call for re-stringing, particularly in the extreme treble register where the strings, even at their best, tend to sound 'dead'. Rusting deadens their tone still further.

The stringing on these pianos is different from that of the smaller ones and tends more to follow the styles used in the conventional piano. Better made instruments have strings which end only at the wrest-pin, the other end forming a 'U' turn round the bottom peg and then coming back up to the wrest-plank again. This means that one broken string must call for the replacement of the adjacent string also, since it is one continuous piece of wire. These pianos also feature a continuous pressure bar or agraffe which holds all the strings down firmly before the wrest-pins and ensures contact with the first bridge. The illustration Fig. 41 shows these points.

Bass strings—the wrapped ones—are single strands per run with eye ends on the bottom pegs. Badly corroded or broken ones must be replaced with new ones. Again, use the old one, where present, as a pattern for the string-maker to copy.

Examine the wrest-plank. Street pianos were exposed to all kinds of weather including rain and snow. The most highly stressed part of the instrument was the harp itself and changes in temperature and humidity caused the total force of the string pull to vary. Whilst this was contemporarily noticed as 'going out of tune', the effects may remain today as a cracked or split wrest-plank. A plank in this condition will neither be stiff enough to resist the string pull nor

132

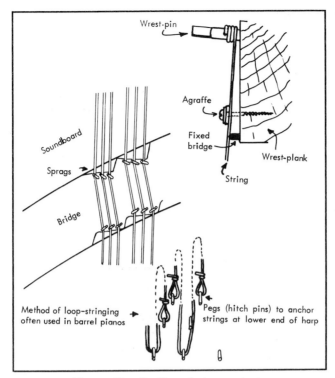

Fig. 41. Detail of barrel piano stringing

will it keep the wrest-pins tightly in place. It must be repaired.

Let us first of all consider how the wrest-plank is made. Most were made of well-seasoned hardwood faced with a veneer about one-sixteenth of an inch thick. The grain of both veneer and plank naturally ran across the top of the harp. The effect of having two, three and even four or more lines of wrest-pins closely spaced along it served literally as the thin end of a wedge hell-bent on splitting the timber. I must admit to having had the horrifying and frustrating experience of seeing a wrest-plank on a newly strung and tuned piano, gradually start to split and, as I watched powerless to do a thing, the crack spread across the centre two feet of timber!

Although the repair necessitated by this catastrophe is a time-consuming job, it is not impossible. The job calls for the clamping together permanently of the top and bottom portions of the wrest-plank over the centre portion. It is extremely doubtful that the split will extend anywhere near the sides of the harp since the wrest-plank is supported at each end by the side posts of the frame. To do the job properly, we must use coach bolts, a length of $1\frac{1}{2}$-inch angle iron (yes! this is no delicate watchmaker's job!), a drill, a brace and bit, a rule, a steady hand and a selection of large washers and suitable nuts.

Begin by slackening off all the piano strings so that there is absolutely no pull on the wrest-pins. Pins which have been loosened by the split or which may even have fallen out must be put carefully back into place and left there. Now strip the back off the piano—this is usually diagonal boarding, screwed to the harp to keep it from distorting, although on some cheaper instruments the frame is held rigid by the boundless faith put into his brainchild by the builder—and but a piece of blue cloth covers the back of the instrument. It should perhaps be

133

added that the sound-board and the piano back are two different things. The sound-board should be left in place and only the back-boarding, where present, removed.

We want to drill a number of holes right down through the wrest-plank from the top to the bottom. Because the wrest-pins are so closely spaced, we cannot drill between them, but must drill clear of them. Take out a pin, measure the length of the portion which fits into the plank, add $\frac{5}{8}$ inch and mark a line across the horizontal top face of the wrest-plank which is this total dimension away from the string face of the plank. The illustration shows this.

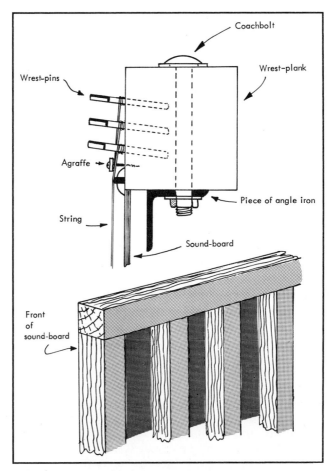

Fig. 42. Repairing the wrest-plank. Better-made pianos had their wrest-planks braced with stout vertical timbers, like this, at the back. The enormous load of the strings tends to twist the plank off its supports

The plank is surprisingly deep and thick; in fact one wonders, on seeing it exposed for the first time, how on earth it could ever split. This demonstrates the terrific load of the strings.

If we drill the bolt holes through first, then loose chippings can enter the gap where the split is, so making it impossible to close it up tightly. Obtain five or six really large, tough G clamps. These are expensive and you will probably find it more practical to beg or borrow some from a local joiners works or a garage. They must have a throat of at least four inches and a gap of twelve inches.

Lay the piano on its back across two trestles so that you can comfortably get to both front and back (now top and bottom) faces of the wrest-plank. Mix up a jam-jar full of synthetic resin adhesive such as 'Aerolite' which has the added merit of being colourless and thus will not stain the wood around the joint. Tend to make the resin mixture a little thinner than normal. Run this mixture into the splits and work it well in with a thin piece of metal to avoid any air bubbles. The glue should be applied liberally and, as it drains into the crack, more applied.

Using stout pieces of timber as caul blocks to prevent the clamps cutting into the plank, fit the clamps along the timber. Do these clamps up really tight and make sure that the splits close up completely. Bear in mind that these synthetic resin glues have a brief 'shuffling' time before they begin curing and during which the joint must be clamped up. Take a damp cloth and wipe off all the excess glue squeezed out of the cracks on the face of the plank. You must now leave the job clamped up for at least twenty-four hours.

At the end of this period, remove the clamps and prepare for the drilling to take the bolts. With the brace and bit, drill $\frac{1}{2}$-inch holes down through the plank, keeping the holes straight, parallel and about six inches apart. It is usual to put about five or six such holes, equally-spaced through the wood. I must repeat the importance of clamping everything up tightly and completing the gluing before boring these holes.

Now carefully mark out and drill your length of angle iron to match the holes in the plank. Aim to have the iron with the right-angled face nearest the sound-board—this gives even better support. Because it is unlikely that you have been able to bore the holes absolutely accurately through the wood, the holes in the angle iron may be slightly larger to ensure an easy fit.

Put the bolts in the holes so that the heads will be on the top of the plank. Put a large washer—about 2 inches in diameter and $\frac{1}{8}$ inch thick—under the head of the bolt, and tighten all the nuts under the iron bar to the same tension. The job is now complete. When you come to try to turn the wrest-pins, particularly those in the split which have been in contact with the glue, they will at first be extremely stiff, but will soon loosen sufficiently to work under the tuning lever. If they are greased in any way prior to gluing, then they will be too loose to hold the string tension.

Whilst the back panels are off the piano, make good any split in the sound-board as described earlier. See that the bridge is not cracked or loose and replace any sprags with headless panel pins one inch long, hammered in at the correct angle.

Restringing and tuning follows, after which weave a strip of thin felt through the string beneath the bridge to deaden them.

At this point it is as well to complete whatever case finishing you may require. Many of these street pianos were varnished and imitation-grained and most received so many coats of paint and varnish during their lives that a covering of paint one-sixteenth of an inch thick is not uncommon. A few were done up very attractively with enamels and decorative lining with barrows to match but these are the exception rather than the rule. There was nothing special about the wood used, so do not enthusiastically scrape down to bare wood and expect to find anything more exotic than fairly clean pine. One of the best modern treatments I have seen on a street piano is one which probably demands far more work than any other—thorough sanding to a dead smooth surface followed by a black mirror finish like a normal piano. Since the case-work is usually well knocked about, chipped and split, such a labour of love is seldom justifiable and the best and simplest finish is probably to strip down to the bare wood, apply a dark stain and then several coats of copal varnish. If the final coat is slightly matted when thoroughly hardened using a fine wire wool, it will take a final coat of household wax polish very nicely.

Now to tackle the key-frame. There can be more work to do on this than on the rest of the instrument put together, so begin by examining carefully to detect the following points: (1) broken or bent hammer-tails; (2) broken hammer blocks; (3) loose hammer-head wires; (4) bent or damaged hammer-heads; (5) loose, missing or badly ribbed felts on the hammers; (6) weak, broken or missing hammer springs.

Where hammer-tails are bent out of alignment, they can usually be eased back into place by gently bending them with a pair of large pliers. Where they are broken off, try to pull out the stump but do not attempt to 'dig' it out—if it cannot be got at or will not respond to a reasonable amount of force, file it flush with the hammer block and leave it. Earlier I described how to make new hammer-tails. The same instructions apply here, save that the pins are larger and a little longer. Be careful driving these new pins in—it is very easy to shear the hammer block right off.

The hammer block may be broken through shearing as described above. If so, and the two mating faces are complete and clean, repair is not too difficult. You will need to obtain two long, thin, brass screws, preferably round-headed and $1\frac{1}{2}$ inches in length by $\frac{3}{32}$ inch in shank diameter. Have a helper hold the top half of the hammer block firmly in place and drill two $\frac{1}{16}$ inch diameter holes from the underside (see the illustration Fig. 43). The holes should be the same depth as the length of the screws. Now drill both holes $\frac{3}{32}$ inch in diameter for a depth of not quite an inch. This ensures that the screws will hold the wood without expanding it and so causing the hammer to bind in its slot in the key-frame. Apply a little glue to the mating wood faces—not so much that it will be forced out in excess to cement the hammer block into the key-frame. Work the two parts together a little to exclude air bubbles and then screw up tightly. Wipe excess glue off the flanks and put a thin strip of waxed paper between the hammer block and key-frame slot on both sides so that they will not stick whilst drying out.

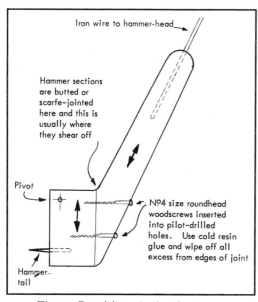

Iron wire to hammer-head

Hammer sections are butted or scarfe-jointed here and this is usually where they shear off

Pivot

Nº4 size roundhead woodscrews inserted into pilot-drilled holes. Use cold resin glue and wipe off all excess from edges of joint

Hammer-tail

Fig. 43. Repairing a broken hammer

The wire extensions from the block which carry the hammer-heads sometimes break off or come loose in the block. They are made of soft iron wire. Where they have just come loose, remove the wire and fill the hole with 'Araldite' adhesive and replace the wire, wiping off excess adhesive before it sets. Where the wire has broken off, do not attempt to remove the broken piece in the hammer block. Remove the hammer-head from the broken wire—it is usually threaded on—and make a new wire. This should be soft wire, as the original, or can be mild steel. A highly suitable wire is that used by oxy-acetylene welders as a filler rod and it comes in a number of thicknesses, one of which is bound to do the job. Thread the end to take the hammer. Drill the hammer block with a hole to take the wire. This hole should be at least $1\frac{1}{2}$ inches deep and must be in front of the old wire and as close to it as possible. See that the wire is the same shape as adjacent wires and that the hammer-head is at the right position and angle and then cement the wire into the hammer block and secure the hammer-head with Araldite.

The hammer-heads usually have felt or leather covers like normal pianos. These vary from maker to maker and most makers used plain wooden hammers of hardwood for the treble hammers or where a tremolo effect was fitted. However, the bass and tenor hammers were invariably felted. The intervening years often cause the felt to spring free from the wooden part of the hammer-head and this must be glued back and held down until set, using a large spring paper-clip. Where the part of the hammer which touches the musical strings is compressed or deeply ribbed, then you should tease up the felt with a small wire brush, moved up and down on the felt in line with the hammer, not across the face, otherwise the felt will spread.

The hammer springs are next for examination. These are like large safety pins and can be removed, if necessary, with a pair of long-nosed pliers. Any missing or broken ones must be replaced using thick piano wire obtainable from model engineers' shops. Draw back all the hammers and see that approximately the same resistance and force applies to each one. Any slow or sluggish hammers will affect the playing of the piano and, where they are stiff through friction in the frame rather than flaccid springs, you should liberally apply powdered graphite to the hammer flanks. Remember, never use oil or grease.

Between the hammers and the key-frame, there is a strip of felt upon which the hammers sit when at rest. If this felt is hardened or moth-eaten, the hammers will not sit evenly at rest and, more important, the hammer-tails may scrape the tune barrel. To examine the felt, hold all the hammers forward with a strip of stiff wood. Tease up the felt with a wire brush if it can be re-used, otherwise strip it off and replace it with a length of $\frac{3}{16}$ inch thick medium piano felt available from a piano sundries dealer.

Finally, look over the key-frame for other damage or defects. The extension lever on the left side which engages with the tune changing mechanism must be a good tight fit; it is screwed to the main key-frame member.

Before putting the key-frame back into the piano, check over the tune-changing mechanism and see that it works properly. This should be lubricated with a good motor grease. If the bearing for the changing handle is worn so that the handle is sloppy, take off the handle, remove the shaft and make a new bearing.

Replace the key-frame on the half trunnions in the case sides, screw back the trunnion-bearing capping pieces, replace the two stout wire springs which press the frame against the changing mechanism and reconnect the tension spring which pulls the frame up against the left side. Hook this over the lug on the key-frame and turn the lug back clockwise to hold it securely. Turn the tune-changing handle to see that the mechanism works properly and then set it so that the key-frame is held out in the between-tune position so the barrel can be replaced.

Treatment of the barrel is more or less as already described, except that, being bigger and stouter, the wooden cog is less likely to have succumbed to wear. Any woodworm can be treated and any bent pins straightened.

Gently slide the barrel back into the instrument, taking care not to catch the pins on the access door or on the hammer-tails. At the end of its travel, check to see that the arbor is located properly on the changing cam and that the drive-worm is correctly engaged in the barrel cog. The end of the barrel may need to be lifted slightly to get it into the proper position.

See that the stout leaf-spring in the access door which pushes the barrel against the change mechanism is free and able to do its job. A light film of grease should be applied with the finger to the working face of this through the hole on the inside. Note that this end bearing of the barrel is adjustable on the access door, for the wooden block, screwed inside the door to support the barrel arbor, can be loosened and moved up and down and side to side a fraction. Unless playing the piano shows that the barrel is in the wrong position, it is extremely unwise to upset the setting of this bearing, so leave it well alone.

Re-fit the door and lock it with the turn-buttons. Let back the key-frame with the change lever, and play the piano. At the end-of-tune position, stop and check that when the hammers are at rest they are just short of the strings, otherwise, as before, the strings will be muted. They are easily bent into the right position.

The piano must now be put into registration, so wind the tune-change handle until the barrel is at its farthest-left position. This should mean that the farthest-right pins are now in the playing position—play the piano and check. If they are not, then the key-frame must be moved laterally, using the horizontal, eye-ended adjuster at the left end of it. This must only be done at the end-of-tune position otherwise pins and tails will be broken. Once the last tune on the right of the barrel has been accurately registered, turn the tune-changer until the barrel is at its farthest to the right, so bringing the last set of pins on the left end of the barrel under the hammer-tails. Play this one and make any necessary adjustments to the lateral position of the key-frame. Note that quite frequently you must strike a practical medium between all the tunes on the barrel so that they all play with more or less equal success.

The fore and aft position of the key-frame is also important. If the hammer-tails are too close to the barrel, rapidly-repeated notes will not be sounded properly, as there is insufficient space or time for the hammer to fly to the strings before the tail catches the next barrel pin. If the hammer-tails are too far away, then the sound will be weak and sporadic. Adjustment for this is by the two vertical, eye-ended adjusters, one each end of the key-frame. Make sure that the key-frame is parallel with the face of the barrel—a visual check, looking down behind the barrel, will show this.

It will probably be necessary to polish up the tuning at this point. It is advisable with these instruments to 'stretch' the octaves a shade in the extreme treble; this means tuning the top four or five notes a *fraction* sharp. Because these top strings are so short, they tend to sound percussive and their often indeterminate tone can be helped by this marginal sharpening. Complete the job by weaving a strip of thin red felt through the dead portion of the strings between the wrest-pins and the top bridge and also between the bottom pins and the sound-board bridge.

When tackling an 'automatic' piano—that is, one driven by a clockwork motor and probably coin-operated, the mechanism is basically the same, with the exception that there is no crank-handle to play the instrument, but an additional handle is fixed usually to the left side of the case, to wind the clockwork.

One word of warning here. The springs used in clockwork pianos are very powerful indeed and any unskilled attempt at dismantling the motor can result in the release of a coil of steel of such power that it could cause very serious injury. If the spring is broken, and unless you are a competent engineer, I do not advise you to try to repair it yourself. It is safer to give it to some small engineering-workshop to put it right. Usually, when a spring does break, it fails at either the inside end (the piece which hooks on to the arbor) or the outer end where it is looped and riveted round one of the assembly posts of the motor cage.

The motor should be cleaned and this can usually be done without taking it from the instrument. Do not try to dismantle the gear train and the endless screw carrying the governor. If you tamper with this, any power left in the motor will immediately be relased and the least that can happen is stripped gears and a broken spring. If it is necessary for some reason to dismantle the governor, then let the motor run right down against its Geneva stopwork and only remove the governor when there is no longer any force in the motor to turn it. Lubricate the motor with grease.

Coin-operated automatics are in no way complex devices. The coin drops down through the piano in a chute until it finally falls into a pan or other form of receptacle which is counter-balanced on an arm. When the coin lands in the receptacle, it tilts the mounting lever, freeing a detent from a check on the governor. Automatics usually play twice (occasionally three times) for one coin and, after the set number of turns, the coin is ejected and the receptacle and its lever return to the 'stop' position, so stopping the works. The number of revolutions and the instruction to start or stop the mechanism come entirely from the motor unit and not from the barrel or any part of it, so it is important that the barrel be inserted in exactly the right position. If this is not done, the music will stop and start in the middle of the tune. Examination of the barrel will show one point on its periphery where there is a clear line along it, devoid of pins. This is the start/stop position and usually you will see also small prick marks or ink dashes to mark the alignment of the hammer-tails at the start of the first tune position.

Positioning the barrel is thus very important. Instead of being rotated by a wide, coarse-threaded wooden cog, the barrel carries on its left end a large diameter gear-wheel, compara-tively narrow, which meshes with a wide pinion carried in the top of the clockwork motor. (Note that I refer here to the more commn type of automatic with the motor fixed at the left end under the barrel; other types will be similar in general arrangement, although slightly different in detail.)

First see exactly where the stop/start position on the barrel is and gently slide the barrel into the case. You will need to lift up the left end of it to seat it on the drive pinion and at this point see that, when the key-frame is lowered into the playing position, the hammer-tails will fall more or less exactly into the centre of the 'no-man's-land' of the barrel. If it does not, then index the barrel one tooth at a time until this is reached—you can easily do this by repositioning the barrel (with the key-frame held clear, of course).

The final check on this positioning is to locate the barrel completely, that is, with the door closed to support the right-hand barrel arbor, and play the instrument. The music should stop exactly at the end-of-tune position with none of the hammer partly lifted.

If the piano plays too slowly or too fast, then you can regulate the speed by the adjustment of the collar which prevents the governor from flying out too far. To make the music play faster, you must allow the governor to fly out farther, so the collar is moved farther down the endless screw carrying the governor. To make the music slower, you must restrict the fly of the governor by moving the collar farther up the shaft.

In conclusion, we will examine some of the things which can go wrong with barrel pianos, both hand-turned and clockwork.

Piano will not play, although barrel is turning. Key-frame held off so that the hammer-tails are not engaging. Cause might be dirt, stiffness or the breakage of the springs which press the key-frame against the tune-changing trip lever.

Barrel will not turn, or turns sporadically when handle is turned to play. This means that the drive-worm on the handle shaft is slipping and can be due to badly-worn barrel cog teeth, or to the breakage of the spring-loaded inner bearing (on small pianos) allowing the drive shaft to ride up.

Clockwork piano plays jerkily. Spring not wound enough (or the Geneva stopwork is wrongly positioned so that the motor cannot be wound enough, or the spring has been shortened/replaced by one too weak). Might also be that the key-frame is too closely engaged with the barrel, so putting a very great load on both the barrel pins and the hammer-tails.

Music barrel shows fresh scoring from hammer-tails. Key-frame too close to barrel or the hammer-rest felt has become hard and compressed, so allowing the odd hammer to come too far back. Rectification is to adjust the positioning of the key-frame or remove it altogether and re-felt the rest rail.

Instrument plays discordantly. Key-frame not in register with barrel pins or the hammer-tails are bent, so picking up pins from the next tune. Check the hammer-tails carefully for vertical and lateral alignment. Note that all the tails must also be exactly the same length otherwise some notes will sound late due to the hammer being held back longer by the barrel pins. The barrel pins must also be straight.

Instrument plays nine tunes perfectly and the last (or first) tune completely unmelodiously. This means that the key-frame is registered one complete tune out of position and you must take the barrel back to the first tune position, check the registration, then repeat the checks at the last tune position. This is a very common fault with pianos where a previous repairer has failed to appreciate what he has done wrong—or omitted to do.

Clockwork piano plays with excessive mechanical noise. Badly-worn gears in motor drive or, most likely, the stop/start detent is not disengaging fully from the governor sprag, causing a rapid 'tick' as the piano plays. Adjustment is to regulate the coin-tray arm or bend the governor sprag slightly.

Repetitive notes do not sound—hammers stop short of strings. This means that the key-frame is too close to the barrel. Adjust the two vertical, eye-ended adjusters. Note that, on tremolo arrangements, every note has its own individual hammer adjustment.

Music sounds dead, particularly in the treble. This may be due to very rusted strings which are now useless and must be replaced, or due to the fact that the hammers are striking the strings too close to the bridge. It is practice for the hammer to strike the strings at a distance between one-seventh and one-eighth of their length (this is the 'speaking length' between the bridges, of course), to produce the best and purest tone. Demonstrate this on a string near the centre of the piano by plucking the string at various positions along its length. Barrel piano makers were not so fussy about this fact, but a dead string usually means that you must make the hammer hit the string a little farther out from its end. Try resetting the hammer by bending the wire slightly whilst maintaining the correct clearance between the hammer and the string when at rest—about one-sixteenth of an inch.

Music sounds dead and tinny in places. Check the hammer clearance. If the hammers are actually touching the strings when at rest, the string is muted and cannot sing out. Bring all hammers to within one-sixteenth inch of the strings.

If you have understood all these points, and appreciate how the barrel piano works, then you can confidently tackle similar barrel-operated percussion instruments. One golden rule, and this applies to all mechanisms. It is better to spend time thinking about the job carefully before starting work than to dash ahead and risk irrevocable damage by over-enthusiasm and lack of understanding.

CHAPTER 7

How the Player Piano Works

I T is not my intention to describe in detail the workings of the ordinary piano (which is the basis of the player-piano) for such description has no place in a work of the present compass. This information is readily available from more specialized reference works. I must therefore assume the reader to have a basic knowledge of the action of the piano, both in upright and in grand format, and to possess a fair idea as to 'how it ticks'.

Before going deeply into the whys and wherefores of the pneumatic action, however, it is as well to have a brief look at the piano action and just see which parts have to be automated by the pneumatic system. The illustration of the upright action, reproduced on this page, shows

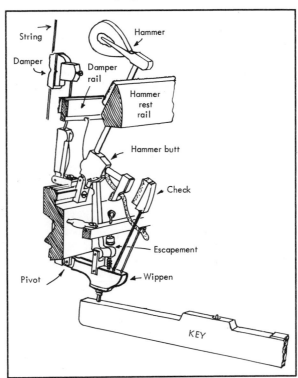

Fig. 44. The basic action
of an upright piano

the various bits and pieces which go to making one key action. You can see how, when the pianist depresses a key on the keyboard, the action is set into motion, causing the hammer to fly forward and strike the string. Two important features to observe are the rest-rail and the damper rail. Even if the pianist holds the key down, the hammer does not stay in contact with the string, but falls back, clear of it (observe here that when I refer to 'string' I am using this collectively to refer to one note on the piano which may consist of two, three or even four separate wires or strings tuned in unison). By holding down the key, all the pianist succeeds in doing is to hold off the damper which is provided to mute the string before it may be struck again. In holding off the damper, the string is permitted to vibrate for longer duration than if the pianist were to play the note *staccato*. All the dampers can be moved individually in this way, working separately for each note. But all the dampers are freely located upon a rail which itself can be moved away from the string. The action which moves the dampers collectively is called the 'sustaining pedal'—the right one at the lower front of the ordinary piano—and which is so often miscalled the 'loud pedal'.

The rest-rail is the second of our important features. This is simply the rail against which the individual hammers rest and it can be moved either away from the strings, so allowing the hammer to fly forward a good distance and hit the string hard, or moved closer so that the hammers have only a short distance to travel to do their work and thus hit the strings without great force. This action, controlled by the left-hand pedal at the lower front of the ordinary piano, is called the 'soft pedal'.

Another point has to be considered and that is that the pianist has two hands which normally each play on only half of the keyboard and he can also play loudly or softly by regulating the force with which he strikes the keys. He can also accentuate certain notes, even certain notes in an *arpeggio* or an *appoggiatura* and change with alacrity from delicate tones to strident ones or to *sostenuto*. All these features, separately and collectively, have to be capable of worthy reproduction using the pneumatic system.

As we shall see, the execution of these functions by mechanical means is quite easily achieved. But to return to the ordinary piano action once more, we must make sure that we understand exactly which parts of it we have to set in motion by our mechanical or pneumatic means. It is pointless to try to make something which will move the keys (assuming that we are thinking in terms of an inner player as compared with a piano-player), for the keys are, so to speak, a further step beyond the parts we want to move. The key is purely a lever to move the hammer action and the part we have to get at is the hammer action itself. If we want to modernize a steam locomotive, we find a fresh way to drive the wheels, not a better way to light the fire which heats the water which makes the steam which drives the wheels. One part of the hammer action lends itself admirably to taking both normal keyboard operation and mechanical inducement in its stride and this is the rocking lever which is called the wippen. Everything above the wippen is required to set in motion the sequence of string-hitting; everything below it is but a means of moving the wippen, which is the starting point of the chain of sequences ending with a string sounding.

The wippen is also convenient from another standpoint. It is at such a position that it can be pushed or pulled up without interfering with any other function of the piano and, most important, does not interfere with the manual use of the instrument at other times.

What we have now discovered are the parts of the action which must be moved and also the junction in the road from key to string at which we can build our pneumatic services.

Now we must look into the basic pneumatics and try to see just why the pneumatic player works, what it does and how it does it.

The player-piano in essence comprises an assortment of small functional devices connected to a chamber in which the air pressure has been reduced to below that of the surrounding atmosphere. Each device is operated by the controlled admittance of air through it and, because the atmospheric pressure is being allowed access to the reduced state of air pressure within, this air can be used to move a valve on its seat or to deflate a bellows to perform mechanical work, or to permit access of other components to the pressure variations taking place.

Expressed in even more simple terms, the player-piano is a machine containing a partial vacuum into which air is continually trying to find access. In entering the instrument, it is made to perform a mechanical function. Place a player-piano in an atmosphere which is itself a vacuum, or put it on the moon, and it will not work. Nature abhors a vacuum—and the player-piano needs to be able to create a partial vacuum in order to be able to work.

Air has one characteristic which is particularly important to us if we are to use it to power a piano. Regardless of its pressure, it will always fill a given space at an equal density. Suppose you have a box representing a one foot cube and into this you put a cubic foot of sand. The box will naturally be filled and the sand particles will be tightly packed together. Now supposing we empty out of the box three-quarters of the sand, the remaining sand will lie at the bottom of the box, its particles still tightly packed together, the rest of the box being 'empty'. Supposing that instead of sand we now fill our cubic foot box with air from the atmosphere—all we have to do is lift the lid and then close it again and we can be certain that the air around us is also in the box. The box is now full of air. If we now make the box air-tight and, using a pump, begin to draw the air out of the box, as we reduce its pressure relative to the atmosphere, the pressure of the air all over the inside of the box falls to an equal level. Air does not pile up, lie in masses of different density or behave in a lumpy way. Air will always fill the space allotted to it and fill it completely, regardless of its pressure and thus density.

So far, our demonstration of the properties of air has been theoretical, using a proper box. Now we can actually see this interesting property of air at work if, instead of having a box with fixed sides, a top and a bottom, we make one side into a movable diaphragm, or, better still, hinge that side along one edge and make a flexible bellows-type of wall between the edges of the side and the rest of the box. If we make a simple non-return valve, such as a leather flap on the inside to cover a small hole, and then blow air into that hole, the increased air pressure inside the box will push out the hinged side. If we now put our non-return valve on the outside of the hole, and suck air out of the box, the hinged side will collapse.

Air exists all around us at a constant pressure equalling about 14·75 lb/sq. inch. We are accustomed to this pressure and do not notice it. In the same way that deep sea fish are accustomed to the tremendous water pressures at the bottom of the sea and, when trawled to the surface, expand and actually explode, the human body, to a lesser extent, suffers extreme discomfort if the air pressure around it is greatly varied. High-flying airliners have to have pressurized cabins both to provide enough oxygen to breathe and also sufficient air so that the first symptoms of too low an air pressure—bleeding from the ears, nose and eyes—can be avoided. Divers quickly accustom themselves to the increased pressure on the sea-bed but, on returning to the surface, have to be re-accustomed slowly to normal pressure. From this we can see not only the importance of air to us to enable us to live, but also that air exerts a pressure.

We can demonstrate another aspect of air with a further piece of schoolboy science. Air can be made to move a cork in a flask or tube. If we take a flask and place a loose-fitting cork in the neck and then draw air out of the flask, the cork will move down the neck of the flask. If we

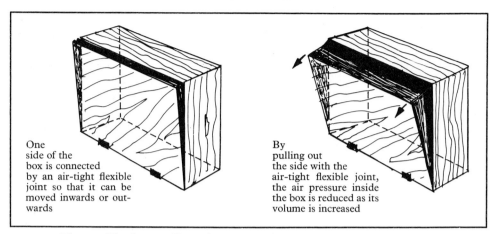

One side of the box is connected by an air-tight flexible joint so that it can be moved inwards or outwards

By pulling out the side with the air-tight flexible joint, the air pressure inside the box is reduced as its volume is increased

Fig. 45. The theory of how air pressure can be reduced in a player action

pump air into the flask, the cork will move upwards. It is this fervent desire of air for equality in pressure that causes this to happen. As air is drawn out of our flask, the remaining air is continually expanding to fill the space, rarifying as it does. The air the other side of the loose-fitting cork, however, is still at 14·75 lb/sq. inch and this pressure pushes the cork down to try to equalize the pressure.

A further vital point materializes here. If you place a vehicle having four smooth wheels on a smooth surface, it requires a certain initial effort to start it moving. This is required to over-come mechanical friction. One man can propel a large coal truck in the railway sidings by pushing it, yet it requires three or four men to set it going from a stationary position. Supposing that you put an object on a sloping surface, it does not immediately rush downwards, but stays put until the slope is increased beyond a certain point. These two examples illustrate the effect of friction and show that there is both a time lag between there being a change in a set of circumstances desired to affect equilibrium, and also an excess of power needed to initiate the change from immobility to motion.

Air is by no means so prone to the manifestations of friction. The moment there is a pressure variation at one point, the entire mass of air rapidly sets about adjusting itself either to equal pressure, or to a suitable volume to suit the pressure. A mass of air, suitably contained, can be made to do a surprising amount of work, even when the pressure differential from the surrounding air is only a matter of a few ounces per square inch.

It is thus not strictly true to say that a player-piano works by vacuum, for were there to be a complete vacuum within the instrument, the air pressure of the atmosphere would be so great as to implode the instrument, squeezing up all the tubes, compressing the air passages and chests, and achieving pressure equality in so doing. Of course, you could build a player mechanism so robustly that conditions of total vacuum might be achieved and utilized, but it is obviously unnecessary. The conditions, whereby the mechanism can and will play, are achieved by the development of a *partial* vacuum inside the instrument. The lower the air pressure inside (the greater the vacuum), the quicker will be the response of the instrument and the greater the power exerted by the pneumatic system on the hammers which strike the musical strings. Precise control of the processes of pressure-reduction within the instrument is thus very important to enable the artistic rendering of a piece of music.

144

We have seen that a high vacuum condition is not necessary to work a player-piano. Under ordinary conditions, the instrument will operate perfectly by the existence of a pressure difference of eight ounces per square inch, which is equivalent to less than a four percent vacuum. Thus only about one-thirtieth of the air inside the instrument must be withdrawn to set in motion the piano action and produce music of about middle strength. An audible sound can actually be achieved using a vacuum of only half this amount. The average player-piano is constructed with an air pump capable of operating for short periods of time at a suction of up to two pounds per square inch. This is far in excess of the amount needed under normal circumstances.

Paradoxically, we speak of the 'pressure' of a vacuum when really we mean the 'suction' of a vacuum. The pressure referred to here is the amount of pressure which the surrounding atmosphere is induced to offer to the mechanism, by virtue of there existing inside it a reduced state of pressure relative to the atmosphere. Thus a working pressure of two pounds per square inch is the same as a vacuum which produces a rarification of the air to two pounds per square inch below that of the atmosphere.

With a player-piano, the quantity of air to be moved is comparatively large and does tend to vary over a wide range according to the parts of the piano action which have to be moved at any one time. A loud, full chord, for example, will require the shifting of more air than, say, a *pianissimo* passage for a few short notes. The air pump employed is thus a slow-moving, low-pressure piece of apparatus. Its operation, in a piano controlled by the performers' feet, must not require excessive physical effort.

This air pump, commonly referred to as 'the bellows' but more properly termed 'the exhausters', consists, broadly, of a chamber having one wall arranged so that it can be moved inwards and outwards by a linkage from a foot-operated treadle. Assuming the chamber to be sealed, as the movable side is pulled outwards, so the air inside the chamber is rarified. The air in the chamber is thus at a lower pressure than the outside, free air, because it has been made to fill a larger area than the space it naturally filled at atmospheric pressure (Fig. 45). Supposing a pipe from the chamber is led to another, smaller bellows assembly, the air pressure difference in the inside of the chamber will also affect the bellows. This is illustrated in the accompanying Fig. 46 and represents the rudiments of the player action.

Hitherto, all we have done is to reduce the pressure in our chamber. But as the action of playing is to admit air, and since air seeps into the chamber however well we try to seal it, we have to devise a way of repeatedly taking air out of the chamber.

A method of flying, fervently believed in by the ancients, was that if you jumped, and then jumped again when you reached the highest point of that jump, you could just keep on going up and up, jumping and jumping. They omitted to realize that the action of jumping demanded a reaction to the force—something solid to apply the work of jumping to. You could jump up a flight of steps one at a time, but where there were no steps, you could not keep jumping upwards. Now the player-piano poses a problem of a similar type. Using the exhausting bellows, we have drawn one lot of air out of the chamber, but we have to keep on doing it. If we just move the movable side in and out, all we are doing is alternately stretching and compressing a unit mass of air and doing a lot of work to get nowhere. There has to be a means of taking a bite out of the air and being able to go back for more without replacing the first bite.

One way in which we can make this work is to separate the movable side from the chamber by another compartment. What we will have in effect is a box to which is connected an extra side fixed over an existing side with a flexible diaphragm or bellows. We can now draw air out

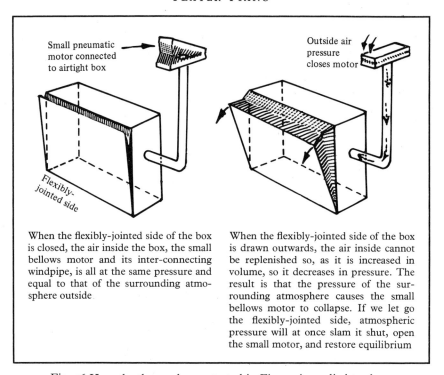

When the flexibly-jointed side of the box is closed, the air inside the box, the small bellows motor and its inter-connecting windpipe, is all at the same pressure and equal to that of the surrounding atmosphere outside

When the flexibly-jointed side of the box is drawn outwards, the air inside cannot be replenished so, as it is increased in volume, so it decreases in pressure. The result is that the pressure of the surrounding atmosphere causes the small bellows motor to collapse. If we let go the flexibly-jointed side, atmospheric pressure will at once slam it shut, open the small motor, and restore equilibrium

Fig. 46 Here the theory demonstrated in Fig. 45 is applied to show how a mechanical function can be achieved by reducing the air pressure in the box. A small bellows, called a 'motor', is made to collapse. In fact, a large number of similar motors could be made to work from one such flexibly-jointed side to an air-tight box. Pressure only has to be reduced very slightly in order to allow a mechanical function to be performed in this way

of the main chamber, through a hole in the proper side, into the chamber created by moving the extra, hinged side away from the box. But still we must solve the problem of the need to take continual sucks without simply pushing the same amount of air in and out.

The answer is the flap valve, surely the simplest and most efficient air valve one could wish for and as useful today as it was when first used by the organ-builders in the Middle Ages. This valve is purely a strip of leather secured at each end over a portion of our movable side which has several holes in it. When the side is pulled outwards, the pressure of air lifts the leather clear of the holes and allows the air to pass through. However, when the side moves the other way, the air pressure now acts upon the other side of the leather strip, pressing it firmly against the holes and so sealing them. The sketch shows this and as this is an important fundamental of the pneumatic operation of a piano, you must understand how this operates before proceeding further. Air pressing on to one side of a movable seal will move that seal to close an opening against atmospheric pressure; air at atmospheric pressure will close the same opening when there is air at a lower pressure on the other side of the seal. The seal can

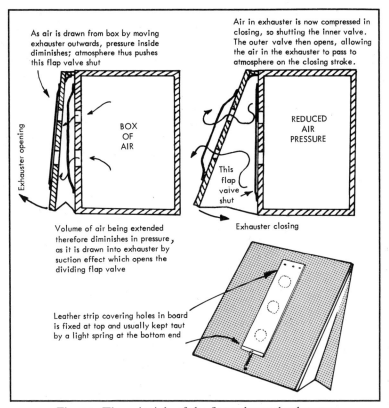

As air is drawn from box by moving exhauster outwards, pressure inside diminishes; atmosphere thus pushes this flap valve shut

Air in exhauster is now compressed in closing, so shutting the inner valve. The outer valve then opens, allowing the air in the exhauster to pass to atmosphere on the closing stroke.

BOX OF AIR

REDUCED AIR PRESSURE

Exhauster opening

This flap valve shut

Volume of air being extended therefore diminishes in pressure, as it is drawn into exhauster by suction effect which opens the dividing flap valve

Exhauster closing

Leather strip covering holes in board is fixed at top and usually kept taut by a light spring at the bottom end

Fig. 47. The principle of the flap valve and exhausters

be a leather flap as we have seen here, or it can be a piston, diaphragm, bellows, or pouch which the air can move.

We have now got as far as seeing that we can make a device whereby we can move a side of an air-tight box in and out, systematically reducing the air pressure within by the use of a simple flap valve. We can work the movable side with a foot treadle. To make the operation easier, we can fit our main chamber with two movable sides, each quite separate from the other, so that they will work alternately as the piano operator presses first with one foot and then with the other upon the foot treadles. So far so good, but still our pressure-reducing mechanism is short of something. As we pedal, there is a brief moment in each cycle when one of the two movable walls—exhausters as they are called—is at one extreme limit of its position, and the other exhauster is at the other extreme. Under these conditions, the vacuum created inside the chamber will suddenly decrease momentarily. Although this variation is only very brief, it will be quite sufficient to affect the playing performance of the piano. If, for example, this momentary change-over coincided with a rapid passage of music, we would probably lose one or two notes, the music would suddenly change from normal to soft and then back again, and the speed of the music-roll, itself driven by an air motor as we shall see later on, would fluctuate.

All these snags are overcome by the provision of a reserve power of suction—a vacuum accumulator. This is another movable wall to the main chamber, only this one is usually at the side opposite to the exhausters and it is also larger. It is normally held wide open by internal springs. Now, as we treadle, air is drawn out of the main compartment still, but the difference in pressure causes the atmosphere to press on the large movable wall and push it in against its internal springs. This makes an air buffer to cater for the moments of lost motion in treadling, since it gives an extra quantity of vacuum pressure aided by the internal springs. In operation, assuming there to be no function of the instrument working, as one treadles, so the large movable wall begins to close up against the main compartment until finally it is almost completely closed. If we then stop treadling, the large movable wall will gradually open outwards until it comes to rest at its widest open position. During all the time it is opening, a working vacuum is being maintained within the compartment. The duty of this portion of the system is to equalize the suction pressure which would otherwise fluctuate with each stroke of the exhausters. For this reason, the portion is called the 'equalizer'.

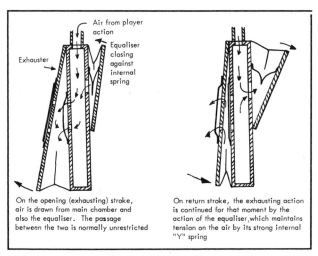

Fig. 48. The equaliser

The equalizer is thus a stand-by exhauster which comes into operation when, for the reasons already explained, the foot-operated exhausters are momentarily inoperative. The steadier and more regular the operation of the exhausters, the less work there is for the equalizer to do.

Our 'bellows system', therefore, comprises a central, main vacuum chamber from which vacuum power can be taken to the playing mechanism, two foot-operated exhausters and the equalizer.

Under certain conditions of playing, it is possible to build up an excess of suction power in the bellows system. If we treadle at a steady rate through a roll of music which contains a pause or a soft passage comprising only a few notes, then we might build up so much suction in the exhausters and equalizers that actual damage could result. This is taken care of by the provision of a spill valve—a device to let in air from the atmosphere when the partial vacuum begins to assume excess proportions. The valve is mechanical and is often just a small flap valve somewhere in the system so that, as the equalizer opens to its extreme, a linkage draws back a simple, hinged pallet.

The loads imposed on the bellows system during playing are quite considerable. For this reason, the various components of the system are robustly built in hardwood, whilst the equalizer and exhauster panels are made of thick plywood. At a maximum playing pressure of

$1\frac{1}{2}$ lb/sq. inch, an exhauster having a surface area of 300 square inches must resist atmospheric pressure equal to a weight of 450 lb, which must be moved by the action of pumping the foot treadles. Whilst constructionally this is a considerable load to resist, the player performer may be truly thankful for the fact that, as already explained, the air in this connection offers but infinitesimal resistance due to friction, and thus his task is readily accomplished.

It is common practice for the exhausters to be assisted from the open to the closed position by springs. These are 'V'- or gull-shaped and serve to prepare the exhausters for another stroke as quickly as possible. The pressures of these springs vary from 12 to 20 lb. The flexible portions of the bellows are formed in a heavy rubberized twill or duck cloth which is impervious to air.

Player-pianos, although working generally to the same system, are all different in detail construction and the first thing which becomes apparent is the large variations between the proportions of the bellows components. Exhausters and equalizers vary in area and W. B. White has made an interesting study of the reasons why these components do differ so greatly.

The equalizer serves as a pneumatic flywheel to the pneumatic system, supplementing the interrupted action of the to-and-fro cycle with a reservoir of power. This is very much like the flywheel of an engine, where the mass of a solid flywheel is used to take the crankshaft over the top and bottom dead centre positions. The heavier the flywheel on the engine, the smoother will be its running characteristics. But also it will be slow to accelerate (develop power) and also its power output will be diminished by virtue of the amount of power being absorbed in the task of driving a large mass of flywheel.

This same state of affairs can be translated into the interpretation of the duties of the equalizer. Some makers believed that the easier it was for a completely unskilled, insensitive person to play their instrument, the better it was. Others thought it preferable for the player to feel the fluctuations of air pressure beneath his feet. The first viewpoint could easily be accomplished by having a large equalizer. The second trend of thought dictated that the equalizer be smaller. The same effect could be achieved, of course, by varying the size of the exhausters as well. As it is, the more sensitive a piano is, within certain limitations, the better the instrument is for the serious music lover. Ernest Newman detected these variations from the point of view of the listener, and Grew exhorted his pupils to keep one foot always prepared for use to produce a *fortissimo* passage or to accentuate one note—an almost impossible task with a piano having a large equalizer.

Since the equalizer is such a bone of contention, could it not have been dispensed with? The answer is, unfortunately, no, for no matter how astute the performer, he would be unable to maintain conditions of anything like constant vacuum pressure with his treadles, and his music-roll speed would fluctuate considerably.

Having understood the method of driving air out of a chamber to create a partial vacuum, and accepting that the act of playing a piano by a pneumatic system admits atmospheric air into the partial vacuum (hence the need for continual effort to maintain that partial vacuum), we can turn our attention to how the bellows system already described is made to control musical sounds.

We have, in effect, two pressures of air to play with—one is that of the atmosphere around us and the piano, and the other is a lower pressure which we have created inside the instrument by using the foot treadles. It is the difference between these two which is continually applied in various ways to make music.

The piano has 88 notes. In the early days only some of these were played from the music-roll, but, after 1912, rolls were standardized at 65-note and the full-scale 88-note. It does not really

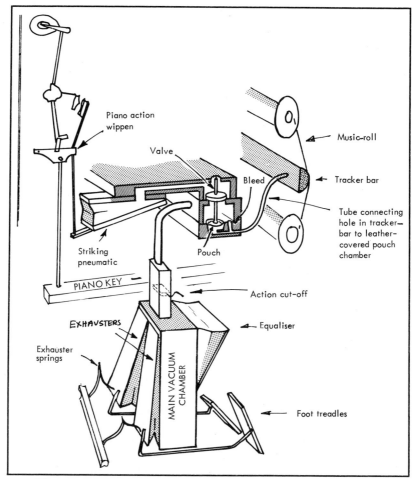

Fig. 49. Section through simple player action showing applied principles for one note in part section

matter which of these we consider—the mechanism is largely the same. Now, to play 88 notes we have 88 separate little mechanisms of the piano to be operated, just like that shown in the cross-section in Fig. 49. We have the power to control these as we have a pressure-reducing device. What has to be done is to convert one chamber containing reduced pressure into a system which will move those 88 little mechanisms individually or severally and to a pre-determined pattern corresponding to a musical composition.

This is achieved by using two components. First of all is the valve chest and pneumatic stack. Secondly there is a facility for the provision of a sliding valve to control each of the 88 valves and pneumatics in the stack. The valve chest and pneumatic stack have a physical connection to the piano sounding mechanisms (the hammers). The sliding valve device comprises a terminal block at which end all the control pipes for the valves. The sliding valve itself is the music-roll.

Valve chests operating the pneumatics are to be found in two types, the simple single-valve system, and the double-valve system consisting of primary and secondary (sometimes called

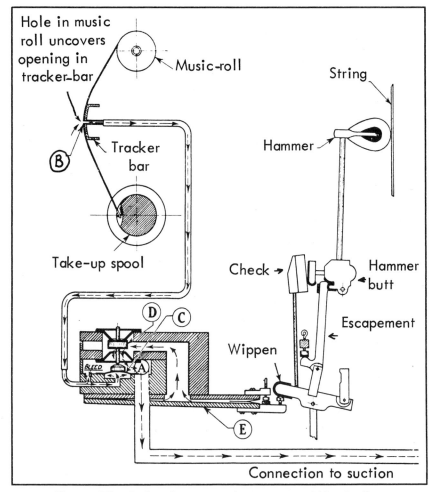

Fig. 50. The single-valve pneumatic system as used by Aeolian

servo and principle) valves. The illustration (Fig. 50) shows a section through a simple, single-valve system. This consists of a pouch in a base-board above which is a suction chamber. Resting lightly on the leather pouch is a stem carrying on it a circular disc which forms a seal on the outside of the suction chamber. By lifting the valve, such as will happen if the pouch is inflated, the suction in the chamber is permitted access to the air contained in an airway above the valve which connects to a pneumatic motor. The air at atmospheric pressure is therefore drawn out of the pneumatic motor, causing it to collapse. By connecting the moving part of this pneumatic to the wippen of the piano action, using, say, a push rod or a wire pull-link, a note can be struck. The method of controlling the movement of the valve via the pouch is the perforation in the paper music-roll. The pouch covers a small secondary chamber in the pouch board, which is connected by a thin pipe to the tracker-bar. This secondary chamber is connected to the vacuum chamber by a tiny open passage called a bleed hole. This at first seems to nullify the whole purpose of having separate chambers and an inflatable pouch. But let us detail precisely what happens and how the assembly functions.

Because this is an important feature of the player mechanism—the principle of the valve chest and pneumatic motor—I would advise the reader to proceed no further with this chapter until he is absolutely conversant with the workings of the system illustrated in Figs. 49 and 50.

The valve stem carrying the valve disc is free to move up and down. It is lightly made and carries a button at its lower end, sitting just a fraction above the pouch, which is made of soft, pliable leather and is glued over the secondary, or control chamber. The main chamber through which the valve passes is connected to the partial vacuum produced by the bellows system. The actual sealing disc of the valve is outside this main chamber and in a further compartment which is normally under atmospheric pressure. The valve seal is thus free to move between the aperture in the main chamber and the aperture connecting the upper compartment with the atmosphere.

Beneath the leather diaphragm called the pouch is a small chamber which has an outlet to the music-roll tracker-bar. This chamber, as already mentioned, is linked to the main vacuum chamber by a small orifice—the bleed hole.

Above the main chamber the further compartment is connected to a pneumatic motor which, by its own weight, remains in the extended or open position under normal conditions.

Now we will apply a suction to the main chamber, as in use, and close off the orifice in the tracker-bar, as by a non-perforated piece of the music-roll. The valve closes the chamber at the top both by its own weight and also by the difference between atmospheric pressure and the suction of the vacuum pressure. The air beneath the leather pouch is also extracted, as is that in the tube to the tracker-bar, through the bleed hole.

The moment a perforation in the music-roll comes into line with the end of the tube at the tracker-bar, the partial vacuum in the tube and in the small chamber beneath the leather pouch is immediately replaced by air at atmospheric pressure. This at once inflates the pouch, pushing up the valve which now makes a seal between the upper compartment and the atmosphere. The suction from the main compartment is thus applied to the air in the pneumatic motor which, exhausted of air, rapidly collapses. This collapsing of the motor is translated into the operation of one of the piano actions and thus the sounding of a note, by the use of a connection to the wippen.

Why isn't all this spoiled by the open connection between the two sides of the leather pouch— the bleed hole? This hole is too small to allow the pressures to equalize when faced with the amount of atmospheric pressure rushing in relative to the amount of suction in the main chamber. The quantity of air in movement is always greater than the capacity of the bleed hole.

However, the moment the hole in the end of the tube at the tracker-bar is once more sealed, as by the perforation in the music-roll coming to an end, the bleed hole serves to reduce the amount of atmospheric air trapped in the pouch chamber and tube. This reduction only has to be fractional before the atmospheric air pressing on the top of the valve sees a chance to equalize things, and pushes the valve and the pouch down. This seals the aperture in the top of the main chamber and reinflates the collapsed motor, returning the system to equilibrium once more.

This valve system is repeated for as many notes as there are to be played on the piano—65 or, more usually, 88. The only common passage is the vacuum compartment beneath which are positioned the individual pouches, each with a separate connection to a different hole in the tracker-bar, and above which are placed one valve and one pneumatic motor for each note.

The tracker-bar serves as the control for the whole mechanism of producing music. Each tube ends in a small orifice in a brass bar over which the sliding valve (more properly travelling valve) of the music-roll passes. On early instruments playing 65 notes and less, the bar was often made of wood but with the advent of the full-scale 88-note action, it was impossible to arrange the openings (nine to the inch spacing) accurately or sufficiently airtight from each other, so metal was adopted. Each hole in the tracker-bar connects with a pouch in the pouch board, the far left one being the extreme bass note of the piano and successively to the extreme treble at the far right. (Note that this relates to the number of notes played as, particularly with the reproducing pianos described later, the scale was not strictly 'full'.)

Because the strings of the piano and the hammers which strike them are fairly close together, it would be impossible to mount a workable action in one straight line, so it is common for the valves and pneumatics to be staggered. Pouches are arranged in staggered lines in the pouch board and pneumatics are arranged in two or three horizontal rows, vertically staggered.

In the foregoing I have described (a) the device whereby a partial vacuum is created as a wherewithal for playing, and (b) the pneumatic valve system which is arranged to interpret a perforated music-roll into a musical performance. There are a number of other aspects to be detailed—the roll-driving mechanism, the controls for giving individual interpretation, the double-valve pneumatic system and the reasons for its use, the regulation of speed, the facility for rerolling a music-roll after playing and the method of keeping the music-roll in perfect alignment with the tracker-bar holes.

The foot-operated upright piano, certainly the most common amongst the breed of player-pianos as well as being the cheapest application of the player principles, will serve as a good illustration of the application of the parts already detailed, and as a good vehicle for showing these further aspects to be described. The illustration Fig. 49 shows a side elevation of an ordinary upright player-piano. It might be as well at this point to state that, generally speaking,

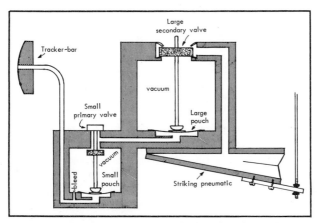

Fig. 51. Section through simple double-valve action

player actions are placed transversely across the front of the instrument above the keyboard. On some players, the action is fitted beneath the key bed (see the cross-section of the Hupfeld piano, Fig. 53). With these, the player action moves the wippen by pushing up under the backs of the keys and, with this and similar actions, the keys are moved in the action of playing. Because, however, piano keys are weighted to provide a balanced action for the manual pianist, it is quite usual for the key to move under its own weight when the wippen is moved by the playing pneumatic. Some makers considered this an undesirable feature and arranged for all

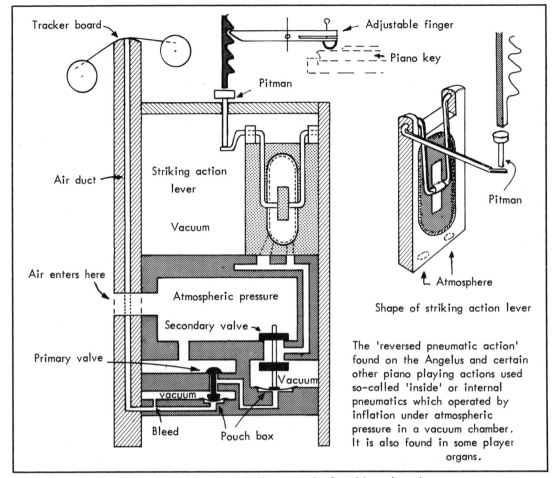

Tracker board

Adjustable finger

Piano key

Pitman

Air duct

Striking action lever

Vacuum

Pitman

Air enters here

Atmospheric pressure

Secondary valve

Atmosphere

Shape of striking action lever

Primary valve

Vacuum

vacuum

Bleed   Pouch box

The 'reversed pneumatic action' found on the Angelus and certain other piano playing actions used so-called 'inside' or internal pneumatics which operated by inflation under atmospheric pressure in a vacuum chamber. It is also found in some player organs.

Fig. 52. 'Inside' or 'reversed' pneumatics found in early actions

the keys to be locked when the player was in operation and the method of locking the keys was controlled by the hinged flap at the front of the key bed, which is moved down to uncover the manual expression controls for the player. With this flap open, the keys are locked and the piano cannot be played upon by hand.

The bellows system on the treadle piano is always sited beneath the key bed, this being an obviously convenient position. Connections from the tracker-bar, which is most commonly situated at a convenient level in the front fall of the piano case so that the music can be watched, are made to the pouch board by rubber tubing or, in the case of better-made models, by lead tubing. It might be worth mentioning here that, whilst a lead-tubed player piano will probably never need to be re-tubed,* it is so alarmingly heavy as to pose a serious disadvantage to the collector.

The connection between the bellows system and the upper or player action is by large-diameter flexible rubber hoses.

We have seen that the production of musical sounds is controlled by a suitably-perforated

* Lead tube often oxidizes, though. All lead tubing should be replaced by rubber on rebuilding the instrument.

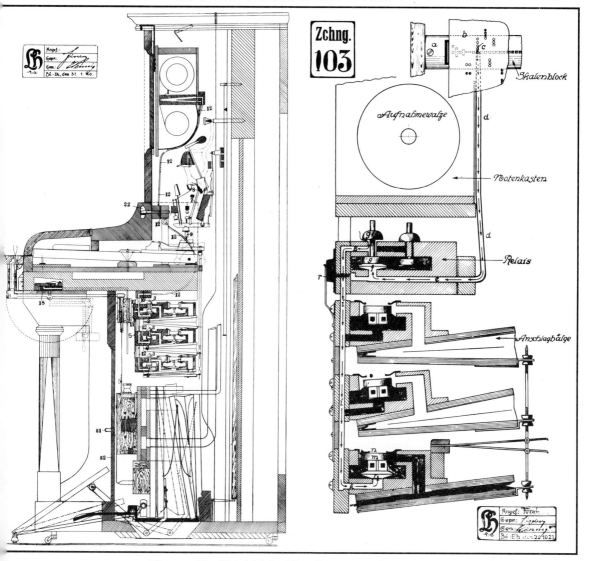

Fig. 53. The Hupfeld double-valve pneumatic system

paper roll. This paper roll comes wound on to a spool having suitable ends, which engage with a free-turning centre at one end, and a chuck drive at the other, both of these being features of the spool box on the piano. The central feature of the spool box is the tracker-bar whose function we now understand. The roll travels from the top of the box downwards to the take-up spool which is fixed permanently in the box. (On some instruments, the roll travels from bottom to top but the principle is just the same.) The end of the music paper has a loop on it to engage with a hook on the take-up spool. When the roll of paper has transferred from the music spool to the take-up spool, to the extent that the music perforations have come to an end, the paper must be rewound back on to the music spool. The end of the paper remains stuck firmly to the music spool, so all that has to be done is to disengage the drive to the take-up spool and move a suitable mechanical linkage, so that the music spool is now driven through the provision of the chuck holding one end.

This is nearly always achieved by mechanical means, such as the moving of a free-turning sprocket wheel on a shaft so that it engages with a dog clutch. Such a system is illustrated in Plates 79 and 80. The spool mechanism is driven by an air motor. This is, in effect, an inlet to the partial vacuum of the bellows system. As the air at atmospheric pressure rushes into the vacuum chamber, it is made to produce rotary motion which is applied to the spool box mechanism through chainwheels and sprockets. The air motor is an ingenious piece of mechanism which fulfils its functional requirement under extreme variations of pressure. It is, for example, required to maintain a constant speed from the very gentlest suction up to the maximum suction created for a *forte* passage of music. It must produce a constant amount of power to keep the music-roll moving across the tracker-bar, against the suction created between tracker-bar and paper by the playing mechanism. Above all, it must have the ability to be controlled by the performer to give instantaneous changes of *tempo* and smooth *accelerando* and *ritardando*, even to the degree of being stopped momentarily and instantly restarted back to a predetermined speed.

We have already seen that the use of an air pressure differential can cause a simple pneumatic

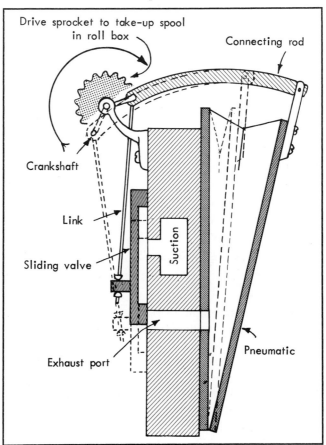

Fig. 54. The air motor showing one pneumatic and valve in section

156

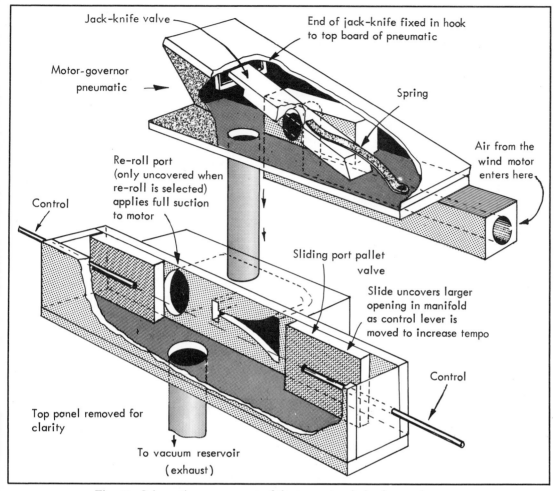

Fig. 55. Schematic arrangement of the tempo/rewind valves and governing pneumatic. Compare these details with the application in Fig. 56

motor to open and close. The air motor works on just this principle and features a number
of pneumatics which alternately open and close in sequence. Their motion drives a crankshaft
and the cycle of each pneumatic is reversed automatically by a sliding valve, one for each
pneumatic. In this manner, the rotary motion imparted to the crankshaft is constant, smooth
and continuous.

Figure 54 shows a cross-section of one pneumatic of the motor and from this can be seen
the chamber through which atmospheric air is sucked, and the way this is affected by the sliding
valve. To ensure perfectly smooth operation, the air motor works in exactly the same way as
a car engine only in place of cylinders, the air motor uses pneumatics and for fuel it uses the
atmosphere as compared with the reduced pressure within the system. As with a car where a
number of cylinders is used to give smooth motion, the air motor has a number of pneumatics—
never less than three, usually four, occasionally five or six.

An important feature of the air motor is this ability to be able to regulate speed within very precise limits and an easy way to achieve this is to throttle the motor, as one throttles the internal-combustion engine, to regulate the amount of air passing through it. If we allow the motor to draw the maximum amount of atmospheric air into the bellows system, then it will move quickly. By reducing the amount of air, we can slow down its performance and adjust the *tempo* of the music being played from the music-roll. This is done by a sliding port linking the suction side of the motor to the suction of the bellows; the port is, in effect, wedge-shaped so that, at one extreme of its movement, it presents the maximum sized opening, whilst at the other it shows a much smaller hole. Control of this sliding port is by a lever or knob, which also operates a pointer along a scale near the music-roll so that the player operator can immediately follow any speed direction printed on the music.

The sliding port also has another feature and this is associated with the re-roll mechanism. At the end of a piece of music (or at any other time to suit the will of the player operator), the drive to the take-up spool in the roll box can be disengaged and the music-spool drive engaged, so applying the motor power to rerolling the music. Because the music could still actually play regardless of the direction in which the roll travels, the principal airway between bellows and valve chest is cut off during reroll, so that there is no suction power in the valve chest. To speed up rerolling, the sliding port also has a very large orifice which immediately applies full power to the motor, and this is only brought into operation during the reroll procedure. The air motor always rotates in one direction—the apparent change of direction of drive is achieved by the mechanical gearing. Thus the movement of the reroll control lever (a) shuts off the suction power to the valve chest and pneumatic stack, and (b) opens a very large port between motor and bellows so that reroll can be accomplished in the quickest possible time, and (c) alters the drive to the roll-box, through gearing.

Now this system of regulating the motor speed would be quite perfect were it not for the fact that, as we have already shown, the amount of suction, and thus the amount of potential power for the motor, is varying continually during playing. So varied is the suction pressure available, that the music-roll drive would fluctuate continuously. Even by the expedient of the equalizer, it is not possible to guarantee the speed of the air motor within the precise limits needed without some other means being brought to bear; for whilst the equalizer 'irons out the bumps' in playing, it cannot cope with quantitive differences such as that between soft treadling and hard treadling. This additional refinement is accomplished by the use of a pneumatic motor fitted between the motor suction and the bellows, so that the air sucked in through the air motor passes through the pneumatic on its way to the bellows. Its course through the pneumatic, however, is subject to the control of a jack-knife valve. This is a secondary throttling device, only this one is quite automatic. Whilst the operator of the player can control the general amount of air regulating the overall speed of the motor, the rapid pressure fluctuations are smoothed out by this self-acting valve which is called the *tempo* governor. Its principle of operation is quite easy to follow and the illustration Fig. 56 shows the components. The pneumatic motor is normally held open by a spring. The air connection into the pneumatic is through a block in one side, across which is arranged a moving pallet-valve pivoted on the bottom board of the pneumatic and connected to the top board. This is called a jack-knife valve and we will find it occurring again in other applications, particularly with the reproducing piano described later. When the performer begins to treadle, the amount of suction produced will normally be balanced by the spring force holding the *tempo* governor open. Supposing now the performer wishes to provide more power to his performance, such as might be required to accentuate a passage, he treadles harder and creates a suction greater than that which the *tempo* governor

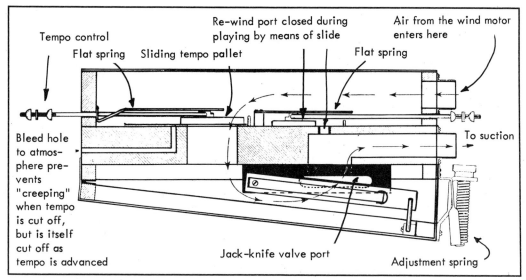

Fig. 56. The speed *(tempo)* governor (Duo-Art action)

spring can resist. The governor closes a little, in so doing allowing the jack-knife to cover part of the inlet hole.

The effect is to allow an increase in the suction force acting on the air motor (which in turn must draw more air from the atmosphere), but to restrict this taking of more air from the atmosphere by reducing the aperture through which it must pass to the bellows. The air motor thus continues to run at a constant speed governed by the over-ruling control offered by the ordinary *tempo* control.

It will be appreciated that the setting of this valve is extremely important and, indeed, although the pneumatic should always be in a state of partial collapse during playing, it may well be that, for normal setting, the jack-knife may be called upon to cover part of the hole so that the player performer can achieve musical effects on both sides of this arbitrary half-way mark.

Associated with the provision for driving the music-roll, so that it is drawn over the tracker-bar, must be the certainty that the paper is going to 'track' properly, its holes aligning with the holes in the tracker-bar. If the paper is not aligned the right way, then the note holes may either miss the tracker openings altogether or partially allow two adjacent holes to open. In either case the effect on the music will be disastrous to the ear. The principles of governing tracking are quite simple. To keep the paper passing across the tracker in the proper position, you must have an automatic means either for moving both music spool and take-up spool from side to side, or you must make provision for the tracker-bar itself to move. The amount of lateral shift will be small and should be prompt in operation, without any tendency towards over-correction. Both the systems hinted at have been successfully applied in player-piano construction although it is more usual to move the spools. Operation is very simple. Two pneumatic motors are used, normally made back to back with one central fixed board and two hinged sides. The tracker-bar is provided with an extra opening at each end, larger than the note holes and square in shape. The connection from one side of the tracker runs to one side of the double motor, and that from the opposite end of the tracker to the other. Normally the music-roll partially covers the holes. If the roll is warped, unfortunately an all too frequent occurrence, then one of the holes becomes covered, fully opening the other. Previously, the air pressure exerted on each side of the motor was equal, but now it is set off balance and so the motor begins to move. A linkage moves the paper spools over until the closed tracking-hole is once more opened, restoring the air balance to the motor and bringing it to rest. To achieve smooth operation, without over-correction, the airways and openings in the motor are comparatively small so that the air shift is slow.

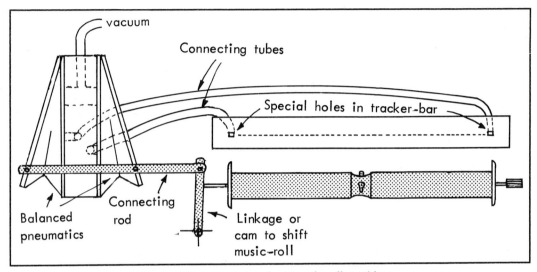

Fig. 57. The principles of automatic roll-tracking

This is important for another reason. Quite often the edge of a roll may become slightly split or damaged. Were the action of the automatic tracking to be very prompt, each of these splits would at once cause the music-roll to be shifted willy-nilly. Naturally, where the edge of the roll is badly damaged or has been folded over (a feature known to one member of the Player Piano Group as 'the Aeolian Pleat'), then the principles of automatic tracking are disrupted and the roll may not play properly at all.

There are at least three common types of automatic tracking device, but all work on this same principle of balanced pressures controlled by the edges of the paper roll passing between certain defined limits. The Aeolian Duo-Art earlier models used two small feelers which gently touched the edge of the roll during playing. If the roll moved, the feeler would also move but, in so doing, a small pallet at its other end would shut off an atmosphere vent, upsetting the balance of pressures in the double-acting motor. Another system employed small fences at the edge of the music. The roll passed between these two delicately-adjusted, sprung strips and again any tendency for the paper to wander was converted into an adjustment of the roll.

Where the tracker-bar is itself moved, it is made to slide by the self-same type of mechanism. Whichever system is used, automatic tracking calls for movement of not more than $\frac{3}{32}$ inch each side of the mean position and usually far less than this.

Automatic tracking must not be confused with *transposition*, where the whole roll is allowed to be played in a different key by re-aligning it with other holes in the tracker-bar. This *en bloc* adjustment is nothing to do with tracking and is usually achieved by moving the tracker-bar so that accompaniment for singing can be arranged in a mutually convenient key. It is

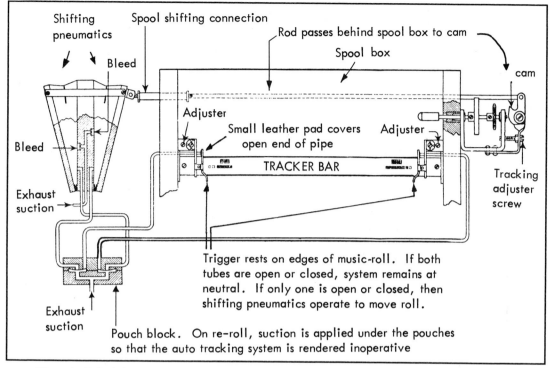

Shifting pneumatics

Spool shifting connection

Rod passes behind spool box to cam

Spool box

cam

Bleed

Adjuster

Small leather pad covers
open end of pipe

Adjuster

Bleed

TRACKER BAR

Tracking
adjuster
screw

Exhaust
suction

Trigger rests on edges of music-roll. If both
tubes are open or closed, system remains at
neutral. If only one is open or closed, then
shifting pneumatics operate to move roll.

Exhaust
suction

Pouch block. On re-roll, suction is applied under the pouches
so that the auto tracking system is rendered inoperative

Fig. 58. Principles of automatic tracking applied—the Duo-Art system using 'balanced air'

controlled mechanically by a knob or lever on or in the roll box.

The features we have now examined are all associated one with the other and are thus best considered under one grouping. Starting with the air motor we have (a) the *tempo* control, governing the speed of the music; (b) the *tempo* regulator, applying automatic speed conformity to the *tempo* selected by the *tempo* control; (c) the system used for rerolling the music; (d) the device for maintaining the proper tracking of the roll; and (e) the transposing control, whereby the key of the music may be changed at will.

Let us now examine how the player performer can play his roll of music with expression and put into it his own shades of colour, accentuation, *forte* and *piano*. To be able to do this, he must have control over those expressive devices which are normally to be found fitted to a piano—the two pedals controlling the position of the hammer rest-rail and the dampers. He is prevented from being able to use his feet for these as would a manual pianist, because his feet are already called upon to provide the suction power to drive the mechanism. The form of control has therefore to be left entirely to his hands on suitable control buttons or levers. These controls have to be placed within comfortable reach of the player operator and thus it is common practice for them to be mounted in a hinged portion of the forward rail of the key bed. By opening the key bed rail downwards, the controls are found mounted in the control rail.

Returning to the fourth paragraph of this chapter, we considered that the pianist playing manually has two hands and can thus vary the force with which he applies the hammers to the strings from one hand to the other. The action of the soft pedal is to move the hammers closer to the strings so that, not having so far to travel before striking the strings, the sound produced is less loud than with the pedal in the normal position. However, the pianist can achieve a combination of tonal effects largely independent of the pedal control by varying the force with which he can strike any individual keys or group of keys on the keyboard. In this way, he can achieve a distinction between a soft accompaniment and an accented melody.

Remembering that the 'soft pedal' controls the hammer rest-rail position relative to the strings, the mechanical operation of this is easily achieved by pneumatic means. However, to make possible the distinction between melody and accompaniment, it is better resolved by dividing the rest rail into two portions, each being free to move independent of the other and each having a separate control. Now this control can be mechanical, by a lever connection, or, more usually, by the employment of a pneumatic motor. One method of pneumatic control is to provide a button on the control rail which controls a small pallet. The pneumatic which controls the rest rail works on exactly the same principle as the motor which is used to move the piano action at each string in normal playing. The difference is that the operating valve, instead of being a travelling one made of paper (the roll), admitting suction to the pedal pneumatic, is a pallet covering the end of the tube open to atmosphere. When the pallet is opened, atmospheric air rushes in, the motor contracts, and the rail is moved.

The other control which has to be established is the operation of the dampers. This is, in effect, the sustaining pedal action and, because all the dampers are moved together throughout the range of notes operated, and because they require considerably more force to move than the rest rail, the operating pneumatic motor is usually larger than that for the rest rail. Furthermore, since the performance of the music must call for prompt operation of the dampers, it is fairly common for the pneumatic to be governed by two valves. Do not confuse this with the double-valve pneumatic system, to be described further on. This is still a single-valve system, but the valve is duplicated in the same chamber so as to provide a more positive and rapid suction connection to the motor. Again, the atmosphere end of the control tube can be closed off by a small pallet valve operated by a button on the control rail. This is shown in Fig. 59.

At this point, you will observe that both the functions of the pedal action of a normal piano can be controlled by pneumatic means and that the method of control is exactly the same as that used to play the piano mechanically. Each pedal-action pneumatic has the same type of control tube leading to atmosphere and governed by a valve, as are the pneumatics in the pneumatic stack. Thus if we take the ends of the control tubes from their valve pouch chambers to the tracker-bar instead of to the control rail, we can operate these functions by punching additional perforations in the music-roll instead of having to rely on the player operator to press the right buttons at the right moment.

Having found a way of doing these things automatically from the music-roll, we find that most player-pianos have a device—usually a small lever in the roll box—which disengages these features and brings back into operation the buttons and levers on the control rail.

So far we have dealt with the overall replacement of the pedal action by pneumatic means. The adroit pianist will have detected one major shortcoming—the ability to change very rapidly the playing intensity, perhaps only for one note or a chord. Even the best player performer, operating his foot treadles with the utmost subtlety and understanding, could not achieve this and thus the player-piano might soldier on, resigned to being nothing but an obvious mechanical interpreter of music. Happily this is not the case, thanks to a further device contrived to affect dynamic changes. This is the *power-governor*, which really holds its own on grand player-pianos. Now in the grand action, there is often no rest rail and thus it is not possible to move the

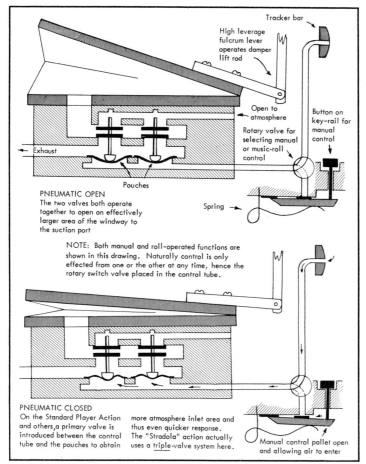

Fig. 59. Pneumatic control of dampers

hammers backwards and forwards relative to the strings. In fact the soft pedal action on the better-class grand shifts the whole action sideways, so that the hammers strike only one or two of the strings which together make up one note. In the player-grand the control of the 'soft' pedal effect is achieved by dividing the common suction chamber in the pneumatic stack at the position where the rest-rail on an upright piano might be divided, and applying suction to the end of each half through a pneumatic power-governor valve. This is shown in Fig. 60. This is, again, controlled by a button on the control rail.

The parts of the power-governor comprise the single-valve suction system, controlled by a pouch operated by a control pipe ending with a valve (either pallet at the control rail or hole in the tracker-bar). All these features we have already dealt with. Inside the pneumatic motor we find two openings. The first is above the valve controlled by the pouch, and is so arranged that, when the valve lifts, it seals off this port altogether. The second opening is smaller than the first and can be restricted by a pallet valve, hinged to the base of the motor and connected with a link to the top in such a way that, as the motor collapses, so the pallet gradually closes up the port. The motor is held in the normally open position by a tension spring which can be adjusted.

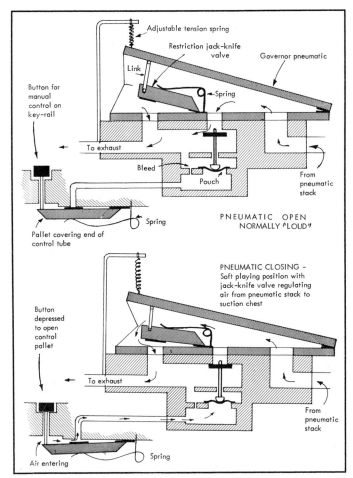

Fig. 60. The power governor

In operation, the air from the atmosphere must pass through the large port (under which is the rising valve) on its way to the bellows. Both this port and the valve are of such a size that, even though the pneumatic is in a state of partial collapse against the spring tension, there will be no reduction in the area of the opening. So long as the control button is not touched, the system will be doing nothing in the way of regulation.

Supposing the button be depressed on the control rail, it will immediately cause the valve to rise and seal off the large port. The air must now pass through the smaller port, which is controlled by the pallet valve. As the pneumatic collapses, so this pallet valve will reduce the size of the port and thus the amount of air which passes through this metered opening is always constant. Remember the *tempo* governor for the air motor? This is a similar piece of equipment. The operation of the pneumatic is controlled by the tension of the spring, which offers a resistance to the suction from the bellows. The stronger the spring, the greater the resistance offered and the less it collapses under any given condition of suction in the bellows system. From this we can see that the reduction of playing power can be regulated by the adjustment of the spring. This form of automatic governor can be upset at any time by the depressing of the button, permitting instantaneous changes from governed to ungoverned pressure and thus from *piano* to *forte* playing.

So prompt in action is this device that one note or chord in a group can be accented, the dominant in a bar brought out or any other effect achieved by its use. The power-governor, an important part of the grand action, is fitted to almost all actions and serves to provide this over-riding expression control.

The principle of the power-governor is such that, so long as the control button is depressed, the action can be controlled to play relatively softly. When the button is released, the effect is to provide a *forte* crash instantaneously, assuming all other aspects of control and the amount of suction in the bellows system to be adequate. However, it is far easier if, instead of holding down a button for normal playing and releasing it for accented notes, the control could be the other way round, e.g. the mechanism playing relatively softly at all times, but accents being effected by depressing the button or covering the open end of a normally-open nipple (Fig. 61). This is easily accomplished and indeed is the most common principle in use. The playing is at all times relatively soft, no matter how much effort is put into the bellows system. However, if the open end of the control tube is shut off either directly with the finger or indirectly by a button-operated pallet, the operation of the governor will be reversed and the flow of air will be through the main opening inside the pneumatic, thus allowing an instantaneous response to the vacuum conditions created by the player operator's feet.

It is important to fix in one's mind the definition of 'normally soft'. This really means the median of the level of sound being produced; the central path to the left of which is very soft and to the right of which is loud.

Now if we can control our playing from normally soft to loud by the sudden opening and

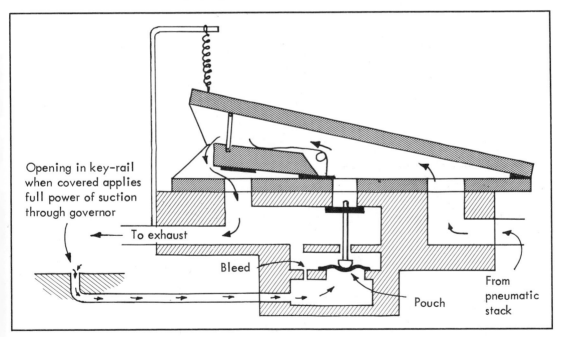

Fig. 61. The 'normally soft' power governor. When the open hole in the key rail is closed with the finger or a pallet, the governor changes to full power

closing of the vent of a control tube, then this can be just as easily accomplished from the music-roll, thereby obtaining accented notes quite automatically. The operation of the power-governor is achieved by the use of two small marginal perforations leading to a common control tube to the valve pouch. With a divided valve chest, there is a power-governor at each end and thus their automatic operation is achieved by there being two sets of controlling music-roll perforations, one set at each side of the roll. This is a method of control which forms the fundamental of the mechanisms within the reproducing piano.

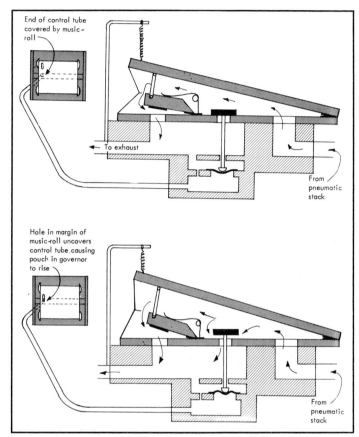

Fig. 62. Automatic power control from the music-roll

One method of theme accentuation, used by Aeolians for a while, was to make provision for the pouches to start inflating before the note was to be sounded. The idea was that if the chamber under the pouch could be filled with just enough air at atmospheric pressure so that the pouch came up to and stopped at the end of the valve (a distance of but a fraction of an inch) when the note was to be sounded, most of the work of inflating the pouch was already done and the note could thus be sounded with greater force, the valve lift being just that tiny bit quicker. In practice, the tracker-bar was equipped with a number of short vertical slots just above the normal tracker holes. These slots were connected directly with the openings in the tracker-bar beneath them, so that air admitted would be passed into the tracker control tube to the pouches. Naturally, they were very thin slots and they were placed to the side of the tracker hole so that

Fig. 63. Ungraduated type of pedal control the 'Soloist' system used in the Standard Player Action

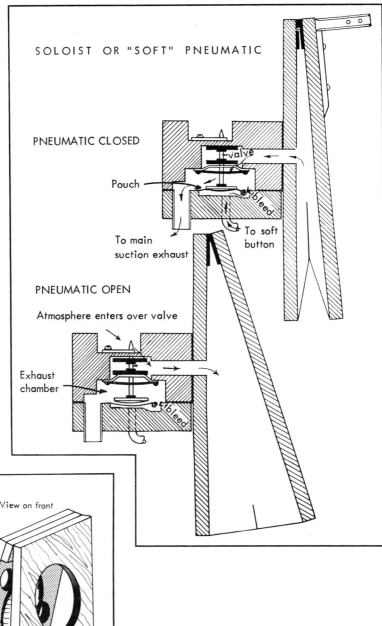

SOLOIST OR "SOFT" PNEUMATIC

PNEUMATIC CLOSED

valve

Pouch

bleed

To main
suction exhaust

To soft
button

PNEUMATIC OPEN

Atmosphere enters over valve

Exhaust
chamber

bleed

Position in bass equaliser

View on front

Wind chest

Spring

Four small windways in back
Central closing valve
Main windway in front

General arrangement of
valve with covering re-
moved for clarity

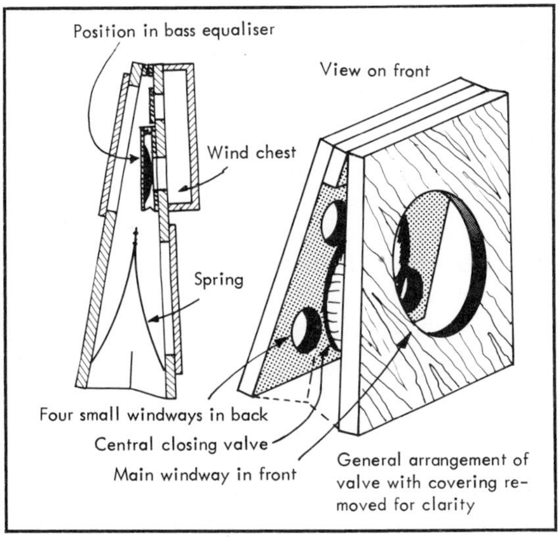

Fig. 64. The crash valve as used in
the Standard Player Action

the ingress of air would be fractional. The arrangement was fitted over the central tracker-bar holes only.

To be considered along with the power-governor is another device which, although not really in the same category, is also used to create emphasis. This is the *crash valve*, used by a number of makers to enable the player operator to obtain a *forte* accent by the sudden vigorous use of the player treadles. To illustrate this, we will detail the use of this as applied by the American Standard Player Action Company. In this instrument the crash valve is placed over the opening between the bass equalizer and the main suction chest, where it is connected to the upper action. It consists of what appears to be an ordinary pneumatic motor having a large opening in one side and four small openings in the other. Inside is a fixed valve pad, which is connected to the moving wall of the pneumatic itself and so arranged that, so long as the motor is at rest, air within the crash valve can be exhausted through the large opening, but it can be replaced by air entering through the four small openings on the other side so that the pneumatic will not move. Supposing, however, that a sudden pressure is applied to the foot treadles, causing the exhausters to work more quickly, the air within the crash valve is withdrawn faster than it may be replaced, so the pneumatic closes and the valve inside it seals the large opening. The effect now is the complete isolation of that equalizer. The treble equalizer, having collapsed against its internal V-spring and also a special coil spring provided inside, has become momentarily inoperative and so the situation exists wherein the action has no equalizers at all and a sudden forceful push on the treadles operates directly on the channels of the player, without the absorbing and equalizing effects of the equalizers. The result is a heavily struck or accented note or series of notes. The instant vigorous footwork is ended, the crash valve opens and the equalizer is recommissioned.

Another control within the player-piano is the 'cut-off' or silencer by means of which the air motor can still draw the music-roll over the tracker, but the action will not operate. This is a desirable feature where portions of a roll are not required to be played. All this feature does is to operate the slide valve over the large air-transfer port between pneumatic stack and the bellows system. Again, the slide valve cut-off can be made to operate automatically by a perforation in the music-roll.

Hitherto, we have only examined the single valve pneumatic system. In the early days of player-piano manufacture, designers were faced with the virtual non-existence of materials suitable for use in their instruments. Lightness and compactness had to be coupled with the ability to remain air-tight. Whilst the principles of the player action were understood, very little of the science had been discovered, with the result that the proportions of various components such as pneumatic motors and valves relative to their weight had not been evolved. It is understandable, therefore, that the makers of such instruments should tend to err on the side of reliability in making their player-pianos, contriving a mechanism in such a manner that it would be dependable. By far the main drawback was the lack of suitable materials and, to be able to accept a certain amount of air seepage, it became necessary to use components of such a size that the mechanism could no longer be built practically. In the early years of this century, a 65-note player action took up more space and was considerably heavier and less powerful than the 88-note action of the 1920's.

Much of this problem concerned the amount of air which could be called upon to operate the valves and this was directly governed by the amount of air which the tracker-bar holes could accept. Even with the comparatively large holes in the 65-note tracker-bar which came at six to the inch, as compared with nine to the inch in an 88-note action, the intake of air

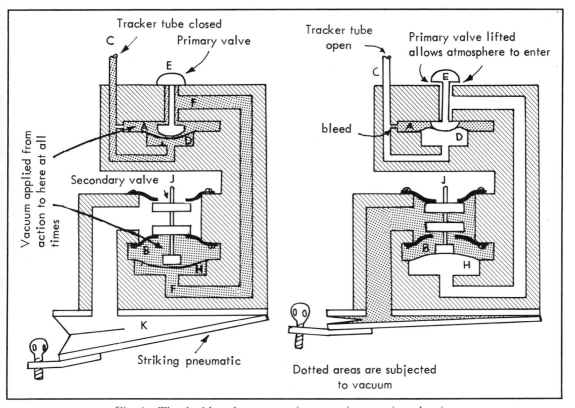

Fig. 65. The double-valve pneumatic system in operation, showing how the relatively small opening in the tracker-bar is used, via the primary valve, to admit a large volume of atmosphere to the secondary valve. Air is exhausted from chambers A and B by the action of treadling. When the music-roll uncovers an opening in the tracker-bar, a pulse of air is admitted through tube C. The equal state of vacuum in tube C and chamber A is thus upset and the vacuum causes the primary pouch D to be lifted, so lifting the primary valve E. A much larger volume of atmospheric air is then admitted past the primary valve E, down channel F and into the secondary pouch chamber where it lifts pouch H thereby causing the suction in chamber B to be applied to the striking pneumatic K. Once the tracker-bar opening is closed again, equilibrium is almost instantaneously achieved through the bleed hole

through one hole was often far short of that necessary to raise the valve quickly enough for all conditions of playing, unless the pump or bellows system was operated at a much higher vacuum pressure than was practical or comfortable for the operator. The action worked well on loud, but poorly on soft playing. A considerable amount of thought was given to this and the upshot was the provision of a small, light valve placed between the tracker tube and the valve which operated the pneumatic motor in the stack. This valve would be light enough to lift instantaneously on even a light pressure and it could by this means uncover an air passage large enough to lift the heavier valves which worked the motors. This extra valve was, then, to be used as a 'lever' in the system, so that a light force at one end of the system could be made

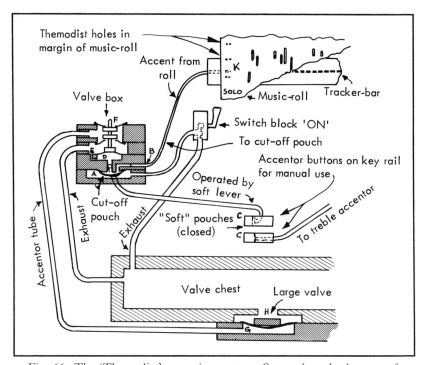

Fig. 66. The 'Themodist' accenting system. Screwed to the bottom of the valve chest is a small panel, into which run two rubber tubes and a large exhaust tube. This panel contains the Themodist accenting valves marked G. The action is as follows: With the Thermodist in the 'ON' position, the cut-off pouch A is drawn by the exhaust clear of the air channels B, thus preparing them for action under control of the Themodist perforations in the music-roll margin. The two 'soft' levers are then moved to the 'ON' position, thereby closing the two small pallets marked C which shut off open air. The pouch D is thus deflated by the bleed hole E, and the valve F comes to rest. Open air enters over the top of F, inflates the large pouch G and closes the port H. All this is achieved in a fraction of a second. When a marginal roll perforation K admits air down through the tube B, pouch D is lifted. The valve F is raised and G is instantly deflated, opening H to heavy suction. The illustration shows it in this condition. By cutting the marginal holes very slightly ahead of the note to be accented, the melody can be picked out very effectively, even individual notes in an *arpeggio* can be accented. When the Themodist is selected 'OFF', open air is admitted through the switch block to the pouch A, which is thus drawn against the channels B by the bleed hole E and the valves F and G can be operated only by the two manual soft levers. When these levers are not in use, they hold pallets C open so that under normal suction power the valve F is raised and the pouch G is lowered

to move a 'heavy' valve at the other. The tracker-bar hole thus moved a valve which opened up a much larger atmospheric air-pressure inlet to the pouch and attendant valve.

The 'double valve' pneumatic system came as the only solution to the inherent player-piano problems and so was adopted immediately by all makers. However, in later years, with the gradual availability of better materials, the *raison d'etre* behind the double-valve system was

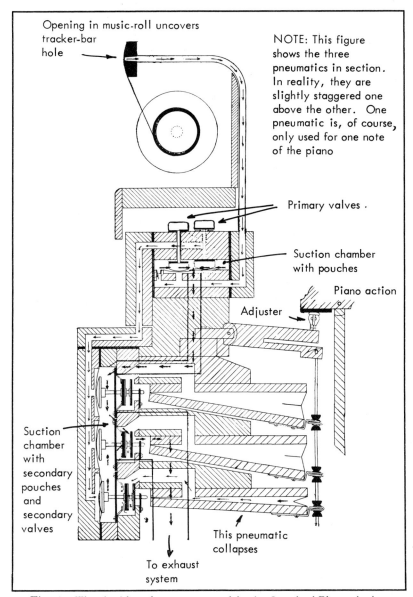

Opening in music-roll uncovers tracker-bar hole

NOTE: This figure shows the three pneumatics in section. In reality, they are slightly staggered one above the other. One pneumatic is, of course, only used for one note of the piano

Primary valves .

Suction chamber with pouches

Piano action

Adjuster

Suction chamber with secondary pouches and secondary valves

This pneumatic collapses

To exhaust system

Fig. 67. The double-valve system used in the Standard Player Action

no longer valid and several makers reverted to the single-valve system. Most makers, though, believed that the double-valve system, although more complicated to make, was a good insurance policy against the malfunctioning of their instruments. Today, with modern materials and an understanding of the dynamics of player mechanisms, we might build a thoroughly reliable and prompt action using single valves.

The pneumatic action, whether of the single valve type or the double valve type, is extremely prompt and rapid and will repeat its cycle of operations at least ten times per second under normal conditions.

With the double-valve system, the valve chest is divided into two portions—the primary and the secondary chambers. The valves in the first are termed primary valves; those in the other become the secondary valves. The way the system works should be self-evident if the foregoing descriptions of pneumatic systems have been understood. Fig. 51 shows a schematic arrangement of the double valve pneumatic system, and Fig. 67 a section through an actual system. As the pneumatics are normally arranged in three banks, they are drawn thus.

You will see that there is no vent or bleed hole in the secondary chest. In the single-valve system the bleed is a vital part, being necessary to reduce the atmospheric pressure in the tracker tube so that the pouch will collapse, closing the valve. In the double-valve arrangement, the atmospheric pressure in the secondary channel is allowed to be reduced by leakage into the primary chamber when the primary valve is closed. Remember that the pressure difference has only to be very slight before the valve will close. We will have more to say on this type of system in the next chapter when we look closely at repair and overhaul.

Of the pneumatic devices, I have left until last to make brief reference to some of the patent systems devised to simplify the valve chest and pneumatic stack. These are usually referred to as Unit-block systems or just Unit Valve Pneumatics. Several American manufacturers devised their own particular variants, among them Amphion Action Company and Simplex. Of the European makers, J. D. Phillips & Söhne and also Kastner produced unit valves, the last-mentioned making a big thing of the fact that their valves and all components were of metal. Briefly the systems all employed valves and pneumatics (or chamber cylinders which served as pneumatics) which, instead of each being installed in a common chest, were individually made and screwed into place so that, for servicing, they could be removed *in toto*. The Standard system is shown in Fig. 67. Large, wooden unit valves were used on Broadwood grands c.1910.

Finally to the construction of the chest for the valves. The best quality actions used maple for the walls of the chambers and, because it was necessary to provide facilities for servicing the double-valve systems, these usually have boards which are faced with buckskin or similar leather so that they may be air-tight. Oak and ash are other woods frequently found. Interiors of all chambers and pipes are liberally coated with shellac which fills the pores and minute grain cracks. The leather used for the pouches is a very fine, soft kid which meets the need for being completely air-tight, yet at the same time extremely flexible. Primary pouches are usually about $\frac{3}{4}$ inch diameter and secondaries about $1\frac{1}{4}$ inch diameter, each being glued over a chamber, bored in the pouch board, which is slightly smaller than the leather disc. Primary valves are often made by gluing small wooden button-shaped turnings on to a wooden spindle. Secondary valves, on the other hand, have a steel spindle on which are threaded inner and outer discs comprising a thick card body faced each side with leather, the thickness of the total not being above $\frac{1}{16}$ inch. A light wooden button is fixed to the end nearest the pouch, and rests in front of the pouch. The spindle is carried in guide slots to prevent any distortion in motion and these guides are usually made of fibre bushed with action-bushing felt. Single valve actions, made in the later years of the industry, dispensed with guides by making the spindles the same diameter as the orifice, and then grooving or scolloping out the spindle to provide an airway, whilst still leaving shoulders to bear on the walls of the hole as a guide. It is probably as well to note that brass screws are used throughout—certainly in the better-made actions—to resist corrosion and to facilitate dismantling and servicing.

I hasten to add that, in the same way it would be impossible to write a detailed description to cover the servicing of every type of motor-car ever made, so it would for the player-piano. Indeed, as the motor-car has a wheel at each corner, an engine, gearbox, transmission, steering

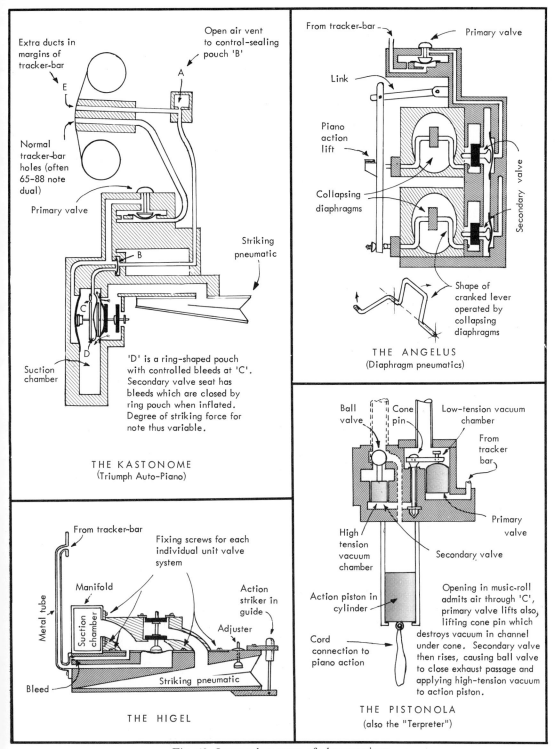

Extra ducts in margins of tracker-bar E

Open air vent to control-sealing pouch 'B' A

Normal tracker-bar holes (often 65-88 note dual)

Primary valve

Striking pneumatic

B

Suction chamber

C

D

'D' is a ring-shaped pouch with controlled bleeds at 'C'. Secondary valve seat has bleeds which are closed by ring pouch when inflated. Degree of striking force for note thus variable.

THE KASTONOME
(Triumph Auto-Piano)

From tracker-bar

Primary valve

Link

Piano action lift

Collapsing diaphragms

Secondary valve

Shape of cranked lever operated by collapsing diaphragms

THE ANGELUS
(Diaphragm pneumatics)

From tracker-bar

Fixing screws for each individual unit valve system

Manifold

Metal tube

Suction chamber

Action striker in guide

Adjuster

Bleed

Striking pneumatic

THE HIGEL

Ball valve

Cone pin

Low-tension vacuum chamber

From tracker bar

High tension vacuum chamber

Primary valve

Action piston in cylinder

Secondary valve

Cord connection to piano action

Opening in music-roll admits air through 'C', primary valve lifts also, lifting cone pin which destroys vacuum in channel under cone. Secondary valve then rises, causing ball valve to close exhaust passage and applying high-tension vacuum to action piston.

THE PISTONOLA
(also the "Terpreter")

Fig. 68. Some other types of player actions

173

and brakes, so has the player-piano a bellows system, a valve chest, pneumatic stack, tracker-bar, basic expression pneumatics, roll drive and controls. But makers chose to differ in their approach to problems and so every make of action differs in some way or another. However, an understanding of what the player-piano is for and what it does and how it works is the key to the ability to tackle work on any make of instrument. There are today few specialists in this field. Many piano-tuners try to avoid working on player-pianos, primarily because to tune a player-piano it is advisable to remove the player action first and this can add several hours to the job. Those who do work on players prefer to work on nothing else and there are at least two firms who will undertake to rebuild instruments like new. Again, the British enthusiast has the facility of the Player Piano Group—a unique association of devotees who, among other more practical aspects of pneumatic piano appreciation, have gathered together a rare assortment of player-piano literature and information. Founder of the Group is Mr Frank W. Holland who established the British Piano Museum—an amazing collection of mechanical musical instruments at Brentford, London. Thus the player-piano enthusiast may never feel 'out on a limb' and, should he find himself in difficulties, there are always fellow enthusiasts who are willing to advise.

CHAPTER 8

Rebuilding the Player Piano

THE player-piano is a carefully engineered piece of mechanism (the player) installed in a well-developed and carefully made instrument (the piano). It operates by reduced air pressure allowing atmospheric air to enter, performing functions on its way to the inside of the action.

In extension of this definition, we can see that, if air is allowed to enter elsewhere than through the proper places, or if ill-fitting or damaged pieces are used to control the air transference, then air will rush in and rapidly try to equalize the pressure inside the instrument with that of the outside atmosphere. This means that the player will not operate properly, nor will it sustain its necessary partial vacuum. Hard pedalling will thus be needed to try to maintain an operational pressure differential.

From this it is easy to see that the valve of an air seal, or the attachment of a tube or airway must fit properly and the repairer must exercise meticulous attention to detail if the pneumatic action is to be restored to perfection. The importance of this care cannot be over-emphasized.

The player-piano has one unfortunate secondary characteristic in that it works in exactly the same way as a vacuum cleaner. It draws air in from all around it and passes it back into the atmosphere, having extracted most if not all the dust particles on the way. Dust and dirt are thus the main enemies of the instrument. Another point to note is that the player action of a piano can be no better than the piano in which it is fitted. This is to say that if a piano is a poorly made specimen, or suffers certain inherent defects as a piano, then, no matter how good or how perfect the player action, it cannot improve the performance of the instrument.

The acquisition of a player-piano must therefore be prefaced by a careful examination of the instrument *as a piano* in addition to its condition and capabilities as a mechanical interpreter. A damaged frame, poor sound-board or badly-worn key action is seldom worth the amount of work necessary to restore it to good order.

It is preferable to buy an instrument by a good maker so that you can be fairly certain of its potentials. Many players are still in working order or are advertised, hopefully, as 'needing slight adjustment'—a delightful piece of vendor's jargon to describe a valetudinarian piano in need of anything from the reconnection of a loose tube to a total rebuild. Even more players are of unsound action, tubercular-bellowed and faint-hearted. Restoration can thus take anything from a few hours up to many weeks of work. For the purpose of the present chapter, I am assuming the worst and therefore will go right through the procedure of stripping, repairing and regulation. Naturally, if a player is in fair order, it would be foolish to dismantle the thing completely. Nevertheless, it is always a good idea to remove the player action, clean both it and the piano, check over the piano and tune it, and then replace and regulate the player.

To tackle player-pianos you will need ordinary handyman's tools plus a long 'watchmaker's' screwdriver and a pair of long-nosed pliers. Now you should also have certain specialist tools for attending to the piano action, but I suggest that you have this side of things tackled by an expert, unless you are well-versed in the practicalities of piano overhaul—in which case you will already have these piano tools! For player action rebuilding you will require a good, sharp pair of scissors—ideally barber's narrow, pointed scissors—a selection of small paintbrushes to be used for dusting and glue-spreading, a broad putty-knife for separating the pneumatics from the stack, an angled screwdriver for getting at screws in awkward places (this is a cranked rod having a 90° blade at one end and a 45° one at the other) and a sharp scalpel for cutting leather and pneumatic cloth *in situ*. Most important of all, you should buy a tracker-bar sucker from a piano-sundries house—this is like a large cycle pump and is used to draw dust out of the tracker-bar openings.

You will also probably need some thin leather for pouches and for seals, and some pneumatic cloth for pneumatics and bellows. It is important to match the original in quality and thickness at all times. Pouch leather, for example, must be soft, supple and very thin, and any other quality just will not do the job properly. The same goes for pneumatic cloth. Never be tempted to use thinner or thicker—it will affect the response of the action and probably the durability of the finished job. Rubber cloth and leathers can be bought from any piano-sundries house, or from an organ-builders. Piano felts, leather buttons for limit adjusters, tubing and all such parts, all come from piano-sundries suppliers.

A word about rubber tubing. There are two types of rubber—red and black. Now black tubing contains a high percentage of carbon and this causes the rubber to harden and deteriorate far quicker than the red quality. There is very little difference in price and red rubber tubing has almost twice the life of black tube under normal conditions. Tubes used to transfer vacuum from bellows to action are normally of fabric-reinforced rubber hose and this is the same quality as car radiator pipe. Unlike tracker-bar and service tubing which can be stretched on to a pipe or nipple, the main suction trunks are not so flexible and are held firm by hose clips. The 'Jubilee' clip is an ideal replacement for the original wire clips.

A number of people have re-tubed pianos using plastic or neoprene tubing on the grounds that it is often cheaper and certainly more durable than rubber. Be that as it may, these substances are affected by temperature, tending towards being hard and inflexible in cold weather and the opposite in summertime. Also, they are not endowed with the same properties of stretching as rubber, which means that once fitted to a nipple they can develop a 'set' and work loose or leak. On the standpoint that it will outlast rubber, I would say that it is more than likely that a player action should receive fairly thorough attention probably every ten to fifteen years of its life. Rubber tube can certainly last that time and it is no great hardship to re-tube the action on such occasions if necessary. It is probable that there will always be two schools of thought on this subject, so it must be left to the restorer as to which he chooses.

A vital accessory is a proper player-piano test roll which is available for either 65- or 88-note actions. These rolls are specially contrived to provide a thorough test for the operation of the action for each note, as well as demonstrating the proper valve setting and bleed hole size which will ensure that the note will repeat adequately and quickly. The roll is also used to regulate the speed of the player action in conjunction with the air motor and the *tempo*-control scale.

Test rolls are still available today from good piano-sundries houses the world over. They are not expensive and you cannot hope to do your job properly without one. Reproducing pianos, as we shall see in the next chapter, require to have their own special tester rolls.

We will now start work on the piano and, as already said, detail the complete dismantling. The first job is to unscrew and remove the bottom panel (to expose the bellows system), the upper front fall, the fallboard and the top of the piano. This will expose the complete workings. Removal of the player action necessitates the disconnecting of the controls to the hand levers and varies from instrument to instrument in detail. The pneumatic stack is fixed into place by two thumb nuts, one each side, and sometimes by a central bracket. Having removed the air hose into the chest, it can be undone and taken out. It is advisable to remove it with extreme care, tilting it backward and easing it gently out from the bottom, so that the pneumatics clear the wippens. Note that the action comes out complete with the roll box and all tracker tubing untouched.

The bellows are removed, after having removed the control linkages, by undoing the bolts holding the centre board into place. Wooden spacing blocks are sometimes used in each side and these, too, must be removed. The bellows can now be withdrawn complete.

Before proceeding further, it is as well to have a qualified piano-tuner come and regulate the action, take up any lost motion in the key/hammer linkage and also put it into tune. It is important that lost motion be rectified here and now, whilst the key action is readily accessible. I repeat that no player action made can make a bad piano sound good and thus a thorough overhaul of the piano is absolutely vital if anything like perfection is to be sought. Rusted or otherwise corroded piano strings will always sound dull and it is well worth having them replaced. Hammers which are deeply grooved may need replacing if it is not possible to needle the felt back to life. The action should be checked carefully for moth, since moth grubs cause more damage to pianos than may be appreciated. The grubs hatch in the felts and systematically eat their way through. This reduces the felt to a hard, lumpy mass, non-existent in places, and makes all the hammers lie at different positions. The throw of each hammer is thus different and the action noisy. Where traces of moth are present it is vital that *all* felts be replaced. It is utterly false economy to ignore these points and then spend much time and effort on the player action only to have it work fitfully due to a bad or damaged piano action. It is your instrument—take a pride in it from the start if you intend to restore it.

Having either had the piano overhauled or having done it yourself, if you have the knowledge and ability, you can either close it up or cover it with a dust sheet until the player action is ready to be replaced. To leave a piano open can do nothing but harm.

We can now start work on the player action. As we might imagine, having read the foregoing chapter, the assembly known as the upper action comprises two parts—the valve chest and the pneumatic stack—which are usually connected by wood-screws or screwed brackets. The dismantling of the action will call for a certain amount of careful examination, as all manufacturers constructed their actions along different principles. By removing the front board and the top board, where fitted, the primary valve tops will be revealed, also the screws which secure the pieces forming the lower ducts and airways. The illustration, Fig. 67, shows the Standard Player Action in part-section and from this can be seen the valve chest and the pneumatic stack which must be separated.

Begin by removing the action linkages which run between the striking fingers and the pneumatics. On most actions these are fixed to the pneumatics with small metal brackets, held in place by woodscrews. Others, like Aeolian, use wooden ones. Disconnect all these brackets but do not remove the brackets from their wire links unless it is necessary to clean or replace them. The decks carrying the pneumatics can now be unscrewed from their common location board and the fixing screws can normally be found running from the front of the location board back into the decks. Before this, however, mark each deck clearly at one end, say 'a', 'b' and 'c', to aid re-assembly. Now mark each individual pneumatic with a ball-point pen or similar, to ensure that each may be replaced in exactly the original position. Always number from left front to right to avoid confusion.

The seal between the decks and the location board (which also carries the secondary valves board) is normally of soft leather. Occasionally, a previous repairer may have thoughtlessly glued them together, in which case you must split them apart very carefully using a broad-bladed knife. Never use a narrow chisel or screwdriver to separate glued parts—this will compress the wood locally and forever spoil the seal. Use a putty-knife.

Carefully remove the decks one at a time, remembering that a while spent thinking about each move beforehand can ensure both the proper way to complete a job and also aid re-assembly later. Skill comes with practice and never be guilty of fooling yourself. Take your time—it will pay in the long run.

Examine the pneumatics for deterioration, hardening of the rubber cloth and flaking of the rubberized surface due to the hard surface cracking. If the cloth crackles when fingered, then it is useless and must be renewed. In checking these pneumatics, do not deceive yourself into believing that perhaps they are all right when in fact they are suspect. Nothing is more exasperating then to complete the replacement of a player action only to find that careless work dictates that it must all be torn apart once more. If the rubberized cloth on one pneumatic has deteriorated, then it is both a safe assumption and a wise decision to consider that all of the pneumatics must be re-covered. At the most it will add eight hours' work to your task—if you are practised in the art it will take you much less. The risk you run by leaving them alone is that, at any time, one or more notes may just cease to play and the whole player action lose power. It is a quirk of personalized mechanisms of all sorts that they always choose to mal-function when their proud owners are demonstrating them to an admiring (or critical!) audience. Rest assured that your carelessly-restored player-piano will pack up on you just when you are hopefully serenading someone of importance.

Occasionally one does find just one or two pneumatics which have sustained physical damage, although the remainder of the stack is genuinely serviceable. If it is not possible to remove the defective pneumatic for re-covering, and if the hole is small, it can be patched using a small disc of rubberized cloth at least twice the size of the damaged part. Only glue around the edge of the patch—never glue in the centre as this will result in a stiff lump being formed which may well affect the operation of the pneumatic.

Now comes the removal of the individual pneumatics. These are sometimes glued in place and the adhesive originally used was hot animal glue, which tends to be rather brittle. Drive the point of the putty-knife between the deck and the pneumatic, taking care not to allow it to dig into the wood. A few taps with a hammer are usually enough to cause the pneumatic to crack free. A word of warning here. A number of players, including those of European origin, and also some player-organs which employ single-valve systems, have the pneumatics screwed to the deck from underneath. This type of attachment is easily recognizable by the fact that there is a white soft-leather seal between deck and pneumatics, and they all come free as soon as the fixing screws are removed from beneath.

In removing the glued pneumatics, you may find some are more obstinate than others.

These should be left until last so that, with the others out of the way, you can approach them from three if not four sides. If they still prove unwilling to separate from the deck, paint methylated spirits round the edges of the glue line or tear open the pneumatic, fold the hinged board back, place a penny centrally on the fixed board and rest a hot soldering-iron on top. The transmitted heat will soften the glued joint after a few minutes.

Having taken off all the pneumatics, resist the temptation to clean off the deck and remove the old glue from the pneumatics, as this slightly irregular surface is matched on both deck and pneumatic and is necessary to provide a fresh seal on re-gluing.

Rubberized cloth is available in several thicknesses and only the thinnest must be used for re-covering the pneumatics. Before removing the old cloth from them, find one which still has its cloth reasonably intact and open the motor fully so that the cloth is taut. Measure the span of the motor in this position; this is the width which the newly covered motors must measure on completion. Remove the old cloth by sanding, ideally on a belt sander.

If this is not available, you can hold a sheet of medium sandpaper flat on a level table surface and, gripping the pneumatic tightly in the other hand, rub it briskly up and down the paper a few times. This will effectively remove the old cloth down to the wood, the folded cloth in the middle being pulled out afterwards. Try not to damage the fabric hinge to the pneumatic boards as this is invariably intact and in any case is covered by the rubber cloth.

Cut your new rubberized pneumatic cloth into strips just a little wider than the finished span required and long enough to wrap right around the pneumatic with an overlap of about $\frac{3}{8}$ inch at the back, or hinge, edge. Some repair-men advocate tearing the new cloth into strips to save time. If you do this, allow at least an extra $\frac{1}{8}$ inch in width so that the ragged edge which invariably remains may be removed completely afterwards, since the act of tearing strains the rubberized fibres and can affect the air-tightness.

The steps in recovering pneumatics, all 88 of them (65 in a 65-note player), can be done progressively throughout the lot to speed up the work and relieve the tedium. The job takes but an hour to do and you must use hot brown glue. One of the best glues available is cabinet-maker's 'Pearl' glue which comes in pellet form and must be dissolved with water and just a few drops of methylated spirits. Alternatively, 'Duraglue' in tins should be used. Avoid white or clear glues, synthetic resin glues—these will ruin the chances of success for any subsequent repairer. It is as well to bear in mind that, properly looked after, a player-piano should last indefinitely if it is rebuilt, say, every twenty years or so, and thus you must consider the ease with which your work can be ultimately replaced in the future.

Dissolve your glue in a small jar such as a cream bottle ('Duraglue' can be kept in its own tin) and place the glue container in an old saucepan full of hot water to keep the glue soft. It should be maintained at the consistency of thin syrup; any thicker and it will not spread properly; any thinner and it will not adhere. You will tend to get plenty of glue on your fingers, which you should not be afraid of using as glue spreaders, and, because you must also maintain the glue warm enough, it is not a bad idea to do this job on the kitchen table near stove and washing facilities.

Lay all the strips of cloth on the table so that none is overlapping and approximately mark the centre of each length. See that all the pneumatic boards are clean and not cracked or split (remembering not to clean off the surface which is later to be glued back on to the deck). With a small stiffish brush, apply glue evenly to the open ends of the boards of the first pneumatic and then press them firmly on to the cloth (rubber side on the outside, of course!), moving them slightly so as to exclude any trapped air. The boards should now be standing vertically

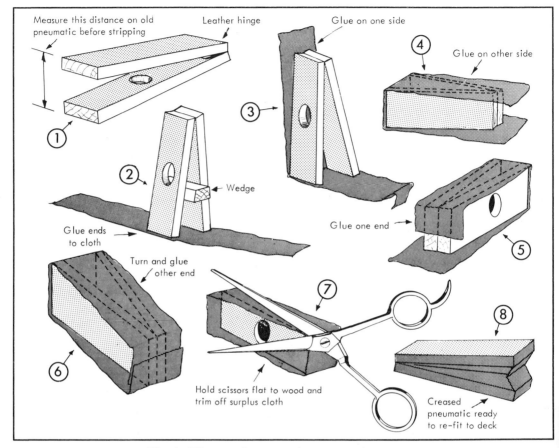

Measure this distance on old pneumatic before stripping

Leather hinge

Glue on one side

④ Glue on other side

③

② ← Wedge

Glue ends to cloth

Glue one end

⑤

Turn and glue other end

⑦

⑥

Hold scissors flat to wood and trim off surplus cloth

⑧

Creased pneumatic ready to re-fit to deck

Fig. 69. The steps in re-covering pneumatic motors

at the approximate centre of the strip, as shown in the illustration.

This work is all very important and, at the risk of appearing pedantic, I must make reference to the spreading of the glue on the boards. You should apply the coating evenly but neither too thickly nor too sparsely. Cover the surface and then gently smear the surface with the finger to spread it. Try not to let any get on to the inside edges of the boards and certainly do not allow any to run over the inside of the boards or over the cloth. Glue on the inside edge will form a hard ridge; glue on the free portions of the cloth will harden it. Both these serve to inhibit the free movement of the pneumatic in use. It all sounds involved yet in the time taken to read these words, you may complete the covering of several pneumatics.

Having glued all the open boards to the strips, go back to the first one you worked on, lay it on its side, glue the edges and lay the cloth evenly over that side, taking care not to over-stretch the cloth whilst at the same time ensuring that it is properly down at the corners. Turn the pneumatic over and repeat the process on the other side, completing the job by gluing and lapping the ends of the cloth to the hinge edge of the pneumatic. Set this on one side to dry, so placing it that it will not stick to the table. Proceed in this fashion through all the pneumatics. Now take a hot, damp cloth and quickly wipe the edges of all the pneumatics, keeping the cloth hot and moist from time to time, to remove any excess glue which might cause tackiness.

A player left in a moist atmosphere, bad at the best of times, may well have its motors gum up through neglect of this point remembering that it is difficult to avoid some glue transferring from the fingers on to the outside of the cloth.

Once they have all been wiped off, return to the first one again and trim it along all its edges using a pair of long, narrow-bladed scissors. I use special barber's scissors, which are readily available from good hardware shops, and by the use of which a whole edge can be cut in one go. The final job is creasing and this is done by opening the pneumatic fully and then pushing in the sides with the thumb and middle finger whilst the forefinger pushes in the top. Press the motor firmly closed and this will induce a permanent crease in the new cloth. Finally, lightly dust French chalk over the rubberized surface of each one. This ensures that there is no chance of the cloth sticking in the folds.

To replace the pneumatic motors on their decks, first of all sort them out to follow the original marking or numbering for each deck. Where they have to be glued on, obtain some spring clamps or large 'Bulldog' clips wide enough to clamp the pneumatics to the deck. Apply hot glue to the mating surface of the first pneumatic, press it into place and exclude all air bubbles, then apply the clamp. Avoid over-tightening and, if you resort to using 'G' clamps, make sure you put a block of wood between the jaw of the clamp and the pneumatic to spread the pressure, and do not tighten more than is necessary to hold it steady whilst the glue sets. In actions where the pneumatics are not glued but held in position by just woodscrews, tease up the intervening leather seal with a wire suède-brush before refitting the motors. Once all the decks have been attended to and their motors replaced, put them to one side and attend to the valve chest assembly.

The state and condition of the valves, their operating pouches and the vents or bleed-holes is vital to the operation of the player action and thus you must use meticulous care in completing the steps of reconditioning.

As already said, there are many different styles of player action and although all have the same salient features and ultimate function, the details of assembly vary greatly and thus some thought must be devoted as to the way in which an action interprets the principles and how best to take it apart. Dismantle the chest, setting each piece on a clean, clear bench. It is a good idea to cover your working surface with white or brown paper; it not only looks neater but it makes it easier to trace and find small parts which may otherwise hide themselves by process of camouflage.

Begin work on the pouch board. If the leather pouches are cracked, torn or hardened in any way, then you must replace the lot. Fortunately, this special leather, being closed up in the dark and with limited access to air, retains its life much longer than might be imagined. Pouches in good condition should feel smooth and pliable. Run the finger tip around the inner surface. Again, don't try to fool yourself that they are serviceable if there is any doubt. Press your finger on to a pouch and just see if you can push your finger through the leather by exerting a little force. Good leather will easily resist tearing in this way. On some single-valve actions, the leather will have, glued to its centre, a disc of thick cardboard which engages with the button on the end of the valve stem to prevent its ultimate penetration of the leather. Most player actions used a fibre disc or washer for this purpose. Where a pouch is defective, pull off these discs and clean off any remnants of the old leather from their undersides together with the old glue and set them aside for subsequent replacement. Removing the old leather from the board is best done with a flat scraper. Work down to the bare wood where each leather pouch disc was originally glued. Thoroughly dust off the board and clear the bleed holes of leather and glue dust. Ideally, use a vacuum cleaner for this, alternately sucking and blowing (by reversing the hose in the cleaner) through the vents and also through the pouch recesses.

In cases where the pouches are not readily accessible and where it is believed that they may be in such good condition that it does not justify massive dismantling to get to them, each one can be tested by using a length of rubber tube. Arrange the position of the pouch board so that the valves are vertical and gently blow through the tube. The pouch should inflate and move the valves easily. Its operation must be prompt, sensitive and quite free.

The bleeds—they are often found as small, brass pressings fitted into the pouch board, adjacent to the pouches—must be clear of dirt. Some actions, particularly early ones, used discs of stiff paper or celluloid, stuck flat over a hole in the pouch board. These discs would have a small central piercing through which the air could pass.

Pouch leather is a soft, thin brown skiver and is obtainable from piano-sundries houses and also from organ-builders. It is expensive and in short supply. Because of this, don't be tempted to use substitutes. You might use a white skin, but it will be at the expense of the promptness and repetition of the action.

The leather must be cut into discs approximately $\frac{3}{8}$ inch greater in diameter than the diameter of the pouch borings in the pouch board. Originally, these discs were punched but, unless you have a press and a sharp punch, you will be better off with a pair of sharp scissors. Examine the leather closely for imperfections and rough, hard patches on the underside. The edges of a skin often include irregular material having sharp variations in thickness and also small holes. Obviously, you must not use these pieces. Make a pattern in stiff card and mark round it on the leather using a ball-point pen. Carefully cut out each leather disc.

I have already laid emphasis on the application of glue regarding other reconstruction work; now I must once more stress the importance of careful gluing. If too much glue is used to fix the leather discs over the pouches, it will form a hard rim around the inside, reduce the effect of the pouch, limit its movement and generally spoil the performance of the action operated by that particular pouch and valve. You should spread the glue around the pouch opening with the forefinger and in such a way that the extreme edge of the opening *remains dry and unglued*. Aim to apply a concentric ring of glue around the opening—if it spreads outside the area it is of no consequence. By using the finger, a fairly even glue coverage can be achieved. Place the leather disc centrally in the hole and with the left forefinger press it gently down in the extreme middle so that it touches the bottom of the pouch boring. With the fingers of the right hand, gently and evenly smooth out the edge of the disc so that it lies flat and unwrinkled. You can make up a tool to do this so that each pouch is dished exactly the same. Make it from hardwood and machine a dome on the end $\frac{1}{32}$ inch less in diameter than the pouch boring, and about $\frac{1}{32}$ inch less than the depth of the bore. The sketch (Fig. 70) shows such a tool. You will appreciate that, as the valves should all move an equal distance in the performance of their duties, the pouches should all move a similar amount, one to the other. If you find that successive leather discs overlap, this is quite acceptable so long as the edge of one disc does not actually come to the edge of an adjacent bore or become glued near the vital unsupported part of an existing, adjacent pouch-disc leather. Where this happens, it is perfectly acceptable to trim a piece off the leather. Do not let glue get on to the free leather of the pouch, and, if you make a mistake in positioning a disc so that it gets glue on the vital part underneath, then scrap it and use another or thoroughly wipe it off with a damp cloth.

Refit the card or fibre central valve-contact discs to the leather where originally used and now refit the valve stack over the pouch board. Do not overtighten the screws or strip the

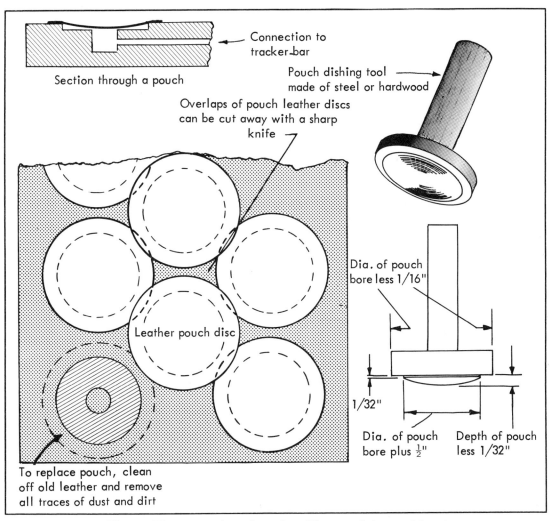

Section through a pouch

Connection to
tracker-bar

Pouch dishing tool
made of steel or hardwood

Overlaps of pouch leather discs
can be cut away with a sharp
knife

Leather pouch disc

Dia. of pouch
bore less 1/16"

1/32"

Dia. of pouch
bore plus $\frac{1}{2}$"

Depth of pouch
less 1/32"

To replace pouch, clean
off old leather and remove
all traces of dust and dirt

Fig. 70. The re-covering of pouches. The use of the special tool
speeds the work where many have to be replaced

screw threads from the wooden pieces. Adopt the policy of always inserting the screws by
hand and starting them as far as you can with your fingers. In tightening screws, start at each
end alternately and tighten adjacent ones in opposite rows gradually so as to close the boards
evenly and without strain. An engineer refits the cylinder head to a motor-car engine in the
same fashion so that the mating faces do not distort and the joints leak. Apply the same care
to the screwing of wooden pieces where the joint must be tight. Where leather is used to face
a joint, it is always glued with the natural outside surface to the wood, the soft, furry inside
face being the one which seals to the mating component. When you have such a seal to replace,
strip off the old leather and clean off any residue, particularly any traces of the skived surface
of the old leather.

Your new piece of leather should be soft, white skin, free from hard lumps or ridges on its surface. Ideally, you should adopt the organ-builder's technique of sanding the soft inner side of the skin and then rubbing powdered chalk into it, but, as this refinement is seldom found on pianos, you can be excused from following suit.

If the piece is to be used to face, say, a windway with an opening in it, or if the piece has screw holes in it, cut neither the opening nor the holes before gluing. Using hot brown glue such as Duraglue, evenly coat the wood and then press the leather, natural outside to the glue, and apply hand pressure until the glue will hold it—normally a couple of moments. Trim off the outer edges with a very sharp modelling knife and then cut round the openings. Where the screw holes are, cut out a small square hole with the point of the knife.

Whilst you can use ordinary modelling knives in this work, it is well worth spending a few shillings on the purchase of a Swann-Morton scalpel. You can order these from both artists and drawing-office supplies shops and chemists. The blades to use are No. 11 which are slender, pointed—and surgically sharp.

Assemble the valve chest to the pouch board. Since each make of action differs in detail, the only guidance I can give here is that the sequence of operations in dismantling should now be reversed. The regulation and adjustment of the valves can now be made at this point. This is made easy on some actions by the valve stem being threaded so that the valve head may be screwed up or down a little. With the pouches in the normal, 'silent' position, the pad or button which is provided on the end of the valve should be just a fraction clear of the pouch disc. If you can pass a strip of thin notepaper between pouch disc and valve button without the valve being lifted from its seat, this is ideal. The final adjustment of primary and secondary valves is dealt with further on but there is one point to watch and that is that, if the valves were originally locked to the screwed stem with a drop of shellac or glue and if you have disturbed them, then you must relock them with a spot of glue.

Replace the pneumatic stacks, making sure that the securing screws are all replaced and tightened evenly. Do not rely on the screws to draw up the wooden pieces by their threads alone—this way you can strip the threads in the timber. Hold each pneumatic deck in the correct position, start the screws by hand and tighten them evenly, gently drawing the deck back into place. It goes without saying that all dirt and dust must first be removed from all mating surfaces, otherwise the seal of the joint will be affected.

Having refitted all the decks, you must now replace the connecting links attached to the pneumatics. These are carried on a bar or guide and if you removed this bar earlier, then you must replace it now. Where the links are attached to metal brackets, each is now screwed back on to its pneumatic and the trick here is to place a drop of hot glue between the metal link and the wood before bringing the two pieces together and tightening up the little woodscrews. Naturally the metal is not glued to the wood by the hot glue, but the glue, being forced out from under the link, forms a reinforcing key to steady the links from sideways play and prevents them from working loose. With wooden brackets, this is not necessary.

Replace all cover boards and refit any control levers and their cranks ('squares') to the underside of the action, as necessary. The action can now be re-tubed, as the last job before fitting back into the piano. The subject of tubing has been covered earlier in this chapter. Although at first sight the mass of tubing and its apparent complexity appears as insoluble as a Chinese puzzle, replacement of the tubes is not a difficult task. The tubes run from the first hole in the tracker-bar to the first hole in the action pouch board and thence along to the other end and if each tube is replaced individually, the job is easily done. When automatic pedal controls are fitted, these tubes run from the tracker-bar to a valve block. Wherever possible, cut your new tube using the old one as a pattern. If it is not possible to do this, run the new tube between the two nipples and cut it so as to allow a little slack—there must be no strain on the tube nor must it be either so tight or loose that it can kink. Sometimes a tube will become so hard that it no longer appears to be made of rubber. This can best be removed by shattering it, using a pair of pliers to squeeze it, taking care not to press so hard that the metal pipe or nipple beneath is damaged. The metal can then be cleaned up with wire wool. Rubber can also be transformed into the exact opposite—a nasty sticky mess. This you can remove by scraping with your fingers and afterwards washing the nipple (and your fingers) in petrol. Re-tube auto-tracking devices at the same time.

Lift the action back into the piano. You should have someone help you so that a hasty move does not undo all the work you have so far accomplished. The exact method of replacement you will have to find by experiment, but normally you should tip the action so that it leans backwards slightly as it goes into place, so that the lifting pieces of the player action do not foul the wippens. Secure the action into place with the studs and nuts provided and see that they are done up tightly.

Most actions feature an adjustment to the lifting pieces so that they can be brought into the proper position relative to the wippens. With the action at rest, the lifting pieces should just be in contact with the wippens. If all the piano hammers were properly set before replacing the player action, then they should remain all perfectly in alignment with the action in place. Test the action of each note manually from the keyboard, to see that nothing is being fouled. In lieu of a proper tool, adjustment of the lifting pieces can usually be made using a length of stiff wire with a $\frac{3}{8}$ inch long, right-angle bend at one end.

With the upper action now restored and installed once more, turn your attention to the bellows system. Examine the exhausters and equalizer(s) for deterioration of the covering, paying close attention to the corners and folds and not forgetting the bottom hinge line. I refer here to equalizer(s) because the early player actions and those of the cabinet-style push-ups used only one large equalizer; the later players often employed one for the bass action and one for the treble, each with a different 'power' as governed by the internal springs.

Bellows cloth can be very deceiving. It must not feel hard, nor must it flake when rubbed. However, even cloth which seems satisfactory may, on test, be shown to be useless. Quite often, rubberized cloth develops thousands of tiny pin-holes through which air can pass, and these holes are only visible when the cloth is held up to the light. If the bellows system will not hold vacuum, i.e. if the equalizer opens fully very quickly after the exhausters have been operated, then it is quite likely that the cloth is porous. When one piece of cloth is found to be porous, you are safe to assume all to be porous and you should re-cover all the moving bellows parts. A serviceable bellows system should maintain its vacuum for between six and eight seconds.

Should it be necessary to open up an equalizer at any time, either to renew the flap valves or to re-cover, take great care that the internal springs do not fly out and hit you. They are extremely powerful and the haphazard stripping off of the old cloth could lead to a serious accident. It is a good idea to leave a wide strip of the original cloth still in place along the wide top edge of the equalizer so that the spring tension can remain held. In re-covering, this strip can be left in place, the new covering passing over it. So long as the new cloth is not glued to the old piece (except at the edges of the equalizer of course) it will not interfere in any way with the operation of the unit. You might resort to a 'dodge' such as holding the boards of the equalizer between rigid floor-braces whilst re-covering but, whatever you do, an appreciation of the vicious bite which an equalizer spring can give is the most important thing.

Notice that the shape of the bellows cloth is very important if a free and strain-free movement of the finished unit is to result. You must cut it evenly about a centre-line representing the whole length of the wrapped-round cloth.

Fix the new cloth with hot glue well worked into the weave. On some players the cloth was originally tacked on as well. It is not good practice to have even headed tacks passing directly through the fabric and if you choose to replace using glue and tacks, and provided that there is enough room when the units are assembled, adopt the organ-builders' bellows technique and tack through thin strips of wood about $\frac{1}{2}$ inch by $\frac{1}{8}$ inch. Whether just glued on, or glued and tacked, pay close attention to the forming of the new cloth at the corners to ensure a freely-moving, close fit.

When restoration is complete, refit the bellows to the piano and seal off the main outlet trunk. Now test the bellows for leaks. After four or five strokes of the exhausters, the foot treadles should offer considerable resistance up to the point of the opening of the relief valve where fitted.

Final assembly of the player action can now proceed together with the attachment of hand-operated controls.

Testing, fault-finding and regulation can all be classed under one heading—adjustment. However, assuming that perhaps you have obtained a player in working order I shall include some pointers towards major defects which should already have been taken care of during rebuilding. Although the player-piano is at first sight a complex of piping, motors and valves, we learned from the preceding chapter that this complexity is but an assembly of functional parts all basically working in a similar manner, and therefore, armed with an intimate knowledge of our piano-player, common sense will largely dictate what has to be done in the way of adjustment.

First of all, you should test for leaks by sealing off the tracker-bar either by placing a roll of music in position and stopping on the unperforated leader part, or by sticking a strip of sellotape across the openings in the bar. Place the *tempo* lever at the pause position (normally to the far left) and put the re-roll lever to 'play'. Now treadle evenly. If the action and bellows are sound, there should be a mounting resistance felt through the feet, culminating on some pianos by the opening of the spill valve, the effect of which can be felt as a release of some pressure. If, however, there is little or no resistance, then there is a leak somewhere which can often be heard as a rushing or whistling. Have a friend treadle whilst you locate the leak. It may be a hole or split in the bellows, a disconnected air tube or a badly-fitting joint somewhere in the action.

Some leaks are very stubborn to locate and in these cases you must resort to a process of elimination. First disconnect all the connections to the bellows system, such as the main trunk to the upper action, the motor airway, the supply to the sustaining-pedal pneumatic or hammer rail motors and so on. Plug these open ends and try treadling again. If there is no great resistance, then you know the defect lies in the bellows system. Check all the wood screws for security and then examine the cloth of the bellows folds very closely—it is most likely that the cloth will have deteriorated along one of the crease lines (don't forget the hinge strip at the root of the bellows) or at one or more of the folding corners of the cloth.

Proceed with this elimination method, connecting and testing the various functions one by one. Check the air motor carefully to see that the leak is not being caused by an uneven sliding surface to one of the valves.

Finally reconnect the upper action and if this leaks, try tightening all the screws but beware of over-tightening which will only result in stripping the threads of the screws and making matters worse. (Stripped threads must be plugged with a softwood peg and the screw replaced in the centre of the peg.) If this does not cure the trouble, then one can be fairly certain that the primary or secondary valves are not seated properly. If the secondary valves do not make a good seal against the exhaust seats, there will be a leak and this can be due to a particle of dust, or the buttons on the other end of the valve stem may be adjusted so that they are touching the pouches, so preventing them from lifting the valves sufficiently. In the case of primary valves, they may not have the proper range of movement or again dust may have lodged beneath the buttons.

There is a good way to short-circuit these tests and that is to move the re-roll lever to the 're-roll' position and hold the motor against turning whilst treadling. If there is a strong resistance offered by the treadles, then the indications are that the bellows system is serviceable and that the leak is in the upper action.

Now comes the test for notes that may not play. The use of the tester roll is called for here and it should be watched closely as it travels over the tracker-bar to see that each note sounds. If any do not, then it may well be that the tube from the tracker-bar to the primary pouch is blocked with dust or fluff from the music-rolls. This can be sucked out with the suction pump. If the note does play but will not repeat, the bleed hole is probably obstructed, or the valves may be sticking, playing once but not repeating. Remove the front board from the valve chest and, using a length of rubber tubing, blow into the suspect tracker hole to check that the valves move. If the primary valve does not move, the tracker tube may be blocked, or the valve held down by some mechanical defect such as corrosion, dampness or dirt. Try next the secondary valves. The action can thus be tested thoroughly by following the path taken by the air in playing. Using a note which plays well as a yardstick, observe how its valves function and compare with the defective ones.

If the bleed hole is blocked, use a piece of fine wire, bent to suit, and gently insert it into the little hole. This will clear any obstruction. Be careful not to enlarge the bleed or, in actions where the bleed is in the form of a small metal cup or celluloid disc with a hole in the centre, take care not to dislodge it.

The bleed hole is also to be suspected if the action displays slow or sluggish repetition. If a good sucking out from the tracker-bar fails to remedy this, the bleed holes must be cleaned out by carefully probing each one. Now it may be necessary to enlarge a bleed hole and whilst this is good for repetition, since it allows rapid equalization of pressures after a note has been sounded, it adversely affects playing power, since, by the same premise, the air inflating the pouch is being vented faster. Generally speaking, the action should be arranged so that the notes on the test roll should repeat well on light pumping at a *tempo* setting of 80.

Supposing if, on test, it is seen that one or more hammers are not falling right back to their proper place (assuming the piano action to be in perfect order), then this is due to the secondary valve remaining open. The cause can be dirt under the primary valve, thus causing it to remain open, keeping the pneumatic in a state of collapse.

If the primary valve functions properly but the hammer-action pneumatic remains motionless and inoperative, it may be that the channel between the primary valve and the secondary pouch is blocked. If the secondary pouch works, then the trouble must lie in the secondary valve which may be stuck by spread glue or dampness. Satisfactory primary valves coupled with inoperative pneumatics always indicates trouble in the secondary pouch or valve. Valves and pouches can always be checked by blowing them with a rubber tube, holding one end of the tube in the mouth. The pouches should inflate under the merest breath but do not forget that the air is being bled away through the bleed hole. Secondary pouches, on the other hand, should show a positive resistance when blown, for there is no bleed hole between the channels. Primaries should, by comparison, offer a slight resistance.

Sometimes after re-assembly of an action, some notes will appear inoperative for no other reason than that the valves have not seated properly. These can be detected with the test roll and quite often the staccato repetition of the note, as instructed by the roll, will be sufficient to cause the valve to drop back into place. The test roll is also of assistance in the reseating of player action valves after a piano has been moved. Generally speaking, it is harmful to tip a player-piano on end but removal men often find it necessary to do just this when shifting an instrument. The result is that the valves become unseated, and, on righting the instrument, some may not return to their proper place. A few plays with the test roll can often save tears, disappointment and unnecessary work.

When all valves and pneumatics seem to work but the piano will not play certain notes, then the trouble lies in the linkage between the pneumatic and the piano action which is usually a wire.

Should there be a leak at the exhaust side of the secondary valve, the pneumatic will either not work or, if it does, it will work weakly and slowly. If the secondary valve has too much movement, then the movement of the pneumatic would be very weak and the normal playing resistance to the foot treadles would diminish, calling for more rapid pumping. On the other hand, if the secondary valves have too little motion, the pneumatic action will be slow and the player would not sound very loud. Primary valves need not rise more than $\frac{1}{64}$ inch and secondaries between $\frac{1}{32}$ inch and $\frac{1}{8}$ inch, depending on the action. An average is $\frac{1}{16}$ inch and it is imperative that all valve settings, whatever they are, are repeated throughout the valve system otherwise there will be a variation in the apparent striking force of each note. The single-valve system should be adjusted to lift between $\frac{1}{16}$ inch and $\frac{1}{8}$ inch depending on the action.

On the bellows system, if there is a leak in the flap valve of the exhausters, there will be little resistance to the treadles and little work done for each stroke. If the valve on the inside of the exhauster leaks, there will be normal resistance on the downwards stroke, but an immediate tendency to kick back at the end of the stroke. Another indication of the deterioration of the inside flap valves is if one treadle is lightly held fully down and the other pumped, there should be no feed-back of motion to the down treadle. If the stroke of one has a counter effect on the other, however slight, then the inside valves are leaking.

As already indicated, dust and dirt are the enemies of a pneumatic action and the presence of foreign matter between the valves and their seats can cause a whole host of malfunctionings such as expression-pneumatics operating all the time, notes sounding or not sounding, motors running at high speed even with the *tempo* control closed, inoperative tracking devices and so on. Ciphers, the bane of the organ-builder, also affect pianos and a ciphering pneumatic is one which allows a note to be played when there is no note indicated by a corresponding hole in the music roll. The trouble is usually something elementary such as dirt holding a valve open, a disconnected tracker-bar tube or one with a leak in it. The magnitude of the effect of dirt is best appreciated when you realize that it only takes a few bits of dirt, holding a few valves open, to cause a pneumatic action to be inoperative, for, as fast as air is pumped out, air is drawn straight back in again.

Another defect can be the opposite of a cipher. Here a note remains silent when it should sound. The pneumatic will not collapse. The cause can be a blocked air passage, a twisted or kinked tube, or the pneumatic may be loose on its seating, so being deprived of its operating vacuum by an unintentional air inlet.

If the action cut-off is not working properly, then the music will play on re-wind. If the cut-off is mechanical, then the trouble should be easy to locate—a broken linkage, a stripped thread or similar. If the cut-off is pneumatic, then the defects which can plague such a system should be sought after—a sticking valve, blocked or kinked tube, broken tube.

If you find that the pneumatic stack will show no vacuum—in other words there is no operation of the pneumatics when the bellows are operated—then the trouble can be the incorrect setting of the primary valves or perhaps they have been unseated. This is fairly common when a piano is shifted, as mentioned earlier. If it worked well beforehand, it is only necessary to keep the instrument playing for an hour or so to enable the valves to drop back. However, where this is not the case it may be due to valve-guide corrosion where the valves have guide pins, or perhaps the pouches have lost their suppleness. The pouches must be soft and pliable and the valves seating correctly.

If the action just does not play and no other cause can be found, then it is fairly obvious that the action cut-off valve is remaining closed. This can be due to a detached suction hose in which case the treadles would offer no great resistance. Alternatively, if the valve is closed, and the hoses are all present and correct, then there will be heavy resistance to the foot treadles.

The most sensitive and important feature of the player-piano is the air motor and it is to this that we must look for the ability to be able to give an individual performance. Its failure to give of its best will thus have a drastic effect on the music played. Music-rolls are arranged to agree to certain pre-arranged *tempi* and these correspond to certain numbers which are indicated on the *tempo* scale forming part of the motor control, and which are also called up on the music-roll. The following table shows first the *tempo* pointer setting and then the proper distance which the paper should travel over the tracker-bar measured in feet per minute:

Number	Ft/min.
10	1
20	2
30	3
40	4
50	5
60	6
70	7
80	8
90	9
100	10
110	11
120	12
130	13

During manufacture, the air motor was originally calibrated at at least three points in this speed range but for the purpose of repair it is normally adequate to see that the paper travels 7 feet in one minute with the *tempo* setting at 70. Test rolls are normally intended to be run at 70 but—and watch carefully for this—it is usual for reproducing-piano test rolls, as mentioned in the next chapter, to run at 80.

Supposing that the motor runs faster than it should, then the spring in the motor-governor must be slackened off slightly and, conversely, if the motor runs too slow, then the spring must be tightened. All speed calibrations are best done either with the test roll marked off at 1 foot intervals with a pencil, or with any suitable music-roll. A watch with a sweep second-hand can then be held by the roll whilst playing to check the speed setting.

Supposing the motor runs too fast immediately you start to treadle hard, then this shows that the motor-governor is not closing sufficiently. The adjusting screw for the jack-knife valve should be brought out a fraction until this is cured. Do not alter the spring setting unless the motor also races on normal pumping.

If, as soon as you start to pedal hard, the motor slows down, the governor must be closing too much. Again, the regulation of the jack-knife setting screw is the answer. Screw it in a little so that the governor closes a fraction more. If the motor drags on light pumping, then the spring tension needs to be increased.

Should the motor run irregularly (visibly moving erratically or momentarily stopping, particularly when carrying a heavy load such as at the end of a long roll, and emphasized by a slow *tempo* setting to begin with), this usually means that the sliders of the motor are not seated correctly. They may be warped or the surfaces need re-graphiting. Where there is a chance that they are warped or roughened, rub down both sliders and their mating surfaces on a sheet of fine glasspaper resting on a dead flat surface, such as a piece of plate glass. After sanding, they can be burnished by rubbing hard on the plate glass. To re-graphite, gently breathe on the surface to make it very, very slightly damp and then dust on graphite and rub it into the wood with the finger. Continue in this fashion until the whole surface is 'bright' with graphite and the wood grain completely filled. Never use any form of oil, either on its own or mixed with the graphite. The essence of graphite is that it is a perfectly dry lubricant which minimizes drag between moving mating-components. Some people claim to achieve the same results with talcum powder or French chalk. Admittedly, the initial effects are similar, *but* both talcum and French chalk are basically the same substance and they absorb moisture. A talcum-lubricated motor will work well for a while, but will rapidly slow up and become gummy and erratic. Use only graphite of the type made for locksmiths, although, as a 'running repair', you can rub a very soft pencil, such as a 6B grade, over the surfaces so long as the pencil point does not indent the wood.

Other problems which can lead to irregular running of the motor are badly adjusted or bent connecting rods and, of course, leaking pneumatics. Dealing first with pneumatics, they are often found to have been strengthened in manufacture by the addition of small corner gussets in the central folds. These patches are usually of leather glued to the rubber cloth and they deteriorate rapidly. If you endeavour to replace or patch these patches, you will only serve to increase the friction of the motor and it is far better to re-cover the pneumatics completely with thin rubber cloth. Regarding connecting-rods, it is important that each slider should move the same distance each side of the central position. Most connecting-rods have threaded ends and, by disconnecting one end, the rod can be screwed in or out to make it longer or shorter. Some cheaper pianos had fixed wire links and all you can do with these, if they need adjustment, is to bend them carefully to the desired setting. Other instruments had wooden links and these featured felt bushes in their ends. These harden or disintegrate in time and thus produce the same effect as incorrect lengths. The bushes are made of thin piano felt glued to form a bearing lining in the hole of the link. The link is usually split and secured with a tensioning screw to facilitate both renewal of the bush and also assembly.

Should the motor run fast continuously, the speed valve connected with the rewind device in the *tempo* box is failing to close or else the *tempo* valve is not seating properly. If there is a silent control lever or button, this may be operating the speed valve due to a leak in its tube. If the action has an automatic, pneumatic rewind device worked by a hole in the tracker-bar exposed at the end of the roll, look to this for any signs of leakage or broken tubing.

The spooling and unspooling of the music-roll can cause trouble. If the motor turns at speed without a roll in place, but will only shift the music slowly when in place, even at top speed, then the small brake-pad which bears on the spool drive to keep the roll under slight tension on rewind may be affording friction. It should be disengaged from the brake plate during playing. Again, if the music respools loosely, then it is due to this brake not offering enough resistance and it must be adjusted so that it just bears on the plate.

If the action dampers remain in the lifted position (the so-called loud pedal effect), then there may be a leak in the tube from the tracker-bar if it is automatically controlled. Where control is pneumatic from a key-bed button, look for leaks in that tube. The leak may be in the shut-off lever in the spool box. This lever works a valve block which may be leaking. Occasionally, air can enter under the pallet below the key-bed control button and in this case either a stronger pallet spring is needed, or the leather facing has become hard and distorted and must be replaced.

When the damper works slowly you must achieve a compromise between the valve settings. The damper-lifting pneumatic requires a great deal of power so that, if it is adjusted to work quickly, it will use a large amount of the available vacuum power which will be felt on the treadles and also, possibly, in the music. When adjusted to work slowly, there will be no noticeable side-effects to playing. Adjustment is governed by the pneumatic valves. Given long travel and with a suitable, large bleed hole, operation will be very quick but with the objectionable side-effects mentioned. Adjusted to give short travel, the damper pneumatic will be slow to move.

Sometimes the piano action will not repeat properly when the soft controls are operated and this is usually found where the pneumatic stack is divided with an expression-governor controlling each half from a manual control. Adjustment is to vary the spring tension on the governors, making it greater if the effect is too soft, less if the result is not soft enough. The same rules apply where the soft-pedal action is controlled from marginal perforations in the music-roll.

Bellows have been dealt with earlier in the rebuild section but it sometimes happens that minor defects are developed in an otherwise satisfactory system. Flap valves sometimes leak and this is either due to slack or broken stretcher springs (or perhaps the leather strip itself has become excessively stretched), or dirt has wedged between the board and the leather. Where the leather has actually curled at the edges, it should be replaced but you can get by for a short while by removing the strip, holding it tight between the hands and rubbing it back and forth, mating surface lowermost, over the edge of a board. Finally, rub chalk well into the soft surface of the leather and refit. If the bellows board is bowed, there is not much that can be done and, if it is very bad, then you must remove it and make a new one from thick plywood. Small cracks can be sealed with hot glue and covered with a strip of pneumatic cloth.

Although not strictly an adjustment solely in the province of the player-piano, it is sometimes found in an instrument that one or more of the bass strings—those which are wrapped—produces a decidedly peculiar sound. Whilst this sound may be detected sometimes as a buzz or tinniness, it can take the form of a 'beat' which defies correction by the tuner. It is a fairly well-known defect and is due to the copper wire wrapping of the string having become loose. If the string is otherwise serviceable, it is not essential for the string to be replaced; all you need to do is slacken the string right off at the wrest-pin until the eye loop formed at the opposite end of the string can be slipped off the peg. Now twist the string half a turn in the direction of the copper winding. This serves to tighten it on itself. Replace the string twisted in this way, make sure it is located through the bridge pins correctly, then re-tune. Nine times out of ten, you will have cured the fault at the expense of a few moments of work. Stubborn strings may want a full turn of twist but if this still does not cure the trouble, then the winding is so loose that the string must be scrapped.

There is a saying that prevention is better than cure and, to this end, the manufacturers of the modern motor car recommend that after every so many miles it should go to a garage for servicing and overhaul. It can do nothing but good to adopt the same principle of 'preventive maintenance' with the player-piano. Depending on the amount of use it has, it should be serviced regularly. Piano-tuning, ideally a thrice-yearly job, is usually considered by piano owners as a once-a-year task. Be this as it may, each time the piano is tuned, it is sound policy to go right over the player action, first of all sucking out the tracker with the tracker pump and then systematically going through the whole mechanism looking for defects. Periodic cleaning and dusting inside is also advisible.

Properly cared for, a player-piano, whether it be an early model or a late 1930's specimen, will continue to give faultless service for many, many years to come.

53. This attractive-looking piece of furniture is in fact a Keyless Red Welte Feurich piano, made in 1908 and sold by Steinways in Paris. It is related that the piano was installed in a mansion which was specially panelled and ornamented in oak, to match in every respect the fine cabinet work of the piano. Restored to mint order, it now stands in the home of Mr Norman Evans in Tottenham, London

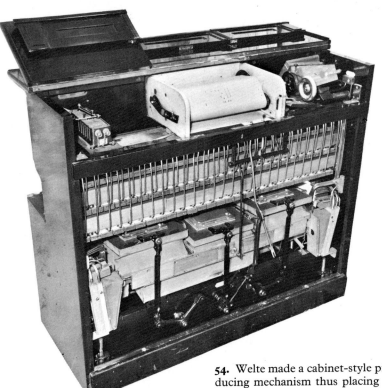

54. Welte made a cabinet-style piano-player which was a full reproducing mechanism thus placing it on a completely different plane from all other piano-players. Introduced about the same time as the Keyless Red Welte, this instrument remained in production until the 1930's. It was electrically-driven and played 13½-inch wide red paper rolls. This instrument illustrated is from the collection of Norman Evans, London, and was formerly in Hampton Court Palace. See Fig. 30 on page 95

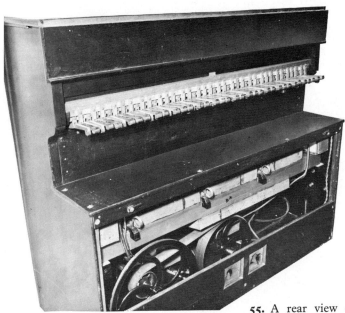

55. A rear view of the cabinet-style Welte Reproducing Player shows the full-compass, 88-note player fingers and some details of the robust, well-engineered belt-driven mechanism

Norman Evans collection

56. Another European instrument was the Hupfeld Dea-Rönisch made in Leipzig. This expression piano was electrically driven and incorporated many novel features found on no other player or reproducing piano. One of the few instruments to play its music-roll from bottom to top, this instrument was made in 1913

57. Detail of the Hupfeld Dea mechanism. The player action can be seen under the keyboard, with the automatic expression mechanism beneath it. Below that again are the characteristic horizontal exhausters and equaliser. The action pneumatics (soft and dustaining control) are to be seen in the top left of the case and, just visible in the centre of the tracker-bar, are the three expression control openings

58. The Steinway Welte-Mignon reproducing action in a grand piano *c.*1922. 13½-inch wide red paper rolls are used. Note the patented Welte trefoil roll-drive motor, characteristic of all original Welte player actions

Norman Evans collection

60. Richard Strauss seated at the Welte-Mignon recording piano in the studio of the Welte organisation in Freiburg about 1918. The recording machine for the music-rolls is in the cabinet to the left of the special piano. In this a master roll travelled at a constant speed, whilst a series of special pens recorded each note and its characteristics upon the moving paper

Picture from the Author's library

61. A pianist in one room plays on a special piano which is connected pneumatically to a roll perforating machine in the next. This picture was taken in July, 1909, at the works of the Perforated Music Company

Picture copyright: *Radio Times Hulton Picture Library*

62. The largest manufacturer of music-rolls in England was the Perforated Music Company (q.v.). During the early hours of Saturday, March 16th, 1918, their City Road premises in London caught fire and, despite the use of '3 hydrants, 15 water pumps and 42 firemen', the six-floor building was engulfed in a fierce blaze, the roof collapsed and adjacent premises, including Lipton's tea factory across the road, became involved. The picture (right) was taken by an insurance surveyor and shows the desolation as two workers stand amidst the charred remains of more than a quarter of a million piano rolls. The damage was put at £48,750 and the Perforated Music Company, although continued in other premises on a much smaller scale, never recovered. The illustration comes from the unique collection of Mr Ron Benton by whose permission it is reproduced

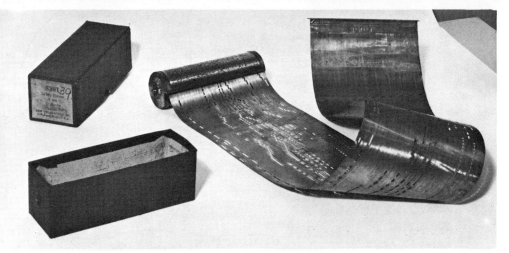

63. The 6-inch wide brass music-roll used by the Telektra electric piano-player. To play, it was drawn out of its casette, being re-wound back in again at the end of the music, rather like the film in a camera

By courtesy of Gerry Planus

64. The Boyd Pistonola player-piano worked on a totally different system from all other instruments. Every function of the player action was operated by pistons in cylinders

Ron Benton, Shanklin, collection

65. The neat and compact installation of the Pistonola action is clearly seen here. The foot treadles operate pistons in two cylinders with a central, spring-loaded reservoir cylinder

Ron Benton, Shanklin, collection

66. This detail view of the Pistonola shows the extremely small piston and cylinder roll-drive motor and also the flexible linkages between the action cylinders and the piano action itself. This revolutionary action was not altogether a success, for the mechanical player was very hard to adjust if it went wrong. In good order, the Pistonola and its later variant, the Terpretor, were very good instruments

Ron Benton, Shanklin, collection

C. R. TAYLOR,
34, COMMERCE ROAD, WOOD GREEN,
LONDON, N.22.

Established 1903.   Telephone: Palmers Green 1031.

PLAYER GRAND.

Length 4' 6"   7¼ Octaves.   Schwander Action.   Ivory Keys.

67. Typical of the cheaper treadle-operated player grands was this model produced by a North London firm in the late twenties. The action was the 'Higel' which was a very good and cheap British-made player

68. A 1910 model Steinway-Welte reproducing piano, the entire action for which is mounted above the piano itself. The music-rolls are 13½ inches wide and travel from bottom to top, unlike most other instruments. An electric motor drives the mechanism
British Piano Museum
Brentford, Middlesex

69. The mechanism of the Steinway-Welte reproducing piano seen from the back of the piano with the electric motor at the far right. Along the top of the case can be seen the four air exhausters. The electric light bulbs have been added by the Museum who have thoughtfully fitted a transparent back to this part of the piano so that its complexity can be watched whilst in motion
British Piano Museum, Brentford, Middlesex

70. The House of Blüthner was the first to introduce the Hupfeld reproducing piano into this country. Hupfeld actions being fitted into their pianos. This illustration, from a catalogue of about 1918, shows a Blüthner/Hupfeld grand.

By courtesy of Blüthner Pianos Limited.

1. An early Steinway Duo-Art Pianola which features triple exhausters, belt-driven from a large electric motor mounted to the right of the case. On the left of the piano, next to the exhausters, can be seen the expression box for this reproducing piano.

By courtesy of Phelps Pianos Limited.

72. This Steinway Duo-Art Pianola grand was formerly the property of Princess Beatrice, at Kensington Palace. It was made in 1926. The foot treadles are housed in the compartment beneath the instrument, when not in use

British Piano Museum, Brentford, Middlesex

73. One of the finest reproducing pianos ever made was the Grotrian-Steinweg fitted with the Ampico action. This one, beautifully restored by Norman Evans of North London, dates from 1927, and shows the roll drawer in the open position. For normal playing, the drawer fits snugly under the keyboard and it may also be closed whilst playing

Norman Evans, London, collection

74. A detail view of the Grotrian-Steinweg Ampico drawer with the roll-drive motor visible to the left, and the control levers for manual expression and reproducing control to the front. The mechanical parts seen here are covered by decorative cover-boards, which have been removed for the camera
Norman Evans, London, collection

75. In addition to the Hupfeld action, Blüthner for a time fitted their own player action known as the Carola. Because it offered no saving in cost over the imported actions of better quality, its production was discontinued. This illustration shows the Style U 'Upright-Grand'
Picture from the library of the Author

76. The new 1968 model player-piano is available in several different styles. Sold by various companies within the Aeolian Corporation, the P–102 Musette is stylishly modern and plays both new and old 88-note music-rolls

REPAIRING THE PLAYER-PIANO. I

77. This is a derelict pedal-operated player action of the Duo-Art type. Note the details of the tracking device (left of spool box), three-valve motor (right of spool box), the junction boxes from which tubes run to the expression devices (left) and the connections for the control levers. The action is supported in the piano by down-bolts in the ends of the main deck plank

REPAIRING THE PLAYER-PIANO. 2

78. This is a rear view of the action seen in Plate 77. Most of the rubber tubes have been broken, through perishing, but their replacement is an easy job. The two horizontal bars below the roll box keep the tubes tidy and clear of the piano action. The pitmans which lift the piano action wippens are clearly seen in this two-bank pneumatic installation

REPAIRING THE PLAYER-PIANO. 3

79. Detail of the roll-drive mechanism. The gear-shift lever (left of centre bottom) is in the 'drive' position. The rod which presses against it just above its pivot point is the brake lever, which allows a slight resistance to be maintained on the top spool chuck so that the paper roll is always under tension during playing. The brake pad bears on the wheel to the left of the sprocket wheel at the top

80. Compare this view with the preceding illustration. Here the gear lever is in the 're-wind' position, the drive pinion having been slid to one side on its shaft. At the same time, this pinion engages with the free chain sprocket, which connects to the top spool via a simple engagement clutch. Also the brake lever has been moved so that (a) the top spool chuck is quite free, and (b) a brake is applied to the lower or take-up spool to provide slight friction during rewind

The action is now upside down he locating rail for the pitmans noved

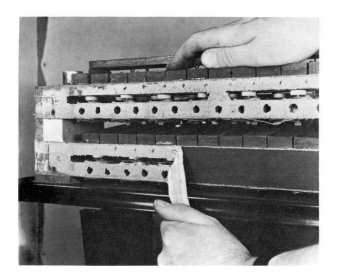

82. The rubber cloth sealing strips are now
off the back of the valve chest. This reveals
valve units (seen between the two pairs of
boards) and the bleed holes, set back inside
recessed small holes in the boards at the top
of the deck in this view. The pneumatics are
between the two decks and under the right h
of the mechanic

83. The decks are supported
at several points along their
length by brackets which must
be removed. One is seen in the
centre of this picture indicated
by the screwdriver blade. The
adjustments for the action pitmans can also be seen; those
on the first deck having drilled
bollards which can be screwed
in or out using a small tommy
bar and limited by eye-ended
set-off pins. Those on the top
deck are limited by a rail along
their length and adjusted by
set-off pins. Remember the
action here is upside down

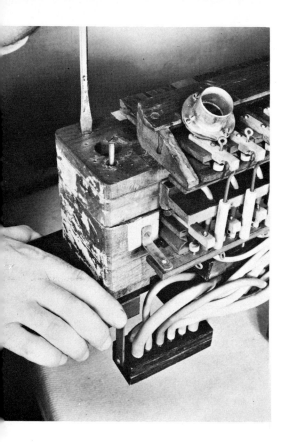

84. Separation of the decks is achieved by removing the main air-trunk connections at each end (one is seen here resting on top of the pneumatics check rail) to give access to the long screws which pass right down through the decks. Different actions vary in detail

With the decks separated, the
vs are removed which separate
valve chests. These screws
all be different lengths, so note
h one goes where to aid re-
nbly. The valve units are seen
from their tops, the action now
g the right way up again. Just by
screwdriver can be seen one of
leck attachment links mentioned
cture 7 of this set. The rubber
ig to the lower valves has been
en or cut to aid dismantling; it
afterwards be carefully removed
its attachment nipples and re-
d as the final part of recon-
tion

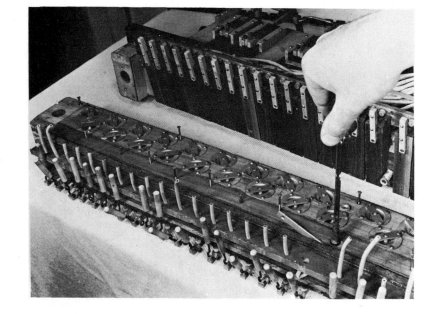

86. Here the valve chest has b
opened up and the top board tur
back on itself. One complete v
unit has been removed and is s
lying on the pouch board. Note
large disc on the valve which r
upon the leather pouches. The scr
driver is now removing the sc
which secures one of the pneuma
As a matter of secondary inter
observe the division in the c
(top left) which separates the th
from the accompaniment side of
Duo-Art action. This is a strip
metal cemented into two woc
blocks and sealed on a leather s
on the pouch board. This is
found in ordinary players.

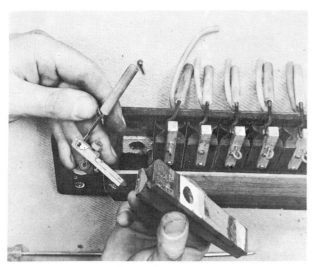

87. One pneumatic is seen here after rem
from the deck and the wooden extension w
carries the pitman has been unscrewed and
glued joint carefully broken away. The eye-en
set-off screw limited the amount of collaps
the pneumatic by bearing on the felt strip run
along immediately in front of the pneumatic

88. The manufacture of music
rolls. The copying machine,
seen here, is a multi-purpose instrument which works in conjunction with the perforating
machine to make copies from
existing rolls, or to produce the
special 'master rolls' which it
then uses for making a relatively
large number of copies of a
new piece of music set on an
original roll. Owner of the
Artona factory, Mr Gordon
Iles, is seen regulating the
machine.

89. When a new music roll is first made, the initial step is the punching of the 'master roll' (made on the copying machine). After leaving the copying machine, it is set up and corrected and checked by hand before being put on to the punching machine

90. Fifteen lengths of paper are laid out one on top of the other ready to pass through the perforating machine in which they are to be transformed from plain paper into punched music rolls to be sold to enthusiasts everywhere under the trade name 'Artona'

91. Mr Gordon Iles, of Artona Music Rolls Ltd, Ramsgate, watches the perforating machine cutting through fifteen copies at a time. The punches which cut out the notes are locked and selected by an automatic process in the electrically-operated machine

92. Manufactured to patents taken out by Claude Gavioli, this 1890 Organophone Expressif was made by the Paris firm of Jerome Thibouville-Lamy. A book of punched card music can be seen on top of this reed-playing instrument, which has four stops controlled by the knobs on top of the front fall of the case. These stops are celeste, saxophone, clarinet and viola

Conservatoire des Arts et Métiers, Paris

93. M. Welte & Söhne of Freiburg made a l number of orchestrion organs in many s prior to producing the Welte-Mignon re ducing piano. This 46-note instrument restored by the Author and plays 13½-inch paper music-rolls

Graham Webb collec

94. Working on the same principle as the Un was the Arno musical box patented jointl Arno and Paillard in America in the 1880's

R. Moss colle

95. The Chordephon was a mechanical zither made in the 1890's. Its 14-inch metal discs had projections on their undersides which engaged in plectrum linkages, which in turn plucked the strings in the ornate, decorative harp. The clockwork driving motor was housed to one side. This instrument is a direct descendent of the disc-playing musical boxes and sold for £8 8s

National Museum, Prague

96. The Triola mechanical zither was invented by Reissner who was responsible for many improvements to the Polyphon disc-playing musical box. This featured an ingenious reciprocating plectrum frame, worked by turning a crank handle. The handle on the side (at the top of the picture) is for rewinding the music-roll

Graham Webb collection

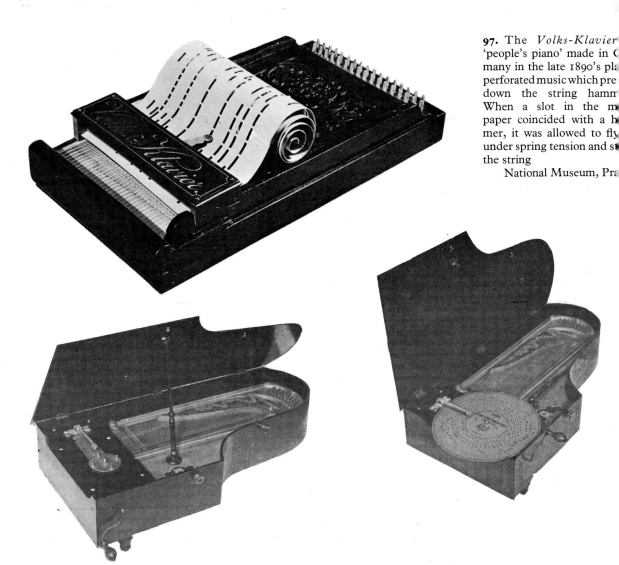

97. The *Volks-Klavier*
'people's piano' made in G
many in the late 1890's pla
perforated music which pre
down the string hamm
When a slot in the m
paper coincided with a h
mer, it was allowed to fly
under spring tension and s
the string

National Museum, Pra

98. The Orpheus was an interesting device which played a proper piano in minia
by means of a perforated cardboard disc. It was the product of the Ehrlich fir
Leipzig who also made the Ariston organette. Tune discs for the Ariston could
be played on the Orpheus

Gerry Planus collec

99. An interesting organette was the Manopan
which played an endless band of perforated cardboard. The case contained powerful exhausters
and the reeds were mounted in the extension by
the music band. The volume of sound could be
varied by the opening of a small 'swell' door in
the end of the reed housing. It was made by the
Leipzig firm of Otto Helbig & Polikeit who made
the Celeste disc-playing musical box

National Museum, Prague

MILITARY BANDS
FOR SKATING RINKS AND DANCING SALOONS
PLAYING BY PERFORATED MUSIC.

The only instrument that **successfully** replaces a band at a **minimum of cost** and **no trouble.**

Then, WHY ENGAGE A COSTLY BAND?

OUR MILITARY BAND "ORCHESTRAPHONES"
will do all you require at a quarter of the cost and always remain **a valuable asset.**

A large repertoire of perforated music always in stock.

Price - - £400.

CHIAPPA & SONS,
6, LITTLE BATH STREET, HOLBORN, LONDON, E.C.
TELEPHONE: 12930 HOLBORN.   TELEGRAPHIC ADDRESS: "CHIAREZZA, LONDON."

100. One of the many very large mechanical organs made in various parts of Europe at the beginning of this century was this Orchestraphone sold by Chiappa in London

101. Mechanical concertinas such as this German *Tanzbär* were popular for many years with music-hall artists. This instrument, complete with dummy note buttons on the ends, plays a narrow music-roll by flicking a reciprocating lever with the fingers of the right hand

Graham Webb collection

103. The thick music paper used for the Tow Ballroom orchestrion in place on its spec tracker fitted at the back of the organ. This i Welte-designed action fitted in 1914 to play mu cut by Wurlitzer

City Museum & Art Gallery, Birmingh pict

102. An attraction at the Tower Ballroom, Blackpool, for many years was this fine Imhof & Mukle orchestrion organ. Originally barrel-operated, it was converted to perforated music action and is now preserved in the City Museum & Art Gallery, Birmingham, by whose permission this picture is reproduced

104. Of the many different models of the Aeolian Orchestrelle paper roll-playing reed organ, this, the Model F, was the finest made. 116-note rolls were used on the tracker-bar which had two rows of holes, each slightly staggered. Twenty-four speaking stops were used on this pressure model (see Chapter 10 for description)

City Museum & Art Gallery, Birmingham, picture

105. Rare in this country is this 'Nickelodeon' made by the German firm of Gebruder Weber GmbH

British Piano Museum collection

106. Inside the Nickelodeon there is a piano, mandolin, xylophone and violin organ pipes. Standing 100 inches high, it is 74 inches wide, 35 inches deep and plays music-rolls 32·5 cms wide

British Piano Museum collection

107. The Reproduco was one of the many instruments made in America to provide accompaniment to the silent motion pictures. Made by the Operators Piano Company, it comprised an organ and piano with percussion and other effects and played two perforated paper rolls

108. Another of the breed of Nickelodeon was the Coinola with its mission oak finish and decorative glass front panels. This type of machine was never seen in England.

109. A number of different models were produced by most makers of these so-called 'photoplayers' and this one, the Super Junior, was made by the makers of the Reproduco range and featured a separate cabinet to house 41 stopped diapason organ pipes, 32 open flute pipes, 49 Viola diapason pipes and 37 quintadena pipes. A pedal bass of one octave was also included. Larger models were made with two matching cabinets, one each side of the console

110. A remarkable and imposing instrument – the Hupfeld Phonoliszt-Violina. Basically a Rönisch piano, the upper work contains three violins mounted inside a circular bow. In this view, the three-panel top doors are open and the circular bow can be seen

111. Widely acclaimed as a 'wonder of the world', and publicised by the American Government, was the Mills Violano-Virtuoso. In this view, with the access doors open, can be seen the piano, the violin and, beneath, the roll-playing mechanism. In the bottom of the cabinet are several spare rolls in their original cardboard boxes. The ornamental top is detachable and is probably the only one to survive

Norman Evans collection

112. An attractive part of the Dutch street scene today is the *pierement* or street organ, properly termed *draai orgel*. Many of these delightful instruments are to be seen and heard in the streets of Amsterdam, Rotterdam and Utrecht. Playing perforated cardboard music, these organs are operated by turning a large wheel at the back

CHAPTER 9

The Reproducing Piano

T HE reproducing piano is simply a player-piano wherein the last vestiges of human control are mechanically performed. It is an instrument which may be switched on and left to play a roll of music, with the self-same certainty of the resulting interpretation as we have today when we switch on a record player. Not that the reproducing piano is in any way a characterless and introspective device where human participation is neither welcome nor necessary to play music. With the exception of the Keyless Welte and the Welte cabinet player, all of the reproducing pianos made, whilst quite capable of performing without any manual effort other than the motions of switching it on, could also be played using manual controls as with the ordinary player-piano, and they would play ordinary music-rolls if required. Of course, they might also be played upon by hand. It is a quirk of ethnic development that, whatever we succeed in making automatic in action, we always make provision for it to be achieved the old way—manually. The auto-pilot in an airliner can and will fly the aeroplane without the aegis of the pilot, yet, for various valid reasons, he can chip in and override the controls. Automatic transmission and pre-selector gears on cars verge on the same design concept—let them work on their own, but also let the man have the facility of doing it himself.

I have said that the instrument we are now looking at can do all these things, but it is nevertheless only a player-piano which has been taken a stage further. What of its mechanisms? Its complexities? And its adjustments?

Examination of a reproducing piano shows that all the parts we are already familiar with in the ordinary player are still there. There is the pneumatic stack, the valve chest, the wind motor, the *tempo* control, the *tempo* governor, the cut-off valve—in fact just about everything that we have already detailed in Chapter 7. One large difference may be detected—and that is the power section. Where we had foot-treadled exhausters and a bellows system, our reproducing piano usually has in place of all that impedimenta either an electric suction pump in a metal case, or a square-shaped suction pump driven by a separate electric motor. Early models retained the exhausters system and drove them with a motor-operated series of cranks and belts. Some models are dual-purpose in that they can be treadled in the ordinary way, or driven electrically and these are called 'pedal-electric' pianos.

We must realize that, although so much of the reproducing piano is basic and almost elemental, the system by which expression is put into the performance and the touch of the original pianist recreated is extremely sensitive, critical in adjustment and demanding of skill and intelligence in servicing.

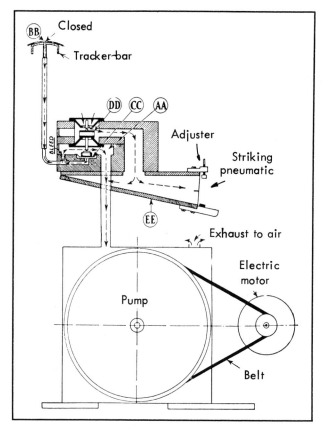

Fig. 71. The operation of the pump-driven single-valve action, showing the particular note at the 'silent' position. Compare valve positions with those in Fig. 50 (page 151.)

Key: AA = suction chamber
BB = end of tube at tracker-bar
CC = leather pouch
DD = valve
EE = striking pneumatic

Unlike the ordinary player-piano, where the operator is required not only to put the expression into the music, but also to regulate the *tempo* as necessary, the reproducing piano music-roll travels at a constant speed. Where an ordinary roll might have a 'sustain' instruction printed by some notes, the reproducing piano roll will have them perforated to the proper length relative to the speed of the music-roll as printed on the leader of the roll and set before the instrument begins to play. Where a silence or rest comes in the music, the ordinary roll will show a 'pause' instruction (probably to save paper!), but the reproducing roll will continue to travel in blank paper for the length of time which the pianist who recorded the roll chose. The roll drive speed is thus set at the beginning of the music and left alone.

Having established that the instrument is basically an ordinary player, all we have now to understand is the mechanism by which it is elevated to the class of the finest type of mechanical piano ever produced. Air remains the motive power, the pressure differential, which we now understand, being used in a more delicately adjusted manner than before. Instead of admitting the full power of the partial vacuum, created inside the instrument, to the piano functions, this power is transferred through monitoring and metering valves which allow varying amounts of suction power to operate the functions. These regulating devices (we have already met them in simplified form with the ordinary player action) are instructed in the work they must do, not by a manual lever, but by more valves which are in turn given their orders from special holes in the music-roll.

We saw in Chapters 7 and 8 how the pedal action (soft and sustaining) could be controlled from the roll. We saw how music could be accented or themodized, to use Aeolian's phraseology. The reproducing piano has to do just the same but—and here is the great difference—it has to interpret the *amount* of pedal movement and the degree of force used to accentuate a theme or note. As we shall see, all this is done very ingeniously by using components which, in their basic form, we are already familiar with.

There are three main types of reproducing piano which are most common and most likely to be found by the collector or enthusiast. These, in order of probability, are the Aeolian Duo-Art, the American Piano Company's Ampico, and the Welte-Mignon. There were quite a few others, of course, but they are so few and far between now that the chances of finding them are slim. The operation is always the same, though; only the detail as to how that operation is achieved may differ.

Fortunately, servicing and overhaul manuals for the three actions listed above are still available to enthusiasts today as reprints. Armed with a piano, a service manual and a thorough experience and knowledge of an ordinary 88-note player-piano, the average person can restore a reproducing instrument without too much difficulty. What I propose to do in this chapter is to describe the principles of these three makes of action and show you just how they work. But, beforehand, some more of my words of warning! Never attempt to tackle a reproducing piano without first having three special things—first, a proper tester roll *for that make of instrument*, second, the overhaul manual and, finally, a vacuum pressure-gauge. Having got these three adjuncts to your work, make sure you use them!

Another word of warning! It is common to find electric pianos fitted with female socket plugs at the piano so that a male mains plug can be fitted in. This means that there has to be a live two-pin plug on the end of a cable which can be accidentally pulled out with obviously dangerous risks. It is vital that you rewire the mains connections to instruments of this type so that the piano has a *male* plug. Electric pianos were never earthed and so it is a good idea, whilst rewiring the mains lead, to use a three-core cable and connect the earth wire to the case of the motor. In an earlier age, electricity was treated in a surprisingly lighthearted manner and modern thinking on the subject is one of the few manifestations of present-day civilization which is unquestionably acceptable. Happily, the newspaper headline, albeit amusing, has not yet appeared which reads: 'Pianist killed by Electric Piano', but neglect of the power-supply leads could well precipitate a disastrous happening.

Most common in the field of reproducing pianos is the Duo-Art made by Aeolians from 1913 onwards.

The Duo-Art system works by dividing the music into the theme and the accompaniment. Compared with most other reproducing pianos where the music is separated between bass and treble sections, the divided expression system of the Duo-Art operates by two variable vacuum pressures. The division of the valve chest comes between the 43rd and the 44th note on the piano keyboard, and can be seen in the illustration Plate No. 86. In use the pressure to the left can be vastly different from that on the right. Regulator pneumatics control each at a different fundamental setting so that the theme setting is fractionally stronger than the accompaniment when under identical conditions. This is an acceptable basis, since the theme is usually louder than the accompaniment when both are performed at their softest.

The *theme* side is normally the treble or right-hand side; the *accompaniment* side the bass or left. I refer to *normally*, since there is provision made for the control of either side from the opposite end of the pneumatic stack so that, if called upon so to do, the theme side can operate

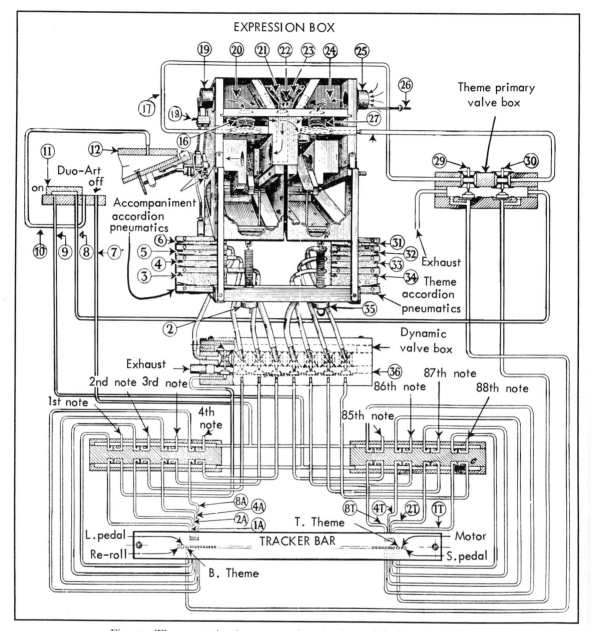

Fig. 72. The expression box connections in the upright Duo-Art action

on the bass half of the stack, the accompaniment on the treble. Alternatively, the entire stack can be governed from either side.

The system operates through the functions of four special expression perforations and a theme perforation in each side of the music-roll, bass and accompaniment. The ingenious operation of the expression holes will be described in a moment, but before this we will have a look at the function of the theme perforations which are narrow, horizontal openings in the tracker-bar and are the holes immediately preceding and succeeding the music-playing holes. Under normal playing conditions, the loudness level of the whole piano is determined by the accompaniment expression system. When a theme perforation in the paper crosses the tracker-bar, whether it is on the treble or the bass side of the roll, the other side of the pneumatic stack becomes under the control of the theme side of the expression mechanism. This can apply to either bass or to treble, or simultaneously to both sides. By this means, each half of the piano can be controlled by its own tracker-bar theme duct—virtually two separate tracker-bars. However, the moment the duct is opened by a music perforation, the same suction pressure is applied to both halves of the piano.

Expression dynamics are controlled by an expression box which contains so-called *zero* pneumatics by which the foundation level of the music (with neither expression nor theme modification) is determined. Each zero pneumatic has its own jack-knife valve to cope with the

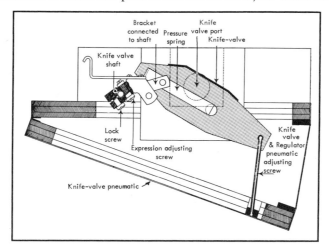

Fig. 73. Side view of the Duo-Art knife valve

variations of suction pressure which occur in performance (as in an ordinary player-piano). These jack-knife valves are controlled by the 'accordion pneumatics', which are so simple in concept yet so perfect in operation. There are two sets of accordion pneumatics, one for each jack-knife valve—one for each side of the piano, bass and treble or, if you prefer it, theme and accompaniment. These comprise four parallel motors each joined to the other, the upper one having a small opening, the next larger and so on until the fourth has the widest opening. The top one is made to collapse only $\frac{1}{16}$ inch, the next one $\frac{1}{8}$ inch, the third $\frac{1}{4}$ inch, and the fourth $\frac{1}{2}$ inch. If all are arranged to collapse together, the jack-knife valve is moved $\frac{15}{16}$ inch. Now, by using these pneumatics in combinations such as numbers one and two, one and four, two and four and so on, fifteen separate combinations can be achieved (sixteen if we include the zero position), each a shade louder or softer than the other. As there is a set of accordion pneumatics for each side of the piano, one half can be playing *fortissimo* and the other *pianissimo* or any stage between the two.

The accordion pneumatics have numerical values corresponding to the number of sixteenths of an inch which they open, hence they are referred to as numbers 1, 2, 4 and 8. There is another feature of the expression box which we must note and this is the 'spill valve'. As we can under-

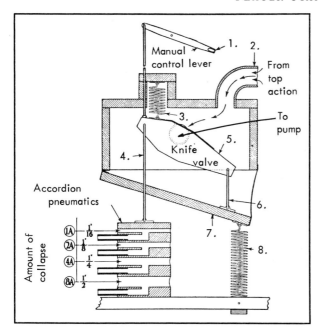

Fig. 74. Accordion dynamic control of the knife valve showing Duo-Art expression control

Key: 1. manual control lever
2. exhaust from top action
3. knife valve tension spring
4. accordion pneumatic and knife valve connecting rod
5. knife valve
6. knife valve and Regulator pneumatic connecting rod
7. regulator pneumatic
8. regulator pneumatic coil spring

stand from Chapter 7, air is continually being drawn out of the expression box by the exhaust system—in reproducing terminology always referred to as the 'pump'. It is being removed from both sides of the pneumatic stack through the pump. To achieve a suitably low vacuum point norm, air is continually bled into the system through what is called the spill valve. This is arranged so that it can be gradually reduced in opening via our old friend the knife-valve, which in turn is worked by the movement of the main knife-valves controlled by the accordion pneumatics. Under normal playing conditions, then, a metered quantity of atmospheric air is fed into the system to reduce the normal vacuum pressure. As the accordion pneumatics begin to collapse, so this amount of vacuum modulation is reduced until a point is reached when accordion pneumatics numbers 2 and 8 have collapsed (two plus eight sixteenths equalling $\frac{5}{8}$ inch moving either of the knife-valves that amount). When this happens, the spill valve knife-valve closes completely and stays that way during any further increases in movement of the main knife-valves as dictated by the accordion pneumatics. So it is that the vacuum norm can be said to be reached at a position corresponding to an opening of $\frac{5}{8}$ inch on either side of the expression box.

Control of the accordion pneumatics is effected through four openings in each side of the tracker-bar which are placed above the first four and the last four musical note openings (see Fig. 72). The openings appear as large, vertical holes and, when operating with Duo-Art rolls, the four music note holes beneath, at each end, are disconnected. To play ordinary 88-note rolls, a lever in the roll box is moved which changes over a valve block, cuts out the Duo-Art expression openings and reconnects the musical note holes.

The collective operation of the above-mentioned parts can be better understood by the following description of the functioning of the system as a whole. Starting with the accompaniment side, if neither the accompaniment nor the theme hole in the tracker-bar is uncovered, the air from each side of the pneumatic stack enters the expression box, passes through the flap valves and passes out through the opening to the accompaniment passageway, past the accompaniment regulator knife-valve and so on to the pump where it is exhausted to atmosphere. The speed of the air from the pneumatic stack to the pump depends on the position of the knife-valve which can be modified by the accordion pneumatics on that side. As we have already seen, there are sixteen different amounts of regulation which the accordions can apply to the knife-valve. Assuming that neither of the theme openings in the tracker-bar are uncovered, this accompaniment regulation will control the whole keyboard.

Now, if the bass theme hole remains closed, but a perforation in the music-roll opens the theme hole in the treble, atmospheric air enters and shifts the treble theme primary-valve and closes the corresponding secondary-valve in the expression box. Air entering the expression box from the treble side of the pneumatic stack is thus made to pass out over the top of the closed secondary valve and thus to the theme-regulator passageway past the knife-valve. The exact position of this valve will now be under control of either setting of the accordion pneumatics on the theme side.

If the treble theme opening stays closed, air flow from the treble side passes through the accompaniment side of the expression box and if, at the same moment, the bass theme opening in the tracker-bar is uncovered, the bass air flows through the theme regulator.

For manual application of expression on ordinary music-rolls, hand controls are fitted together with a device called the 'temponamic' lever which has a large, circular knurled handle to it. When moved bodily from side to side, this is used to adjust the *tempo* both in Duo-Art and

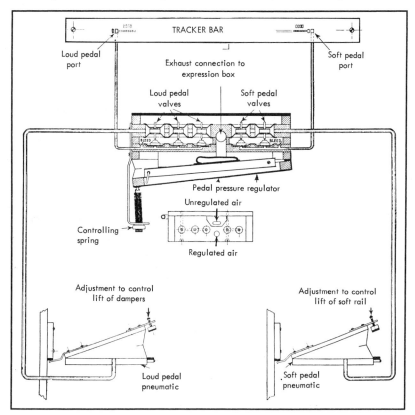

Fig. 75. Loud and soft pedal control for upright action—the Duo-Art

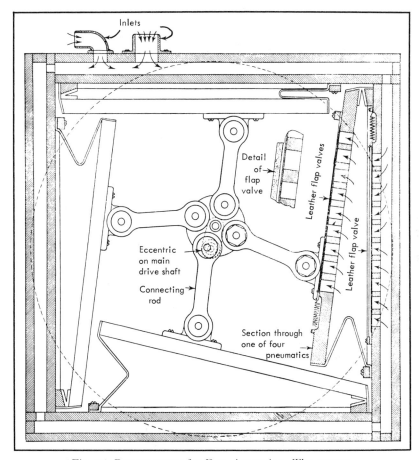

Fig. 76. Rotary pump for Duo-Art action. The centre
shaft must turn at between 120 and 125 r.p.m.

manual playing. If the knob is pulled outwards, it is also used to apply manual expression to
the accompaniment of ordinary rolls by twisting the knob in a clockwise direction. This serves
to regulate the accompaniment knife-valve directly.

Duo-Art pianos were made with two types of pump (excluding early models which used
electrically-operated belt-driven exhausters). The earlier models used a four-lobe exhauster
pump pulley driven from a motor. As the pump rotated, so a crankshaft inside alternately
opened and closed each of four bellows motors applied to the main suction trunk. This is shown
in Fig. 76. The other type of pump, usually applied to later models, was a self-contained
cylindrical pump. Although far neater and lighter than the lobe pump, it tended to be noisier
and more liable to overheat. Hung from a hook within the underside of the piano case, the
fully-enclosed aluminium housing contained the electric motor and a suction fan. Frequent
lubrication of the grease-bearing pads at each end of the motor shaft is necessary with this
type of pump.

The grand installation of the Duo-Art called for the expression box to be constructed along
different lines due to the intrinsic differences between the two instruments—grand and upright.

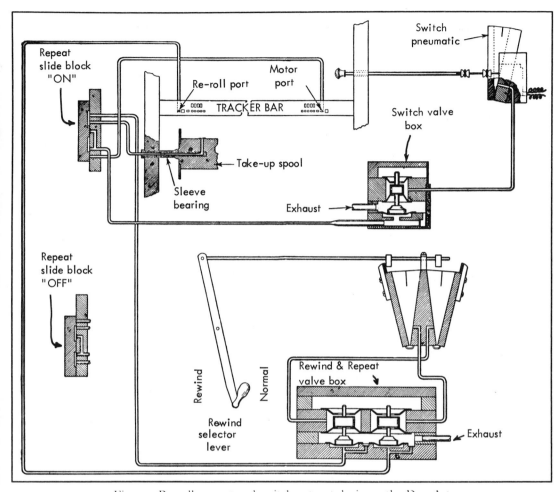

Fig. 77. Re-roll, repeat and switch cut-out devices—the Duo-Art

The basic principles remained the same but the grand box incorporates a crash valve which functions when the accordion pneumatics reach power number 15 on the theme side as called for by the music-roll.

In operation, it connects directly the channel from the pneumatic action to the pump, by-passing the theme knife-valve so that very quick, loud accents can be obtained.

Another feature, special to the grand installation, is the modulator pneumatic. This provides a means whereby the normal Duo-Art may be modified or softened, without losing any of the dynamic gradations provided by the accordion pneumatics. It also serves as a supply regulator for the sustaining pedal and accordion pneumatics and it is equipped with a cut-out valve for the pneumatic action on re-roll.

The third special control is the keyboard shifter. As already noted, there is normally no rest rail in a grand action (controlled by the soft pedal) but the grand action couples the soft pedal to a cam which shifts the keyboard laterally so that the hammers only strike two of the trichord strings. The key-frame shifting in the Duo-Art is effected by the use of a pneumatic acting

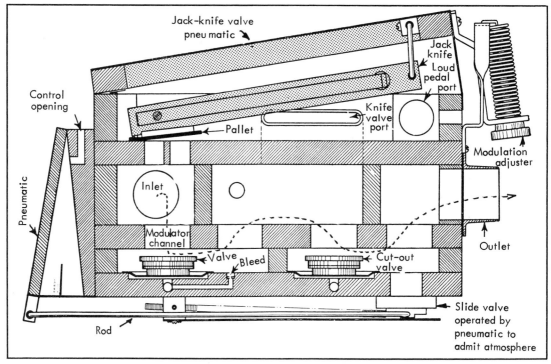

Fig. 78. The Duo-Art Modulator pneumatic for the grand installation.
This serves to soften the piano without losing the Duo-Art gradations

on a lever as shown in the illustration, Fig. 79. On some grands which are fitted with 'half-blow' rails, this is not used.

Mention should be made of the experiments which were going on at the Aeolian Company's Hayes, Middlesex, factory to improve the Duo-Art action. In the early 1930's, they were on the threshold of perfecting a method of bringing out the melody or accenting any note anywhere in the music, even in an *arpeggio* or counter-theme. Called the 'isolated theme', it involved the use of two sets of valves to operate the striking pneumatics plus a further valve, which was subjected to supplemental pressure, for notes to be affected. The isolation of such notes was achieved by Themodist-type music-roll perforations. Unfortunately, the cost of the apparatus coupled with the piano slump, directed that it was never put on the market.

The regulation and adjustment of the Duo-Art mechanism is well set out in the service manual and therefore will not be repeated here.

The Ampico reproducing action, introduced prior to 1913, is a more complex mechanism and was produced in three distinct variants. The Model A action was produced for both grand and upright actions, the expression unit and other detail components being re-engineered in 1920 from double to single-valve systems. In 1929, the action was completely redesigned, there being very little resemblance between the earlier Model A and the new Model B. With the introduction of the Model B, the production of upright actions was dropped, so whilst all Ampico uprights were Model A, Ampico grands were made as Models A and B.

Operating on an entirely different system from the Duo-Art, the essence of the Ampico expression system is the delicate balancing of a regulating valve between two sets of pneumatics.

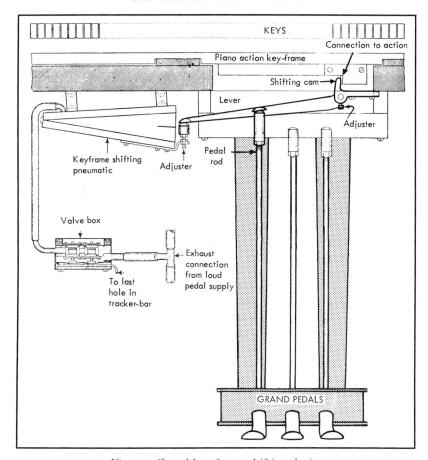

Fig. 79. Grand key-frame shifting device

The dynamics of the Ampico system are measured in the terminology of fast and slow *crescendo* valves, intensity pneumatics, lock and cancel valves.

Ampico designers claimed that they found by experimentation that the ear could distinguish about six different degrees of accents when the playing was soft, and naturally less as the playing became louder. It was also found experimentally that no number of steps produced a smooth *crescendo* effect; to say nothing of expression shades. When the Ampico first appeared, it had sixteen steps to work with, to produce dynamic effects, but these were soon found to be entirely inadequate to give smooth *crescendo* or expression effects. The mechanism was, therefore, redesigned to enable it to produce these effects. Subsequently it was found that sixteen steps of loudness were unnecessary to produce accents.

The Ampico system of dynamic control, subsequently developed, provided just seven steps of loudness. By means of side perforations in the music-roll, the intensity of the playing can be set to any of these seven steps and remains so-set until a subsequent perforation, or combination of perforations, sets it to another step. The change in intensity takes place practically instantaneously. By quick changes in intensity settings, melody notes or accented notes can be brought out without affecting the loudness of the surrounding notes. The effect of using the

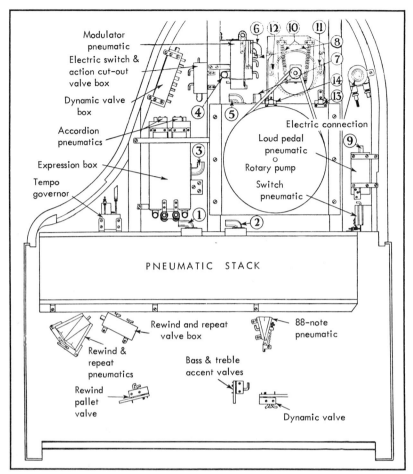

Fig. 80. Bottom view of Duo-Art grand installation.
Numbers refer to the overhaul manual

steps and the *crescendo* at the same time, made it possible for perfectly smooth *crescendos* to be played at the same time as clearly defined accents being given.

The function of the dynamic mechanism is to control the loudness of the playing. The system of dynamic control makes it possible to get sudden changes of loudness or gradual fluctuations, *crescendos* or *diminuendos*.

The seven degrees or intensities of loudness are used to produce accent and sudden stepping-up effects, while the spring pneumatic mechanism makes it possible to increase smoothly the power of the playing from the softest to the loudest at any speed required. Both of these mechanisms can work simultaneously and produce accent or step effects during a *crescendo* effect.

The regulator valve is secured to the regulator valve stem which is in turn fastened to the lever arm. Three little intensity pneumatics, fastened to the under side of the lever arm, are fed by vacuum pressure, so are the striking pneumatics. The spring pneumatic, which is fastened to the upper side of the lever arm, is fed with air from a regulator pneumatic controlling the softest intensity. This pneumatic functions during *crescendo* effects and is therefore

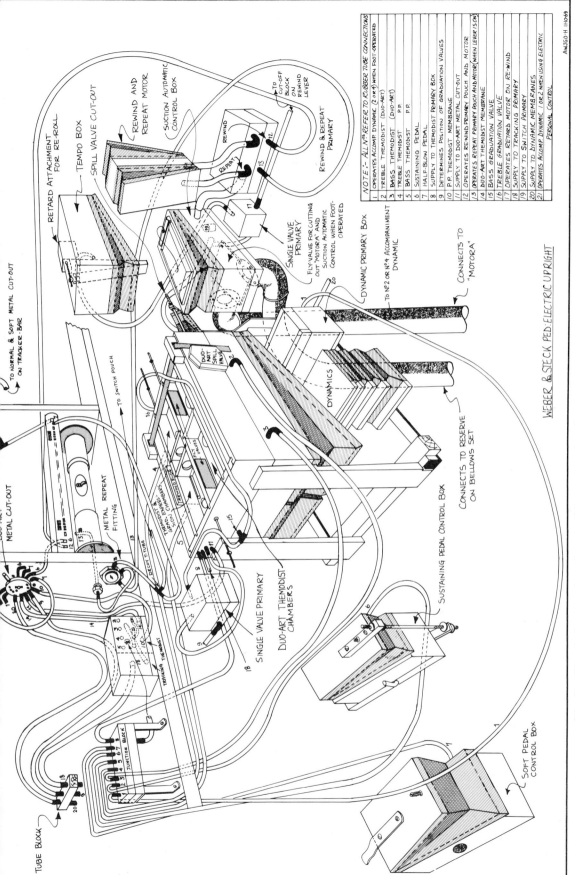

Fig. 81. Sketch showing the primary tubing connections for the Duo-Art. In practice, the connections from the action stack are often via connector blocks to facilitate dismantling and removal for servicing

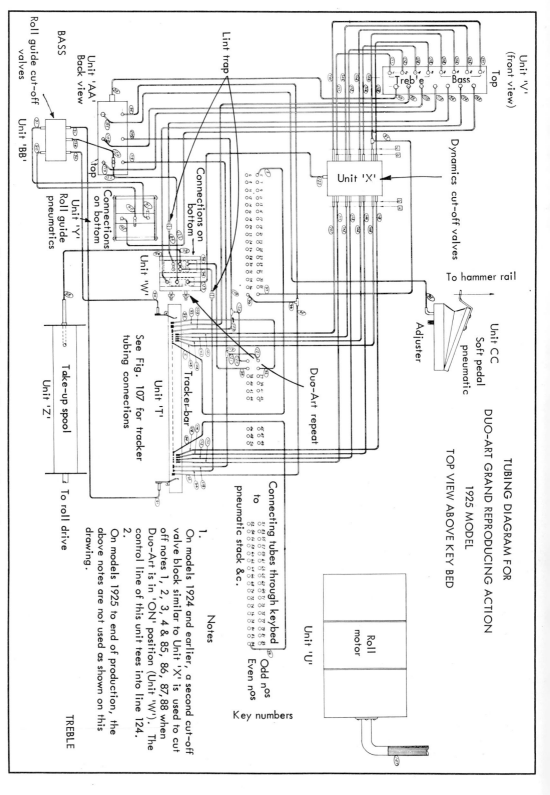

Fig. 82. Tubing diagram for Duo-Art grand installation

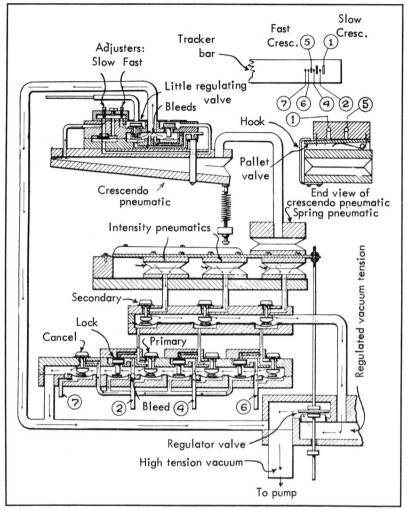

Fig. 83. Dynamic mechanism—Ampico Model A

conveniently called the *crescendo pneumatic*. This *crescendo pneumatic* in turn gets its supply, through a constricted channel, from a little regulating valve. The rubber tube leading from the top of the little regulating valve is a muffler tube.

The three little pneumatics pull down on the lever arm and tend to close the regulator valve, while the spring pneumatic pulls up and tends to open it. When there is no *crescendo* taking place the up-pull of the spring pneumatic is constant and even. When a *crescendo* is taking place the up-pull of this pneumatic gradually increases.

The dynamic mechanism not only controls changes in the loudness of the playing bᵤ has the very important function of maintaining an even pressure of vacuum, regardlesᵣ many notes are being played.

If no notes are being played, the regulator supplies just enough air to makᵣ When a note is played it causes the vacuum tension in the wind chest to ᵣ it is this same air which supplies the three little intensity pneumatics

PLAYER PIANO

regulator valve is lessened and the valve opens slightly, thereby letting more air pass through it, but only enough to increase the down-pull of the intensity pneumatics to a point where it just equals the up-pull of the spring pneumatic. The regulator is so sensitive that it will correct a drop in the tension which is imperceptible in the playing and barely noticeable on a water gauge.

If atmosphere is admitted to one of the intensity pneumatics, the down-pull on the valve is lessened and it raises until the pressure is great enough to make it possible for the down-pull of the remaining two pneumatics to equal the up-pull of the spring pneumatic. It will readily be seen that the different steps are obtained by admitting atmospheric air to the different intensity pneumatics singly or in combination. Quick accents are produced by stepping the pressure up just as the note to be accented is played, and instantly stepping back again.

The operation of the step mechanism is as follows.

Regulated air is admitted to the three intensity pneumatics through three valves, which are located on a wind chest supplied with vacuum pressure the same as goes to the striker pneumatics. These three secondary valves, as they are called, are in turn controlled by three primary valves located in a high vacuum wind chest exhausted direct from the pump.

It can readily be seen that decreasing the down-pull on the regulator valve is equivalent to increasing the up-pull. To produce a quick step change, the down-pull of one or more of the intensity pneumatics is suddenly released by admitting atmospheric air to it.

The function of the intensity pneumatics is an interesting application of the lever. By arranging the pneumatic motors under a lever so that one is near the fulcrum, another is in the centre and the third at the greatest distance from the fulcrum, the pull of each one upon that lever is different.

The intensity pneumatics thus exert different pulling powers on the regulator valve, due to their different locations on the lever arm. The one nearest the valve stem has the greatest effect while the one nearest the fulcrum has the least.

The valve nearest the fulcrum is called the No. 1 intensity valve and is controlled by the No. 2 hole in the tracker (counting from the treble end for the treble regulator and from the bass end for the bass regulator). With no intensity valves raised, the loudness of the playing is called No. 1 intensity.

The following table shows the settings for the various intensities of playing:

Intensity of Playing	Intensity Valves Open	Holes in Tracker Open
No. 1	None	None
No. 2	No. 1	No. 2
No. 3	No. 2	No. 4
No. 4	No. 3	No. 6
No. 4	No. 1, No. 2*	No. 2, No. 4
No. 5	No. 1, No. 3	No. 2, No. 6
No. 6	No. 2, No. 3	No. 4, No. 6
No. 7	No. 1, No. 2, No. 3	No. 2, No. 4, No. 6

*(Alternative setting.)

In order that the sides of the music roll will not be filled with expression or intensity perforations, a lock valve is provided for each primary valve, and a single cancel valve controls all the lock valves. Each primary valve is supplied with a bleed but this bleed is not placed

208

directly between the wind-chest and the tracker duct, as is the case with the bleeds of the primary valves of the striker pneumatics.

A channel from the primary valve leads to the lock valve and thence to the bleed. When the primary valve is down, suction is admitted to the underside of its pouch through the bleed, but when the valve rises, atmospheric air passes over the lock valve and through the bleed to the pouch, thus locking the valve open.

When the lock valve is raised, it shuts off the channel from the primary valve and connects the bleed with the wind-chest thereby neutralizing the pouch and allowing the valve to come back to its seat.

The cancel valve acts as the primary valve for all three lock valves and, when it is sprung from the No. 7 hole in the tracker, all three lock valves are raised, and any primary valve which is up will drop back. If, however, a primary valve tracker hole is open simultaneously with the lock valve, the primary valve will remain up because more air is admitted to the pouch than can be withdrawn through the bleed. If the cancel valve hole in the tracker is closed before the primary valve hole, the lock valves will drop, and the primary valve which was open will remain locked open.

This is accomplished by having the primary valve perforation in the music roll a little longer than the lock valve perforation. For instance: if the alternative setting of No. 4 intensity is on, No. 1 and No. 2 valves will be open. Now if we wish to drop back to No. 3 intensity, the cancel valve hole No. 7 will be open at the same time as the No. 4 hole, but the No. 4 hole in the music roll will be extended a little beyond the No. 7, so that the No. 2 valve will be held open not only while the No. 7 hole cancels the No. 1 valve, but long enough to let the lock valves return to their lower seats, when the No. 2 valve will then keep itself locked open. This kind of setting is very frequent in the music-rolls.

The loudness of the No. 1 intensity is adjustable as will be explained further on, but the other steps are not adjustable in their relative loudness to the No. 1.

The functioning of the spring pneumatic mechanism works in the following manner.

As was explained before, the three little intensity pneumatics tend to close the regulator valve, while the spring pneumatic pulls up and tends to open it. By admitting atmospheric air to any of the intensity pneumatics, an instant decreasing in the down-pull on the regulator valve takes place, and therefore an instant change in the loudness of the playing is achieved.

Increasing the up-pull on the valve produces exactly the same effect as decreasing the down-pull and it is by gradually increasing the up-pull that *crescendo* effects in the playing are obtained. Step effects or accents being caused by changing the down-pull on the regulator valve, and *crescendo* effects being caused by changing the up-pull on it, makes it possible to produce both these effects at the same time.

The spring pneumatic is connected by a rubber tube to the *crescendo* bellows. This *crescendo* bellows is in turn connected to a little regulating valve by means of a small tube. After entering the valve board, the channel passes into the metal speed-regulating block which contains two little, pointed adjusting screws, which are for the purpose of timing the slow and fast movements of the *crescendo* bellows.

The air passes first through the slow adjustment, then through the fast adjustment, then to the little regulating valve. The pouch of this valve is connected by means of a channel to a pallet valve which is operated by a hook connected to the movable board of the *crescendo* bellows. There is an ordinary bleed connecting the pouch channel with the high tension wind-chest. The hook is of such a length that it engages the pallet valve just before the *crescendo* pneumatic becomes fully distended. The *crescendo* bellows is pulled open by a spring which is adjustable. This adjustment is for the purpose of setting the No. 1 intensity to the right loudness.

Now let us go back to the channel leading from the *crescendo* bellows to the little regulating valve. As already stated, this channel passes through the slow adjustment, but there is a by-pass around this adjustment which is controlled by a by-pass valve consisting merely of a pouch, which normally has atmospheric air under it so that it is distended against the by-pass channel, thereby keeping it closed. Normally all the air flowing to the *crescendo* bellows must pass the slow adjustment, which is so set that it takes the bellows eleven seconds to close. Likewise it takes about the same time to open.

When the *crescendo* bellows is open nearly to its full extent, the hook engages the pallet valve and opens it, thereby admitting atmosphere to the little regulating valve pouch and raising the valve. As soon as the *crescendo* bellows begins to close on account of the regulating valve being raised, the hook allows the pallet valve to close and the valve again seats itself. The regulating valve actually floats between its upper and lower seats, mixing just enough atmosphere from above it with suction from below to produce the right degree of reduced pressure on the air in the *crescendo* bellows to counteract the spring.

The by-pass valve around the 'slow' adjustment is controlled by an inside working primary valve, which in turn is controlled by the same pallet valve that controls the slow *crescendo* valve. If there is a sudden demand for exhaust, caused, for instance, by the playing of a heavy chord, there will be a perceptible movement of the regulating valve and likewise the spring pneumatic will close a little and the *crescendo* bellows open slightly, thereby lifting the pallet valve away from its seat further than normal. The channel from the inside working primary valve is located nearer the fulcrum of the pallet valve, so that it does not open effectively until after the other hole is wide open. When this sudden demand takes place, not only is the latter hole opened wide enough to cause the little regulating valve to go up against its upper seat, but the primary valve hole is also opened and this causes the primary valve to open, thereby admitting suction to the pouch of the by-pass valve which allows the air to flow through the by-pass around the slow adjustment. The flow of this air is then only constricted by the fast adjustment, which allows the *crescendo* bellows to close much faster. This faster motion brings the movable board of the *crescendo* back to its normal position very quickly, so that normal conditions are almost instantly restored.

Crescendo effects are obtained in the following way. From the two ducts controlled by the pallet valve there are two branches. The one leading from the little regulating valve duct connects with the No. 1 hole in the tracker, while the one leading from the inside primary valve duct connects with the No. 5 tracker hole.

The vacuum pressure of the air in the spring pneumatic is of course the same as that in the *crescendo* bellows, and as the setting of the spring determines the vacuum in the *crescendo* bellows and spring pneumatic, it likewise determines the loudness of the playing. When everything is normal, the pallet valve controls the position of the *crescendo* bellows, but, when the No. 1 hole in the tracker is opened, atmosphere is admitted to the little regulating-valve pouch faster than the bleed can exhaust it, and the valve is raised so that suction, without any mixture of atmosphere, is admitted through the fast and slow adjustments to the *crescendo* bellows, which is slowly collapsed. If the No. 5 hole in the tracker is opened at the same time as the No. 1, the *crescendo* bellows will collapse at a much faster speed.

As the bellows closes, it stretches the spring, thereby causing it to pull harder. This spring is designed so that its pull, when the *crescendo* bellows is almost completely closed, is just sufficient to produce tension enough on the air within the *crescendo* bellows and spring pneumatic to pull up on the main regulator valve enough to raise the loudness of the playing to the level of the No. 7 intensity which is the loudest.

As the *crescendo* bellows closes *gradually* the pull of the spring likewise gradually increases and thus is produced a gradual rise in the loudness of the playing—a *crescendo*.

Under these conditions the little regulating valve ceases to perform its function as a regulator and becomes the controlling valve of the slow *crescendo*. It is therefore generally called the slow *crescendo* valve, while the inside primary valve when operated from the tracker becomes the fast *crescendo* valve, and is usually so called.

To produce a slow *crescendo* the No. 1 hole in the tracker is opened. When the hole is then closed a slow *decrescendo* takes place. To produce a full speed *crescendo* the No. 1 and No. 5 holes in the tracker are opened. If both holes are then closed a slow *decrescendo* takes place, but, if only the No. 1 hole is closed and the No. 5 kept open, a full speed *decrescendo* takes place. If the No. 1 hole in the tracker is opened by a series of perforations 2 inches long separated by about 1 inch, a half-speed slow *crescendo* is produced, for the *crescendo* is on for 2 inches of the music roll and off for 1 inch, then on again for 2, etc. If an unbroken slow *crescendo* perforation is in the music roll, and with it are a series of short fast *crescendo* perforations, the effect will be a *crescendo*, the speed of which is intermediate between the slow and fast. By varying the intervals between the short fast *crescendo* perforations, different intermediate speeds are obtained.

Connected to each side of the wind-chest is a small pneumatic with a long spring. Inside this

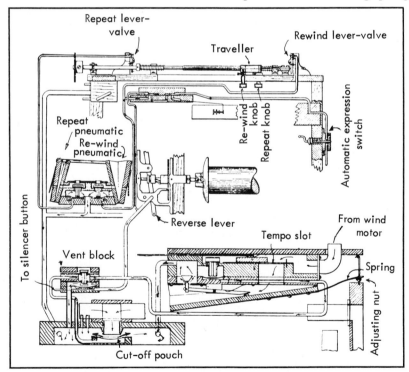

Fig. 84. Diagram of automatic rewind—repeat system, air motor governor and reverse cut-out for the Ampico Model A

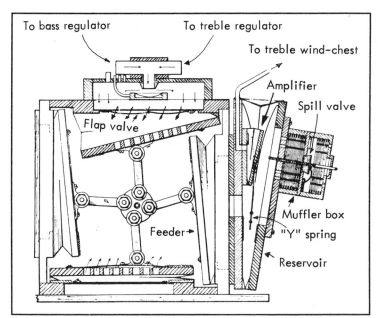

To bass regulator
To treble regulator
To treble wind-chest
Amplifier
Spill valve
Flap valve
Muffler box
"Y" spring
Feeder
Reservoir

Fig. 85. Diagram of pump

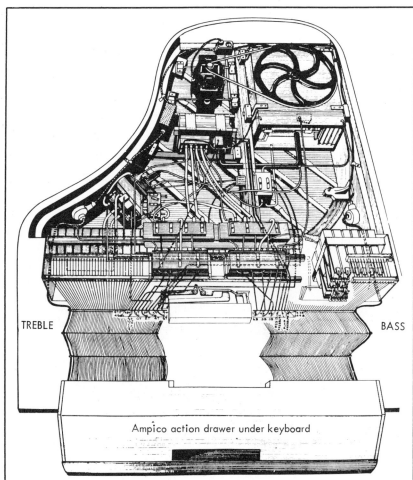

TREBLE

BASS

Ampico action drawer under keyboard

Fig. 86. Ampico grand
installation viewed from
underneath

pneumatic is a small bumper spring. This pneumatic is a regulated tension reservoir and is for the purpose of taking some of the work of regulating off the regulating valve, when various numbers of notes are being played at low intensities. It keeps the regulator from 'jumping' and operates very much as does the equalizer in an ordinary player-piano.

The Model B Ampico, introduced in 1929, represented a complete rethinking of the reproducing action. The salient points of difference are as follows.

The expression regulator is constructed to entirely new principles and contains only one moving part—a rubber diaphragm. The elimination of moving parts from the expression regulating apparatus makes for more rapid, silent action.

The *crescendo* apparatus is incorporated in the pump assembly and controls both the bass and treble sections of the action simultaneously. Two steps of pump amplification are employed —the second one providing for louder *fortissimo* effects than possible with the earlier model. Both steps of pump amplification and the *crescendo* are produced by the same mechanism, which itself is part of the pump assembly.

The intensity valve system, controlling the expression regulator, is greatly simplified by the elimination of the intensity lock valves. This elimination does not involve any change in the function of the intensity valves themselves. They serve exactly the same purpose as before but are cancelled by a less complicated mechanism. A pedal regulator is employed, which at all times supplies the pedal-actuating apparatus with constant power, irrespective of the vacuum pressure generated by the pump.

The unit valves which control the striker pneumatics are modified so as to eliminate the primary valve system, whilst at the same time preserving the precision and speed of valve action obtained by the double-valve system (this followed suit with Aeolian's engineering of the Duo-Art which reverted to being a single-valve system). Each striker pneumatic was adjusted in manufacture, so that its power was exactly suited to the individual piano-action element which it operated. This adjustment was accomplished by varying the normal opening of the pneumatic, so achieving a far greater evenness of playing under *pianissimo* conditions.

An additional intensity valve, known as the 'sub-valve', is added for the control of the expression regulator in both the bass and treble sections of the action. This, together with the striker pneumatic adjustment, provides *pianissimo* effects which were not possible with the Model A. A small hand lever, situated under the piano, adjusts the first intensity within limits to suit the room in which the piano is being played.

The wind motor of the Model A is replaced by a specially-designed electric motor which drives the music-roll through a centrifugal governor. The control of the governor is far more precise than can be obtained with an air-motor governor. Ample power for driving the roll under all conditions is provided by the electric motor, and *tempo* registration and alteration is instantly achieved and maintained within very fine limits. Added to all this, music-rolls which play for thirty minutes are available for this instrument.

Now let us examine the detail parts of this action and see how they work.

The expression regulator is illustrated in Fig. 88 and consists of a perforated partition or grid B forming a seat for the rubber cloth pouch A which controls the flow of air from the wind-chest F to the chamber G, and thence to the pump.

The chamber C, under the pouch, is connected to pump suction through the adjustable opening E and to atmosphere through the variable opening D. If E were open and D tightly closed, pump suction through E would pull the pouch completely away from the grid and full pump suction would be admitted to the wind-chest F. If these adjustments were reversed, with

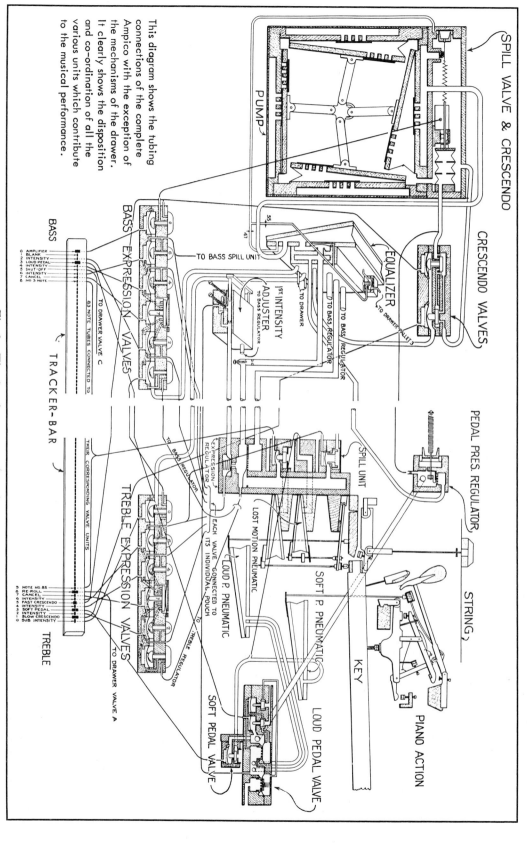

This diagram shows the tubing connections of the complete Ampico with the exception of the drawer. It clearly shows the disposition and co-ordination of all the various units which contribute to the musical performance.

Fig. 87. The Ampico pneumatic action

SPILL VALVE & CRESCENDO

PUMP

CRESCENDO VALVES

BASS EXPRESSION VALVES

BASS

TO BASS SPILL UNIT

EQUALIZER

TO DRAWER PALLET 3

PEDAL PRES. REGULATOR

STRING

PIANO ACTION

55

47

1ST INTENSITY ADJUSTER
TO BASS REGULATOR

TO DRAWER

TO BASS REGULATOR

TO BASS REGULATOR

0 AMPLIFIER
1 BLANK
2 INTENSITY
3 LOUD PEDAL
4 INTENSITY
5 SHUT-OFF
6 INTENSITY
7 CANCEL
8 NO 3 NOTE

83 NOTE TUBES CONNECTED TO

TO DRAWER VALVE C

TRACKER-BAR

THEIR CORRESPONDING VALVE UNITS

TO BASS REGULATOR

EXPRESSION REGULATOR

SPILL UNIT

LOST MOTION PNEUMATIC

LOUD P. PNEUMATIC

SOFT P. PNEUMATIC

SOFT P. PNEUMATIC

KEY

EACH VALVE CONNECTED TO ITS INDIVIDUAL POUCH

TREBLE EXPRESSION VALVES

TO TREBLE REGULATOR

TREBLE

9 NOTE NO.85
8 RE-ROLL
7 CANCEL
6 INTENSITY
5 FAST CRESCENDO
4 INTENSITY
3 SOFT PEDAL
2 INTENSITY
1 SLOW CRESCENDO
0 SUB INTENSITY

TO DRAWER VALVE A

SOFT PEDAL VALVE

LOUD PEDAL VALVE

PEDAL PRES. REGULATOR

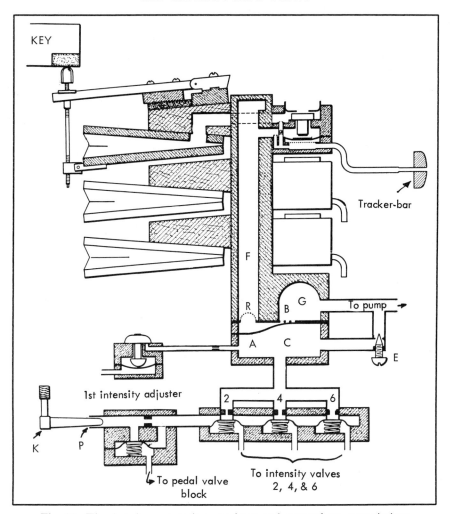

Fig. 88. The Ampico expression regulator and atmosphere constrictions

E tightly closed and D open, pump suction in chamber G would cause the pouch A to seal the holes in the grid and no suction would be developed in the wind-chest F.

Without changing the pump pressures, adjusting the openings E and D between these extremes will produce a suction in the chamber C, which is a fractional part of that developed by the pump, and this fractional suction will peel the pouch away from the grid, until there is developed in the wind-chest the same degree of suction that exists in chamber C. The pouch will then be in balance and any change of suction in the chest F, due to the playing of notes, etc., will be instantly rectified by a movement of the pouch A. Any increase in pump suction will give a corresponding fractional increase in suction in the chamber C. This is used in producing amplification and *crescendo* effects.

The opening E is adjusted at the time of manufacture to fit the scale of intensities to the particular piano into which the Ampico is installed. The opening E can also be adjusted to even up the No. I intensity pressures, Bass and Treble.

The size of opening D is variable and is automatically controlled from the note sheet. The opening is actually made up of four different sizes, o, 2, 4, and 6 (Fig. 89), which may be opened or closed, either singly or in combination, from the note sheet. Three of these openings are arranged longitudinally along the bottom of chamber C and one connects into the side of this chamber.

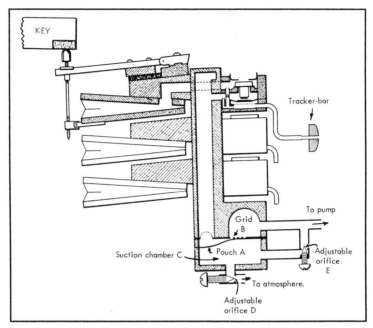

Fig. 89. Expression regulator, showing atmosphere constrictions

For the purpose of making this figure perfectly clear, all parts are shown in transverse section, except the openings and valves which are diagrammatic and are shown in longitudinal section. The three openings and pouch valves are actually built into the bottom board of the regulator and not isolated as shown.

Disregarding for the moment the parts of the appartus at H and I of the First Intensity adjuster (see under Loud Pedal Valve Block), atmosphere enters tube P around the tapered pin K, flows through J and then through 2, 4 and 6, any or all, into chamber C. With 2, 4 and 6 open and o closed, the suction maintained in chamber C produces the First Intensity. The closing of 2, 4 and 6 singly, or in combination, reduces the atmosphere influx to chamber C and produces different degrees of suction in it. These different degrees of suction cause the regulator A to open different amounts and produce the same suctions in the wind-chest F. This gives the different steps in the intensity scale.

With 2, 4 and 6 and o open, the suction, maintained in chamber C, produces an intensity which is lower than the No. 1 intensity. This is called the 'sub' intensity and is used to obtain extreme *pianissimo* effects. The pouches controlling 2, 4 and 6, as well as the opening o, are operated by valves in the expression valve block. All of these openings, o, 2, 4 and 6, are of fixed size, each having its proper and constant effect upon the intensity scale. They are manufactured to accurate limits and must never be altered.

216

Two regulators as described above are used—one for the Bass, and one for the Treble. The entire regulation is accomplished by the balance of pressures established on both sides of the regulator pouch, by means of the relationship between the respective fixed orifices. There are no mechanical parts to be moved during the process of regulation, when action suction must be accurately maintained, or instantly changed. All of this is accomplished by the slight movement of a thin rubber cloth pouch, the weight of which is only a few thousandths of the weight of the moving parts of the other regulating systems.

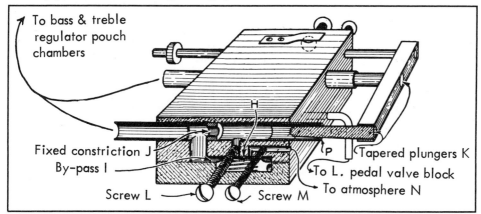

Fig. 90. First intensity adjuster

The First Intensity adjuster, shown in the diagram Fig. 87, is shown in detail in Fig. 90. It serves to provide a method whereby the owner of the piano can vary the soft intensity to compensate for climatic conditions, the size of the room and so on.

The opening at P is controlled by a tapered plunger K, inserted into the open end of a tube leading from the chamber C through a fixed constriction J to atmosphere. Movement of this plunger increases or decreases the atmosphere admitted through 2, 4 and 6 to the chamber C and provides a ready means of adjusting the first intensity. It does not affect the higher intensities. The bass and treble plungers are mounted together and are provided with a handle which projects slightly through the hiding curtain just behind the action stack. Pulling the handle out admits more atmosphere to the chambers C, and further reduces the lower intensities; pushing the handle in reduces the atmosphere influx to the chamber C and raises the lower intensities.

The handle should be set as far out as possible, so that the softest notes, which are played with the 'sub' intensity and the soft pedal, will just barely speak.

This block also contains the loud pedal compensating device described further on.

The expression valves are built in three blocks—bass intensity valves, treble intensity valves, and *crescendo* valves.

The bass and treble intensity valves are in two separate blocks and are located on the bottom side of the action stack just in front of the expression regulators. They are interposed between the tracker-bar and the expression regulators, and are used to obtain sudden changes in loudness of playing.

In the treble-intensity valve block, Fig. 91, there are six valves: the sub-primary valve oT, three intensity valves 2T, 4T, 6T, the cancel valve 7T, and the treble sub-secondary valve. The bass intensity valve block is interchangeable with the treble block and all valves, but one, function the same.

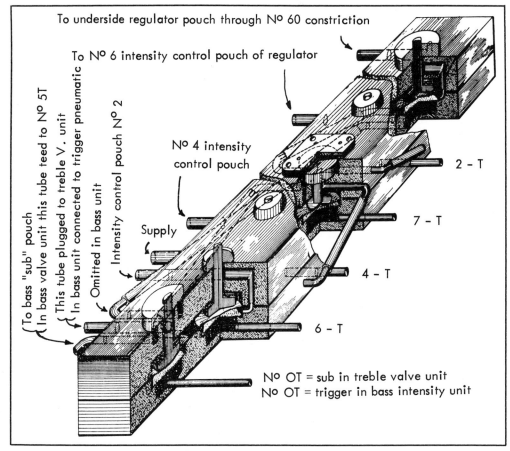

Fig. 91. Intensity valve block

The valve which is used in the treble block as the sub-primary, is used in the bass block to control the amplifier trigger. The three intensity valves in each valve block lock themselves open when sprung by a short hole in the note sheet. The sub-secondary valve locks itself open when sprung by the sub-primary valve oT. These four valves are unlocked by the same cancel valve.

This locking and cancelling is best understood by referring to Fig. 92 which shows diagrammatically one intensity valve and the cancel valve.

Normally, suction is communicated to the underside of the intensity valve pouch through a small bleed A, thereby allowing the pouch and valve to rest in the 'down' position. When the intensity hole in the tracker-bar is opened, the valve raises and atmosphere is admitted from the upper seat to the pouch through the small bleed A. When the tracker-bar hole is closed, this atmosphere, through the small bleed A, holds the intensity valve locked up. With this valve locked in the 'up' position, atmosphere is admitted to its corresponding regulator pouch valve, which allows the spring to raise it and close its constriction to the chamber C, Fig. 89.

When the cancel hole in the tracker-bar is opened, the cancel valve raises and admits suction through the large bleed B to the under side of the intensity valve pouch. This suction overcomes

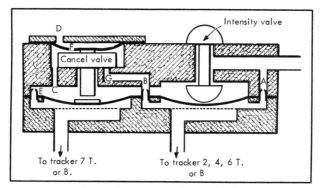

Fig. 92. Intensity and cancel valve

the effect of atmosphere coming through the small bleed A, and the intensity valve returns to its 'down' position. When the intensity valve resumes its 'down' position, suction is admitted to the under side of the regulator pouch valve, which lowers to its normal or 'down' position. In this position, atmosphere is admitted through the constriction to the regulator pouch chamber.

The cancel valve is provided with a bleed E, to return it to its seat after the tracker-bar hole is closed. This valve is held firmly against its lower seat by a small pouch F above it, which receives its suction through a small hole C leading to the suction chamber of the valve block. The upper side of this pouch is always in communication with atmosphere through a small hole D. The cancel valve has four holes under its head, instead of the one G as shown.

These four holes communicate through large bleeds to the four valve pouches which the cancel valve controls. They are the three intensity valve pouches, 2, 4 and 6, and the sub-secondary valve pouch.

A diagram of the sub-primary, sub-secondary and cancel valve connections is shown in Fig. 93. The sub-secondary valve operates in the same manner as the intensity valve, except that it is sprung from a hole under the head of the sub-primary valve instead of directly from the tracker-bar.

The bass sub-secondary valve is sprung from a second hole under the head of the sub-primary valve. When the 'sub' hole oT in the tracker-bar is open, it springs the sub-primary

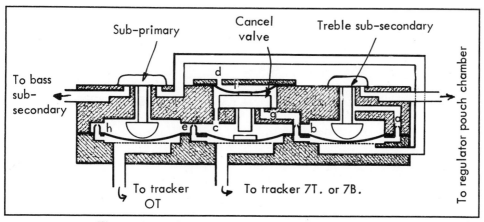

Fig. 93. Sub-primary, sub-secondary and cancel valves

219

valve which, through the two holes under its head, springs the bass and treble sub-secondary valves. They both lock up and have their corresponding effect on the regulator pouches. Either one of these valves may be cancelled at will by the use of its own cancel valve.

The valve, which in the treble intensity valve block is used as the sub-primary, is used in the bass block to operate the amplifier trigger. The actual arrangement of these valves in their block is shown in Fig. 91.

The use of a series of valves controlled by one cancel valve makes it possible to control the entire expression mechanism with very few tracker-bar holes, and does away with a great many extended perforations in the music roll. Furthermore, the design of the intensity valves ensures quietness of operation.

The chambers of all pouches operated from the tracker-bar are equipped with strainers which keep dirt, coming in through the tracker-bar, from obstructing the bleeds.

The intensity valve blocks are held together by means of springs which ensure tightness under all climatic conditions.

The pump spill-valve mechanism determines the degree of suction generated by the pump. It is located directly on the pump and consists of three major parts: (a) the governor, which holds the suction at any predetermined degree; (b) the *crescendo* pneumatic, which can gradually increase the pump suction as desired; (c) the amplifier trigger which can lock the spill valve spring in either of its two amplified positions.

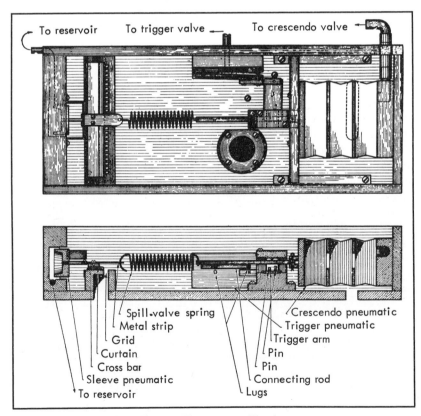

Fig. 94. The pump spill valve

Figure 94 shows a plan and elevation view of the mechanism. A lead from the pump terminates in a chamber covered by a 'grid' C, the amount of opening of which is controlled by a curtain valve D. This curtain valve is a strip of rubber cloth a little longer than the grid, one edge of which is secured to the face of the grid. It is doubled back on itself and the other edge is fastened to a light cross-bar E. The cross-bar is pulled by the spill-valve spring A in the direction which rolls the curtain valve over the grid. It is pulled in the opposite direction by a sleeve-type pneumatic F which unrolls the curtain off the grid. The sleeve pneumatic is connected to pump suction by a tube G from the high-pressure reservoir. This tube contains a small constriction.

With the pump in operation, pump suction increases until the pull of the sleeve pneumatic, as it uncovers the grid, is the same as the opposing pull of the spill-valve spring. The point at which they balance is the regulating point. If the pump suction increases, the sleeve pneumatic F opens the curtain valve D, and spills more atmosphere into the pump, and so reduces the suction to the valve determined by the spring A. If the pump suction drops, the sleeve pneumatic is weakened and the spring rolls the curtain valve over the grid holes. This reduces the atmosphere spill into the pump and brings the pump pressure back to where the spring and sleeve pneumatic are again in balance.

During re-roll it is desirable to increase slightly the pump suction. This is accomplished by spilling a small amount of atmosphere into the sleeve pneumatic, which reduces the tension of the air therein. This makes it necessary for the pump to generate a little higher vacuum so that the pull of the sleeve pneumatic will balance the pull of the spill-valve spring.

The tube connecting the cut-out primary to the action cut-out pouch is linked, through a constriction, into the tube leading from the high-pressure reservoir to the sleeve pneumatic. This connection is made between the sleeve and the small constriction.

When the cut-out primary valve is raised, atmosphere is spilled into the sleeve pneumatic, through the constriction, and thus causes the pump pressure to be increased. Due to the fact that a sleeve pneumatic has practically a constant pull throughout its travel, and to the extreme lightness of the moving parts, its action is instantaneous and the pump suction is maintained uniform.

Instead of spilling outside atmosphere directly through the grid, an opening is provided, connecting the pump housing chamber with the sealed pump spill box, whereby most of the atmosphere exhausted from the mechanisms is again used for spilling purposes. This reduces air noise.

The *crescendo* pneumatic—H is connected to the spring A by means of a connecting rod M. When the pneumatic H is gradually collapsed, the pull of the spring on the curtain D will gradually increase and produce a corresponding increase in pump suction, which is communicated to the regulator pouch.

As this pump suction gradually increases, it raises the suction in the chamber C and produces a gradual raise or *crescendo* in the scale of intensities.

There are two speeds of *crescendo*: the *Slow Crescendo*, in which the pneumatic takes about four seconds to collapse, and the *Fast Crescendo*, in which it takes about half a second. By combining the two, many different speeds of *crescendo* are obtained.

The slow *crescendo* is operated by a valve controlled from the 1T hole in the tracker-bar, and the fast *crescendo* is operated by a valve controlled from the 5T hole in the tracker-bar.

The No. 1B hole, in the bass end of the tracker-bar of the Model 'B' Ampico, is not used. The No. 5B hole is used in conjunction with the shut-off mechanism, which stops the motor when the music-roll has been rewound and if the 'Repeat' switch is not set to by-pass it and play the roll again.

The amplifying mechanism makes use of the *crescendo* pneumatic and its connecting rod M to the curtain valve, a trigger J and a trigger pneumatic I. The trigger pneumatic is normally held collapsed by suction from its operating valve, which, as previously explained, is located in the bass intensity-valve block.

When the amplifier hole oB in the tracker-bar is opened, atmosphere is admitted to the trigger pneumatic which is opened by its spring. This brings the pin K on the trigger arm in line with the lug N on the connecting rod M. When the *crescendo* hole 1T is opened simultaneously with the amplifier hole oB, the lug N will strike the pin K thus allowing only a partial collapsing of the *crescendo* pneumatic. When the holes oB and 1T are closed, the trigger bar is pulled back before the *crescendo* pneumatic opens and the pin L on the trigger arm J is drawn in, back of the lug N, and this holds the spill-valve spring stretched to its mid position. This holds the pump pressure at what is called the First Amplification.

To raise the pump pressure from First Amplification to Second Amplification oB and 1T holes are opened simultaneously. This allows the trigger arm to move forward, until the pin K rests against the fin connecting the two lugs. In this position pin L is out of the path of lug O and the *crescendo* pneumatic pulls lug O beyond the pin L. On closing oB and 1T holes, the trigger pneumatic pulls pin L against the pin beyond lug O and, as the *crescendo* pneumatic releases, the pin is caught behind the lug and the spring is locked in the Second Amplification position, or highest pump pressure.

To bring the spring back to the First Amplification position, the oB tracker-bar hole is opened by a short perforation in the music roll. This moves the pin L out from behind the lug O for just an instant, and gets it back behind the lug N before it passes, thereby stopping the travel of the connecting rod at the First Amplification position. A somewhat longer perforation in the music roll is required, to bring the spring from the Second Amplification position back to Normal. A hole under the head of the trigger valve is joined into the fast *crescendo* tracker tube 5T. This causes the *crescendo* pneumatic to operate quickly, whenever the amplifier hole oB is opened simultaneously with the slow *crescendo* hole 1T.

It will be seen from the foregoing, that pump suction regulation, *crescendos*, and the two degrees of amplification are obtained by one piece of mechanism whose moving parts are very light and frictionless.

The intensity scales are illustrated in Fig. 95, which demonstrates the three intensity scales of Normal, First Amplification and Second Amplification. The lines represent the approximate pressures of the various valve settings when the Normal No. 1 intensity is 5·6 inches and the Normal pump pressure is 20 inches. The Normal No. 1 intensity may be set slightly higher or lower than 5·6 inches, according to the heaviness of the particular piano action used, or climatic conditions.

Each of the eight valve settings give three gauge pressures, i.e. the normal pressure; a higher pressure when the First Amplification is set; and a still higher pressure when the Second Amplification is set. Thus by the use of the expression valves alone twenty-four different gauge pressures may be obtained. In addition to these twenty-four fixed pressures, the *crescendo* mechanism makes it possible to obtain any intermediate pressure desired.

The Ampico normal scale is not an arbitrary succession of steps, but is based on the different degrees of loudness that are perceptible to the ear. These different, perceptible degrees of loudness are called 'audibility steps'. The factory setting of the pump pressure is marked on the

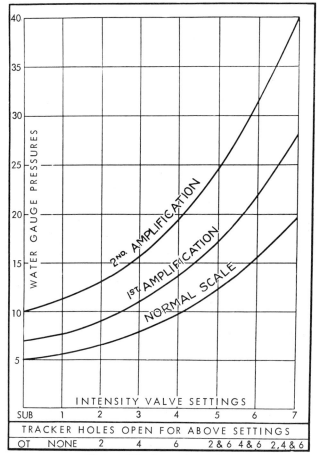

Fig. 95. The Intensity scales

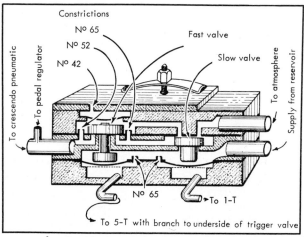

Fig. 96. The *crescendo* valve block uses the characteristic Ampico control system of differing rates of bleed through different diameter constrictions or bleed holes

pump spill box. The only way to alter the pump setting is to modify the spring.

In reading gauge pressures on the Model B Ampico, always connect at the tap-plate under the centre of the piano.

The *crescendo* valves are used to control the pneumatic which produces gradual increases and decreases in loudness of playing. The slow and fast *crescendo* valves are mounted in one block, which also contains the constrictions which govern the speed of operation of the *crescendo* pneumatic.

Figure 96 shows a section of the *crescendo* valve block. The 'fast' valve is equipped with an auxiliary pouch to return it to its seat. This pouch connects to atmosphere at all times by a small inlet. Slow *crescendo* is produced by opening 1T hole in the tracker-bar. The *crescendo* will continue as long as this hole is open, or until the pump suction reaches its maximum value.

Opening the 1T hole raises the slow *crescendo* valve, thereby shutting off atmosphere, and exhausting the *crescendo* pneumatic at a low speed through the No. 52 bleed, over the top of the fast valve and through the No. 65 bleed. When the 1T hole is closed a slow *decrescendo* takes place, but the slow *decrescendo* is a little faster than the slow *crescendo*, because the atmosphere comes in across the top of the slow valve, across the top of the fast valve and thence through the No. 52 bleed. During slow *crescendo*, the air passes through two constrictions. During the slow *decrescendo* it only passes through one constriction.

For a fast *crescendo*, tracker-bar holes 1T and 5T are opened simultaneously. Both valves are thereby raised, permitting the *crescendo* pneumatic to be exhausted, without passing the air

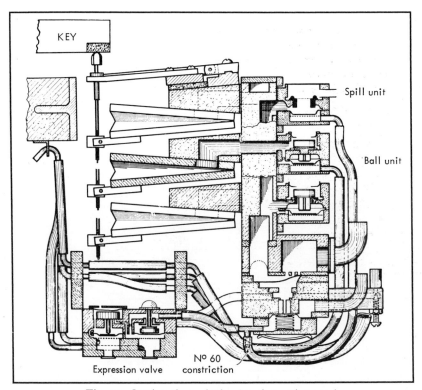

Fig. 97. Section through the Ampico action stack

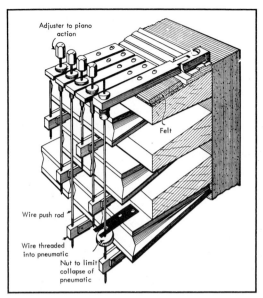

Fig. 98. Striker pneumatic connections

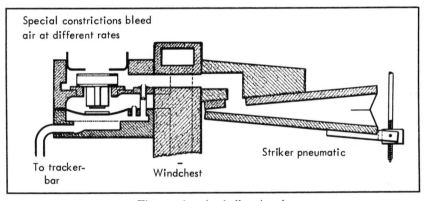

Fig. 99. Ampico ball-unit valve

through either the No. 52 or the No. 65 constrictions. When the tracker-bar hole 1T is closed and the 5T is left open, a fast *decrescendo* is produced.

A tube from the pedal-regulator, containing a No. 70 constriction, is connected to the tube leading to the *crescendo* pneumatic. Through it is supplied a minute amount of pedal suction to the *crescendo* pneumatic at all times so that when it is in the open position, its fabric is held taut. By having no slack in its cloth, the pneumatic responds instantly when the 1T hole in the tracker-bar is opened.

The *crescendo* valves, by controlling the pump spill-valve, automatically produce *crescendos* or *decrescendos* in both the bass and the treble side of the action simultaneously. This lends itself to reproducing the artist's interpretation as shown by the method of Ampico recording.

Although the expression system of the Model B is different from that of the Model A, the ability to accent notes during *crescendos* by means of the intensity valves is retained.

The action stack comprises the wind-chest, two expression regulators, three decks of action

T

pneumatics, lost-motion action adjusters, the tracker or poppet wires, two action spill-valves, two intensity valve blocks and the so-called ball-unit valves.

All these parts are manufactured in one complex (see Fig. 98) and the components are closely spaced.

The wind-chest is built of a solid piece of maple and is extremely rigid. It features a main windway along the bottom edge and a supplementary windway along the top. These two windways are connected by a series of vertical holes, from which are led the supply channels to the ball-unit valves. The high-pressure chests, with their grids, are glued to the wind-chest and form an integral part of it.

Atmosphere is drawn from the main windway directly into the expression regulators, through a series of round holes each protected by a sieve. These sieves prevent any particles of dirt from reaching the grids of the expression regulators. Each high-pressure chest, bass and treble, is exhausted through two $\frac{5}{8}$ inch tubes which run direct to the high-pressure reservoir.

The ball-unit valves are accurately located by guides and studs so that their holes will register exactly with those in the chest.

The decks are made of maple and are secured to the wind-chest by heavy springs, to reduce chances of leakage at the joints.

The poppet wires, shown in Fig. 98, are threaded top and bottom: the top thread provides adjustment for the hexagon head A to take up lost motion which comes from the packing of the felt pads under the keys. It is taken up in two ways: first, to remove general lost motion, the whole action can be raised by screwing 'in' on the hanger screws. These screws are located in the action bracket at each end of the stack. Second, after the general lost motion has been taken up, individual adjustment to the poppets can be made with the hexagon nuts A on the tops of the poppet wires B.

To make the above adjustment, remove the piano action from the piano and place it on a table. With a gauge, measure the height from the bottom of the key-frame to the bottom of the depression made in the pad under the key.

With this distance obtained, check the height of the poppets from the key-bed to the top of the hexagon nut. Any lost motion that may be found is taken up by screwing the hexagon nut upward. Hold the poppet wire above the head with pliers and turn the hexagon nut with a spanner.

The bottom thread on the poppet wire passes through the pneumatic tip C and provides for the adjustment of the striker pneumatic opening.

Differences in the piano action, due to the different weights of hammers, varying frictions at pin joints and rubbing points may make the soft playing uneven. In rectifying this, advantage is taken of the varying power of pneumatics at different openings, bearing in mind that a wide-open pneumatic gives more power than one half closed.

Making the opening of the striker pneumatic greater when more friction is encountered in the action, and reducing the opening when there is little friction, compensates these differences and so obtains an evenness of soft playing.

This was adjusted in manufacture and should not need to be changed until after it is found necessary to regulate and voice the piano action.

Once the piano action has been regulated and voiced, it may be found that some of the pneumatic openings may have to be readjusted, to even out the soft playing. The use of the tester roll will show up any such deficiencies and also serve to show when adjustments have been properly made.

The action pneumatics are controlled by the ball-unit valves. Their construction is shown in Fig. 99.

Each unit consists of an 'inside' valve with a very small fixed bleed connecting from under its pouch to the suction chamber, and an additional larger bleed, provided with a ball check valve, connecting from under the pouch to the valve chamber.

When the tracker-bar hole is open, atmosphere enters under the pouch and works with maximum efficiency to raise the valve, because at the outset air can leave the pouch chamber only through the No. 70 bleed. As the valve approaches its top seat, suction in the valve chamber increases until air flows from the pouch chamber upward through the ball check valve, as well as from the open number 70 bleed.

As the upward travel of the valve nears completion, both bleeds are open and the valve reaches its outside seat, not suddenly but slowly and with no perceptible noise.

When the tracker hole is again closed, the valve starts downward. Its stem is in contact with the pouch, and during the first portion of the valve's downward travel, air may escape from the pouch through two paths. One of these is the No. 70 bleed, which is always open; the other is the ball check bleed, which is open when the valve starts downward. As the valve proceeds towards its inside seat, atmosphere enters the valve chamber, and, before the valve completes its travel, atmospheric pressure and gravity seat the ball, closing the No. 60 bleed. Thereafter, air can escape from the pouch through the No. 70 bleed only, and the valve is retarded in its downward travel, so that it reaches its inside seat while travelling at a relatively slow speed, and thus, again, produces no noise.

This bleed system was claimed by Ampico engineers to be the most effective and efficient method of venting a pouch. During most of the upward travel of the valve, the smallest bleed consistent with efficiency is open. Therefore, the maximum amount of energy admitted by the tracker-bar is used for lifting the valve promptly. As the valve completes its upward travel, the venting of the pouch is augmented greatly by the opening of the ball check bleed, whereby the speed of the valve is reduced at the last end of its stroke, and it comes to rest, noiselssly, against its seat.

Similarly, during the reverse of this operation, the maximum venting is available through the two open bleeds during the start of the downward travel of the valve, and, toward the end of its motion, the venting is again changed and reduced to the point where the valve cannot make undue noise when it contacts with its inside seat. The advantages of the double valve control of the striking pneumatic are all embodied in this single unit valve.

Because screens R are placed in the pouch chamber of the units to protect the bleeds from dirt, it is never necessary to clean them out. Besides the intensity regulator, this valve is one of the most highly developed pieces of apparatus in the Ampico.

For a more detailed account of the operation of the Ampico together with servicing instructions, you are referred to reprints of the original manuals which are available.

The Welte reproducing action comprises two distinct types—the so-called 'Original' Welte-Mignon which plays only special music-rolls $13\frac{1}{2}$ inches wide, and the Welte-Mignon (Licensee) which was produced in America by the Auto Pneumatic Action Company, to Welte patents. This latter action used standard-width music-rolls. Original Welte-Mignon actions comprise three basic types—the cabinet reproducing player which is a 'push-up' instrument made up until the 1930's, the grand action which was always made to fit above the keyboard in the upper portion of the piano (as compared to the underneath installation of the Duo-Art and Ampico pianos), and the action used in upright instruments. The principles of the three variants are

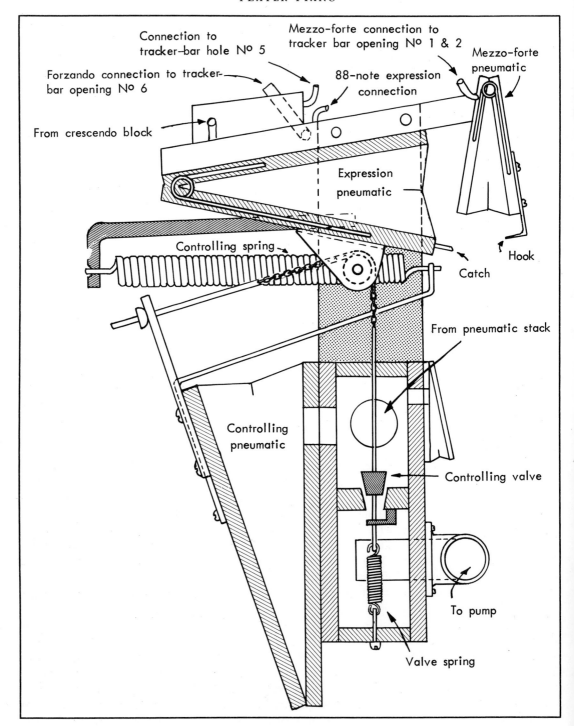

Fig. 100. The Original Welte-Mignon expression system

to all intents and purposes identical. All Original Welte-Mignon actions are powered by an electric motor driving exhausters and the power installation is always characterized by sound, solid engineering and, in the upright and cabinet players, by the use of flat drive belting instead of round leather or 'V' rope drive favoured by other makers.

Dealing first with the Original action, the amount of available playing power can be pre-set by adjustment to a spring governing a spill valve. The essence of the Welte expression system is a system of mechanical locks controlling the expression pneumatics. These locks—one is shown in Fig. 100—comprise a plate attached to the moving board of a pneumatic motor, which can engage in a hook attached to the moving board of another, smaller motor mounted at right-angles to it. As the motor controlling the expression function collapses, the lock motor is also made to collapse, so trapping the plate beneath its hook. To cancel the function, the suction is bled from the lock pneumatic, allowing it to open, thereby releasing the expression pneumatic. This avoids the need to apply continual suction to the expression pneumatic, which would call for impossibly long perforations in the music-roll. It is interesting to note that this system of mechanical locks had already been used by Welte. The Welte pipe orchestrion organs had employed a similar method for the selection and cancelling of organ stops.

Eighteen expression holes are used in the Welte tracker-bar—eight on the left and ten on the right—plus the two openings for the automatic roll tracking. These holes work in pairs, the left side using the odd numbers to set an expression operation, and the even numbered holes to cancel, whilst the right side uses the even numbers to set the operation and the odd to cancel. The two sides of the piano are divided and self-contained and each operates a conical valve which controls the level of suction for that side. The valve is lifted by a controlling pneumatic, the equilibrium of the valve being maintained by a tension spring fixed beneath it. A *mezzo-forte* pneumatic—in fact the hooked locking pneumatic—is arranged so that, if the expression pneumatic be only partly collapsed, this may also collapse and hold the expression pneumatic from further movement (Fig. 100). It can also be employed to reduce overall volume by preventing the full movement of the controlling pneumatic, which would result in the loudest playing level. These functions are set in operation by the tracker-bar perforations.

The controlling pneumatic serves to balance and maintain a level of suction, regardless of the number of functions which are taking suction power to operate, and it does this by regulating the suction by means of the conical valve. The expression pneumatic has the ability to move suddenly to produce *forzando* or slowly to produce a *crescendo* and it does this by pulling on the conical valve. The expression pneumatic is normally open, allowing the conical valve to be maintained at its lowest position. Under these conditions, the playing power is normally at its minimum and almost all degrees of playing call for the opening up of the passageway restricted by the valve. The inlets into the expression pneumatic comprise one small and one large inlet for the rapid or slow movement of the motor.

To govern the position of the main expression pneumatic, four functions are used from four tracker-bar openings. These are *crescendo* on, *crescendo* off, *forzando* on and *forzando* off.

An unusual feature of the Original action is that, unlike the other reproducing actions described, it contains no definite steps of volume increase. As we have seen, the normal playing intensity is with the conical valves governing each half of the piano at their minimum setting. All volume is built on the movement of pneumatics to add more power to that minimum setting. Now, this is all very well for a mechanical datum, but, for the practical playing of the piano, it was found too nebulous to rely on building everything except the most *pianissimo* of tones on a low suction pressure. For this reason, a further point was established by which the

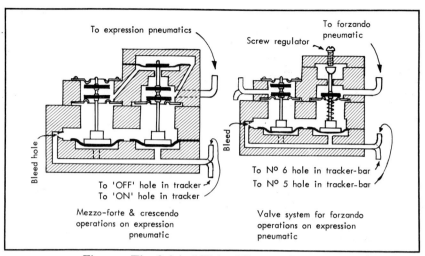

Fig. 101. The Original Welte-Mignon valve system

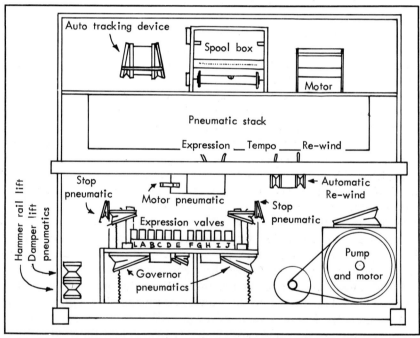

Fig. 102. The arrangement of the Welte-Mignon (Licensee) parts

operation of the expression system could continually be checked and regulated. This point is provided by the *mezzo-forte* pneumatic with its locking hook. By allowing this to interact with the controlling pneumatic, as dictated by the normal musical expression, the level of sound could be monitored and the controlling pneumatic kept in its proper range of movement. Because, in the normal playing of a piece of music, the piano plays for much of the time at something like medium volume, this *mezzo-forte* pneumatic may operate at frequent intervals, and there is no perceptible sense of the instrument 'hunting' in volume.

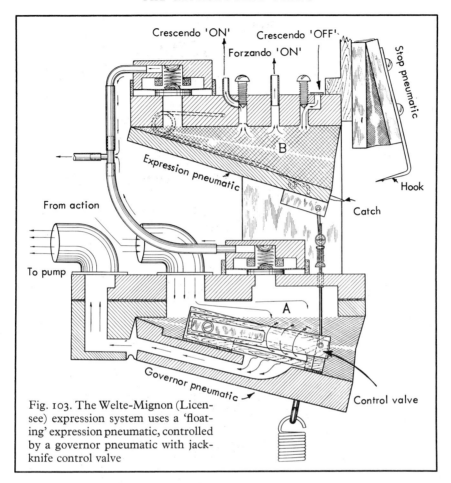

Fig. 103. The Welte-Mignon (Licensee) expression system uses a 'floating' expression pneumatic, controlled by a governor pneumatic with jack-knife control valve

When the Welte-Mignon (Licensee) action was re-engineered by the Auto Pneumatic Action Company in New York, the major visible alteration was the substitution of music-rolls made of ordinary paper and cut $11\frac{1}{4}$ inches wide. The unusual 3-pneumatic roll-drive motor, characteristic of all Welte instruments, appears in both variants. The divided pneumatic stack remains and this is controlled by a 'pressure regulator', which serves as the governor pneumatic in the Original action, an 'expression regulator' and a 'stop pneumatic'—all parts which, by comparing Fig. 100 with Fig. 103, show a strong similarity. The conical valve is replaced by a spring-balanced knife-valve, which is a far better method of regulating suction when you consider the analogy of endeavouring to close off the waste-pipe of a bath full of water by slowly lowering the bath plug—the closer it gets to the hole, the greater the pull until finally it goes home with a jerk.

Control of the *crescendo* expression system is fundamentally the same but the *fast crescendo* and *slow crescendo*, instead of relying purely on the tension spring to the valve, as directed by the expression pneumatic, this spring tension in the grand installation is continuously varied under the guidance of a 'modulator pneumatic'. The working pressure of the action is maintained at whatever level may be required by the 'governor pneumatic' and this is continuously

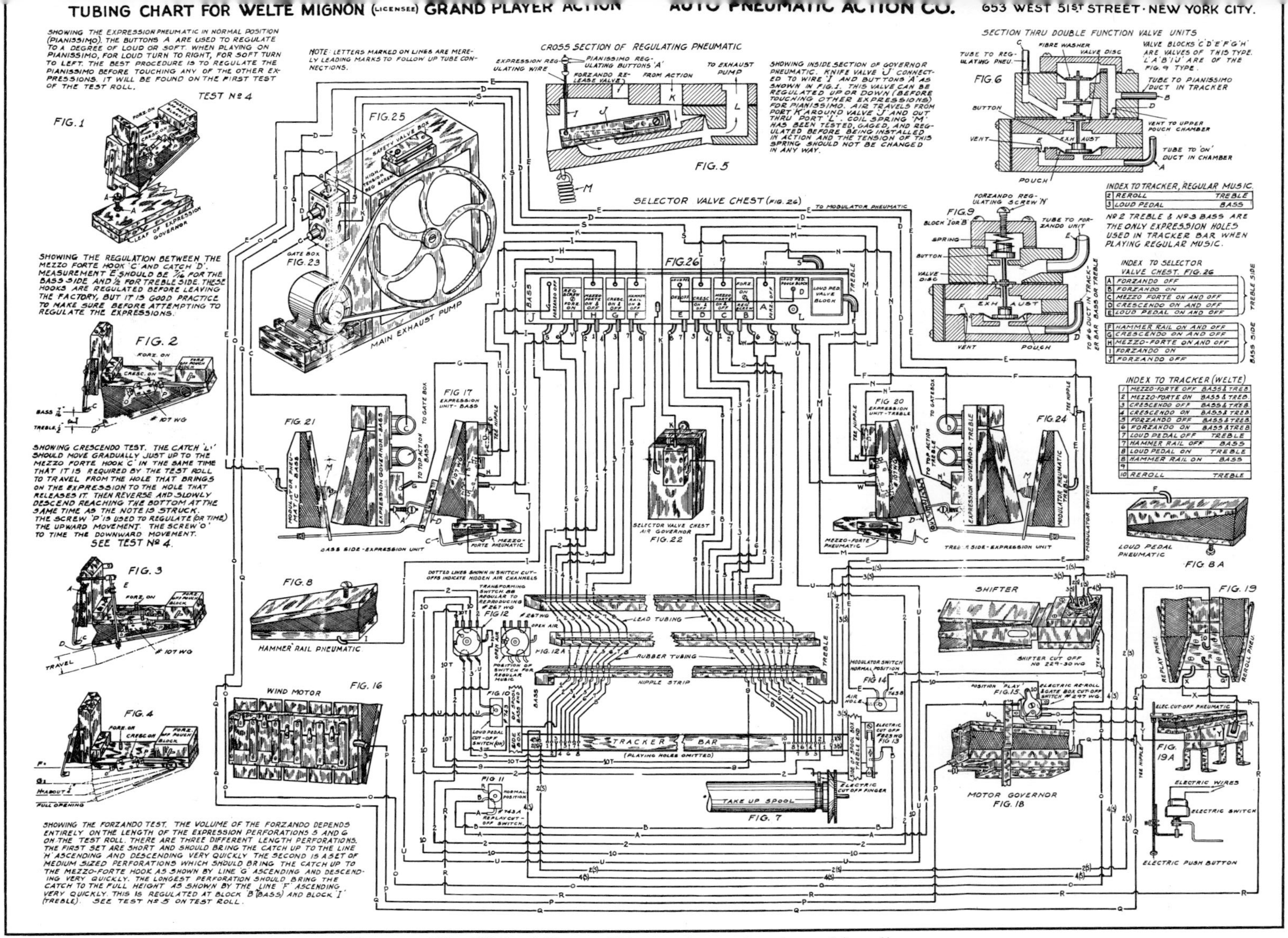

Fig. 104. The Welte-Mignon (Licensee) grand action tubing diagram

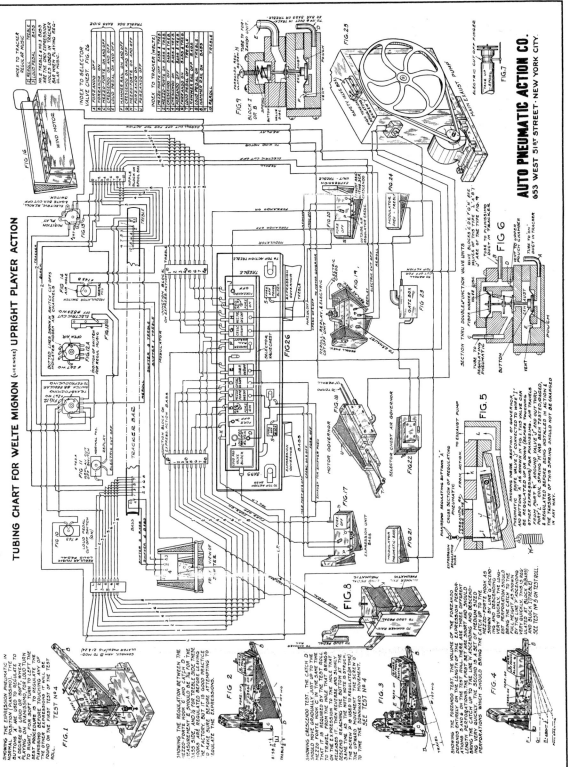

Fig. 105. The Welte-Mignon (Licensee) upright action tubing diagram

under the guidance of the 'expression pneumatic'. We will examine the functioning of this in detail.

The Welte-Mignon (Licensee) action makes use of two expression units, both being identical. One is used to control the bass, and the other the treble. The first may be considered as representing the left hand of the pianist and the second as the right hand.

Each expression unit comprises three units: the governor pneumatic (marked A in Fig. 103), the expression pneumatic (B), and the stop pneumatic (C). The governor pneumatic is connected directly to the suction by the tube marked D and to the pneumatic action through the tube E. The purpose of the governor is to maintain an even flow of air from the pneumatic action, so that the 'touch' is the same regardless of how many notes are being struck at any one time.

The even flow of air is maintained by the control valve, which covers the opening of the channel F leading to the suction, through the moving board of the pneumatic. This special knife-valve, when in normal position as shown in the illustration, allows the piano to play *pianissimo* and to produce the softest hammer blow at which the notes will repeat.

The expression pneumatic is the smaller motor placed directly above the governor. Its moving board, which is kept normally open by a spring (G), is connected with the control valve by the connecting rod (H). The expression pneumatic serves to control the flow of air from the top pneumatic action.

The differences between the expression system of the Original and (Licensee) actions are now fully apparent. The difficult control of the conical valve of the former is overcome by the smooth and easy operation of a jack-knife valve.

The governor, marked (A) in Fig. 103, maintains the flow of air at a given point. The expression pneumatic regulates or controls the flow of air to a desired point. The flow of air is, of course, adjusted by the opening or closing of the expression pneumatic and its incumbent knife-valve. Side perforations in the music-roll are employed to move the expression pneumatic in several ways, separately or in concert, to produce a wide range of expression. The pneumatic may be closed slowly by allowing suction through the small opening marked (I), which has the effect of causing the action gradually to play louder—the *crescendo* effect. Alternatively, the pneumatic may be closed very quickly by allowing suction through the large opening (J) which has the effect of causing the hammers to strike a quick, sharp blow. This is called *forzando*. A combination of the two may be employed so that, whilst the pneumatic is gradually closing under the suction of opening (I), a momentary opening of the suction (J) will produce a subtle fractional accent as in the original playing of the artist.

Control of *diminuendo*, achieved by the reverse procedure, can likewise be varied, all combining to enable the action to play the very lightest to the very heaviest blow almost instantaneously, or to build up to *crescendo* or decrease to *pianissimo* as slowly as may be required.

From this it can be seen that the level of the piano is infinitely variable and without fixed steps in graduation. Here we have basically the same characteristics as with the Original action, but both improved and simplified.

In the Original action, we had the so-called *mezzo-forte* pneumatic. The same feature applies with this action except that it is termed the 'stop pneumatic'. This motor, with its engaging hook, can be used to stop the opening or the closing of the expression pneumatic beyond a certain point, so limiting the maximum volume or minimum *pianissimo* if required.

The connections for the operation of the expression system are easily related by referring to the tracker-bar diagram for this action shown in Fig. 107.

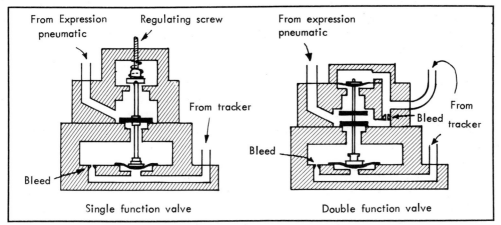

Fig. 106. The Welte-Mignon (Licensee) valve system

The *forzando* system comprises the *forzando* valve unit through which the expression pneumatic is emptied rapidly. This is illustrated in Fig. 106. The reverse of this operation is provided through a similar valve which is under the control of the *forzando off* duct in the tracker-bar. The *forzando* valves are single-function valves.

To enable the action to be controlled manually, when using ordinary rolls, a valve block is placed between tracker-bar and pneumatics into which connect pipes leading to the hand controls. Changeover from manual to automatic expression is achieved in the normal way by the use of a switch valve.

The tracker-bar has the same hole pattern as the Original and the expression valves are of two basic types—single function and double function (see Fig. 106), and they are arranged on the valve board as follows: L, A, B, C, D, E, F, G, H, I, and J. The single-function valves are A, B, I and J. C, D, E, F, and G are double-function valves and H, L and E together operate the sustaining-pedal pneumatic motor. This combination is necessary because the sustaining-pedal tracker hole is No. 3 in the bass end for Welte (Licensee) rolls, and No. 8 in the treble end for other rolls. Tracing the pipelines from the tracker-bar to the valves, we find the following:

On the bass side, tubes 1 and 2 lead to C; 3 and 4 lead to D; 5 leads to A; 6 leads to B and 7 and 8 lead to F. On the treble side, tubes 1 and 2 lead to H; 3 and 4 lead to G; 5 leads to J; 6 leads to I and 7 and 8 lead to E.

Having understood how the single and double function valves operate, the operation of the instrument should now be fairly obvious. To delve further would be to repeat much that has already been said.

What I have attempted to do here is to outline how these instruments work. With service manuals readily available through the enthusiastic endeavours of Mr H. Roehl, whose New York business—The Vestal Press—is entirely devoted to mechanical music and its literature, the owner of one of these instruments has the fullest available information to draw upon to aid his restoration.

In concluding this chapter, brief mention should be made of the best of the other reproducing actions.

The Solo Carola, produced by The Cable Company of Wabash, Chicago, in 1916, was a foot-treadled reproducing instrument, which made particular point of its ability to strike solo and accompaniment notes simultaneously or independently throughout the entire length of the keyboard and with any degree of power required.

Each opening in the tracker-bar was matched with a narrow slot coinciding exactly with it and just above the note holes (not to be confused with the Aeolian theme slots found on some instruments and placed over the central notes). These slots were connected to a small bellows which could independently select the position of each hammer relative to the strings, before the striking pneumatic was brought into operation. Unfortunately, the Solo Carola was not to catch on to any great extent, and specimens are very rare in America.

Wilcox & White, who produced the Angelus players and player-pianos as well as the Symphony player-organ, produced the Angelus Artrio reproducing piano. This was an interesting instrument inasmuch that almost the entire action was mounted in a drawer under the keyboard (it was mainly made for grand pianos). Unlike the Ampico, the drawer contained, in addition to the transmission music-roll box and controls, the complete pneumatic stack and expression system. The action depended on thirteen expression openings in the tracker-bar— five in the controlling governor, four in the treble governor and four in the bass governor. Melody and accompaniment playing-levels could be controlled by the main governor, or by either of the side governors.

The Angelus action was made by the Hallet & Davis Company, of New York, until the late 1920's. Even so, it is still rarely come across today.

The Artecho was produced by the Amphion Piano Player Company, a subsidiary of the American Piano Company. It used a divided chest and a system of intensity valves, lock and cancel valves and in some respects resembled the Ampico early action made by the parent company. The Artecho was also known as the Celco and the Apollo.

The Aria Divina was another unplaced runner in the race to win the largest chunk of the market for a reproducing instrument.

European contributions to the reproducing piano market consisted of the Hupfeld Duophonola and Triphonola actions, and the Carola action made by Blüthner in London. The latter was dropped as being too costly as compared with the competition, and the Hupfeld was certainly a success even if only on a limited scale in Europe.

My earlier words in this chapter may justly be rephrased here. The chances of finding an instrument of one of the lesser-known makes is now extremely slim—that is why I have concentrated on the 'big three'. However, acquisition of one need not present insuperable problems thanks to the endeavours of a few collectors both in England and in America, who have preserved rare literature on these pianos. The British Piano Museum is a first-class starting position for any enquiries.

TABLE OF TRACKER-BAR OPENINGS FOR REPRODUCING PIANOS

(Bass reads left to right: Treble reads right to left)

DUO-ART

TREBLE
1 = Soft pedal
2 = Motor switch-off
3 = Treble theme
4 = First accordion degree
5 = Second accordion degree
6 = Third accordion degree
7 = Fourth accordion degree

BASS
1 = Re-wind
2 = Sustaining pedal
3 = Bass theme
4 = First accordion degree
5 = Second accordion degree
6 = Third accordion degree
7 = Fourth accordion degree
Accordion pneumatics

AMPICO MODEL A

TREBLE
1 = Slow crescendo
2 = First intensity valve
3 = Soft pedal
4 = Second intensity valve
5 = Fast crescendo
6 = Third intensity valve
7 = Cancel valve
8 = Re-roll

BASS
1 = Slow crescendo
2 = First intensity valve
3 = Sustaining pedal
4 = Second intensity valve
5 = Fast crescendo
6 = Third intensity valve
7 = Cancel valve

AMPICO MODEL B

TREBLE
1 = Sub-intensity valve
2 = Slow crescendo
3 = First intensity valve
4 = Soft pedal.
5 = Second intensity valve
6 = Fast crescendo
7 = Third intensity valve
8 = Cancel valve
9 = Re-wind

BASS
1 = Amplifier trigger
2 = Not used
3 = First intensity valve
4 = Sustaining pedal
5 = Second intensity valve
6 = Switch-off after re-wind
7 = Third intensity valve
8 = Cancel
83 playing notes

WELTE-MIGNON ORIGINAL

TREBLE
1 = Mezzo-forte 'OFF'
2 = Mezzo-forte 'ON'
3 = Crescendo 'OFF'
4 = Crescendo 'ON'
5 = Forzando 'OFF'
6 = Forzando 'ON'
7 = Damper pedal 'OFF'
8 = Damper pedal 'ON'
9 = Not used
10 = Re-roll

BASS
1 = Mezzo-forte 'ON'
2 = Mezzo-forte 'OFF'
3 = Crescendo 'ON'
4 = Crescendo 'OFF'
5 = Forzando 'ON'
6 = Forzando 'OFF'
7 = Hammer rail 'ON'
8 = Hammer rail 'OFF'

(odd number openings cancel: even number openings set)

WELTE-MIGNON (LICENSEE)

TREBLE
1 = Mezzo-forte 'OFF'
2 = Mezzo-forte 'ON'
3 = Crescendo 'OFF'
4 = Crescendo 'ON'
5 = Forzando 'OFF'
6 = Forzando 'ON'
7 = Sustaining pedal 'OFF'
8 = Sustaining pedal 'ON'
9 = Electric cut-off
10 = Re-roll

80 playing notes

BASS
1 = Mezzo-forte 'OFF'
2 = Mezzo-forte 'ON'
3 = Crescendo 'OFF'
4 = Crescendo 'ON'
5 = Forzando 'OFF'
6 = Forzando 'ON'
7 = Hammer rail 'OFF'
8 = Hammer rail 'ON'

Relationship of tracker-bar openings to valve blocks:

BASS SIDE	TREBLE SIDE
1 & 2 with C	1 & 2 with H
3 & 4 with D	3 & 4 with G
5 with A	5 with J
6 with B	6 with I
7 & 8 with F	7 & 8 with E

Fig. 107. Table of tracker bar openings for reproducing pianos

CHAPTER 10

Player Organs and their Overhaul

THE reader may well query the justification for inserting a chapter on Player-Organs in a book on Player-Pianos. Such a query is warranted on the basis of general terms and terminology, but there are several very real reasons for this inclusion. First of all, both instruments are played pneumatically from a perforated paper roll. Secondly, you must accept the fact that people who love player-pianos also seem to love player-organs, in the same way that salt is quite different from pepper, yet they go together on the table.

Having excused myself, I feel bound to say that all I intend to do is outline briefly the operating principles, expecting my readers already to have digested the principles of player action pneumatics contained in the preceding chapters. I do not intend to delve deeply into the history and derivation of the various instruments, although some of their history has of necessity already been told as part of the story of the pneumatic piano. By the same premise, I shall not go to great lengths to tell you how to dismantle and resurrect a player-organ. This is to be a short chapter, giving pointers to overhaul.

Let us make a start by detailing these points of similarity between the player-piano and the player-organ. There is the obvious one, of course—both have keyboards and both can also be played manually as well as automatically. Both play music from rolls of perforated paper. Another similarity is that both rely on a difference between the air pressure inside the instrument and the pressure of the surrounding atmosphere. Both, therefore, have foot-operated treadles, or electric motors which provide the necessary pressure differential. Both instruments have a pneumatic system with a tracker-bar as a visible common feature. And both have the familiar spooling and rewind mechanisms. From the point of view of the collector, both are decidedly heavy to try to shift.

These instruments play on reeds and there are three basic makes of player-organ which the collector may come across. First there is the Aeolian Orchestrelle, made in at least sixteen different sizes and styles between 1900 and about 1920. Aeolians also made a Pipe Orchestrelle which was a true reproducing organ. Wilcox & White of Meriden, Connecticut, produced the Symphony which again came in several different sizes and styles. The date of this instrument is from about 1888 to 1900. The Maxfield organ, stemming from the basis of McTammany's patents and the Munroe Organ Reed Co., was a British contribution patented in 1896 and models cost up to £25. The Maxfield, invented by the man who gave us the Celestina organette, played rolls much narrower than the others—only 5½ inches—and was altogether a smaller instrument, having only 31 of its 61 manual notes automatically operated as compared with 58 notes on both the Orchestrelle and the Symphony.

There were a number of other makes but these are seldom to be found, particularly as they were of such a size that they were nearly always built in to a house to fit the available room, hence their being termed 'residence player organs'. These larger instruments, emanating largely from America, were indeed wonderful things and were classed not only as excellent mechanical organs, but also as first-rate finger organs. Larger examples were fully automatic (stop control and swell action operated from the roll perforations) and had two or sometimes three manuals. Manufacturers included Aeolians with their 65-tracker perforation Universal, 116-hole Double and 167-hole Duo-Art, Welte with their 150-hole model, Skinner with 120 and finally the leviathan Austin Quadruplex, which played rolls $21\frac{1}{4}$ inches wide and having no less than 240 apertures in the tracker-bar. It is interesting to record that the attendant problems of tracking with so wide a music-roll were solved by making the tracker-bar in five sections, each of 48 holes. The central section was fixed and the other sections could move laterally one way or the other to suit.

But to return to the more common types of player-organ, let us begin by taking a look at how these instruments function and why.

From the foregoing chapters on pneumatic actions, we have learned how air, either at a pressure greater than that of the atmosphere, or at a pressure reduced from that of the atmosphere, can be made to perform certain duties in order to operate the mechanical parts of a playing mechanism in a piano. In the player-organ there are two separate air systems—one to operate the necessary valves and pneumatics to instruct a certain note to speak, and another to provide that note with the ability to respond to the instruction. In the latter system, the air must be used to blow the reed. Both pneumatic systems rely on foot treadles to provide the differing air pressure.

A reed can be sounded only by allowing air to pass through it, but there are two distinct methods by which air can be caused to make a reed produce sound. One is by creating a suction on one side of the reed, so that, when a valve is opened, atmospheric air pressure rushes in, sounding the reed in passing. The other is to create a pressure on one side of the reed so that, when a valve is opened, the pressurized air rushes out to atmosphere, making the reed sound on the way.

This is the basic difference between the harmonium, which blows air through its reeds, and the so-called 'American Organ' which has a more strident or prompt tone because it sucks in air through its reeds. The term 'American Organ' can confuse, however, for both the Aeolian Co. and the Wilcox & White Co. made different models with blown reeds and sucked reeds.

The suction models of these reed organs are relatively simple devices, although it does not necessarily follow that they produce inferior sound. Indeed, my own suction Orchestrelle produces very pleasing music of excellent and varied tonality and is quite up to the standard of some of the pressure models.

In the suction model, air is exhausted constantly from the inside of the instrument by means of large exhausters similar to those used in the player-piano. Because, though, the volume of air at atmospheric pressure released into the inside during playing, particularly when sounding a heavy sustained chord on all stops (i.e. full organ), is quite large, the player-organ has exhausters and a suction reservoir or equalizer which is of considerably larger proportions than that which we are accustomed to finding in the piano.

There is another point to be remembered and that is that the pneumatic system, which forms part of the automatic playing of the instrument, is also a vital part of the organ for manual playing. One still has to treadle when playing by hand so that there is an air pressure differential inside the instrument, to allow the reeds to speak. From this we can readily see that there must be some form of shut-off or by-pass valve, which cuts out the keyboard for automatic playing, yet may readily bring it back into function whilst at the same time shutting off the mechanical part of the action—that is essentially the tracker-bar and roll-winding air motor.

This dual function is achieved very simply. When manually playing the Aeolian Orchestrelle, a leather-covered bar, normally stowed in the roll box, automatically slides out and covers the tracker-bar holes. As this comes out, under the control of a 'manual' stop knob, a set of small spring-loaded pallet valves is raised *en bloc* to touch the bottom of the keys in the keyboard. When a key is depressed, a corresponding pallet in the system is raised, opening a small piston and plunger in an airway. This allows air to enter a small windway and inflate a pouch on the pouch-board. For manual playing, this piston is controlled by the key as we have seen. When automatically played, the piston and its special pallet is swung away from the keys, the tracker-bar sealing strip moved, and the pouches in the pouch-board become under the control of the perforated music paper over the tracker-bar, as in a player-piano. On the Wilcox & White Symphony suction models, the tracker-bar sealing is effected manually by lifting up a leather-covered bar hinged to the tracker-bar.

The suction system is illustrated in Fig. 108.

Pressure models operate on a different principle. As mentioned earlier, here we have a positive pressure exerted inside the organ to play it. This means certain complications arise in the instrument. Whereas before, with the suction model, the foot treadles worked exhausters which drew air out of a reservoir, which was kept normally open by heavy springs, the bellows now compress air into a reservoir, which is held open against heavy springs by the pressure of air inside it. Added to this, the air motor for driving the roll mechanism is still of the suction type, and has to be driven from the suction side of the bellows. This means that, in order to cater for varying air pressures and to maintain an even motor speed, the motor must be driven through both a knife-valve and its own suction equalizer, controlling, in most cases, another knife-valve. This equalizer on the pressure Orchestrelle is a long, thin air-motor bellows normally held open by 'Y' springs and controlling a valve from an adjustable wire in its centre back-board.

A further problem with the pressure models is that there is no suction to operate the primary pneumatics. Since they cannot be operated by normal atmospheric pressure, the difficulty is overcome by operating the pouches which control the valves by air at pressure. This means that the tracker-bar and music-roll must be contained in an air-tight box, into which air is pumped from the pressure system. Access to the roll is thus achieved by a sliding glass door in this roll box and the instrument will not play with this door in the open position. This pressure supply to the roll box is also equipped with a cut-off valve, so that, for rewinding and for manual playing, a sliding valve can be made to seal the windway. Again, to prevent there being a 'buffer' of air in the tracker-bar and also because manual playing uses separate valves in the windway from tracker-bar to pouch, the tracker-bar is sealed by a leather-covered flap for manual operation as on the suction models.

Because, by now, I hope that I have dealt with the question of keyboard pneumatics and primary valve systems to the point where they can be taken for granted, I shall confine myself to describing the details which are placed above the pneumatic stack and which relate only to the player-organ.

Since the Aeolian Orchestrelle is the most common of the player-organs, and since the basic principles can be applied to the other styles and makes, we will have a general look at the two types of such an instrument—the suction and the pressure.

The suction model comprises a large vertical chest which is divided into narrow, vertical compartments, fifty-eight in number (one for each note of the keyboard), and running from front to back. Along the front of all these vertical compartments is arranged a number of rows of reeds, each reed mounted individually in a wooden cross member and each corresponding with one of the vertical passages. There may be four, six, seven or eight of these rows of reeds and each row comprises reeds of a slightly different form or shape, so as to produce a sound of different characteristic, and the chambers in the wooden cross-members, and in which the reeds are mounted, are arranged to be a different shape in each row, so as to impart different tonal characteristics to the reeds inside. In this way, subtle variations in tonality can be engineered so that one row of reeds sounds entirely different from another—i.e. French Horn, Oboe and Trumpet. Each row of reeds is provided with a hinged, tight-fitting flap which seals off all the reeds and which is connected to a stop knob on the keyboard fascia. When a certain bank of reeds is required to speak, the performer draws the respective stop which opens this hinged flap. Air can now be drawn in through the reeds, when a note is required to be sounded.

Reverting to our large vertical chest divided into fifty-eight compartments, the back of each compartment is sealed by a pallet. In fact, because the vertical passage is so long—about twelve inches from top to bottom—the pallet is made in two halves, put together so that both operate as one. The opening and closing of these pallets is controlled from small pneumatic motors or bellows provided, as in the piano, on a windway controlled by pouches and valves. The difference is that these pouches and motors can be controlled both by the holes in the tracker-bar and also by the keyboard. Between the pallets and the motors run wire pull-downs or, sometimes, cranked rods. All the pallets and, in fact, the entire back of the vertical chest is enclosed in an air-tight casing and the operating rods or pull-downs pass out of this through felt seals on their way to the pneumatic stack. Air is continually exhausted from this enclosed chest. When a note is required to sound and the respective motor collapses, it opens one of the pallets, via the pull-down, inside the chest, which contains air at a reduced pressure to that of the atmosphere. If one of the reed-carrying members on the front of the chest now has its hinged flap opened (by drawing the stop on the keyboard fascia), then air will immediately be sucked into the vertical compartment through the reed. If more than one row of reeds is opened, then air will rush in through several reeds, producing the same note from several reeds of different tonalities.

This chest is supported by, and fixed to, a horizontal platform which is built just below the keyboard level of the organ. Consider, if you like, that this is a table. Beneath the table are fitted the treadle-operated air exhausters and the exhaust reservoir. Above the table is mounted the chest. The airway into the exhaust reservoir is matched by a slot in the table which also matches a slot in the chest, so that the air pressure differential in one is directly united with the other. Part of the air inlet system comprises the air motor, which provides rotary motion to the mechanism for transporting the music-roll, and this is controlled and governed in exactly the same way as in the player-piano.

We will now turn our attention to the pressure-operated instruments, and perhaps the best start is to forget all that we have learned about suction systems and exhausters, for here we are dealing with air at pressure. The action of treadling operates feeders instead of exhausters—feeders which are continually pumping air into a reservoir, which supplies a large quantity of

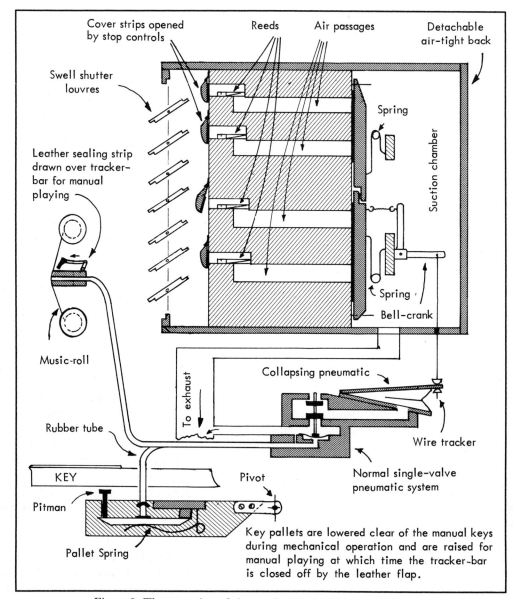

Fig. 108. The operation of the suction model 'Orchestrelle' player
organ showing the action for one keyboard note, one rank of reeds
open to speak

wind to circulate inside the chambers of the instrument, and by means of which the many
reeds can be blown adequately.

The pressure Orchestrelle comprises a table upon which the mechanics of the organ may be
located, such as wind motor to drive the music-roll, stop linkages, pneumatic valves and so on.
This table also contains the windways for the keyboard operation of the instrument and thus
ends with a double, staggered row of pouches along the back edge. Beneath the table is the

242

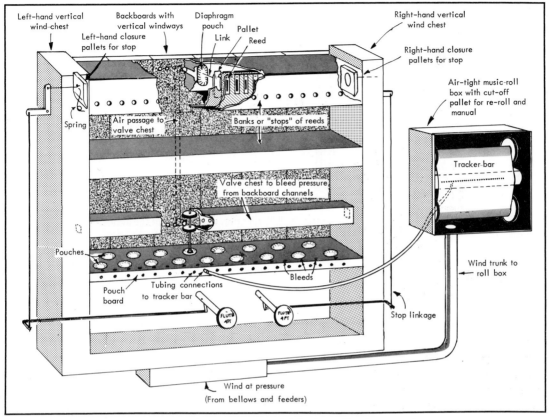

Fig. 109. Diagram of pressure model Orchestrelle player reed organ
(only one stop indicated for clarity)

centreboard, having upon one side the wind reservoir and on the other the two treadle-operated feeders. Wind from the reservoir is taken to two vertical trunkings of wood, which run from each end of the table to the top of the instrument. The inside faces of these trunkings have certain openings, between which fit first of all the pneumatic valve stack above the pouch board, and then successive narrow boxes, one on top of the other, each containing one rank or 'stop' of reeds. From this you will appreciate that air is admitted from both of the trunkings to the reed boxes at the same time. Similarly, air is admitted to the pneumatic valve stack from both sides.

The passage of air from the vertical trunking into a reed box is controlled by a large pallet valve which in turn is controlled by a linkage to the stop-knob on the keyboard fascia. As a precaution against excess air pressure in a reed box causing the momentary sounding of a reed in that box, after the stop has been shut off, the stop linkage is also connected to a felted hinged flap, rather like that which we have already seen on the suction models, to cover the air exit from the reeds.

Thus we can summarize the actual speaking part of the organ as comprising two vertical wind-chests, between which are fixed banks of reeds, each bank voiced in a different way. Air is passed into the reed boxes from both ends, and may be shut off by master pallets which close

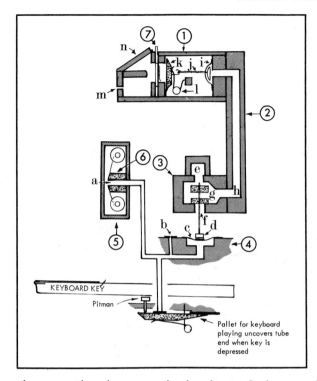

Fig. 110. Detail of the action of the pressure model Orchestrelle.

Key: 1. one typical reed box
2. back board with individual air-ways
3. valve chest
4. pouch board
5. music-roll box (with air-tight sliding front)
6. tracker-bar
7. reed

the respective air passage in the chests. So long as the feeders are being treadled, air pressure exists in these two vertical chests.

The speaking part of the organ—the method in which a note is made to sound, is rather more complex. Each bank of reeds, as well as being fixed to the side chests, is fitted to the back of the organ and this back is made up of panels of timber containing vertical passages. Each reed in each bank is matched by an opening in the back of the reed box which matches an opening in the backboard of the organ. At the bottom of the backboard the vertical passages end with another opening, which lines up with openings in the pneumatic valve stack. The purpose of this is that air will be under pressure in the passages in the backboard, at all times whilst the instrument is being operated. When a note is to be played, a valve in the pneumatic stack is pushed up by the pouch in the pouch-board, so closing off the air-pressure inlet to that valve, and opening the backboard passage to atmosphere, so bleeding out its air pressure.

We now have two functions explained—air pressure in the reed box and the exhausting of a column of air relative to every reed, in all the banks of reeds, which represents one predetermined note.

Inside the reed box there are two sections. The first is a section common to all the reeds (this actually is not entirely true as we shall explain further on, but it will suffice to accept this for now) and the other is made up of small compartments, one for each reed, along the back of the box. It is these compartments which are in communication with the windways in the backboard. The compartments are separated from the main portion of the chest by a soft leather diaphragm, into which is cemented a small bearing block carrying a wire hook. Each reed, fixed into the front edge (the common passage) of the reed box, is covered by an inwards-opening pallet and the wire hook is connected to the pallet by a piece of linen thread. Move-

244

ment of the leather diaphragm therefore causes the reed pallet to open and shut.

Now we can see how the system works. So long as air exists at an equal pressure inside the reed box and also inside the backboard windways, the reed pallets are kept closed by a light spring. The moment the pressure is exhausted from one backboard windway, all the diaphragms connected to that windway will collapse under the pressure of the air in the reed box, so opening the respective pallet in each reed box corresponding to the note to be sounded. The air pressure can now escape through the reed, making it speak.

The apparent complexities of this system are best explained by illustration Fig. 110. For clarity, this functional drawing shows one particular note (one hole in the tracker-bar) and only one box of reeds. In practice, a number of reed boxes are connected to the backboard airways.

Referring now to the drawing, air chambers (5) and (3) are subjected to air pressure at all times whilst the machine is being operated, i.e. the feeders being treadled or the electric blower in operation. When a stop is drawn, the respective reed box (1) is also subjected to pressure. Chambers (5), (3) and (1) are common to the whole keyboard compass. Airways (a) and (h) are relative only to one keyboard key or one note in the keyboard scale, and each hole in the tracker-bar is connected, via its own airway (a), to its own pouch (c), thereby controlling its own valve assembly (g). This in turn regulates air to an individual passage (h) and operates separate diaphragms (i) and pallets (k).

When the instrument is at rest, meaning when it is not making any sound, the roll box (6), the valve chest (3), the backboard (2) and the reed box (1) contain air at pressure from the bellows. In this state, the lower of the two valves (g) seals the vent (f) to atmosphere, and at the same time pallet spring (l) seals pallet (k) from the reed.

When air is admitted to a pouch (c) through the tracker-bar (a), the pitman (d) is raised, the upper of the two valves (g) closes off pressure airway (e) and exhausts air from the airway (h) through the vent (f). This causes the pouch (i) to contract, thereby drawing open the pallet (k) against the spring (l) via the link (j). In this condition the reed (7) will speak.

To ensure prompt return of the action to silent condition the moment the tracker-bar airway (a) is once more closed, air in the tracker-bar passage is allowed to escape quickly via the bleed hole (b), thereby allowing the pouch (c) to contract under pressure of air from airway (e) on to the upper of the two valves (g). The moment the exhaust vent (f) is once more closed, air is immediately admitted into airway (h), pouch (i) is extended, and pallet (k) closes. Because the pressure in the reed-box is equal to the pressure in the backboard, pouch (i) is free to take up a position on its own, equal to the closed position of pallet (k).

If the action becomes sluggish and cannot produce a rapid staccato, the travel of the valve assembly (g) may be too great, the clearance between (d) and (c) too small, or the bleed hole (b) too small. Because air is admitted at constant pressure through (a) when a note is speaking, bleed hole (b) can be slightly larger than optimum, but, of course, this again may delay speech by making the operation of the valve assembly (g) too slow.

Variation of tonal colour is achieved by the various ingenious methods of mounting the reed (7) in its box (1). A typical installation is shown in the illustration. In this a hinged flap (n) covers the major sound passage. When the reed speaks normally, the sound is allowed to pass into a comparatively large chamber, the only exit from which is a small hole (m). The shape and size of the chamber, the size and positioning of the hole (m) and the relative position of the reed (7) assist materially in providing tonal variation. If the hinged panel (n) is opened, the reed speaks more or less freely to atmosphere through a large chamber, thereby producing a completely different tone.

It will be seen that, regardless of which stops are drawn, the operation of the pouch (i) via the airway (h) continues all the time the instrument is being played. Only when air is admitted into the reed-box (l) will the system speak. The main entry into the reed-box (l) is via a hinged pallet at the sides of the vertical wind-chests. It is these pallets which are controlled directly by the stops.

In dismantling the pressure Orchestrelle, the first point, having removed the upper half of the case, is to take off the back-board. This is actually comprised of a number of sections which fit next to each other. Each section is dowelled with small wooden pegs to the table and is then screwed with a large number of wood screws to each reed box. When removing and replacing these sections, they are a tight fit and you should try not to break the locating dowels, although it is not too important if a few do snap off. Take off the end boards first as these can be reached from the front of the organ with a length of 1 inch square wood. The boards can be tapped free of their dowels, using a mallet on the piece of wood. Remember that these boards are laminated into windways and are thus not as robust as they appear, so do not use excessive force in tapping them free. The boards are all numbered, but it is as well to make your own mark to ensure that they go back in the same position. Each of the screws has a washer under its head and all these screws and washers should be kept separate from other screws.

With all the back-board sections off, unscrew the side panels from the vertical side chests. This allows access to the screws which secure each end of each reed box to the chests. Some of these reed boxes are very heavy—you will see that they are asymmetric in shape and each one differs in shape and proportions. Have someone support the weight of the boxes one at a time, starting from the top, as you unscrew and remove each of them. Note that there is a soft leather seal between the ends of the boxes and the mating portion of each chest. If this sealing gasket is broken, then it must be replaced, using soft white skin available from an organ-builder. So long as the gasket is not too hard, you can reconstitute it by brushing with a stiff wire brush, to restore the knap to the leather. The same treatment should be applied to all pallets which are disturbed or which look as if they are not able to seal properly. The ideal is to replace all leather pallet faces but this is not always essential. Having removed all the reed boxes, the last item to be removed is the pneumatic valve stack and this needs to be handled carefully, as otherwise it may puncture the pouches or bend the valve stems, unless lifted straight out once the screws have been removed.

The sequence of reassembly is the reverse of dismantling and the first item to be replaced is the pneumatic valve stack.

The adjustment of the primary valves tends to be critical. Assuming that the leather of the pouches is in good condition and supple enough, and also that the small, circular pressure pad, cemented into the centre of each pouch, is present, the clearance between the bottom of the valve stem and the top of the pad must be about $\frac{1}{32}$ inch and certainly no more than about $\frac{3}{64}$ inch. Since the valve stems are threaded in the actual valves, it is possible to screw the valves down to this clearance, extremely precise though it may sound. In this position of rest, the bottom of the two valves on the stem must seat evenly on the vent hole of the valve chest. The top valve must be open between $\frac{1}{16}$ inch and $\frac{3}{32}$ inch, for proper operation. These valve adjustments must be made with the pneumatic stack properly fixed in its final position, between the vertical side chests. Since there are two distinct pneumatic systems in the organ—the keyboard and the mechanical—the operation of these valves can be checked before the back-board is replaced and, if the organ has been fully dismantled, before the reed boxes are fitted. All you must do is make sure all the other air vents in the vertical chests are closed and then have someone select 'manual' on the stops and depress each note on the keyboard by hand, whilst pumping the feeders. You can now watch the functioning of the pouches and valves from the back, making any necessary adjustments as you go. Ensure also that all the bleed holes are clear of dirt or other obstruction, and see that the valves move freely in their guide rails.

Having completed the adjustment of the valves, proceed with replacing the reed boxes from the bottom upwards, again having somebody take their weight until the side screws are in place. Once all the boxes are refitted, you can turn your attention to the pieces which form the backboard. See that all the circular leather or fibre washers, which are placed around each opening, are present and in good order. Tease up their surfaces with the wire brush. If one is missing, before replacing it, make sure that it has not stuck to the matching hole in the reed box.

Position the centre section of the backboard first and replace all the wood screws loosely. Now position both the end sections and again put back the screws finger-tight. The remaining boards are next put back, if necessary carefully springing them into place. Only when all the screws are already in position loosely, should you start to tighten them up. You will find that each reed box has two rows of screws, one along the top of the back edge and one along the bottom of the back edge. Tighten the screws for each box alternately, one top, one bottom, one top, and so on all the way along in a zig-zag fashion. When all the boxes are secured in this manner, tighten the intermediate screws. Make sure all are firmly home. The remainder of stripping, servicing and reassembly is straightforward.

Earlier, mention was made of the fact that the reed boxes receive air from both ends of the vertical wind-chests. This is correct but the reed boxes are, in fact, divided into two unequal portions by a thin plate of steel, which is placed between the twenty-first and the twenty-second note up from the bass end of the keyboard—the A below middle C being the first of the upper division and the immediately preceding G being the last of the lower division. This break in each rank of reeds enables the performer to make subtle use of his controls to play music with a 'heavy' bass accompaniment on several stops, whilst at the same time playing the melodic tenor and treble theme on a 'solo' stop. The converse of the technique is also possible, bringing out the melody on several stops whilst sketching in a soft bass on different stops.

The break in each bank of reeds is therefore used to achieve two stops from each bank. To explain this, one rank may be divided so that the upper portion is controlled by a stop marked 'Oboe', whilst the lower is controlled by a stop marked 'Bassoon'. This represents a fairly logical tonality between these two instruments of the orchestra. Another rank will be divided into 'French Horn' at the upper part and 'Gemshorn' at the bass, whilst another may be 'Cremona' and 'Melodian'. The performer may choose to have all three upper parts of the reed boxes playing, whilst he may select only 'Gemshorn' out of the bass portions to bring in a bass which may not drown the music. This characteristic, of breaking the rank of reeds into two separate stop controls, is also found on the suction models but, of course, there, the reeds are all mounted together into the vertical common chest and only the cover strips need to be divided.

The player-organ has several other features such as a 'Vox Humana' stop, which controls a small air turbine which can be set to revolve in the upper portion of the reed boxes adjacent to the reed openings of one rank of pipes. This turbine turns a paddle which breaks up the sound and produces a wavering effect on each note. Another feature is the 'Swell', which consists of a number of closely-spaced louvres or venetian blind shutters which close off the entire front of the organ inside the case. When these shutters are closed, the organ speaks quietly or muffled. By opening the shutters, the volume of sound can be made to increase. The swell is controlled by a knee-board worked by the right knee of the performer. A further feature is the 'Full Organ' or 'Great Organ'. This is worked by a knee-board for the left knee and as it is moved, it takes control of all the stop linkages and gradually opens up each stop. So long as this board is held over by the knee whilst treadling, all the stops are open and free to speak, regardless of the stop knobs which are drawn. As the board is released, so the stops close, leaving once more only those for which the knobs are drawn.

Armed with this explanation of the operation of the player-organ mechanism, the repairer should have a fair idea as to how he should set about repair and restoration. As a guide, here are the principle snags which you are most likely to find, together with the correct action to take:

When played manually, one or more notes sound continuously. This can be due to one of three things: (a) the key sticking in the down position, (b) the pallet beneath the keyboard, which operates for manual use, has a loose or broken spring, (c) there is a hole in the leather sealing strip over the tracker-bar or it is just not seating properly. It can also be due to a perforated rubber tube or a missing tube.

When played from the roll, one or more notes do not speak at all, even when sustained. This means that either there is a broken tube connection, the tracker hole is blocked (it should be sucked out with a pump), or the valve clearance is incorrect. It could also be due to a perforated pouch.

When played from the roll, one or more notes are slow to speak. This means that the bleed holes are too large or the valve clearance is too great.

When played from the roll, one or more notes are prompt in speech but will not repeat staccato, producing one long note instead or a number of short notes. This means that the valve clearance is too little or the bleed holes too small.

When one note speaks, an adjacent one 'whimpers'. This means that air from one windway in the backboard is getting through to another windway, and can be due to the board not being tightly screwed to the reed boxes, dirt trapped between backboard and reed box so preventing it from being tightened properly, or the small leather washer between reed box hole and backboard hole being torn or missing.

Organ will not play at all mechanically. This means that the keyboard manual-playing stop-knob is disconnected from the keyboard manual-pallet rail underneath, so leaving open both the mechanical airways in the tracker-bar and the key pallets.

When played manually, certain notes suddenly begin to screech. This means that a pallet is not closing in a stop. A common feature amongst suction organs, this can be rectified by locating the reed, and then removing the controlling pallet at the back of the vertical chest and either re-leathering the sealing face, or teasing it up with a fine wire-brush.

Air motor to drive music-roll is sluggish, erratic or inoperative. This can be due to damp affecting the sliding seals, a disconnected airway, or the control valve being disconnected.

On pressure models, the rewind for the roll is very slow and requires heavy treadling. This is due to the shut-off valve, which cuts air pressure from the roll box, not closing properly. With the roll box open, the rewind will speed up, but air is still being wasted. If you can hear and feel air at pressure coming from the windway into the roll box during rewind, remove the cover of the box (it is attached with simple hooks along all sides) and check the operation of the valve when the 'rewind' stop-knob is drawn. If it does not fully close, then adjust the linkage until it closes properly.

If the organ plays on rewind. This is exactly the same as on the player-piano and the same valve selector adjustment should be carried out.

If a reed suddenly produces a muffled, flat tone. This indicates either that a piece of dirt has got on to the reed, or that it has fractured through age. Draw out the reed with a reed hook (use this tool carefully and engage it only in the recess provided, otherwise the reed tongue will be damaged) and examine it. Holding the reed up to the light, you should be able to see an equal amount of light between the tongue and the plate all the way round. Use a soft brush to clean away any dust and dirt. If the reed still sounds flat, then it is probably cracked. Some cracks are almost impossible to see, even with a magnifying glass. A cracked reed must be replaced. Most large piano-sundries houses also carry reeds and, if they cannot match it with an entirely new reed, they can fit a new tongue and re-voice the old one for you, if you send them also the reed an octave above and an octave below the damaged one.

It goes without saying that loose, cracked or otherwise damaged rubber tubing will have a serious effect on the performance of the instrument. Similarly, the feeders, equalizers and exhausters and pressure reservoirs must be in good order and free from cracks and leaks. The main reservoir is covered with a rubberized cloth, considerably thicker than that used in the player-piano, and if you have to re-cover, use material of the same thickness and quality, matched from the piano-sundries house. NEVER USE THINNER MATERIAL—it just will not last.

With this résumé of the works of the player-organ, the amateur should be able to solve his overhaul problems, once he understands the principles of the pneumatic player action common to both piano and organ.

A final word on a subject which, I know, causes much confusion, misunderstanding and speculation. The novice to the organ may be perplexed by some of the terminology used to describe the organ stops as written on the stop-knob faces. He will probably see 'Bourdon 16 ft.', 'Trumpet 8 ft.', 'Flute 4 ft.' and, on some of the larger instruments, 'Piccolo 2 ft.'. He may deduce these dimensions to refer in some way to the reeds or to the reed boxes. In truth, he has no need to concern himself with this part at all. What significance the dimensions have, will become apparent when he begins to play his newly-restored instrument. Suppose you start by drawing 'French Horn 8 ft.', in the upper part of the organ, and matching it with 'Gemshorn 8 ft.', in the lower. If you now play manually, you will find you have a complete scale. You can now select two more stops, again marked '8 ft.', and you will find that this second rank of reeds produces a unison sound—in other words, sound at the same pitch although of a different character. Now pull one of the bass stops marked '16 ft.' and you will find that the bass notes are suddenly reinforced with notes sounding an octave below the others, in other words you are playing two notes, an octave apart, from one key.

On the treble register, you draw a stop marked '4 ft.' and find that you are now playing two notes from one key; this time the '4 ft.' stop is producing a note an octave above the normal. If you draw a '2 ft.' stop, you are an octave above that again, or two octaves above the first note you played with that same one key.

Thus the dimension is related to the pitch of the note. The larger number of stops are marked '8 ft.', so the organ is said to have 'a basis of eight foot pitch'. If you double the number, i.e. 8 to 16, then you decrease an octave from the normal. By halving again, from 4 to 2, you have progressed two octaves from the normal, which is 8.

This characteristic, based on the physical dimensions of a proper organ pipe, and the terminology of a real pipe organ, allows subtle tones in the performance of a music-roll. You can, for example, accentuate the melodic line of a tune by playing it in 'octave unison' in this manner. Likewise, you can accentuate the bass by bolstering up a nominal 8 ft. with a 16 ft. stop.

The middle C on an 8 ft. organ stop is equal to the middle C of the piano, and for this reason a piano is said to be of 8 ft. pitch.

The art of playing the player-organ is perhaps more aesthetically satisfying than that of the player-piano. The skills needed are just as involved if you are to produce a perfect performance. The novice may scoff at the thought that there can be any skill needed to get an interpretation from a roll of music on such an instrument. Give him ten minutes with one though, and he will be a wiser man, if no more technically competent. But the art, for art there is in playing both piano and organ from roll music, is a true art with its own fair share of fundamentals, mechanicals, abstracts and sympathies, and to attempt to do justice to it would require an altogether separate, lengthy work. To some, I am certain, the art will need no interpretation, for the mere possession and fulfilment of such an instrument will cultivate an understanding tantamount to the art spontaneously. To others, it may forever remain a murky mystery.

CHAPTER 11

List of Principal Makers & Patentees

Aɴʏ attempt to list makers of mechanical pianos must of necessity be arbitrary, since there were so very many makers in all parts of the world. The earliest we can trace is the work of Bidermann in the sixteenth and seventeenth centuries, whilst the eighteenth century reveals little if anything in the way of definitely identified makers.

Street pianos or barrel pianos heralded from distant centres such as Bristol and London, and the wandering Italians, who made them, settled in Barcelona, Nice, Paris, London and New York. These barrel-piano makers I have listed as fully as possible.

Perforated music, both in the form of cardboard and paper, played so valuable a part in the development of the mechanical piano that I have listed those who played an important part in its 'invention' and application.

Pneumatic-action pianos emanated from France, Germany and America, by far the greatest advances and the largest volume of products heralding from the last-mentioned. A number of later British piano-manufacturers fitted imported American player actions, particularly that produced by the Standard Player Action Co.

It is thus not only pointless but also impossible to list every maker of these later instruments, or to describe every particular modification employed by various builders. I have therefore chosen to deal only with the makers of player and reproducing pianos who contributed something of importance to history, and have also listed most of the makers of piano-players, since these were part of the formative period of the vast industry which was to follow.

Music-rolls were produced by countless manufacturers and here any attempt at listing in entirety would be impossible. Again, America produced the greatest number of makers—over fifty companies were engaged in the lucrative business of manufacturing rolls in the States— and there were many in England, including subsidiaries of both American and Continental makers. What I have attempted here is to list the more popular types of roll which the British collector will probably come across. To this end, I list the trade name (which will usually be the largest name on the box!) and key this to the name of the maker. The enquiring reader may wonder at first why, in view of the aforementioned problems, I should bother to list any makers of rolls at all. The answer is that, once in a while, the make of roll may be mistaken for the make of piano or, even worse, considered in themselves to be of great value. The only rolls, which are today worth more than a few shillings each on the market, are those made for reproducing pianos such as the Duo-Art and Ampico. Another important point is to be able to differentiate between the 65-note and the full-scale 88-note rolls. Yet again, player-organ rolls, such as Symphony and Orchestrelle, are often taken for piano rolls and vice versa, particularly the Aeolian rolls, for they made both piano and organ rolls.

In conclusion, a listing of makers tends, on the face of it, to be about as entertaining and instructional as an evening spent reading the telephone directory. I have, I hope, overcome this problem by providing a brief synopsis of the activities associated with the various firms, where applicable, usually offering additional data to those given in the preceding chapters. The enthusiast is therefore recommended to include this present chapter in his reading, rather than to bypass it as an occasional reference section.

ADAMS, GEORGE. Published in 1747 his *Adams' Micrographia Illustrated* in which is described, in a catalogue, '. . . a particularly new and curious Machine, containing a Movement which plays either an organ or Harpsichord (or both if desired) in a masterly manner'. The precise details of his device are today unknown.

AEOLIAN COMPANY, THE, Aeolian Hall, Fifth Avenue and 34th Street, New York, U.S.A., and, later, Aeolian Hall, 29 West 42nd Street, New York. The empire formed by W. B. Tremaine from the original Mechanical Orguinette Company, to manufacture the Pianola, originally a 65-note cabinet-style piano-player, which sold for $250. The Company had associates all over the world and the London one was the Orchestrelle Company (also known as the Aeolian Co. Ltd) of Aeolian Hall, New Bond Street. The company produced music-rolls under the registered names Metrostyle (65-note) and Themodist (full-scale 88-note rolls which had automatic pedalling control from extra marginal perforations in the roll). They also made the Orchestrelle player reed organ and later the Aeolian Reproducing Pipe Organ. Manufacturers of the Duo-Art reproducing piano. Still extant in Bronx, New York.

ALBAREDA, PABLO, 36 S. Pedro, Villafranca del Panadés, Spain. Agent and hirer for street pianos, fl. 1903.

ALLERI, FRANCESCO, Corso Carlo Alberto, Porta Milano, Vercelli, Italy. A maker of street pianos who flourished in the early part of this century.

ALVAREZ, JOSÉ, Belmez, Córdoba, Spain. Maker of street pianos, fl. 1903.

AMELOTTI, VVE. Nice, France. An Italian by birth, Amelotti made coin-freed cafe pianos and large barrel-playing mechanical jazz bands. A specimen of the latter by this early 20th century maker has a 39-note wooden-framed, overstrung piano, side drum with four sticks, bass drum coupled with cymbal (one stick), eight tubular metal bells, two temple blocks. The distributor for Northern France was S. Rolleau of Nantes whose name sometimes appears as well as that of Amelotti.

AMERICAN PIANO CO., Knabe Building, 437 Fifth Avenue, Corner 39th Street, New York, U.S.A. Makers of player-pianos who, in 1914, produced an electric player-piano called the Electrelle, which they claimed to have cost half a million dollars to perfect. By 1915 they produced the Flexotone-Electrelle which was a combination pneumatic/electric piano-player. The paper music-roll controlled an air passage which forced silver finger contacts against silver-tipped contact screws. Two or more pianos could be controlled in unison from one instrument. They then introduced the Ampico reproducing piano action, re-forming into the Ampico Corporation (q.v.).

AMERICAN PLAYER PIANO CO., 15–17–19 Canal Place, New York. A large manufacturer of player-pianos.

AMPICO CORPORATION, THE, 27 West 57th Street, New York, U.S.A. Formed in 1915 to produce and market the Ampico reproducing piano action believed by many to be the best action of this type ever made. They formed a London company called Ampico Limited with premises at Regent House, 233 Regent Street, London, W.1.

ANIMATIC. Name given to music-rolls produced by Ludwig Hupfeld (q.v.).

ANTONELLI, DOMENICO, 59 Great Ancoats Street and 2/4 Blossom Street, Manchester. Described as 'Manufacturer of Piano-Organs', Antonelli produced clockwork barrel-pianos and, in November 1901 was granted a British patent for a coin-feed, clockwork barrel-piano, incorporating a method of removing the barrel for changing without disturbing the rest of the mechanism.

ANTONIAZZI, ANDREW. An Italian who established the B.A.B. Organ Co. in Manhattan (q.v.), having spent six years with Maserati (q.v.). He made street barrel pianos.

APOLLO MUSIKWERKE MAX ESPENHAIN & CO., Dorotheenstrasse 27, Leipzig-Gohlis. Makers of pneumatic-action orchestrions and orchestrion pianos, fl. 1903.

APRUZZESE, ANTONIO, Carrera de S. Francisco (El Crande), 7, Madrid 5, Spain. An Italian who came to Spain in 1883, Apruzzese settled in Salamanca where he made street barrel-pianos or 'organillos', as they are known in Spain. In 1906 the firm bearing his name moved to Madrid where it still exists today under Mr Antonio Apruzzese, who was born in 1906 and is the last surviving member of the family, and is the only barrel-piano restorer left in Madrid.

AROSIO, EMILIO, Corso Roma 39, Lodi, Italy. A maker of barrel pianos, fl. 1903.

ARRIGONI & CO., JOHN, 158 Great College Street, London N.W. 'Also at Baden Baden, Steam Works, Bruder & Sons, Waldkirch'. Advertised in 1892 as barrel piano and street organ maker. His association with Bruder, a maker of street pipe organs, suggests that he was an agent and probably not a manufacturer of these. By 1896, he had been absorbed by Cocchi, Bacigalupo & Graffigna at the same address and his position with the firm was that of manager. However, two years later, the firm reverted to J. N. Arrigoni & Co. at the same address. By 1912 Arrigoni was at 62 Halliford Street, Islington, advertising as a mechanical-piano maker. A cabinet-maker by trade, he had come from Italy and begun by doing street organ and piano repairs. He was still in business in 1922, as witnessed by his signature inside a street organ with that date.

ARTISTYLE. Music rolls—see under MARSHALL & SONS, HERBERT.

ARTONA MUSIC ROLLS LTD, 22/24 Westcliff Road, Ramsgate, Kent. This company was founded by Mr Gordon Iles, who at one time worked for the Aeolian Company at Hayes, Middlesex. Strictly a one-man business, Mr Iles produces player-piano rolls, both newly-recorded ones made by himself and copies of existing rolls, under the trade name 'Artona'. His roll-punching machinery was acquired when the old Aeolian Co. went into liquidation. He also makes copies of Duo-Art music-rolls.

AUBRY, EMILE, 200 rue Lafayette, Paris, France. An engineer who, with Gabriel Boreau, invented the Violiniste pneumatic violin-player combined with a piano in 1926.

AUTO PNEUMATIC ACTION CO., THE, 653 West 51st Street, New York, U.S.A. Manufacturers of the Welte-Mignon (Licensee) reproducing player-piano action, which played standard-width white paper rolls, as distinct from the original or 'red Welte' which was made in Germany and played $13\frac{1}{2}$ inch wide music-rolls of red paper. The parent company was Kohler Industries (q.v.) and the original Welte-Mignon (Licensee) patents were in their name.

AUTONA CO., 23 Court Street, Boston, Massachusetts, U.S.A. Patented an 'inner player' player-piano in June 1899, which featured the music-roll attached to a hinged spools frame under the keyboard. It is not known if this was ever built or produced, but it certainly was several years ahead of the successful inner player actions.

AUTOPIANO COMPANY, THE. Established in 1903 by R. W. Lawrence, they made only player-pianos, making one of the first 'inner players' as they were then called in 1904. Their six-storey factory on the banks of the Hudson River was, in 1920, the largest in the world devoted to player-piano production. In 1915, they made one of the earliest electrically-pumped player-pianos.

AUTOPLAYER CO. LTD, THE BRITISH, 126 New Bond Street, London W.1. Produced 65-note music-rolls until the mid-1920's.

B.A.B. ORGAN CO., 336 Water Street, Manhattan, U.S.A. Founded in 1912 by an Italian, Andrew Antoniazzi, who had been with Maserati for six years. Antoniazzi was joined in partnership by Borna and the firm began by making street pianos. Later on, Dominic Brugnolotti, formerly with Molinari, joined, and the firm converted a number of cardboard-playing organs to a new system of their own using double-track paper rolls. Later still, they took over the old Molinari factory in Brooklyn and built organs. Fried relates that Brugnolotti and Borna died, and Antoniazzi sold the remains of the business to former-Senator Charles Bovey of Virginia City.

BACIGALUPI, PETER, 1261 Market Street, Nr Hotel Whitcomb, San Francisco, California, U.S.A. Descended from the street organ-building family of Bacigalupo, this branch of the family altered the name to

Bacigalupi. Peter held the San Francisco distribution rights for a number of American mechanical pianos, including Wurlitzer, Cremona and North Tonawanda.

BACIGALUPO, G., 79 Schönhauser Allee, Berlin N., Germany. Formerly of the Cocchi company in London, he set up in business in 1900 in Berlin and produced six different small street organs. He was also a maker of street barrel-pianos. Survives today as Bacigalupo-Söhne at 74a Schönhauser Allee as street organ repairer.

BAGA, CONSTANTINE, 5a Bakers Row, London E.C. Maker of barrel pianos from 1890 to 1892.

BANSELL & SONS, Albert Works, Clarence Road, Hackney, London N.E. Made the Universal Piano Player c. 1911 which fitted on top of the keyboard yet when not in use was small enough to be kept in the piano stool. It played 65- and 88-note rolls, but how it worked remains a mystery. They also made the Aristos player-piano.

BARRATT & ROBINSON, 288–310 York Way, Kings Cross, London N.7. Established in 1872, this piano company produced a range of small player-pianos for use in boats and yachts. The Pedaleon was one of the smallest player-pianos ever produced and was exhibited by them at Olympia in 1913.

BATES & SON, THEODORE CHARLES. A famous manufacturer of musical instruments, Bates made his name in the field of mechanical musical instruments with barrel organs. However, sometime towards the end of the first half of the nineteenth century, he produced barrel pianos, some driven by clockwork with a heavy descending weight as in the German orchestrions, and others equipped with both finger keyboard for normal playing as well as mechanical action. The firm of Bates underwent several changes and amalgamations and occupied numerous addresses in London, but these instruments have been seen bearing their address at 6 Ludgate Hill which, from research by Langwill, dates them between 1833 and 1847.

BECHSTEIN-WELTE, 65 South Molton Street, London W.1. The London address of Welte (q.v.) and that of the make of piano which specialized in the Welte installation, fl. 1926.

BEHR BROTHERS & CO., 11th Avenue and 29th Street, New York, U.S.A. Maker of the Behr piano-player c. 1899.

BELLOTTI, DITTA, Via Savonarola 17/19, Alessandria, Italy. Maker of barrel pianos, who exhibited two barrel pianos at the National Exhibition held in Turin in the summer of 1884. He was still in business in 1903.

BERGEL, JOSEF, Töpferg 9, Rumburg, Bohemia. Maker of barrel pianos and piano orchestrions, fl. 1903.

BERLINER ORCHESTRION-FABRIK FRANZ HANKE & CO., Berlin, Germany. Maker of piano orchestrions, fl. 1903.

BERMEJO, VICTOR, 50 Avemaria, Madrid, Spain. Maker of street pianos, fl. 1903.

BIDERMANN, SAMUEL, Augsburg, Germany. Born in 1540, Bidermann made mechanical spinets, which had keyboards as well as music pinned to a wooden barrel and played by clockwork motors. He also used water to drive some of his mechanical instruments and built a barrel organ in a clock made by M. Rungell. He died in 1622. At least three of his mechanical spinets are still in existence today.

BIDERMANN, SAMUEL (the younger). The son of Samuel (senior), he manufactured organ-playing sewing baskets prior to 1625 and probably made barrel spinets as did his father.

BIDERMANN, B. Most probably related to the family of Samuel Bidermann, he made mechanical spinets which played from barrels during the 1740's.

BORELLA, JUAN, 8 Tabernillas Commandante and 14 Cirujeda, Madrid, Spain. Established in 1860 as makers of street barrel pianos, fl. 1903.

BOUFFIER, Milan, Italy. Exhibited a barrel piano at the National Exhibition held in Turin in the summer of 1884.

BOURQUIN, EDUARD JACQUES, 10 rue des Petites Ecuries, Paris, France. Bourquin was a Swiss engineer who was making mechanical barrel pianos in Paris and musical boxes from about 1885 onwards. In 1922, he applied the so-called revolver mechanism to a mechanical piano. Each of the multiple barrels played one tune or selection and, as the barrel played, it rotated on a spiral, so allowing long musical pieces to be performed. At the conclusion of one barrel, the revolver mechanism would automatically index another barrel into place and so on.

BOYD PIANOS LTD, New Bond Street, London W. Made the only British cabinet-style piano-player *c.* 1908. Produced an unusual player-piano *c.* 1914 which was called the Pistonola. This all-metal action was designed by two university students and employed, as its name implied, pneumatic cylinders and pistons for all the functions of the instrument. Even the foot treadles were coupled to reciprocating pistons in cylinders and the air reservoir was a further cylinder. The method made for a neat and compact mechanism, but it was said to have been difficult to regulate properly. The instrument was later called the Terpreter. Boyds also fitted conventional player actions into their upright pianos.

BRAUN, FRANZ, Hutbergasse 8, Rumburg, Bohemia. Established in 1895 as makers of barrel pianos.

BROWN, THEODORE P., 7 May Street, Massachusetts, Worcester, U.S.A. Maker of the Simplex piano-player which sold for $225 in 1899.

BRUDER LOOS, 97/98 Seestädtl, Bohemia. Established in 1847 as makers of orchestrion pianos and mechanical organs.

BRUGGER & FURTWENGLER, Staraja Basmannaja, Haus Raichinstein, Moscow, Russia. Established in 1832 as manufacturers of organs and mechanical musical instruments. Were making barrel organs and orchestrion organs in 1903 as well as acting as agents for piano-orchestrions and barrel pianos.

BRUSCO, BARTOLOMÉ, 34 Cadena, Barcelona, Spain. Barrel-piano maker, fl. 1903.

BRUSCO, JUAN, 15 Rosal, Barcelona, Spain. Barrel-piano maker, fl. 1903.

BUSSON, Paris, France. Built a harmonium in 1894 which played six Strauss waltzes among other tunes and which could be played either by a keyboard or by a pinned barrel.

CADINI ET CIE, 13 Rue Assalit, Nice, France. A maker of barrel pianos, fl. 1903.

CAMPODOMINICO, GIUSEPPE, Via Genova, Spezia, Lugria, Italy. Agent for street pianos *c.* 1903.

CAMPORA, FRATELLI, Vico Orti San Andrea 32, Genoa, Italy. A maker of barrel organs and barrel pianos for street use, fl. 1903.

CANOVA, JOSEPH PIANA, 16 Sekforde Street, Clerkenwell, London E.C. Patented a tremolo action for barrel pianos on September 24, 1902. He was probably a technician/mechanic working for one of the manufacturers, since his name is not recorded as a maker.

CANOVA, VINCENT, and HARTLEY, HENRY. See under HARTLEY.

CAPDEVILLE, V., SOCIETE DU 'PIANISTE EXECUTANT', 19 pass. Ménil-Moutant, Paris. A maker of mechanical pianos fl. 1903, who may have been in association with Ullman (q.v.).

CAPRA & Co., ALEXANDER, 11 & 13 Hatton Yard, Hatton Wall, London E.C. Founded by Alessandro Capra, they advertized as manufacturers of barrel pianos in 1890. The firm ceased business in 1894, probably when Capra went into partnership with G. B. Rissone (q.v.).

CAPRA, RISSONE & Co., 30 Warner Street, Clerkenwell, London E.C. Manufacturers of street barrel pianos who advertised in 1886. Alexander Capra was originally in business on his own until taking Rissone as a partner. Rissone subsequently took over the business in his own name (q.v. Rissone).

CAPRA & Co., 20 Warner Street, London E.C. Alexander Capra was advertising as a barrel-piano manufacturer under this title in 1887.

CARCHENA, ANGEL, 4 & 6 Cabestreras, Madrid, Spain. Maker of street pianos, fl. 1903.

CARPENTIER, J. A Frenchman who constructed mechanical musical instruments with pneumatic actions for the International Electricity Exhibition of 1880. Among his inventions was an electric recording harmonium or Melograph by the use of which musical notes could be punched into strips of paper for playing back on a key-top piano-player attachment called the Melotrope. He claimed the invention of both instruments but had been forestalled by Abdank (q.v.). Even so, he can claim to have been one of the fathers of the player-piano, exhibiting his first pneumatic instrument of the piano form in 1887, in which year he placed it before the French Academy. In 1903, he was selling the Melograph and Melotrope at 16/20 rue de Lambre, Paris.

CASALI, LUIS, 38 Amalia and 10 Flores, Barcelona, Spain. An Italian who settled in Barcelona during the 1880's and began manufacturing barrel pianos. His co-workers comprised Pombia, who was responsible for the making of the instruments, and Subiranda who scored and arranged the music for the barrels. The firm was variously at Torres Amati 1, and at Poniente 88. Gold medals for their instruments were awarded in Spain and Brussels in 1886 and 1895. Was still in business in 1903.

CAUS, SALOMON DE. A French engineer who, whilst in the service of the Elector Palatine in about 1600, described in his book *Les Raisons des Forces Mouvantes* the method of pinning music to a barrel and illustrated his words with six bars from a madrigal by Alessandro Striggio.

CESA, CARLO, Casa Bergonzolli, Novara, Italy. A maker of barrel pianos and organs for street use, fl. 1903.

CHANCELLOR & SON, Lower Sackville Street, Dublin, Eire. Advertised as 'photographers, jewellers, watch & clock manufacturers, opticians &c', this firm was distributor of the German *Piano Orchestrion* driven by a hot-air motor and illustrated in Plate 36.

CHIAPPA LTD, 6 Little Bath Street, Holborn, London (now re-named 31 Eyre Street Hill, Clerkenwell Road, London E.C.1). Fair-organ makers and repairers who are still in business. Founded in 1864 by an Italian, Giuseppe Chiappa, at an address near Farringdon Road, he subsequently went to America and started a barrel-piano and fair-organ manufactury in New York. However, he soon returned to London to organize a factory at the present location. He made street pianos, street organs, street harmoniums, skating rink bands, clockwork pianos and café pianos. These last played an improved form of Jacquard card-music as well as being available with barrels. He was a pioneer in the manufacture of cardboard music for street pianos. Also pinned barrels for Imhof & Mukle orchestrions and mechanical pianos at one time. Giuseppe's son, Lodovico, subsequently took over the firm and his son, Victor, now runs the business, producing punched-card music for fair organs and restoring instruments.

CHIAPPA & FERSANI, 6 Little Bath Street, London E.C. Giuseppe Chiappa went into partnership with Fersani, manufacturing street barrel pianos and in 1878 they jointly patented a street piano with cornet accompaniment, the instrument being both piano and organ.

CHIAPPA & SONS. In 1885, this firm was in business at 5 Jersey Street, Ancoats, Manchester, making barrel pianos. It was the northern branch of the London firm.

CHIAPPA & SON, JOSEPH, 6 Little Bath Street, London E.C. In 1881 Giuseppe (Joseph) Chiappa was making street pianos under this name.

CHIAPPO, FELICE, Turin, Italy. Maker of barrel pianos who exhibited three instruments at the National Exhibition held in Turin in the summer of 1884.

CHORDEPHON. See under Fabrik Mechanischer Zithern 'Chordephon' Claus & Co.

CLARK-APOLLO CO., 67 Berners Street, and 119 Regent Street, London. Established in the summer of 1901 with a £12,000 capital to exploit the Apollo piano-player in England. The directors were John Beare, Jacques Ullman (of the Paris firm of Ch. & J. Ullman), Henry Kaim (of F. Kaim & Sohn, the German piano manufacturers), E. Rink (of Ullman's London office) and C. H. Wagener (of the Melville-Clark Co.).

CLEMENTI, COLLARD & CO., 26 Cheapside, London. Musical instrument makers. Muzio Clementi, famed keyboard performer and composer, was formerly a partner with the firm of barrel organ and piano makers, Longman & Broderip, and on the dissolution of the firm he set up in business on his own. Finally, he took into partnership John Collard and in about 1820 the firm produced the Self-Acting Pianoforte barrel piano.

COCCHI, BACIGALUPO & GRAFFIGNA, Schönhauser Allee 78, Berlin N., Germany. After their London barrel-piano business failed, they returned to the Continent, setting up business in Berlin about 1898 as makers of street pianos, barrel organs, orchestrions and 'hand organs'.

COCCHI, BACIGALUPO & GRAFFIGNA ('Successors of John Arrigoni & Co.'), 158 Great College Street, London N.W. Street organ and piano makers, 1896. John Arrigoni (q.v.) was manager for the firm but by 1898 the firm had reverted to the title of J. N. Arrigoni & Co. at this address and Cocchi, Bacigalupo and Graffigna went to Berlin to set up in business. The son of Giuseppe Cocchi, John (q.v.) remained in business in London.

COCCHI, GIUSEPPE, 8 & 9 Farringdon Road Buildings, London E.C. Maker of barrel pianos in 1880.

COCCHI, JOHN, Lychenerstrasse 2/3, Berlin N. Maker of barrel organs and piano orchestrions who was functioning in 1903.

COCCHI & SON, JOHN, 2 Childs Mews, Dirleton Place, West Ham, London E.15. Described as 'manufacturers of Mechanical Organs and Pianos', they specialized in the repair of these instruments and were at this address until at least 1935.

COLDMAN, H. C. See under WEBB, C. F.

COLLARD MOUTRIE LTD, 50–52 Southampton Row, Holborn, London. Was agent for the Ehrlich 'Virtuos' piano-player (see Fabrik Leipziger Musikwerke).

COLOMBO, GIOVANNI, Sobborgo S Andrea, Novara, Italy. A maker of street barrel organs and pianos, fl. 1903.

CONNOISSEUR PLAYER PIANO. Sold by Murdoch, Murdoch & Co., 461 & 463 Oxford Street, London, and exhibited by them at the British Music Exhibition, Olympia, in 1913. There was also the Connoisseur Reed Organ and Pipe Organ, both being player-organs. Murdochs also made the Golden Tube series of music-rolls.

COPPLESTON & CO. LTD, 94 Regent Street, London W. Manufacturers of the Ideal Mignon player action and also the Sterling player-piano c. 1910.

CORVINO, ENRICO, Via S Carco 26, and Strada Trinita Maggiore 27, Naples, Italy. A maker of street barrel pianos, fl. 1903.

COSTA, JEAN, 50 rue du Roveray, Eux Viven, Geneva, Switzerland. Repairer of street barrel organs and barrel pianos, fl. 1903.

COSTA, BARTOLOMEO, Via S Maurizio 25, Turin, Italy. Maker of street pianos, fl. 1903.

COURTEUIL, M. DE. A Frenchman who, in 1852, was granted a patent for a perforated strip of cardboard to replace the planchette-type of piano keyboard player invented by Alexander Debain.

CRASSELT & RÀHSE, Löbau i.S., Berlin. Maker of a piano orchestrion which played perforated paper music-rolls. Housed in an ornate cabinet reminiscent of the style used for the larger Polyphon musical boxes, the instrument sold for 950 marks complete with twelve rolls of music in 1903.

CROUBOIS, A., 48 rue des Juifs, Granville, France. Makers of good-class clockwork orchestral barrel pianos for use in cafés. One seen is marked 'Pianos Automatiques Croubois' and has 51 notes on a semi-iron frame with drum, triangle and two castanets. The date of this instrument is c. 1930.

CROWSHAW, London. A barrel-organ manufacturer c. 1790, who produced an instrument (still extant in the Moss collection) which incorporated a 12-note dulcimer in addition to organ pipes and normal percussion accompaniment. The dulcimer was operated from the pins on the organ barrel using keys on the same key-frame as those of the organ proper. No other example of the work of this maker is known.

CUCCONATO, ANTONIO, Via Torino 11, Turin, Italy. Barrel-piano maker, fl. 1903.

DACHS, JUAN, 41 Rosal, Barcelona, Spain. Barrel-piano maker, fl. 1903.

DAVIS, JOSEPH, 11 Catherine Street, Strand, London (1819–1828); also at Blackfriars Road in 1829 and at 20 Southampton Street, Strand, London (1844–48). Makers of barrel-organs who also advertised 'Self-performing piano harp'.

DAWKINS, THOMAS, Clerkenwell, London. A barrel piano bearing this name was sold in London by auction at Christies in 1967. Measuring 38 inches by 18 inches, it would appear that Dawkins was agent for a manufacturer of Hick-style pianos. He was a well-known musical instrument importer.

DAWSON, CHARLES, Hardinge Street, Islington, Middlesex. In 1848 he produced a mechanical organ worked by perforated cardboard of the Jacquard type in place of the usual barrels. It was not a success, since he used the perforations in the card to affect directly the admission of wind to the pipes, and the gradual opening and closing of the airways which resulted produced a disagreeable wavering at the beginning and end of each note. This organ was shown at the Great Exhibition of 1851.

DEBAIN, ALEXANDRE F., 15 rue Vivienne, Paris. An instrument maker who, in 1846, patented an attachment for a keyboard instrument such as a player or harpsichord which played using wooden planchettes. It was called the Antiphonel. He later made a complete piano with the Antiphonel built in, early examples being of the keyless variety. Models of the Antiphonel cost 55 gns. and 90 gns. Until he opened his own company in London (see DEBAIN & CO.), the Debain agent was Novello & Co., 44 Dean Street.

DEBAIN & CO., 41 Rathbone Place, London W. Founded by Alexandre Debain of Paris, this London office opened during the 1880's and advertised 'pianos-mécaniques' and 'pianos-orgues'.

deKLEIST, EUGENE, Düsseldorf, Germany. Born Eugene Von Kleist in 1867, he was formerly representative in Belgium and, later, in London for Limonaire Brothers, makers of fair and band organs. He was requested, as an organ expert, to establish the North Tonawanda Barrel Organ Factory in North

Tonawanda, New York, U.S.A. The firm was financed by the Tonawanda Carousel Factory and deKleist was its manager. They built their first organ in 1891. DeKleist ultimately separated his company from the North Tonawanda parent company and, in 1903, the barrel-organ factory became the deKleist Musical Instrument Company. Wurlitzer commissioned them to make a coin-freed electric piano and deKleist developed a ten-tune barrel piano featuring pneumatic action which he called the Tonophone. Wurlitzer finally absorbed the firm in 1908.

DELMASTRO & CIA., GIUSEPPE, Corsa Vitt. Emanuele 24, Turin, Italy. A maker of clockwork barrel pianos for use in cafés and public places, fl. 1903.

DENIS, CARLO, Via Giovenone 5, Vercelli, Italy. Barrel organ and piano maker, c. 1903.

DEPONTE, CARLO, Turin, Italy. Exhibited three barrel pianos at the National Exhibition held in Turin in the summer of 1884.

DEPONTI, CAROLINA, Via Della Rocca 1, Turin, Italy. Barrel-piano maker, fl. 1903.

DIENST, E., Langestrasse 39/40, Leipzig. Founded in 1871, Dienst made orchestrion organs, orchestrion pianos, played by barrel and pneumatic actions.

DIRECT PNEUMATIC ACTION CO. LTD, 8a Dorset Street, Baker Street, London W. Makers of the Direct Arrow Action. Also sole British agent for the imported Standard Pneumatic Actions. They produced the Stems player-piano fitted with the Arrow action c. 1911 and shown at Olympia in 1913.

DISTIN, HENRY, 2 Church Lane, Temple Street, Bristol. Maker of barrel pianos who marked some of his instruments 'Henry Distin (from the late Joseph Hicks)'. He was also a piano-tuner. Joseph Hicks died in 1847.

DONADINI & POHL, CESARE, Landsbergerallee 78, Berlin N. A maker of barrel pianos who patented in 1865 a combined manual and barrel piano. This was exhibited at the Melbourne Musical Industries Exhibition in April 1888. Was still in business in 1903.

DORCHIN, ARMAND, 40 Rosal, Barcelona, Spain. Barrel-piano maker, fl. 1903.

DUCHÁCEK, LADISLAUS, Patackygasse 114, Turnau. A maker of musical automatons and mechanical stringed instruments fl. 1903.

EAST ANGLIAN AUTOMATIC PIANO COMPANY. See WINTLE, CANON A. O.

ECKHARDT, J. C., Pragstrasse 72/74, Kannstatt, Germany. Manufacturer of musical Christmas-tree stands who probably also handled barrel pianos and organs, fl. 1903. Was formerly in Stuttgart.

EHRLICH, FRIEDRICH ERNST PAUL, Gohlis, Leipzig, Germany. A prolific inventor of mechanical musical instruments, particularly organettes, who produced disc-playing musical boxes, small reed organs and pianos which played using perforated cardboard or paper music. He manufactured the small 24-note Orpheus disc-playing piano and also the Automat piano player in the late 1880's. This played from cardboard discs very similar to those used in the Ariston organette. Some models also used metal discs. Two distinct models of the Automat were built; one was a push-up style resembling that made by Grob (q.v.) and the second was of similar format but was clamped on top of the piano keyboard. His firm was the Fabrik Leipziger Musikwerke (q.v.).

ELIAS, JAIME, Palma de Mallorca, Baleares, Spain. Modern maker of miniature street barrel pianos (*manubriet*) complete with dog-cart.

ENGLEHARDT PIANO CO., St Johnsville, New York. A subsidiary of the Peerless Piano Player Co. which produced instruments of the same type and under its own name. Also sometime Roth & Englehardt Co.

ENGRAMELLE, THE REV. FATHER, Paris. He devised a notation system and tools for barrel-operated instruments, as well as making musical instruments which worked mechanically. In 1775 he built an automatic instrument called La Tonotechnic.

FABRIK LEIPZIGER MUSIKWERKE, Leipzig-Gohlis. Founded in 1877 for the manufacture of mechanical musical instruments by the brothers Ehrlich, they made the Virtuos pneumatic piano-player c. 1903.

FABRIK MECHANISCHER ZITHERN 'CHORDEPHON' CLAUS & CO., Waldstrasse 20, Leipzig. Makers of the Chordophon disc-playing mechanical zither (see Plate 95) which was played by a perforated metal disc. Examples were made which were both hand-cranked and driven by a clockwork spring motor. It was in production in 1903.

FARRAND ORGAN COMPANY, Detroit, Michigan, U.S.A., also London and Paris. Makers of the Cecilian piano-player which cost $250 in 1901. Later they became the Farrand & Votey Organ Company which was one of the associates of the subsequent Aeolian Co. empire.

FASCH, JOSÉ, 9 Meliodia, Barcelona, Spain. Barrel street-piano agent and hirer in business in 1903.

FEILITZSCH ET CIE, HANS VON, 104 rue de Laeken, Brussels, Belgium. Agent for barrel organs, barrel pianos and electric pianos, fl. 1903.

FEISS BROTHERS, Melbourne, Australia. Agents for Imhof & Mukle's Black Forest orchestrions and mechanical pianos in 1888.

FERNANDEZ, ROMAN, 14 Flor Baja, Madrid, Spain. Maker of street pianos, fl. 1903.

FERRARI, ANGEL, 4 S Pedro, Villafranca del Panadés, Spain. Agent and hirer for street pianos, fl. 1903.

F.I.R.S.T. 'Fabb. Ital. Rulli Sonori Traforati'. An Italian make of player-piano music-roll manufactured under licence from G. Ricordi & Co. The music was 'themodized' with automatic accenting from pedal perforations in the margin of the music-roll.

FOUCHER, GEORGE. Manufacturer of pianos and organs, 'patent barrel organ, new mechanical pianoforte performing by hand and handle' in 1881.

FOUCHER, GASPARINI, 17/19 rue de la Véga, Paris. Maker of barrel organs and pianos for street use, fl. 1903.

FOURNEAUX, NAPOLEON. A Frenchman who patented in 1863 a mechanical piano-player called the Pianista. This is the first-known pneumatic player, the action being controlled by a pinned barrel turned by a handle. Each pneumatic, which received its air control from barrel-organ type bellows, depressed a finger on the piano keys. The instrument, somewhat larger than the pianoforte it was designed to play upon, was exhibited in America at the Philadelphia Exposition of 1878.

FRANCOME, VINCENZO, Via S Dalmazzo 16, Turin, Italy. Barrel-piano maker, fl. 1903.

FRANKFURTER MUSIKWERKE FABRIK J. D. PHILIPPS & SÖHNE Akt.-Ges., Frankfurt, Germany. Manufacturers of player-pianos who perfected, in 1912, a motor for winding two tune sheets at once and, in 1916, a special roll tracking device. Also at Berlin, Essen and Leipzig. See also under PHILLIPPS & SÖHNE, J. D.

FRATI, CHIARO, 5 Farringdon Road, London E.C. Probably a son of the founder of the famous Berlin firm of orchestrion organ makers, Chiaro Frati advertised as a maker of barrel pianos in 1876. He subsequently removed to 19 Great Bath Street, Farringdon Road, London E.C.

FRATI & Co., Kastanien-Allee 32, Berlin N. Well-known manufacturer of orchestrion and barrel organs who also made orchestrion pianos. At the International Exhibition held at the Crystal Palace, London, in April 1884, they were given 'special mention' for barrel pianos.

FUSELLA, GIUSEPPE, Via S Dominico 34, Turin, Italy. Barrel-piano maker, fl. 1903.

FUZELLI, JOSEPH, 379 Great Ormond Street, London W. Maker of street barrel organs and barrel pianos.

GALL, JOHANN, Arnau, Bohemia. A maker of street barrel organs and pianos.

GANTER, KARL, Furtwangen, Bad. Schwarzwald, Germany. A specialist in the making of weight-driven clockwork units supplied to many makers of piano and pipe orchestrions, fl. 1903.

GARGALLO, TOMÁS, 178 Conde del Asalto, Barcelona, Spain. Specialized in pinning music for street pianos, fl. 1903.

GAROLACHI, VINCENTE, 6 Sombreria, Madrid, Spain. Barrel-piano maker, fl. 1903.

GAVIOLI & Co., 1 & 2 Farringdon Road, London E.C. Street-organ makers who were producing barrel pianos in 1880.

GAVIOLI & Co., 5 Jersey Street, Great Ancoats, Manchester, and 2bis avenue de Taillebourg (place de la Nations), Paris, France. Makers of mechanical organs and pianos c. 1888. In 1885 they were at 55 Blossom Street, Ancoats, Manchester.

GAVIOLI & Co., L., 5 Little Saffron Hill, London E.C. Street-organ maker who also advertised mechanical pianos in 1870.

GAVIOLI ET CIE, SOCIETE. Founded in Paris at 2 avenue de Taillebourg by Ludovic Gavioli, an Italian, with his sons Claude and Anselme; the Gaviolis can truthfully be said to have been the fathers of the fair or showman's organ. Their inventions both in the tonality and mechanics of these instruments, along with the practical improvements in perforated music, were to influence all that came after them. The cardboard-music playing piano was one direct result of their associated work. Ludovic Gavioli was a meticulous organ-builder who made very fine secular organs, although he did build one for Queen Isabella II of Spain which played hymns. Ordinary barrel organs represented a steady business but the firm was to find its wealth and success in fair organs and, during the late 1850's, the family concern was joined by P. Yver, a financier. After the war of 1870, the Gavioli factory was moved to Alsace in Eastern France. There followed a period of decline in business and in 1901 the firm lost its foreman, Charles Marenghi, who was their principle expert. Marenghi established his own successful firm in the same line of business. Earlier, in 1892, Gavioli had introduced 'book music' and the book-playing organ which used perforated-cardboard music folded zig-zag fashion to form a thick 'book' of music. This was fed through a pneumatic system named the 'mechanical-pneumatic Touch Key' which operated on a similar principle to the church organ. Gavioli was also responsible for the invention of the portable street organ, many interestingly-voiced organ pipes, organs that used two wind pressures from one air source, primary and secondary pneumatic systems for fair organs, and a 'keyless' tracker box along with automatic stop selectors and cancellers. Most of the famous names amongst Italian/French fair organs and their makers served their apprenticeships with Gavioli. In the irony of things, many of these names continued in business long after Gavioli, among them Marenghi and also Chiappa. Limonaire Brothers took over the remains of the Gavioli concern and continued to supply perforated music until they themselves went out of business in 1918. Gavioli built the 'Guitharmony' which was a barrel-operated guitar with plucking mechanism.

GAZZA, GIOVANNI, 71 Roosevelt Street, Manhattan, U.S.A. Took over the barrel piano and organ business of G. Mina of 2 First Street, Manhattan, on his death. The business did not prosper and was closed by 1902.

GENERALAGENTUR DER CHORALION COMPANY FRANK W. HESSIN, Unter den Linden 71, Berlin N.W. The German company representing the Aeolian Company and handling the Pianola and Orchestrelle instruments.

GETTO, FRANCESCO, Via Marsale N.5, Ivrea, Italy. 'Pianoforte en Organi a Cilindro'. Maker of barrel pianos similar in style to the portable Hicks pattern, but strung much lighter to produce a most pleasing bright tone.

GIACCHETTI, GIUSEPPE, Cigliano, Italy. Maker of barrel organs and pianos, who exhibited two barrel pianos at the National Exhibition held in Turin in the summer of 1884. Was still in business in 1903.

GILONE, GIUSEPPE, Casale, Italy. Exhibited two barrel pianos at the National Exhibition held in Turin in the summer of 1884.

GIOVANNI RISSONI & Co., 30 Warner Street, Clerkenwell, London E.C. Formerly with Capra, Rissone took over the Capra business and continued at the same address from 1887, manufacturing street barrel pianos.

GIULIANO, VITTORIO, Via Monteoliveto 61, Naples, Italy. A maker of barrel pianos, fl. 1903.

GRAY, ROBERT AND WILLIAM, '4 New Road, near the end of Portland Road (London). Maker of Barrel Organs, Harpsichords and Pianos'. Probably built barrel pianos or spinets c. 1800, but no instruments have been discovered.

GRISERI & VARETTO, 14 Warner Street, London E.C. Producers of street pianos, c. 1880.

GROB & Co., J. M., Eutritzsch, near Leipzig, Germany. Manufacturers of street barrel pianos. Founded in the 1880's by J. M. Grob, A. O. Schultze and A. V. Niemczik, they patented a method of playing an organ or piano using perforated tune sheets in 1886. This employed cam-shaped levers which, when lifted through the holes in the music, wedged against a rotating drum and operated the hammer action. In 1888, they patented a tremolo or staccato action for barrel-operated pianos using a revolving, cranked shaft engaging the barrel pin key. They also perfected a system of continuously-beating hammers and associated check action similar to that used by Racca of Bologna. Their disc-operated piano-player, illustrated on page 000, played 36 notes of the piano.

GUILBAUD FRERES, LES ETABts., Labaule (L.inf), 2 rue Charles Baudelaire, Paris. Makers of clockwork barrel pianos which featured overstrung, partly-iron frames. This firm also made orchestrions. A label on one 48-note cafe piano states: 'Mfg. Pianos Automatiques en France & Belgium'.

HAAKE SÖHNE, RUDOLF, Karlsruhe I.B., Furtwangen, Germany. Also at Mannheim. Makers of hot-air engines for mechanical musical instruments including piano orchestrions. These little engines, set in motion by a spirit burner, developed $\frac{1}{60}$ h.p. and cost 38 m each. These details were advertised in 1897.

HALL, R., 19b Wilbury Grove, Hove 3, Sussex. 'Piano Organ Specialist'. A restorer of barrel pianos who also re-pinned barrels. An instrument by Pasquale of 5 Phoenix Place, London, re-pinned and restored by Hall, is in the Lancaster House collection in London. It plays the popular American tune *Davey Crocket*. (See Plate 15).

HARPER ELECTRIC PIANO (1910) CO. LTD, 258, 260 & 262 Holloway Road, London N. Makers of electric self-acting pianos, who exhibited such instruments in 1911 at the Coronation Exhibition (Shepherd's Bush), at the Earls Court Exhibition and also the Festival of Empire at the Crystal Palace. At the Music Trades Exhibition of the same year (August) at the Agricultural Hall they showed one model fitted with xylophone and mandolin attachment which could be turned on or off at will. This was intended for use in cafés, restaurants and hotels. The firm remained in business through the thirties although, judging by the rarity of their instruments today, their production must have been small. Most of their music-rolls appear to have been made by the Up-To-Date Music Roll Co. (q.v.) and were $13\frac{5}{16}$ inch wide.

HARTLEY, HENRY, AND VINCENT CANOVA, 39 Corporation Street, Birmingham. In January of 1911, they jointly patented a player-piano system wherein at the completion of one paper roll, another was indexed into position for playing whilst an independent mechanism rewound the other regardless of the length of either roll.

HAUPT, A. E., Aeussere Weberstrasse 69c, Zittau, Saxony. Barrel organ and barrel piano maker, fl. 1903.

HAYS & CO., ALFRED, 82 Cornhill, London E.C. One-time musical-instrument dealers, this firm exists today as a theatre-ticket agency. Their name and former address (above) appears on a small portable barrel piano in a rosewood case similar to the Hicks style and appearing to date from the second half of the nineteenth century. It is likely that, as with barrel pianos bearing the name Keith Prowse, Alfred Hays did not actually manufacture these instruments. Also sometime at 74 Cornhill, E.C.3, and 26 Old Bond Street (c. 1923).

HICKS, GEORGE, Brooklyn, Long Island, U.S.A. A street barrel piano of the small 'English Hicks' style is in the George Brown, N.J., collection bearing the label: 'George Hicks, Hand Organs and Cylinder Pianos'.

HICKS, JOHN, Cobourg Street, Clerkenwell, London E.C. A barrel-organ maker c. 1850, probably related to the Bristol family of Hicks who were organ and piano makers who made the first street barrel piano in about 1805. Sometime also at Chapel Street, Edgware Road, London. The ramifications of the Hicks family are unknown but various members made many barrel pianos, mainly of the portable, street type, in the first half of the nineteenth century. With the common misuse of the term 'barrel organ'— even contemporarily—John Hicks may indeed have been a maker of barrel pianos.

HICKS, JOSEPH, 13 Penton Street, Pentonville, London N. Maker of barrel organs and cylinder pianos (sic), whose name appears on a particularly fine 41-key piano in a rosewood case with two barrels bearing the watermark date 1846. This piano is 5 feet $9\frac{1}{2}$ inches high, 39 inches wide and 21 inches deep.

HICKS, JOSEPH, Bristol. 1816–47. Whether related to, or indeed, the same as, Joseph Hicks above is uncertain. An early pianoforte has been seen with a label reading 'Henry Distin (from the late Joseph Hicks), Barrel Pianoforte maker, No. 2, Church Lane, Temple Street, Bristol'. Bristol directories, examined by Langwill, list Joseph Hicks as a musical-instrument maker, who was made Freeman of Bristol on October 12, 1812, at the following addresses: 11 Griffin Lane and Trenchard Street (1816–29); Trenchard Street (1830); 3 St Augustine's Place (1831); 16 Lower Park Row (1832–41); 17 Lower Maudlin Street (1842–44); 17 Montague Street (1845–47).

HOFFMAN, JULIUS CARL, 111 Hietzingerkai, Vienna, Austria. Barrel-piano maker, who perfected a pianoforte effect for his instruments in 1905.

HOFMAN & CZERNY, XVIII/2, Sandleitnerg 79, Vienna. Maker of piano-orchestrions 'for public places and private houses, fl. 1903.

HORVILLEUR, H., & GEORGES-PRESBURG 7, rue du Temple, Paris (Hôtel-de-Ville). Makers of clockwork-driven 'automatic' barrel pianos for use in cafes and public places. Typical of the French and Belgian style of coin-operated instrument, pianos by H. Horvilleur & Georges-Presburg usually featured an octave of bells struck by metal hammers, and the strings were struck by leather-covered hammers at the bass end, felt-covered ones in the tenor and bare hardwood at the treble and the barrels often featured popular international tunes including polkas and mazurkas, brightly set up.

HROMÁDKA, AUGUST, Josefstadt-Sterngasse, Temesvar, Hungary. A maker of barrel pianos, fl. 1903.

HÜNDERSEN, A., Dornbush 4, Hamburg. Agent for barrel pianos, fl. 1903.

HUNT & BRADISH, Warren, Ohio, U.S.A. Patented a small pianoforte controlled by a perforated paper roll c. 1880.

HUPFELD Akt.-Ges., LUDWIG, Böhlitz-Ehrenberg, bei Leipzig, Germany. A famous maker of orchestrion organs, who devised in 1892 a pneumatic action for the playing of pianos using perforated paper music. The firm first produced a cabinet-style piano-player and later made the Solophonola, Duophonola and Triphonola player-pianos, the last two being reproducing instruments. Also made the Dea which was a pneumatically-played violin attached to a piano, and the Dea-Violina which was three violins all played pneumatically. Their association with Bluthner Pianos in London led to their sharing the same premises (7 to 13 Wigmore Street) in the 1920's. Prior to this, their London agent had been a Mr M. Sinclair, who established the Solophonola Company at 16 & 17 Orchard Street. By the mid-1920's, the Hupfeld London address and showrooms were at 28–30 Wigmore Street where they displayed the Phonoliszt-Violina, a three-violin and piano unit similar to the earlier Dea-Violina but based on their very fine all-metal player-piano, the Phono-Liszt. Their Leipzig factory with its six floors and large wings, was the largest in Europe devoted to mechanical musical instruments. During the early 1920's, they amalgamated with Zimmermann (q.v.), becoming Hupfeld-Gebr. Zimmermann and changing their address to Petersstrasse 4, Postschliessfach 215, Leipzig C.1, between 1926 and 1928. All Hupfeld music-rolls, including those made under their registered trade-mark 'Animatic', were made on special paper bearing the watermark Phonola and the year of manufacture—a unique feature indeed. Hupfelds excelled in the production of the all-metal player action in later years, dispensing with wood, rubber tubing and cloth. The Hupfeld reproducing actions were widely used in Bluthner pianos. The firm is thought to have remained in existence until the outbreak of the 1939–45 war. Their address in Vienna was VI Mariahilferstrasse 9.

ICART, ANTONIO, 23 San Agustin, Tarragona, Spain. Established in 1875 as a maker of street pianos and also a hirer of these instruments, fl. 1903.

IDEAL MIGNON. The name of a player action introduced in 1910 by Copplestone & Co. Ltd of 94 Regent Street, London, and fitted by them into their Sterling player-piano.

IMHOF & MUKLE. Founded at Vohrenbach in the Black Forest in 1845, the firm was at 46 Oxford Street, London, in 1870 and at 110 New Oxford Street in 1883. They were also sometime at 547 Oxford Street and also had a 'manufactury' at 9 Sandiland Street, Holborn, London, in 1880. They were the London branch of a famous German musical instrument works which specialized in the manufacture of barrel orchestrion organs. Daniel Imhof took out patents in 1866 for improvements 'in the machinery of chimes and the striking of drums and other instruments of percussion by self-acting organs'. A very handsome drawing-room barrel piano has survived complete with two barrels, each of which bear a pre-pinning barrel label stating 'Imhof & Mukle'. Whether or not they actually built the instrument, they were certainly responsible for pinning the music which dates from c. 1846.

IMPERIAL. Player-piano rolls were manufactured under this name by the Perforated Music Co. (q.v.). These 65- and 88-note music-rolls were made in a patented one-piece box and the start of the roll was reinforced with glazed linen, hence the term 'linenised'. Also used a steel spool and a 'D'-shaped tag to the roll end.

JACOB, L., Kgl. Hofl, Stuttgart, Germany. A manufacturer of disc-playing piano-orchestrions c. 1895–1900.

JACQUARD, JOSEPH MARIE, Lyons, France. A straw-hat maker who first conceived the idea of using cardboard strips, suitably perforated, to replace the barrel in organs. His invention was primarily intended as a means to the production of woven patterned carpets and hence he was the originator of the so-called Jacquard Loom. He died in 1834.

JEBAVY, FRANZ, Reichsstrasse 118, Trautenau, Bohemia. Maker of piano-orchestrions and barrel organs, fl. 1903.

JONES, THOMAS LINFORTH, 53a Franciscan Road, Tooting, London. An engineer who devised and patented in 1905 a method of operating a coin-freed clockwork barrel piano in a public place from remotely-situated coin boxes. The slot boxes could be situated anywhere in the building and the release of the piano's clockwork was through 'electro-magnetic contacts'. He was later to improve upon his system in collaboration with G. Phillips.

KAMENIK, JOSEPH, Prague. A maker of street barrel organs and pianos who was the last maker to follow his trade in that city.

KAPS, ERNST, Dresden. Established in 1858, they manufactured a range of self-playing pianos and other instruments, automatons, phonographs, etc. Their London agent was Mr Philip Cohen, 224 Brixton Road, London S.W.

KASTNER-AUTOPIANO Akt.-Ges., 6 Wittenbergerstrasse, Leipzig, Germany. Also called Kastner & Co. Pianos-Apparate Akt.-Ges. Makers of player-pianos and actions. They patented a system of unit valves for the player in 1929 in which each pneumatic and motor was fashioned in metal and could be removed and replaced in a few moments. This dispensed with the wooden action components and wooden valve chest. The company also produced music-rolls and they had offices at 196 Great Portland Street, London W.

KASTNER & CO. LTD, 34, 35 & 36 Margaret Street, Cavendish Square, London W. Later at 191 Regent Street, London W. Produced large quantity of 65-note rolls for player-pianos and was a subsidiary of Kastner-Autopiano.

KEITH PROWSE, 38 Berners Street, Oxford Street, London W. Agents for Swiss musical boxes and Polyphons, who also marketed a clockwork barrel piano for use in public houses, etc., under their trade name of 'The Pennyano' which, as the name implied, was coin-operated. It played ten tunes and had 48 notes. Many other barrel pianos of the coin-freed type bear their name, sometimes even tastefully carved on the front barrel fall, but it is thought that they did not manufacture themselves and commissioned pianos from other recognized makers.

KELLY, GEORGE B., U.S.A. In 1886 he perfected the slide-valve air motor for driving the paper music-roll in player instruments.

KINTZING, PETER, Neuwied, Germany. A clockmaker who moved to Paris and c. 1780 made an automaton featuring a young girl playing a stringed instrument, using two sticks as strikers. He was helped by a cabinet-maker named Roentgen. Kintzing also built a musical clock which featured a dulcimer and a number of flutes and this, dated 1780, is preserved in the Museum of Arts and Crafts, Paris.

KLEIN & CO., HENRY, 84 Oxford Street, London W. Agents for mechanical music work, particularly Polyphon musical boxes and Amorette organettes. Also was agent for Peter's electric pianos made in Leipzig. In 1901, these sold for £128.

KLEPETAR, J., Prague. Produced large café barrel pianos c. 1880–1900. One instrument seen comprised a 37-key piano with drum, triangle and cymbal. This instrument was powered by a large descending weight and featured a sophisticated percussive action, described in Chapter 2.

KNABE & CO., WILLIAM, Fifth Avenue, Corner 39th Street, New York, U.S.A. Piano manufacturers established in 1837 with factories at Baltimore and Maryland, who produced a range of quality reproducing pianos fitted with the Ampico action.

KOHLER & CAMPBELL, 50th Street and 11th Avenue, New York, U.S.A. Producers of the Pianista pneumatic push-up cabinet-style piano-player. Their slogan was 'Knows no technical difficulties'. c. 1899.

KOHLER INDUSTRIES, New York City, U.S.A. Manufacturers of the Welte-Mignon (Licensee) action for reproducing pianos. They also controlled the Auto Pneumatic Action Co. and the Standard Pneumatic Action Co. The Welte-Mignon (Licensee) action was installed in over a hundred different American pianos and their slogan was 'The Master's Fingers on your Piano'.

KUHL & KLATT, Berlin and Vienna. Manufacturers of the Pneuma and Pneumatist pneumatic action piano-player and player-piano.

LACAPE ET CIE, J., Paris. In 1882, patented a treadle-driven mechanical piano, playing either from a barrel or mechanically from a tune sheet. Won a bronze medal for barrel pianos at the Brussels Exposition in 1883.

LAFLEUR & SON, J. R., 15 Green Street, Leicester Square, London W.C. Producers of street pianos in 1880.

LAKIN & Co., R. J., 67 Besley Street, Streatham, London S.W.16. Established at this address in 1934, Lakin came originally from Bristol. He advertised as maker of 'mechanical organs' but it is not known for certain whether or not he did actually make barrel organs or barrel pianos. It is known that he sold both music and mechanical street pianos and organs. He also did repairs until ceasing business in 1943.

LEIPZIGER ORCHESTRIONWERKE PAUL LÖSCHE, Blumenstrasse 10, Leipzig. Makers of orchestrion organs who also for a limited period made orchestrion pianos, fl. 1903.

LIEBETANZ & RICHTER, Grübschenerstrasse 85, Breslau. Established in 1902, this firm made orchestrion pipe organs and orchestrion pianos.

LINK PIANO Co. INC., 183–185 Water Street, Binghamton, New York, and 532 Republic Building, Chicago. Makers of coin-operated pianos and instruments with orchestral effects. The firm was originally the Automatic Musical Company, claimed by Bowers to have been one of the earliest makers of coin-operated pianos in the States. They sold the Encore Banjo and the Hiawatha Self-Playing Xylophone. When the firm went bankrupt in 1910, Edwin A. Link was appointed chairman of the creditors' committee, realized the opportunity to re-form the company and so founded the Link Piano Co., later turning out about 300 coin-operated instruments a year. His son, Ed Link, later took over many of the firm's patents and applied them to the manufacture of the famous pneumatically-operated Link Trainer still in use with many flying schools.

LIPP & SOHN, RICHARD, Weigenburgerstrasse 32, Stuttgart, Germany. Founded in 1831, this firm produced player-pianos including the Duca-Lipp electrically-operated reproducing piano. Introduced in the Spring of 1910, this cost £300. None are known to survive. Their London showrooms were at 56 Berners Street, off Oxford Street, Mr Fritz Willeringhaus being manager.

LLINARES, VICENTE, Castelar, Faventia, Spain. Manufacturer of modern miniature street pianos playing 23 notes on metal rods and known as 'Impuesto de Lujo a Metalico'.

LOCHMANN, PAUL. See ORIGINAL-MUSIKWERKE PAUL LOCHMANN GmbH.

LORENZ, WENZEL, Schillerstrasse 176, Trautenau, Bohemia. Maker of piano-orchestrions, fl. 1903.

MAESTRO COMPANY, THE, Eldridge, New York. Produced the Maestro piano-player c. 1899 at $125—half the price of the Pianola and the Cecilian. A utility player which stood on four spindly legs.

MARIANI, LOUIS AND ANTONIO, 133 Nueva, Figueras, Gerona, Spain. Street piano agent, fl. 1903.

MARKS & HARNETT, 4 & 5 Rosoman Mews, London E.C.1. Advertised as manufacturers of 'piano organs' from 1918 to 1919. No other information has been traced on this maker.

MARQUETTE PIANO Co., 2421–2439 Wallace Street, Chicago. Makers of coin-operated pianos with percussion and orchestral effects, also photo-players.

MARSHALL & SONS, SIR HERBERT, Angelus Hall, Regent House, 233 Regent Street, London W. Makers of the Artistyle player-piano music-rolls which gave printed accenting instructions to the melody notes, to enable the performer to interpret the correct way by reading the roll as he played it. They also made player-pianos and extended the music-roll side to include the Angelus Artistyle and the Artist Song Rolls labels. Later a separate company was formed called The Artistyle Music Roll Company with premises at 204–206 Great Portland Street, London W.1. The Marshall & Rose player-piano which they produced was a good, low-priced instrument.

MASERATI, CAESAR, 92 New Chambers Street, New York, U.S.A. An Italian organ maker who also built street barrel pianos mounted on carts, which he sold and hired out. He was in business in 1906 and his colleague, Antoniazzi (q.v.), was later to establish the B.A.B. Organ Co. (q.v.).

MASTERTOUCH. Name of piano rolls currently produced by the Mastertouch Piano Roll Company, Box 157, Redfern, New South Wales, Australia.

McTAMMANY, JOHN Jr, Worcester, Massachusetts, U.S.A. An inventor who patented a number of ingenious applications of the perforated-paper roll tune sheet in 1868. He made a number of organettes but the venture was not a success and he had insufficient funds to renew his patents. These were then successfully exploited by others. He died penniless in 1915.

LIST OF PRINCIPAL MAKERS AND PATENTEES

MECHANICAL ORGUINETTE COMPANY, U.S.A. Formed to manufacture Mason J. Mathews' 'Orguinette' table reed organ which played perforated paper rolls. They then made the Aeolian player reed organ at which time they were re-formed into the Aeolian Company (q.v.).

MEL-O-DEE MUSIC CO., Meriden, Connecticut, U.S.A. A subsidiary of the Aeolian Corporation, Weber Pianos and the Pianola Company. In 1923 they were the largest music-roll producers for player-pianos in the whole of the United States and had the most modern equipment. Formerly called Universal, their piano rolls were called Mel-O-Dee.

MELOGRAPHIC ROLL CO., THE, Buffalo, New York, U.S.A. Makers of the Melographic music-roll.

MELOTO CO., London. Manufacturers of music-rolls for player-pianos, particularly 88-note rolls which had automatic pedalling control from extra marginal perforations in the paper.

MELVILLE CLARK PIANO COMPANY, Steinway Hall, 409 Steinway Building, Chicago, U.S.A. Melville Clark, a member of the Storey & Clark Company of Chicago, took out patents for his Apollo piano-player in 1899. The first Apollo played 58 notes and used a clockwork motor re-wind system for the music-roll. This cabinet-style player stood 36 inches high, was 41 inches long and 12 inches wide. Introduced in 1900, it also featured a transposing tracker-bar—one of the first. Melville Clark was probably the first to make a piano with the player mechanism inside the case, c. 1901. In 1902, he was the first to make a full-scale 88-note player action and was also the first to fit a player action into a grand piano (1904). In 1909, the Clark company was producing a player action to cater for five different sizes of rolls—58, 65, 70, 82 and 88 notes.

METROSTYLE. Music-rolls—see under AEOLIAN CO., THE.

MINA, GIOVANNI, 2 First Street, Manhattan, U.S.A. An Italian who went to America in 1880 and set up in business making barrel pianos, barrel organs and pinning carousel organ barrels. On his death, the business was taken over by G. Gazza (q.v.) and moved to 71 Roosevelt Street nearby, but the business did not prosper and soon closed.

MOJON, MANGER & CO., Bartletts Buildings, London E.C. Well-known makers of large-size musical boxes, some with dancing dolls and orchestral effects. Also made coin-freed cylinder musical-boxes and, later, mechanical harmoniums and pianos. Their factory, which produced watches and clocks as well as musical boxes, was at Chaux-de-Fonds, Geneva, and they had a branch warehouse at Oxford Terrace, Coventry. Their pianos were most probably manufactured by them in this country. John Manger is described, in a patent application of 1886 relating to musical boxes, as being a 'Musical Box Importer..

MOLA, CAV. GIUSEPPE, Via Nizza 82, Turin, Italy. Barrel piano maker, fl. 1903.

MOLINARI & SONS, G., 112 32nd Street, Brooklyn, New York, U.S.A. Produced many small barrel organs and barrel pianos for street use. The factory was started during the Civil War and for sixty years the family sustained the business, Joseph Molinari running a shop at 153 Elizabeth Street, Manhattan, where all kinds of mechanical musical instruments could be purchased.

MOLLER, H. P., Copenhagen. Makers of street barrel pianos of the smaller, portable type. A surviving specimen is in the shape of a lyre or guitar and is said to date from c. 1850.

MONDINI, VEDOVA LUIGI, Corso Vitt. Emanuele 40, Cremona, Italy. A maker of barrel pianos, fl. 1903.

MORTIER, L. Gandae A°. This name appears deeply etched, in large letters, on one of the brass side plates of a combined flute-playing and harp-playing clock in the Guinness collection. Whether this Mortier was any relation to the Belgian innkeeper who subsequently became a famed maker of show and fair organs is unknown and unlikely.

MULLER, P. A., Pau, France. Built a mechanical recorder c. 1907 and an electric piano-roll cutting machine c. 1910.

MURDOCH & CO., JOHN G. LTD, 91 & 93 Farringdon Road, London E.C. Described as 'sole licensees by Her Majesty's Royal Letters Patent' for the Celestina organette, which played perforated paper music and was patented in 1887 by A. Maxfield.

MURDOCH, MURDOCH & CO., 461 & 463 Oxford Street, London. Agents for the Phoneon cabinet-style piano player first shown in Glasgow at the Musical Trades Exhibition in 1901. They also later handled the Connoisseur instruments (q.v.).

265

NEEDHAM & SONS (later Needham Piano and Organ Co.), 96 Fifth Avenue, New York, U.S.A. Founded by Elias Parkman Needham who invented the upright action used in reed organs, which formed the basis of most organettes and player-pianos, where a perforated sheet of paper passes over the reed opening, allowing the reed to speak through air admitted through the perforations. His inventions were covered by fifteen patents which he later sold to the Mechanical Orguinette Company (q.v.). Produced the Needham Paragon piano-player.

NELSON-WIGGEN PIANO CO., 1731–1745 Belmont Avenue, Chicago. Makers of coin-operated pianos with percussion and orchestral effects, also photo-players.

NIAGRA MUSICAL INSTRUMENT COMPANY, U.S.A. Produced instruments similar to those made by the North Tonawanda Musical Instrument Works factory, which was in the same town—North Tonawanda. These included coin-freed barrel pianos.

NIXON, C. E., U.S.A. Built an interesting modern android, in the form of the reclining figure of the goddess Isis playing a zither. The full-size automaton featured an electrically-controlled zither, but the fingers actually performed on the strings.

NORTH TONAWANDA MUSICAL INSTRUMENT WORKS, North Tonawanda, New York, U.S.A. Founded in 1893 by Eugene deKleist (q.v.) as the North Tonawanda Barrel Organ Factory and incorporated in 1906 with premises at Payne Avenue, North Tonawanda, they subsequently produced a range of band organs selling from $250 to $3,000. These had pneumatic action and were played by endless-paper music. They also made coin-freed instruments including the Pianolin and the Mando Piano Orchestrina. Ultimately taken over by the Remington Rand Company, the premises continued as a fair organ manufactory until the mid-1920's. They produced the Tonophone barrel piano for Wurlitzer.

OPERATOR'S PIANO CO., 715 North Kedzie Avenue, Chicago. Makers of coin-operated pianos with percussion and orchestral effects such as the Coinola range, and the Reproduco Pipe Organ (basically a piano) photoplayer.

ORCHESTRELLE COMPANY, THE, 225 Regent Street, London W. Formed early in the 1900's, this was a British-owned, American-financed subsidiary of the American Aeolian Company. Was later known as The Aeolian Co. Ltd. By 1904, The Orchestrelle Co. was at the Aeolian Hall, 135–6–7 New Bond Street, London W., and was distributing the Pianola piano-player and the Pianola player-piano as well as the Aeolian Orchestrelle player-organs. The instruments were manufactured in America, shipped to England and assembled at the Aeolian factory at Hayes, Middlesex. The company had agents in Edinburgh (Methven, Simpson & Co.) and Glasgow (Marr, Wood & Co.). Early in 1930 the firm was dissolved, the assets being taken over by Harrods. See also AEOLIAN CO. The first address of the Orchestrelle Company was in Elm Street, off the Gray's Inn Road, London W.C. The firm produced a large number of music-rolls including the Metrostyle (which referred to the metronome or speed line printed on the roll) and Themodist (accented rolls), as well as music-rolls for the Orchestrelle and the Aeolian Reproducing Pipe Organ.

ORIGINAL-MUSIKWERKE PAUL LOCHMANN GmbH, Zeulenroda (Thüringen), Central Germany. After the Symphonion musical box success, Paul Lochmann, who had been the first to produce a practical disc-playing musical box, went to Thuringia and opened this company in about 1902. He produced a range of very fine disc musical boxes bearing the name Lochmann Original and also a disc-playing piano-orchestrion called the Original Konzert Piano.

ORPHEUS MUSIC ROLLS. See ROLL MUSIC CO.

OTTINA & PELLANDI, Casa Propria, Via Solferio 3, Milan, Italy. Established in 1884 as manufacturers of street pianos and organs and still in business in 1903.

OTTO MANUFACTURING CO., 107 Franklin Street, New York, U.S.A. A company formed in 1906 by the brothers Edmund and Gustav Otto and Ferdinand Schaub to produce a disc-playing automatic piano patented by Schaub. Schaub had been responsible for the design of the earlier Capital musical box made by the F. G. Otto Manufacturing Co., which played interchangeable conical tune-sheets.

PAIN, R. W., U.S.A. Possibly the first to build a completely self-contained 39-note pneumatic piano action in 1880. He worked for Needham & Sons and he produced for them the first 65-note electrically-operated player-piano.

PARKER, WILLIAM D., Meriden, Connecticut, U.S.A. In 1891 he took out patents for a combination manual and paper-roll operated piano, assigned to his employers, the Wilcox & White Co. He and Needham (q.v.) layed the foundations for all pneumatic actions for pianos and organs.

PASTORE, FREDERICO, Spalto Marengo 4, Alessandria, Italy. Maker of barrel pianos, fl. 1903.

PASQUALE & CO., 73 Basinghall Street, Clerkenwell, London E.C., and also 9 Phoenix Place, London W.C. Makers of barrel pianos both hand-turned and clockwork. A good maker who devised a method of incorporating the driving spring in the end of the barrels for automatic pianos.

PASQUALE & CO., GREGORI, 6 Phoenix Place, London W.C. Barrel-piano maker established in 1894–95. The other partners in the firm were Charles Romano of 6 Victoria Dwellings, Clerkwenwell Road, and Pasquale Amato, 5 Phoenix Place, Calthorpe Street, Gray's Inn Road. By 1914, the firm's address was 9 Phoenix Place, Mount Pleasant, London W.C.

PEERLESS PIANO PLAYER CO., 2 East 47th Street, New York. Also at Windsor Arcade, Fifth Avenue, New York; St Johnsville, New York; 274 Wabash Avenue, Chicago. Makers of ordinary player-pianos as well as coin-operated pianos with percussion and orchestral effects, also photoplayers.

PENNYANO. A clockwork-operated coin-freed barrel piano designed for use in public houses and marketed by Keith Prowse between 1905 and 1918.

PERFECTOR MUSIC ROLLS. Manufactured and distributed by Lockwoods, 76 & 78 City Road, London E.C., fl. 1915, 1920.

PERFORATED MUSIC CO., 197–203 City Road, London E.C. The largest firm of music-roll manufacturers in the British Isles, founded in 1903. By 1913, the annual output had risen to 300,000 rolls, a ton of paper being consumed each week in their manufacture. Rolls for almost every make of player-piano and organ were manufactured. In the early hours of March 16, 1918, the entire premises took fire and were destroyed, the insurance value being put at £48,750. For several years after that, the company continued in business in a small way at 6 St Bride Street, London E.C. At the height of their success the firm had offices at 94 Regent Street with a music-roll library at 81 Beak Street off Regent Street, London. (See Plate 61 and 62.)

PEROTTI, CAV. CARLO, Via Ormea e Galliari 41 (showroom/shop), and Via Cavova e Marocchetti (factory), Turin, Italy. Established in 1870. Large maker of barrel pianos and organs, café pianos, clockwork pianos, etc., fl. 1903.

PESARESI, LUIGI, 30 Warner Street, Clerkenwell, London E.C. Founder of the firm of Pesaresi & Son, manufacturer of barrel pianos.

PESARESI & SON, 30 Warner Street, Clerkenwell, London E.C. A small maker of street pianos, mostly 40- and 44-note tremolo clockwork and hand-cranked models who first set up business in 1898.

PESARESI & SON & SPINELLI, 8 & 9 Early Mews, Arlington Road, London N.W.1. Spinelli, formerly a partner of Rossi (q.v.) and latterly working on his own, joined Luigi Pesaresi and his son in 1930. In 1937, the firm moved to 12 Field Place, St John Street, Clerkenwell, London E.C.1, where they advertised 'piano-hire' before finally going out of business in 1941. Their names appear on many barrel pianos and they were publicised as 'patentees and makers of Symphonia autos'.

PHILLIPS & SÖHNE, J. D., Frankfurter Musikwerke Fabrik Akt.-Ges, Frankfurt a.M-West, Germany. Est. 1877. Makers of pneumatic pianos played by perforated paper rolls and also of perforated music for other types of roll-playing instrument. In 1912 devised a motor for winding two tune sheets together at once, presumably in connection with a photoplayer or orchestrion. They perfected an involved automatic tracking device in 1916 for paper rolls.

PIANISTA, 64 rue Lafayette, Paris. Company formed to exploit Forneaux's Pianista piano-player.

PIANISTA CO., THE, 56 Regent Street, London W. Founded in 1901 by Emile Klaber of the American firm of A. D. Klaber, piano makers. They developed and marketed an 'inner player' called the Pianotist which apparently worked without bellows by 'a simple friction device'. No complete instruments are known to survive.

PIANO, JULES, Rouleaux d'Armand Nallino, Nice, France. A maker of mechanical barrel pianos who specialized in large, coin-freed instruments for use in cafés. He always incorporated percussion effects.

PITCHER, WILLIAM, Stockbridge Terrace, Pimlico, London. A maker of pianos and organs which played barrels c. 1827.

PIZANO, ROQUE, 8 Cirés, Barcelona, Spain. Street-piano agent and hirer, c. 1903.

PLAYANO MFG CO., 12 Osborne Street, Cambridge, Massachusetts, U.S.A. Makers of the Playano piano-player in 1902.

POLYPHONMUSIKWERKE, Wahren, Leipzig, Germany. Produced in 1898 a disc-playing piano called the Polyphon Concerto. Using the expertise perfected in the manufacture of the Polyphon disc musical box, Paul Riessner developed the 'Concerto' which played piano sttings, drums and bells from a 32 inch diameter metal disc. See also under REGINA MUSIC BOX CO.

POMBIA, PIETRO, Borgo 2, Agabia 37, Milan, Italy. Maker of street barrel pianos and organs, fl. 1903.

POPPER & CO., Reichsstrasse 33–35, Leipzig 1. Agents for mechanical musical instruments made in Leipzig and also the German distributors for Racca (q.v.). Makers for a wide range of mechanical pianos, instruments with orchestral effects and so on. Also produced a reproducing piano called the Stella. Branches at rue Nationale 93, Antwerp; Junkernstrasse 4, Breslau, and Bahnhofstrasse 83, Essen.

PORTA, FRANCESCO, Biella, Novara, Italy. Agent for barrel street instruments, fl. 1903.

PORTO, SALVATORE DI ROS, Piazza Delle Guardie, Catania, Sicily. Barrel pianos, c. 1903.

POTTHOFF, LUDWIG, & GOLF, HILMAR, Berlin, Germany. In 1884 they perfected a barrel/keyboard piano which could be played either by hand or by hand-cranked barrel. The piano comprised normal action and the barrel was placed under the keyboard, transmitting playing movement through a series of levers and cams to a secondary key mounted above the normal manual key, thereby setting the complete piano action into motion.

POZZI & FRATELLI, FRANCESCO, Treviglio, Italy. Maker of barrel organs and barrel pianos, fl. 1903.

POZZOULI, VINCENZO, 45 Warner Street, Clerkenwell, London E.C. A maker of barrel pianos who patented, in 1906, a street piano producing a mandolin tone by using four bridges, the first being mandolin, the second piano, the third a second mandolin and the fourth a bass piano. He used hammers with hard-wood heads.

PRADO, EDUARDO, 10 Torrijos, Madrid, Spain. Maker of street pianos also operating as hirer, fl. 1903.

PRADO, THOMAS, 8 Salitre, Madrid, Spain. Maker of street pianos, fl. 1903.

PROWSE, KEITH. See KEITH PROWSE.

PROWSE, WILLIAM. A barrel piano in the Guinness collection, New York, bears the label: 'Patent William Prowse, late Keith, Prowse & Co., manufacturer, 48, Cheapside, London'. See also KEITH PROWSE.

PUGLISI, GIUSEPPE, Catania, Sicily. Established in 1820 as a maker of barrel pianos, Puglisi was the only maker of these instruments in Sicily. He also made or handled other automatic instruments. Still flourishing 1903.

Q.R.S. A famous make of American player-piano rolls, sometimes to be found in England. Roehl states that the Q.R.S. Co. had its beginnings as part of the Melville Clark Company in Chicago and DeKalb in Illinois c. 1902. The company bought up about twenty-five smaller roll companies including Voca-style, U.S., Imperial, Pianostyle, International and Angelus, and opened factories in New York, San Francisco, Toronto (Canada), Sydney (Australia) and Utrecht (Holland). During the slump resulting from the stock market slump of 1931, the firm changed hands, centralized in New York and changed its name to Imperial Industrial Company. It is still in business today.

RACCA, GIOVANNI, Via Milazzo 18, Bologna, Italy. Maker of barrel pianos, who produced some unusual grand-format pianos playing barrels and, later, folded cardboard book-music. He patented an unusual beating-hammer system for his book-music piano in conjunction with G. Seward in 1886 and the trade name for his instruments was 'Piani Melodici'. Four models were produced, ranging from four to six octaves, fully chromatic, and these mostly played serious music from beautifully-arranged scores. These were true piano-fortes, having both sustaining and soft controls. He also made a piano-orchestrion called the Verdi. His products were distributed in Germany by Popper (q.v.) and in France by Stransky Frères (q.v.). In England, Racca pianos were sold by Guldman (see illustration on page 73.)

RAMOS, MANUEL, 16 Palma Dupl., Madrid, Spain, Maker and agent for street pianos in business in 1903.

REGINA MUSIC BOX CO., Rahway, New Jersey, U.S.A. Makers of disc-playing musical boxes who produced, in about 1900, a very large mechanical disc-playing piano called the Automatic Regina Concerto. This weighed 950 lb., stood 8 feet 2 inches high, 45 inches wide and 27 inches deep. In addition to the piano, the 32 inch diameter steel disc played bells, cymbal and snare and bass drum. With its quadruple spring motor, this enormous machine changed its discs from a storage rack of ten contained in the base, in the same way that the Regina and Polyphon musical boxes changed their discs. The Regina was developed from the single-play, 32 inch disc size Polyphon produced in Leipzig. The Regina Company was an off-shoot of the Polyphonmusikwerke (q.v.) and both instruments were from the brains of Gustave Brachhausen and Paul Riessner. Also produced the Sublima Piano Junior which was a piano played using '. . . a large roll of heavy and very durable paper, the power being furnished either by Spring Motor or Electric Motor as desired'.

RICCA & SON, 881–903 Southern Boulevard and 884–904 East 134th Street, New York. A maker of piano-players, piano orchestrions and also an agent for similar instruments, fl. 1903.

RICCI, CHARLES, 21 Merlin's Place, Wilmington Square, London W.C. Also known as Carlo Ricci. Manufacturer of 'piano organs', established in 1914. In 1917, we find . . .

RICCI, CARLO, & SON, 37 Claremont Mews, Clerkenwell, London E.C. Barrel-piano makers who ceased trading in 1925.

RIEMER, BERNARD, Chrastava, Northern Bohemia. A maker of barrel organs which featured a separate drive for the barrel and the bellows, to enable music to be played at whatever speed desired, without losing wind. In 1896 his three sons, Robert, Julius and Jindrich, took over the company and made barrel organs of fine tone and attractive appearance. Then barrel pianos were produced and, after 1903, pianos played by perforated music. Their products were exported to France, Belgium, Germany, Switzerland and Russia. They also made and patented an invention called Automaton, which made mandolin music to the accompaniment of lighting effects and which was driven by an electric motor. This was allegedly a great success and sold well. They won a gold medal for automatic musical instruments at an exhibition at Usti on the Elbe. They also made some fine orchestrions at Chrastava and, later, sold radio sets and pianos.

RISSONE & CO., J. B., Poole's Buildings, Mount Pleasant, London W.C. Barrel-piano makers founded in 1902. Their clockwork or automatic pianos are frequently found with Keith Prowse motors incorporated.

ROBINO, SIMON, 59 Oldham Road, Manchester. Described as a musical-instrument maker, he took out a patent in 1906 for producing a tremolo effect on a barrel piano. In his system, bell-cranks pulled the hammer down against a rotating star wheel, to impart the beating motion. (British Patent No. 14,977, of July 2, 1906, refers).

RODRIGUES, ANTONIO, 2 S Cayetano, Madrid, Spain. Hirer of street pianos, fl. 1903.

ROENTGEN. A cabinet-maker who, c. 1700, assisted Kintzing (q.v.) in building his automaton girl which played a stringed instrument with hammers.

ROLL MUSIC CO. LTD, THE, 1 & 3 Sun Street, Finsbury Square, London E.C. Makers of the Orpheus music-rolls.

ROLLEAU, S. Nantes, France. Distributor of mechanical pianos and mechanical jazz bands. See AMELOTTI, V.

ROMANO-LAEKEN. Maker of large clockwork cafe pianos operated by coins. It is not known for certain whether this maker, certainly of Italian origin, was working in London of France, but surviving instruments appear to date from the mid- or late 'twenties. A Charles Romano was partner in the firm of Gregori PASQUALE & Co (q.v.) in the latter years of the last century.

ROSE, COOP & RISSONE LTD, 135 Regent Street, London W. (1902) and 71 Mount Pleasant, Clerkenwell, London E.C. (1905). Manufacturers of barrel pianos, who subsequently took out patents covering an action operated pneumatically from cardboard music. In 1906 the firm was making piano-players. John Rose was described as 'mechanic' and Thomas Coop as 'musician' and the secretary of the company was Reginald Albert Goodman.

ROSENER, F., Schönhauser Allee 157, Berlin N. A maker of barrel pianos who exhibited at the Melbourne Musical Industries Exhibition in April 1888.

ROSSI, Italy. Rossi returned to Italy from London where he had worked with Pasquale and also Spinelli and, c. 1920 onwards, produced an attractive range of clockwork barrel-playing café pianos which featured dulcimers as well as ordinary strings.

Rossi, N., Via S Maria 11, Turin, Italy. Maker of barrel pianos, fl. 1903.

Rossi, Pasquale & Co., 49 Warner Street, London E.C. Barrel-piano makers c. 1896. This short-lived partnership ended when Pasquale set up on his own the following year and Spinelli took his place with Rossi.

Rossi & Fils, 385 rue du Progres, Brussels, Belgium. The Belgian branch of this firm of barrel piano makers. They received Gold Medals for barrel pianos at exhibitions in 1906 and 1907.

Rossi & Spinelli, P. C., 49 Warner Street, London E.C. Makers of barrel pianos from 1897. Later, after Rossi returned to Italy c. 1919, Spinelli was in business on his own until he united with Pesaresi.

Rossi & Spinelli, 22 Baker's Row, Warner Street, London E.C. Barrel-piano makers established at this address in 1915 and remaining until 1919, when Rossi returned to Italy. They made both wooden and iron-frame barrel pianos.

Roura, Agustin, 20 Arco del Teatro, Barcelona, Spain. Street-piano agent and hirer, c. 1903.

Sächsische Revolver-Orchestrion-Fabrik F. O. Glass, Markneukirchenstrasse 160 M, Klingenthal, Germany. Manufacturers of a 'revolver' type barrel orchestrion in 1903 and also an attractive, large piano-orchestrion.

Salengo, Luigi, Pinerolo, Turin, Italy. Maker of street pianos, fl. 1903.

Salvoni, Pindaro, Cortona, Arezzo, Italy. A maker of barrel pianos, fl. 1903.

Sanchez, Antonio, 30 Abades, Madrid, Spain. Hirer of street pianos, fl. 1903.

Sandell, Henry Konrad. Born during the late 1880's in Sweden, Sandell came to Chicago, U.S.A., at the age of ten. When he was twenty-one, he took out his first patents for a coin-operated automatic violin, played electro-magnetically. He joined the Mills Novelty Company of Chicago in 1904 and for the next twenty years concentrated on the automatic violin, producing the first practical instrument in 1906 called the Violano. By 1912, he coupled his Violano to a 44-note piano and so was born the Violano-Virtuoso, which was designated one of the eight greatest inventions of the decade by the U.S. Patent Office. Roehl suggests that the Violano-Virtuoso must first have appeared in 1909. Sandell went on to develop instruments with two and three violins and then the Violano Orchestra—a separate cabinet containing percussion instruments which could be coupled to the Violano. The instrument was operated by a perforated paper roll. Next he devised the Melody Violin which was not roll-operated, but could be played like a piano from a keyboard. Sandell, who accumulated something like 300 patents for violin-playing mechanisms during his lifetime, died on January 29, 1948, at the age of seventy. A deeply religious man, he refuted claims made on his behalf that he was a genius, claiming dedication to an ideal as being his motivating force.

Sasso, Giovanni, Piazzetta del Carmine, Vercelli, Italy. Maker of barrel organs and pianos, fl. 1903.

Sawin, Mich., Domnikowskaja, Haus Tscheswiakoff, Moscow, Russia. Maker of orchestrion organs as well as church organs who also handled piano orchestrions, fl. 1903.

Schaub, Ferdinand. See under Otto Manufacturing Company.

Schmidt, Johann Gerhard Gottfried, Köpenick, Berlin, Germany. Improved on Potthoff & Golf's system for playing a piano, both manually and by a barrel mechanism and, in 1887, took out patents for a barrel action of great simplicity, wherein the barrel mechanism was called upon only to move the piano hammer when playing mechanically, instead of the complete hammer action.

Schröder, Auguste, Ackerstrasse 68a, Berlin N. A maker of mechanical pianos and organs, fl. 1903.

Schübbe & Co., Uferstrasse 5, Berlin N. Claimed to be the oldest established firm of piano-orchestrion builders as well as the largest in Berlin; they produced an instrument resembling, in appearance and specification, the American 'photoplayer' style of effects piano, controlled by mechanical means.

Schulz Company, M., Chicago, U.S.A. Manufacturers of a reproducing piano fitted with the Welte-Mignon (Licensee) action and also the Aria Divina action.

Scialanti, Alessandro, Piazza Principessa Margherita 161, Rome, Italy. A maker of fair organs, c. 1910, who also made barrel-operated street pianos.

Seeburg Piano Co., J. P., Seeburg Building, 419 W. Erie Street, Chicago. Makers of coin-operated pianos with percussion and orchestral effects, also photoplayers.

SEYBOLD, Strassburg-Meinau. A modern maker of mechanical musical instruments for amusement arcades and cafés. Built Piano-Accordion-Jazz which comprised a piano, accordion and timpani, and which was played by perforated-paper roll music giving 42 notes for both piano and accordion from an 8 inch wide roll.

SEYTRE, CLAUDE FELIX, Lyons, France. In 1842, he patented a system of perforated cardboard strips, on the Jacquard principle, for the automatic playing of mechanical musical instruments and he built an instrument called the Autophone.

SIMPLEX PIANO PLAYER CO. Company formed by Theodore P. Brown (q.v.).

SMEETZ, P., 10 place du Concordat, Curchem, Brussels. Agent for orchestrions, barrel organs and barrel pianos, c. 1903.

SMIDT & CO., ED., Georgstrass 48, Hannover, Germany. Maker of piano orchestrions, who was in business in 1903.

SMITH, BARNES & STROHBER CO. Division of the Continental Piano Company of Chicago. Makers of Chicago Electric Pianos, which were fitted with xylophone and mandolin accompaniments. Made keyless as well as dual manual/pneumatic models.

SOCIETA ITALIANA PER GLI ORGANO A CILINDRO, Via Torniolli 285, Milan, Italy. This name, associated with street barrel organs and pianos c. 1903, is probably that of an agent or distributor rather than a maker or repairer.

SOLÉ, JOSÉ, 18, 21 y 23 Arco del Teatro, Barcelona, Spain. Street-piano agent and hirer, fl. 1903.

SPAETHE, WILHELM, Gera, Reuss, Germany. Spaethe made player-pianos and organs and was also president of the mechanical musical-instrument makers' society, formed in Leipzig to fight the restrictions of the old German musical copyright laws governing music-rolls. Opened a London office at 7 Victoria Avenue, Bishopsgate Street Without.

SPERANZA, FRATELLI, Vico 2, Montesanto, Italy. A maker of barrel pianos, fl. 1903.

SPINELLI, LORETO, 49 Warner Street, London E.C. Barrel-piano maker who was variously associated with Pesaresi (q.v.) and Rossi (q.v.). By 1926 his address was 40 Hollingsworth Street, Barnsbury, London N.7, and he advertised as 'maker of automatic pianos'. He made barrel pianos until 1930, by which time he had united with Pesaresi.

STANDARD PLAYER ACTION COMPANY, 638–650 West 52nd Street, New York, U.S.A. Makers of the famous Standard Player Action used by manufacturers of many player-pianos both here and in America. The action could also be fitted into most existing pianos.

STANGALINI, ANGELO, Via Gal. Ferreris 16, Vercelli, Italy. Maker of miniature barrel pianos, fl. 1903.

STANGALINI, GIUSEPPE, Milan, Italy. Exhibited two barrel pianos at the National Exhibition held in Turin in the summer of 1884.

STEENBEKKEN, FELIX. Maker of mechanical pianos c. 1890–1900. An instrument in a private collection in France has drum, cymbals, castanets and xylophone accompaniment.

STERNBERG-ARMIN ès TESTV-RE Budapest, Hungary. This firm was a general agent and distributor for the Piano Melodici. The name has been seen deeply engraved on the hinged front fall of a 30-note instrument. See also RACCA.

STEUER, WILHELM, Warschauerstrasse 18, Berlin O. Maker of piano-orchestrions, c. 1903.

STOCEK, H., Trutnov, Bohemia. Manufactured an electrically-operated player-piano with bell and drum accompaniment c. 1920.

STRANSKY FRERES, 20 rue de Paradis, Paris. Main agent for Racca mechanical pianos (q.v.) and other similar instruments including the Autopianiste mechanical player, fl. 1903.

STRÁNSKÝ, Vienna. In 1911, this firm manufactured a player-piano with three violins in one cabinet. Each violin had only one or two strings and they were mounted within the limits of a rotating horsehair bow, similar to the system used by Hupfeld in the Dea-Violina. The action of both piano and violins was pneumatically controlled from a paper roll.

STYCHA, J., Prague. Produced a barrel-operated 'piano orchestrion' c. 1890.

SYMANSKI & SÖHNE, Chlodna 34, Warsaw, Poland. A manufacturer of street and fair organs who also built barrel pianos.

TAGLIABUE, GIUSEPPE, Via Sambuco 15, Milan, Italy. A maker of 'barrel keyboard instruments', fl. 1903.

TAYLOR, SAMUEL, Bristol. A cylinder piano in the F. F. Hill collection bears a label reading: 'Samuel Taylor, Musical Instrument Maker, No. 26, Host Street, next to Colston's School, St. Augustine's Place, Bristol. Manufacturers of Barrel Organs and Cylinder Pianofortes. N.B. County Orders punctually attended to'. *Mathews Directory* for 1854 and 1855 lists S. Taylor at 27, St. Augustine's Place and describes him as an organ and pianoforte maker. In the Bristol rate books for 1855–57 he is listed under Host Street but without a number.

TAYLOR, THOMAS, Sheffield. A cylinder piano with this name and inscribed 'Maker, No. 79' (no doubt the serial number of the instrument) and also bearing on the pleated silk front the Royal Arms in brass, exists in the F. G. Turner & Son collection at Horsham. It is likely that this maker was related to the Bristol family but has not been corroborated.

TAYLOR, WILLIAM, Bristol. A cylinder piano in the G. Planus collection bears a label reading: 'William Taylor, 57, Broad Quay, Bristol. Manufacturer of Cylinder or Handle Piano-Fortes and Organs. Extra cylinders set to Piano-Fortes, Organs and Musical Clocks—Old Ones re-set. Harps and Piano-Fortes Tuned and Repaired'. A barrel organ of the same outward appearance and case design was recently rebuilt by the Author. *Mathews Directory* for 1837 lists William Taylor as a musical instrument maker of 69, Stokes Croft at which address he remained until 1840. In the 1841 Directory he is listed as 'musical instrument maker and nautical stationer' at 57, Broad Quay where he lived until his death at the early age of 39. He was buried on December 10th 1847. His home was continued in the name of Ruth Taylor but her precise relationship is unknown.

TAYLOR, W. F., Bristol. A cylinder piano dated 1848 in the F. F. Hill collection bears a label reading 'W. F. Taylor, Musical Instrument Maker, No. 57, Broad Quay, Bristol'. The classified Bristol trades directory lists W. F. Taylor at this address as a musical instrument maker. He was contemporary with S. Taylor but is also listed elsewhere in the same directory as a music teacher. Whether W. F. is the same as William or was brother or father to the latter is not certain. The Taylors were a large family, it seems, with various members in the profession of music in one aspect or another. All Taylor-named cylinder pianos closely resemble the Hicks pattern and it could be conjectured that the Taylors, like Distin, may at some time have worked under Hicks.

TEL-ELECTRIC COMPANY, 12 West 33rd Street, N.W., New York, U.S.A. In 1914 they produced a remarkable electrically-operated player-piano called the Telektra which operated from a completely remote roll-box with controls. This box could be sited anywhere in a room, connection to the piano being by electric cable. The action was extremely simple, being entirely electro-magnetic controlled by the tips of metal fingers making contact through slots in a brass music-roll. (See Plate 63.)

TESTE, J. A., Nantes, France. A mid-nineteenth century instrument maker, who invented the Cartonium which had forty-two free metal reeds and played music from perforated Jacquard-type cards. Patented in 1861, it incorporated a device which could also cut cards for the instrument to play.

THEMODIST. Music-rolls—see under AEOLIAN CO., THE.

THIBOUVILLE-LAMY, JEROME, 68, 68bis & 70 rue Reaumur, Paris, France, and 10 Charterhouse Street, Holborn Circus, London. Old established musical instrument manufacturers, who were makers of musical boxes of the cylinder-playing type from about 1865 onwards and, later, were agents for makes other than their own. In 1884 they advertised two devices. One was the Pianista described as 'an apparatus which can be placed before any piano or organ to perform songs, dances, operatic and sacred music mechanically with the greatest exactitude of expression by means of perforated cardboards'. This instrument, of the push-up player style, played book music by turning a handle. Felt-covered fingers played the piano keys pneumatically, there being a bellow system operated by foot treadles. This device, although superceded by paper-roll music, was still being advertised in 1905. At the same time was offered the Organina Thibouville which 'possesses the tone of a harmonium' and won two gold medals at the International Exhibition of 1885. This again played perforated 'cardboards'. The firm also manufactured barrel organs for street use and, in 1890, they produced reed organs playing Gavioli's design of book-music which they called the Organophone Expressif, and another smaller device called the Coelophone. Their American office was at 15 Great Jones Street, New York.

TOMASSO, A., & SON, 17 Colne Road, Winchmore Hill, London N.21. Clockwork and street barrel-piano manufacturers still in business (1966) repairing and hiring out street pianos at 4a The Broadway, Palmers Green, London N.14. In 1936 the firm was at 18½ Douglas Place, Clerkenwell, London E.C., from where they advertised as repairers of 'automatics' (clockwork barrel pianos).

TOMASSO, EMILIO, 69 Cherry Street, New York City, U.S.A. Barrel-piano manufacturer who advertised himself on his instruments as 'successor to Cesare Maserati & Co., Mechanical Organ Manufacturer'.

TOMASSO, ERNESTO, 1 St Mary's Lane, Quarry Hill, Leeds, Yorkshire. Barrel-piano maker related to Antonio Tomasso who, with his brother, Benedetto, took out patents in 1908 for a tremolo device employing a rotating shaft having four concave flutings.

TOMASSO & PHILLIPO, A., 5a Baker's Row, Clerkenwell, London E.C. Antonio Tomasso, Luigi Vincenzo Tomasso was born in 1862 at Cassino and was brought to England in 1867 with his sister, Niccolina (aged seven), and brother, Antonio (aged three). He became a street musician playing the concertina at the age of eight and, from 1876 until 1882, he was apprenticed to Chiappa making barrel organs and pianos at their Clerkenwell factory. In 1882 he started his own factory making these instruments at Baker's Row. His brother Antonio worked for him. In 1883 he married Domenica Capaldi and, in 1889 at the age of twenty-seven, he started a factory at 1 St Mary's Lane, Leeds 9. The Clerkenwell factory was continued by his brother, Antonio. There was also a factory at Pea Street, Glasgow (1892–93). There were now five sons, all of whom worked in the trade. Although clockwork pianos were made in large numbers, they also produced hand-operated street pianos on carts, and these may frequently be found with a tremolo arrangement on the treble strings as well as travelling picture fronts. Later, electric player-pianos were built. Luigi Vincenzo Tomasso died on Good Friday, 1944, at the age of eighty-two, and all the pianos which had been hired out were sold by auction excepting one which still remains with the family (details from Keith Harding).

TREMAINE, WILLIAM B. Born in 1840, he entered the piano business in America (relates Dolge) in 1868, organizing the Mechanical Orguinette Company in 1876 to market Mason J. Mathews' paper-playing reed organ or Orguinette. In 1883 he acquired the Aeolian Organ Co. and in 1888 the patents and stock in trade of the Automatic Music Paper Company of Boston, Mass. He then established the Aeolian Organ and Music Co. making automatic organs and music-rolls. In 1892 he purchased all the patents of the Munroe Organ Reed Company of Worcester, Mass., and in 1885 introduced the Aeriol self-playing piano. He was succeeded as President of the Aeolian Company in 1899 by his son, H. B. Tremaine, who was also President of the Weber Piano Company. The groundwork of the Tremaines did a great deal to foster the player-piano industry and the ascension of the Aeolian Company, which went from strength to strength, was due entirely to the foresight of William B. Tremaine at a time when there was neither encouragement nor demand for such instruments. He appreciated the power of money, buying not only the patents he needed to put his company in the forefront, but also the best brains such as Kelly, Pain, Votey and others. See also AEOLIAN COMPANY, THE.

TURCONI, JOSEPH, Galata, rue Camondo 11, Constantinople, Turkey. Maker of street pianos who was in business in 1903. Exhibited a barrel piano at the National Exhibition, Turin, summer 1884.

ULLMAN, CHARLES & JACQUES, Paris, Ste Croix (Switzerland) and London. Makers of musical boxes and also the Piano Executant Artiste, a 54-note book-music piano. Charles Ullman also founded the Société du Zonophone.

UNGER, J. F. Invented mechanisms for recording pieces of music for mechanical instruments, using a keyboard and pens on a paper strip (melography) in 1752.

UNIVERSAL. Music-rolls produced in America at Meriden, Connecticut. Later became part of the Mel-O-Dee Music Co., a subsidiary of the Aeolian Co.

UNIVERSAL MUSIC CO. LTD, Hayes, Middlesex. Makers of the Meloto Full-Scale player-piano music-rolls.

UP-TO-DATE MUSIC ROLL CO., King Street, Hammersmith, London. By 1934, this firm, which manu-factured player-piano rolls including those for the Harper Electric Piano with percussion effects, had moved to 4 Leysfield Road, London W.12, at which premises they remained until 1938 when they moved to Netherwood Place, Netherwood Road, W.14. In 1947 they changed their name to the Music Roll Co., finally going out of business in 1949.

VALENTE, ANTHONY, 42 Thompson Street, Oldham Road, Manchester. In 1885 he advertised himself as 'mechanical organ maker' although this was barrel organ or barrel piano ('piano-organ') is unknown.

VAN ROY, PIERRE PAUL, Aalst. Maker of large clockwork barrel pianos.

VANROY, P., Hamburg, Germany. Barrel-piano makers who built large orchestrion-type instruments with percussion effects.

VARETTO BROTHERS, 17 Milton Street, Lower Broughton, Manchester. Described as organ-builders and repairers, they were agents for Chiappa music books and fair organs. They also specialized in the repair of street and fair organs, pianos, etc. A German street organ has been seen bearing the above address and the date August 1931. They were finally bought out by Chiappa.

VARETTO, PETER, 87 Oldham Road, Manchester. Described as a mechanical organ maker in 1885, he was also a repairer of street pianos.

VARETTO, PIETRO, 14 Warner Street, London E.C. A maker of barrel pianos who advertised as such in the London Directory for 1881. Most probably connected with, if not the same as, the 'Pietro' (Peter) Varetto later in Manchester.

VELA, BENITO, Pueblo Español, Barcelona, Spain. Makers of modern miniature barrel pianos, which are more novelties than practical street instruments. These are mounted on detachable dog-carts with shafts and the whole is gaily painted. Termed *pianos a Manubrio*, these have iron frames and are well-made using modern materials and methods such as nylon bushes and moulded parts. They have 32 notes, two clapper blocks and a triangle.

VERBEECK & SON, J., 85 Barnsbury Road, London N.1, and 79 Copenhagen Street, London N.1. Advertised as makers of mechanical organs, Verbeeck was an organ-builder by trade. He sold book music for both fair organs and book-playing pianos between the years 1924 and 1942 when he ceased trading.

VERBEECK, PIERRE, 109 Duinstraat, Antwerp, Belgium. Fair, band and street organ maker. At the outbreak of the 1914–18 war he came to England as a refuge and opened a fair organ factory in Birmingham, selling also book music for both fair organs and book-playing pianos. He advertised as a maker of mechanical organs. In 1924, he moved to 85 Barnsbury Road, London (see VERBEECK & SON), finally selling out to Chiappa in 1942. He died about 1954.

VIAZANNI, Clerkenwell, London E.C. An Italian who used to do maintenance and repair work on organs and, in particular, Imhof & Mukle orchestrions. He is likely to have been associated with the repair of barrel pianos as well.

VICTORIA-MUSIKWERKE TISMAR & BURR, Anklamerstrasse 32, Berlin N. Founded by Berthold Tismar and Willy Burr, this firm produced an electro-magnetic piano-orchestrion in the early part of this century.

VIETTI, PIETRO, Via Madama Cristina 18, Turin, Italy. Maker of barrel pianos, in business in 1903.

VILLA, LUIGI, 18 Granville Square, Farringdon Road, London E.C. Manufacturer of automatic barrel pianos, who patented in 1903 a method of displaying advertisements in the front fall of a street piano. The front fall had a glass central panel and a system of levers and linkages converted the continuous rotary movement of the barrel into an intermittent motion to display signs in the window.

DA VINCI, LEONARDO, Italy. 1690–1730. Built a mechanical spinet with drum.

VIORA, MICHELE, Pinerolo, Turin, Italy. Maker of fair organs and street pianos.

VITTORE, Vicola Consolata 3, Turin, Italy. Maker of barrel pianos, fl. 1903.

VOSGIEN, LUIGI, Fuori Porta Milano, Strada per Pernate 121, Milan, Italy. Advertised as 'successor to L. Colombo', was maker of street barrel pianos, fl. 1903.

VOTEY, E. S. A builder of reed organs, he owned the Votey Organ Company in America and is usually credited with being the inventor of the Pianola piano-player. He and his firm were bought out by W. B. Tremaine and were assimilated into the wealth of brains behind the Aeolian Co.

WALLIS, JOSEPH, 133 & 135 Euston Road, London N.W. A maker of mechanical pianos who, in 1876, was classified in the London Trade Directory as a maker of 'street and saloon' pianos.

WARNIES, LEON, Amsterdam, Holland. In 1875 he started renting out street organs and pianos which he repaired and maintained. He died in 1902 but his widow continued the business until competition from the phonograph forced closure.

WAUTERS, PROFESSOR, Binghamton, New York, U.S.A. Worked for the Automatic Musical Company of Binghamton, which produced self-playing banjos and xylophones playing paper rolls. The firm ultimately became the Link Piano Co. making coin-operated paper-roll playing, keyless café pianos. Professor Wauters produced a self-playing violin for the company in 1907. Pneumatically operated, the instrument took seven years to develop and played special 65-note music-rolls.

WEBB, C. F. Collaborator with H. C. Coldman in the design and development of the Boyd Pistonola player-piano. See under BOYD.

WEBER, GEBR. G.m.b.H., Waldkirch im Breisgau, Baden, Germany. Makers of orchestrion organs, who also produced mechanical pianos and piano-orchestrions such as the Unika, the Grandezza and the Brabo which were basically roll-playing pianos with mandolin, xylophone, string-toned organ pipes and timpani accompaniment.

WEGENER, J., Leipzig, Germany. Built mechanical virginal in 1619 which played three tunes on a barrel and had moving figures. The instrument is now preserved in the Paris Conservatoire.

WEIGEL, C. H., Reichstrasse 30–31, Leipzig 10, Germany. Makers of mechanical musical instruments, who were also agents for Symphonion and Adler disc musical boxes, piano orchestrions and electric orchestrion pianos.

WEISSER, AMBROSIUS, Unterkirnach, Baden, Germany. Formerly the firm of Hubert Blessing established in 1849, this firm made orchestrion organs and also, at the beginning of this century, piano-orchestrions.

WELTE ARTISTIC PLAYER PIANO CO., THE, 18 East 17th Street, New York, U.S.A., and later 398 Fifth Avenue. Marketed the Welte-Mignon keyless reproducing piano c. 1907.

WELTE, EDWIN, New York, U.S.A. Grandson of Michael Welte Snr, founder of the Freiburg (Germany) firm of orchestrion organ builders, and son of Emil Welte who founded the American Welte company in 1865, Edwin invented the reproducing piano action with his brother-in-law, Karl Bockish, in whose name many patents were taken out. Their invention was the forerunner of the Welte-Mignon reproducing piano which first appeared on the market in 1904.

WELTE, EMIL. Eldest son of Michael Welte Snr, he took out the first patents for 'the use of paper music-rolls in connection with a pneumatic action' in 1887. This was to replace the expensive and cumbersome organ barrel with its accompanying paraphernalia and limited repretoire. His work opened up the way to the player-piano.

WELTE & SÖHNE, M., Freiburg, Germany, and 273 Fifth Avenue, New York, U.S.A. Founded by Michael Welte Snr at Vohrenbach and established in Freiburg in 1872, the firm became world famous for its orchestrion organs and later for the invention of the Welte-Mignon, the first reproducing piano, which was called the Phonola. The perforated paper roll/pneumatic system was then applied to their orchestrions and the Welte Philharmonic Autograph Organ, a full reproducing pipe organ. The firm produced a fantastic assortment of mechanical musical instruments incorporating pneumatic action and paper music-rolls, including 'motion picture and cabaret midget orchestra', Brass Band Orchestrion and Concert Orchestrion.

WILCOX & WHITE CO., Meriden, Connecticut, U.S.A. Also had salesrooms at 146 Fifth Avenue, New York. Organ makers who, in 1897, produced the Angelus Orchestral push-up piano-player, the invention of one of their employees, William D. Parker (q.v.). The Angelus was not only a playing device, but had its own set of reeds to accompany the piano automatically. This 58-note player could thus be used on its own as a solo instrument, or accompany itself on the piano, or play the piano 'solo'. A number of different Angelus models were made, some of which were ordinary piano-players. They also produced the Symphony, a large roll-playing reed organ similar to the small suction model Aeolian Orchestrelles.

WILDBREDT, ERNST, Grosse Frankfurterstrasse 44, Berlin N. Manufacturers of electrically-operated pneumatic-action pianos and piano-orchestrions as well as ordinary player-pianos. Made instruments with flute and percussion effects. Patented automatic roll re-winding. Fl. 1908.

WINKEL, DIETRICH NICHOLAS. A Dutchman who was born in 1780 and who invented the metronome, which he showed to Beethoven's friend, J. N. Maelzel, in Amsterdam in 1815. Maelzel promptly copied it and put it into production, taking full credit. Winkle built a mechanical organ called the Componium in 1821, which could compose an almost endless set of variations from a theme presented to it. The instrument is preserved in the Royal Conservatoire, Paris. Winkel died in poverty in 1826.

WINTLE, CANON A. O., East Anglian Automatic Piano Company, The Piano Works, Old Rectory, Lawshall, nr Bury St Edmunds, Suffolk. During the agricultural depression following the First World War, Canon Wintle provided employment for many men home from the war in the repair and renovation of barrel pianos. No pianos were actually manufactured, but old ones were restored and tuned and new barrels made and pinned. The instruments were then sold or hired out to charitable organizations. The name of the original maker was almost always obliterated and the name of the Company marked in place. The barrels were all stamped before pinning with an oval, blue rubber stamp. Canon Wintle died in 1959 and the firm closed, all remaining stock being sold or destroyed.

WRIGHT & HOLMES BROTHERS, Forest Street, Rochdale Road, Manchester. Describing themselves as 'mechanical organ builders and repairers', this firm flourished between the two wars and a fairground barrel organ has been seen with a re-pinned barrel bearing the date 1929, written before the barrel paper was pinned. They probably serviced street barrel pianos as well.

WURLITZER, FRANZ RUDOLPH, Schöneck, Germany. Went to America in 1853 at the age of twenty-two and opened a factory in Cincinatti in 1861, to manufacture military band instruments. Later he undertook selling coin-freed Regina disc-playing musical boxes. He was joined by his three sons, Howard E., Rudolph H. and Farny R. They began by making military band organs in 1907–9. Wurlitzer commissioned the first coin-freed electric player-piano—a 10-tune barrel instrument—from deKleist, which firm he subsequently bought up in 1908 (see North Tonawanda Musical Instrument Works). He made extensive use of electric, electro-magnetic and pneumatic action, paper-roll actuated, for a wide variety of mechanical instruments. The company had warehouses in Cincinatti, Chicago and New York as well as a large factory at North Tonawanda, New York, where the firm still exists.

ZIMMERMANN, JULES HEINRICH, Leipzig, Germany. Manufacturer of the Fortuna disc-playing musical boxes, small portable barrel organs and street pianos. Exhibited an electric piano at the Crystal Palace in 1900.

ZYOB, A. Said by Chapuis to have built a book-playing piano in 1842.

APPENDIX

Some Serial Numbers of Player Pianos

THE following is a list of piano serial numbers given under the name of the maker. This list refers only to the more common types of instrument which the collector may find, and the serial numbers are those relating to the years during which that maker may have produced player-pianos.

Always check the make of a piano by the name cast into the iron frame and do not rely on the name on the fallboard—this may have been altered at some time. The name and number usually appears on upright pianos at the top right-hand side of the piano frame and is visible by the lifting of the piano top. Grand pianos display name and serial number cast into the iron frame, again on the right-hand side. Raise the lid to find this. The author offers grateful acknowledgement to *Michel's Piano Atlas* (by N. E. Michel, U.S.A.).

AEOLIAN-WEBER PIANO CO. and PIANOLA CO. (Worcester, Massachusetts, U.S.A.)

1903— 1900	1911—27000	1919—59000	1927—82000
1904— 3000	1912—31000	1920—63000	1928—85000
1905— 5400	1913—35000	1921—67000	1929—88000
1906— 9000	1914—39000	1922—70000	1930—91000
1907—12000	1915—43000	1923—73000	1931—94000
1908—15000	1916—47000	1924—76000	1932—97000
1909—19000	1917—51000	1925—78000	1933—98000
1910—23000	1918—55000	1926—80000	

ALLISON PIANOS LTD. (50 New Bond Street, London W.1)

1910—38000	1917—43600	1924—48400	1931—52500
1911—39800	1918—44400	1925—49200	1932—53000
1912—40600	1919—45200	1926—49800	1933—53400
1913—41000	1920—46000	1927—50200	1934—53800
1914—41600	1921—46600	1928—50800	
1915—42000	1922—47200	1929—51200	
1916—42800	1923—47800	1930—52000	

AMPICO (AMERICAN PIANO CO., East Rochester, New York)

1920—81000	1923—84900	1926—88800	1929—93700
1921—82900	1924—86600	1927—89600	1930—94000
1922—83900	1925—87800	1928—91500	1931—97000

APOLLO PIANO CO. (Dekalb, Illinois, U.S.A.—successors to Melville Clark Piano Co.)

1903— 5700	1911—17800	1919—36000	1927—80000
1904— 7000	1912—19600	1920—40000	1928—87000
1905— 8700	1913—22000	1921—45000	1929—95000
1906—10000	1914—23200	1922—49000	1930—106000
1907—11500	1915—24400	1923—53000	1931—112000
1908—13000	1916—26800	1924—58000	1932—118000
1909—14500	1917—29000	1925—63000	1933—126000
1910—16000	1918—32800	1926—77000	1934—130000

AUTO PIANO CO. (New York)

1904— 36000	1910— 75000	1916—112000	1922—155000
1905— 45000	1911— 85000	1917—118000	1923—165000
1906— 52000	1912— 89000	1918—125000	1924—185000
1907— 56000	1913— 98000	1919—133000	1925—195000
1908— 60000	1914—105000	1920—137000	1926—205000
1909— 66000	1915—108000	1921—145000	

BENTLEY PIANO CO. (Woodchester, Gloucestershire—made by STROUD)

1919— 3400	1923—13000	1927—25200	1931—32900
1920—10000	1924—15800	1928—27300	1932—34700
1921—10800	1925—18500	1929—29200	1933—36300
1922—11800	1926—21800	1930—31300	1934—38400

BERRY, NATHANIEL & SONS (15a The Grove, Crouch End, London)

1907—11004	1915—13743	1923—19057	1931—28253
1908—11246	1916—14265	1924—19945	1932—29229
1909—11467	1917—14860	1925—20684	1933—30153
1910—12159	1918—16000	1926—21713	1934—31547
1911—12437	1919—16460	1927—22638	1935—32977
1912—12676	1920—17000	1928—24159	
1913—12865	1921—17865	1929—25598	
1914—13347	1922—18272	1930—26699	

BIESE, W. (Weigand, Vier 18, Berlin)

1912—22300	1917—24000	1922—26000	1927—27000
1913—22400	1918—24500	1923—26100	1928—28000
1914—22600	1919—25000	1924—26200	
1915—23000	1920—25300	1925—26400	
1916—23500	1921—25600	1926—26700	

BLUTHNER, JULIUS (Friedrich—Ebertstrasse 69, Leipzig)

1912— 87000	1918— 97000	1924—107000	1930—115000
1913— 90000	1919— 98000	1925—109000	1931—115500
1914— 93000	1920—100000	1926—111000	1932—116000
1915— 94000	1921—101500	1927—112000	
1916— 95000	1922—103000	1928—113000	
1917— 96000	1923—105000	1929—114000	

BORD, A. (1 Rue François, Paris—Made by PLEYEL)

1920—129100	1924—131000	1928—133000	1931—134800
1921—129500	1925—131500	1929—133500	1932—135300
1922—130000	1926—132000	1930—134100	
1923—130500	1927—132500		

BOSENDORFER, L. (Canduagass 4, Vienna, Austria)

1914—21100	1920—22530	1926—24160	1932—25530
1915—21370	1921—22800	1927—24490	1933—25560
1916—21660	1922—23060	1928—24850	1934—25600
1917—21870	1923—23300	1929—25120	1935—25700
1918—22070	1924—23580	1930—25350	
1919—22330	1925—23880	1931—25470	

CECELIAN (made by FARRAND in Holland, Michigan, U.S.A.)

1908— 5000	1913—13000	1918—23000	1923—33000
1909— 6500	1914—15000	1919—25000	1924—35000
1910— 8000	1915—17000	1920—27000	
1911— 9500	1916—19000	1921—29900	
1912—11000	1917—21000	1922—31000	

CHALLEN PIANOS, CHARLES H. (Omega Works, Hermitage Road, Finsbury Park, London N.4)

1908—30423	1915—33778	1923—36630	1930—43205
1909—30852	1916—34170	1924—37761	1931—45346
1910—31309	1917—34675	1925—38152	1932—47684
1911—31842	1918—35362	1926—38608	1933—49673
1912—32356	1920—35814	1927—39060	1934—52424
1913—32767	1921—36167	1928—39885	
1914—33522	1922—36280	1929—41306	

CHAPPELL PIANO CO. (50 New Bond Street, London W.1)

1916—59000	1921—66000	1926—71400	1931—75800
1917—60500	1922—67000	1927—72300	1932—76400
1918—62000	1923—68000	1928—73200	1933—77200
1919—63500	1924—69000	1929—74100	1935—77600
1920—65000	1925—70500	1930—75250	1936—78400

CHICKERING & SONS (Chickering Hall, Fifth Avenue & 18th Street, New York)

1911—117200	1916—126000	1921—133400	1926—141600
1912—120000	1917—127500	1922—134400	1927—143900
1913—121000	1918—128500	1923—137500	1928—145400
1914—122500	1919—130000	1924—137600	1929—147700
1915—124000	1920—132500	1925—139700	1930—148400

COLLARD & COLLARD (50 New Bond Street, London W.1)

1917—185220	1921—188080	1925—190630	1929—192850
1918—186360	1922—188580	1926—191390	1930—193320
1919—186980	1923—189010	1927—191805	1931—193580
1920—187505	1924—189960	1928—192310	

DANEMANN, W. & CO. LTD. (Northampton Street, Essex Road, London N.1)

1918—38300	1922—39900	1926—43000	1930—45400
1919—38700	1923—40600	1927—43500	1931—46000
1920—39100	1924—41500	1928—44000	1932—47000
1921—39300	1925—42500	1929—44600	

ERARD (or GAVEAU-ERARD) (45–47 Rue de la Boétie, Paris)

1912—101200	1917—106500	1922—110000	1927—116300
1913—103000	1918—107000	1923—111000	1928—117600
1914—105000	1919—107500	1924—112500	1929—118900
1915—105500	1920—108000	1925—113800	1930—120000
1916—106000	1921—109000	1926—115000	

FARRAND (U.S.A.)

1910—61000	1920—73000	1928—81000
1915—68000	1925—79000	

GROTRIAN-STEINWEG (Simmerstrasse 24, Braunschweig, Germany)

1912—28150	1918—35069	1924—47337	1930—61235
1913—30169	1919—36390	1925—50250	1931—61903
1914—31541	1920—38076	1926—52506	1932—62268
1915—32100	1921—39802	1927—55788	
1916—33162	1922—42075	1928—58238	
1917—34134	1923—44698	1929—60121	

GULBRANSEN CO. (2050 Ruby Street, Melrose Park, Illinois, U.S.A.)

1915— 90000	1920—140000	1925—218000	1930—301000
1916—101000	1921—150000	1926—240000	1931—303000
1917—110000	1922—165000	1927—265000	1932—304500
1918—120000	1923—182000	1928—282000	
1919—130000	1924—195000	1929—300000	

HARDMAN-PECK & CO. (33 West 57th Street, New York, U.S.A.)

1906—60000	1913—73500	1920—86000	1928—93400
1907—61500	1914—75000	1921—88000	1929—94000
1908—63000	1915—77200	1922—89300	1930—94200
1909—65400	1916—78900	1923—90000	1931—94600
1910—68100	1917—81000	1924—91000	1932—94700
1911—70000	1918—82500	1925—91500	
1912—72000	1919—84000	1927—92700	

HOPKINSON (Paxton Piano Works, Paxton Road, London N.17) (See also ROGERS, GEORGE & SON)

1912—66000	1918—70800	1924—75000	1930—80400
1913—67000	1919—71600	1925—75800	1931—81200
1914—68000	1920—72400	1926—76400	1932—82100
1915—68800	1921—73000	1927—77200	
1916—69600	1922—73700	1928—78900	
1917—70200	1923—74600	1929—79750	

KIRKMAN & CO. (50 New Bond Street, London W.1) (Associated with COLLARD & COLLARD)

1924—49020	1926—49050	1928—49064	1930—52100
1925—49030	1927—49060	1929—49070	

KNABE & CO. (Baltimore, U.S.A.)

1912— 72000	1918— 84000	1924— 95000	1930—107300
1913— 74000	1919— 86000	1925— 97400	1931—108200
1914— 76000	1920— 88000	1926— 99600	1932—109000
1915— 78000	1921— 90000	1927—102000	
1916— 79000	1922— 92800	1928—104400	
1917— 82000	1923— 93900	1929—106100	

KOHLER & CAMPBELL (401–425 East 163rd Street, New York, U.S.A.)

1910—116000	1916—179000	1922—215000	1928—258000
1911—127000	1917—190000	1923—223000	1929—264000
1912—137000	1918—198000	1924—230000	1930—266000
1913—150000	1919—203000	1925—237000	1931—267000
1914—155000	1920—206000	1926—240000	1932—268000
1915—165000	1921—210000	1927—250000	

LABROUSSE PIANOS (33 Rue de Rivoli, Paris)

1910— 7700	1918— 9000	1923—11000	1928—14000
1911— 8000	1919— 9500	1924—11800	1929—14500
1912— 8300	1920— 9800	1925—12500	1930—15000
1913— 8500	1921—10100	1926—13000	1931—15500
1914— 8800	1922—10500	1927—13500	1932—16000

MARSHALL & ROSE (SIR HERBERT MARSHALL CO., Conduit Street, London W.1)

1910— 700	1918— 2400	1925—24100	1932—32000
1913— 1200	1920— 3200	1928—28000	1935—35000
1915— 1800	1923— 3700	1930—30000	

MELVILLE CLARK CO. (Grand Haven, Michigan, U.S.A.)

1901— 2075	1909—14500	1917—29000	1925—63000
1902— 4000	1910—16000	1918—32800	1926—77700
1903— 5700	1911—17800	1919—36000	1927—80000
1904— 7000	1912—19600	1920—40000	1928—93000
1905— 8700	1913—22000	1921—45000	1929—112000
1906—10000	1914—23200	1922—49000	1930—118000
1907—11500	1915—24400	1923—53000	1931—126000
1908—13000	1916—26800	1924—58000	

MONINGTON & WESTON LTD. (Piercefield Street, Malden Road, London N.W.5)

1915—41234	1925—44900	1935—56200
1920—43101	1930—49100	

NIENDORF, GEBR. (Luckenwald, Germany)

1920—18500	1923—22000	1926—26300	1929—31000
1921—19500	1924—23100	1927—28200	1932—34500
1922—20700	1925—24700		

PIANOLA (AEOLIAN CO.)

1904— 3000	1911—27000	1918—55000	1925—78000
1905— 5400	1912—31000	1919—59000	NEW SERIES
1906— 9000	1913—35000	1920—63000	1960—16800
1907—12000	1914—39000	1921—67000	1961—17400
1908—15000	1915—43000	1922—70000	1962—20000
1909—19000	1916—47000	1923—73000	1963—22700
1910—23000	1917—51000	1924—76000	1964—24700

ROGERS, GEORGE & SON (Paxton Piano Works, Paxton Road, London N.17)

1912—25900	1918—28500	1924—34000	1930—40500
1913—26000	1919—29000	1925—35200	1931—41200
1914—26500	1920—30000	1926—36400	1932—42000
1915—27000	1921—31000	1927—37600	
1916—27500	1922—32000	1928—38800	
1917—28000	1923—33000	1929—40000	

STECK, GEO. & CO. (650 East 132nd Street, New York, U.S.A.)

1910— 43000	1918— 58900	1926— 75000	1934—128400
1911— 45100	1919— 61000	1927— 79000	1935—130700
1912— 47200	1920— 63300	1928— 81000	1936—133100
1913— 49300	1921— 65000	1929— 83000	
1914— 51400	1922— 67000	1930— 85000	
1915— 53500	1923— 69000	1931—121000	
1916— 54600	1924— 71000	1932—125000	
1917— 56700	1925— 73000	1933—127000	

STEINWAY & SONS (New York and Hamburg)

1910—140000	1916—180000	1922—210000	1928—260000
1911—150000	1917—185000	1923—220000	1929—265000
1912—155000	1918—190000	1924—225000	1930—271000
1913—160000	1919—195000	1925—235000	1931—273000
1914—165000	1920—200000	1926—240000	1932—274000
1915—170000	1921—205000	1927—255000	

WEBER & CO. (East Rochester, New York, U.S.A.)

1910—64500	1916—72500	1922—77600	1928—79600
1911—66000	1917—74000	1923—78200	1929—80000
1912—67500	1918—74700	1924—78600	1930—81300
1913—69200	1919—75400	1925—78900	1931—82300
1914—70100	1920—76000	1926—79100	1932—82600
1915—71900	1921—77200	1927—79300	

WHEELOCK PIANO CO. (New York, U.S.A.)

1912—27800	1917—32400	1922—36000	1927—41500
1913—28400	1918—33000	1923—37100	1928—42700
1914—29200	1919—33700	1924—38200	1929—44000
1915—30000	1920—34300	1925—39300	1930—45100
1916—31700	1921—35100	1926—40400	

BIBLIOGRAPHY

ADLUNG, JACOB, *Anleitung zu der Musikalischen Gelahrtheit*, Erfurt, 1758.

ATTA, H. L. *The Piano Player* 1914.

BAINES, A., *Musical Instruments Through the Ages*. Harmondsworth, Penguin Books Ltd., 1961.

BEDOS DE CELLES, D. FRANÇOIS, *L'Art de Facteur d'Orgues* (Quatrième partie), Paris, 1778.

BOWERS, Q. D., *Put Another Nickel In*. New York, Vestal Press, 1966.

British Patent Office, *Musical Instruments, 1694–1933*. Abridgement Class 88, London.

BUCHNER, Dr A., *Mechanical Musical Instruments*. London, Batchworth Press, c. 1954.

BUSBY, THOMAS, *Concert Room and Orchestra Anecdotes*. London, 1825.

CHAPUIS, A., *Histoire de la Boîte à Musique*. Lausanne, Edition Scriptar, 1955.

CHAPUIS, A., and DROZ, E., *Automata*. Transl. Reid. Neuchâtel, Editions du Griffon, 1958.

CHAPUIS, A., and GELIS, E., *Le Monde des Automates*. Paris, Société Anonyme, 1928.

CLARK, J. E. T., *Musical Boxes—A History and Appreciation*. 3rd ed. London, Allen & Unwin, 1961.

Conservatoire Nationale des Arts et Métiers, *Automates et Mécanismes a Musique*. Paris, 1960.

Conservatoire Nationale des Arts et Métiers, *Les Boîtes à Musique de Prague*. (Catalogue) Paris, 1966.

DEBAIN, A. F., *Antiphonel-Harmonium Suppléant de l'Organiste*. Paris, 1873.

DEVAUX, P., *Automates et Automatisme*. Paris, Presses Universitaires, 1941.

DRAKE, HARRY, *The Pneumatic Player*. Musical Opinion, London, 1921.

DRAKE, HARRY, *The Player Piano Explained*. Musical Opinion, London, 1922.

ENGRAMELLE, FATHER MARIE DOMINIQUE JOSEPH, *La Tonotechnic ou l'Art de Noter les Cylindres*. Paris, 1775.

Fair Organ Preservation Society, *The Key Frame* (Journal). Northampton, 1966.

FETIS, FRANCOIS JOSEPH, *Biographie Universelle des Musiciens*. Paris, 1860.

FLIGHT, BENJAMIN, *Flight's Practical Tuner for the Organ or Pianoforte*, London, c. 1880.

FRIED, FREDERICK, *Pictorial History of the Carousel*. New York, A. S. Barnes, 1964

GALPIN, FRANCIS W., *Old English Instruments of Music—Their History and Character*. 2nd ed. 1911.

GALPIN, FRANCIS W., *A Textbook of European Musical Instruments—Their Origin, History and Character*. 1937.

GIVENS, L., *Rebuilding the Player Piano*. New York, Vestal Press, 1963.

GREW, SYDNEY, *The Art of the Player Piano*. London, Kegan Paul, Trench, 1922.

GROVE, G., *Dictionary of Music and Musicians*. Ed. Blom. London, Macmillan, 1964.

Harmonicon. London, 1823–33.

HEINITZ, WILHELM, Extract: 'Mechanische Musikinstrumente der Instrumentenkunde' in *Handbuch der Musikwissenschaft*. Potsdam, 1928.

HUPFELD, L., *Dea-Violina*. Leipzig, 1909.

JACQUOT, ALBERT, *Dictionnaire . . . des instruments de musique*. Paris, 1886.

KIRCHER, ATHANASIUS, *Musurgia Universalis*. Rome, 1650.

KOBBE, GUSTAV, *The Pianolist—A Guide for Pianola Players*. London, Sidney Appleton, 1908.

LANGWILL, L. G., and BOSTON, CANON NOEL, *Church and Chamber Barrel Organs*. Edinburgh, 1967.

MAINGOT, E., *Les Automates*. Paris, Librairie Hachette, 1959.

MATETZKI, J., *Uber die Behändlung und Instandsetzung von Pneumatischen Musikwerken*. Leipzig, 1913.

VAN DER MEER, Dr J. H., 'Beiträge zum Cembalobau im Deutschen Sprachgebiet bis 1700', *Anzeiger des Germanischen Nationalmuseums 1966*. Nürnberg, 1966.

MERSENNE, P. M., *Harmonie Universelle*. Paris, 1636.

MICHEL, N. E., *Michel's Piano Atlas*. U.S.A. c. 1963.

Musical Box Society of Great Britain, *The Music Box* (Journal). London, 1962–67.

Musical Box Society International of America, *Bulletin* (Journal). U.S.A., 1966–67.

Musical Opinion, London, 1877–1930.

NETTL, PAUL, 'Ein Spielender Musikautomat aus dem 16. Jahrhundert' in *Zeitschrift für Musikwissenschaft II, 1920*.

NEWMAN, E., *The Piano-Player and Its Music*. London, 1920.

ORD-HUME, A. W. J. G., *Collecting Musical Boxes and How to Repair Them*. London, Allen & Unwin, 1967.

PLAYER PIANO GROUP, *Newsletter*. London, 1964–67.

Player Piano Review. Birmingham, 1912–14.

PROTZ, ALBERT, *Mechanische Musikinstrumente*. Kassel, 1943.

British Institute of Recorded Sound, *Recorded Sound* (Journal): articles by John Farmer, Jan., April, Oct. 1967.

REES, ABRAHAM, *Cyclopaedia of Arts, Sciences and Literature*. London, Longman, 1819.

ROEHL, HARVEY, *Player Piano Treasury*. 3rd ed. New York, Vestal Press, 1964.

S.G.E(arl), *How to Repair the Player Piano*. Musical Opinion, London, 1920.

SACHS, CURT, *Handbuch der Musikinstrumentenkunde*. Leipzig, 1920.

SACHS, CURT, *Real-Lexikon der Musikinstrumenten*. Berlin, 1913.

SCHLOSSER, JULIUS, *Kunsthistorisches Museum* (catalogue). Vienna, 1919.

SCHMITZ, HANS PETER, *Die Tontechnik des Père Engramelle*. Kassel und Basel, 1953.

SCHOLES, P. A., *Oxford Companion to Music*. London, Oxford University Press, 1942.

DE WAARD, R., *Van Speeldoos Tot Pierement*. Amsterdam, 1965.

WHITE, W. B., *Piano Playing Mechanisms*. 1st ed. Ed. Lyman Bill Inc., Chicago, 1925.

WHITE, WILLIAM BRAID, *The Player-Pianist*. New York, Edward Lyman Bill, 1910.

WHITE, WILLIAM BRAID, *A Technical Treatise on Piano Player Mechanism*. New York, Edward Lyman Bill, 1908.

WHITE, WILLIAM BRAID, *Regulation and Repair of Piano and Player Mechanisms*. New York, Edward Lyman Bill, 1909.

WHITE, WILLIAM BRAID, *The Player Piano Up to Date*. New York, 1914.

WILSON, FRGS, DAVID MILLER, *The Player Pianist*. Perforated Music Co., London, 1911.

WILSON, FRGS, DAVID MILLER, *An Introductory Book on The Piano-Player and Player-Piano*. c. 1918, London.

WILSON, FRGS, DAVID MILLER, *Instruction Book on the Piano-Player and Player-Piano*. J. M. Kronheim & Co., London, 1911.

WILSON, FRGS, DAVID MILLER, *The Player-Piano, Its Construction and How to Play*. London, Pitmans, 1923.

DE WIT, PAUL, *Weltadressbuch der Musikindustrie*. Leipzig, 1903.

DE WIT, PAUL, *Zeitschrift für Instrumentenbau*. Leipzig, 1881–1890.

WOODMAN, H. STAUNTON, *How To Tune a Piano*. New York, Corwood Publishers, 1960.

INDEX

In using this Index, please note that the names of agents, inventors, patentees and manufacturers are listed comprehensively in Chapter 11 and therefore references in that Chapter are not included in the Index.

The enquirer is recommended to seek also in the alphabetical listing of Chapter 11 for additional data on names. The plates, indicated in the Index by references in bold, black type, are grouped into two sections as follows:—Plates 1 to 52 between pages 64 and 65; and plates 53 to 112 between pages 192 and 193.

INDEX

INDEX